THE BIBLICAL RESOURCE SERIES

WHAT ARE THE GOSPELS?

A Comparison with Graeco-Roman Biography

• •

SECOND EDITION

Richard A. Burridge

With a foreword by

Graham Stanton

WILLIAM B. EERDMANS PUBLISHING COMPANY
GRAND RAPIDS, MICHIGAN / CAMBRIDGE, U.K.

DOVE BOOKSELLERS
DEARBORN, MICHIGAN

Published jointly 2004 by
Wm. B. Eerdmans Publishing Co.
255 Jefferson Ave. S.E., Grand Rapids, Michigan 49503 /
P.O. Box 163, Cambridge CB3 9PU U.K.
www.eerdmans.com
and by
Dove Booksellers
13904 Michigan Avenue, Dearborn, Michigan 48126
www.dovebook.com

Printed in the United States of America

09 08 07 06 05 04   7 6 5 4 3 2 1

Library of Congress Cataloging-in-Publication Data

What are the Gospels? a comparison with Graeco-Roman biography /
Richard A. Burridge; with a foreword by Graham Stanton — 2nd ed.
        p.   cm.   — (The biblical resource series)
Includes bibliographical references (p.   ) and indexes.
ISBN 0-8028-0971-5 (pbk.: alk. paper)
1. Bible. N.T. Gospels — Language, style.
2. Jesus Christ — Biography — History and Criticism.
3. Greek literature, Hellenistic — History and Criticism.
4. Greek literature — Relation to the New Testament.
5. Religious biography — History and criticism.
I. Title.   II. Series.

BS2555.52.B88   2004
226'.06 — dc22

2004047152

Contents

Contents

PART TWO: THE PROPOSED SOLUTION

Contents

Foreword

This new edition of *What Are the Gospels?* is most welcome, for it makes available for a wider readership a book whose central thesis has to be taken seriously by all students of the Gospels. Over the last decade or so, very few books on the Gospels have been discussed more widely or have influenced scholarly opinion more strongly. This book has played a key role in establishing that the Gospels were read in the early centuries primarily as biographies. Twenty years ago, only a few voices in the wilderness dared to oppose the widely held view that the Gospels reflect the life and faith of the post-Easter church, which had little interest in the past life of Jesus of Nazareth. In terms of their literary genre, the Gospels were considered by most scholars to be without precedent in antiquity. Those who begged to differ had not gathered and sifted critically the mountain of Graeco-Roman literary evidence on which Dr. Burridge rests his case.

To have turned the tide of scholarly opinion in this way is a remarkable achievement, the more so since this book began life as research for a Ph.D. thesis. Most of Dr. Burridge's research into the genre of the Gospels was carried out while he had considerable pastoral duties. During his Ph.D. research, he drew on his earlier Oxford studies as a classicist and developed an impressively thorough knowledge of the primary sources — and that is always the key to a Ph.D. thesis that makes a lasting contribution to scholarship.

There are two further reasons why this new edition deserves commendation. A recently published but rather inaccessible essay in which Dr. Burridge strengthens still further his view has been included. Equally welcome is his lively account of the reception of his book over the past dozen years. No attempt is made to hide the criticisms levelled against his work, so readers of the new edition will be able to judge for themselves whether or not the critics have undermined his case.

Foreword

My own involvement with this book goes back some years. In 1989 I was the external examiner of Dr. Burridge's Ph.D. thesis. I read the thesis with profound admiration, for I had begun to develop a similar line of argument some fifteen years earlier. I realize that I should have been more rigorous and less timid in my own earlier work. When Dr. Burridge submitted his thesis for inclusion in the Society of New Testament Studies monograph series, I was the editor of that Cambridge University Press series. The distinguished scholar who acted as an independent reader was as enthusiastic as I was about its publication in our series. The rest is history!

I am confident that this book will continue to play an important role in discussion of the genre of the Gospels. I do not think it is now possible to deny that the Gospels are a sub-set of the broad ancient literary genre of "lives," that is, biographies. Even if the evangelists were largely ignorant of the tradition of Greek and Roman "lives," that is how the Gospels were received and listened to in the first decades after their composition. And that is a "first order" conclusion, for the interpretation of any writing rests on a decision about its literary genre.

GRAHAM STANTON
Lady Margaret's Professor of Divinity
University of Cambridge

Preface to the Second Edition

I am delighted to have this opportunity to update this book and make it widely available again. I have resisted the temptation to write a completely new book, but I have given chapters 1 to 10 a general overhaul, updating them where necessary. The new additional Chapter 11 is a detailed response to the debates over the decade since first publication, and a discussion of the areas of continuing research. In preparing this revised edition, I am extremely indebted to all those who have responded to my original work over the years, many of whom are detailed in Chapter 11; without their interest and stimulation none of this would have been possible. I am very grateful to Sam Eerdmans and Michael Thomson of Wm. B. Eerdmans publishers for their interest in this work, and for their help and support in preparing this revised edition. Professor Graham Stanton continued his constant encouragement, right from the original viva examination, through my arrival to become a colleague of his as Dean of King's College, London, to his continuing enthusiasm for this new edition; I particularly want to thank him for his kind Foreword, written at a time when he had many other pressing concerns. Dr. Eddie Adams and Dr. Steve Walton have been particularly helpful, especially in their comments on the draft of the new material. The actual work of revision was undertaken during some study leave in the autumn of 2003, which would not have been possible without the support of my secretary, Alison Shapton, and the Chaplain of King's College, Tim Ditchfield, and my other colleagues. Many friends encouraged me through those months with their concern and prayers, but once again the burden of my struggle to write fell as always upon my wife and daughters. I can only reiterate to Sue, Rebecca and Sarah the debt of thanks already described in the original preface but just as real these many years later, and hope that they will accept this new edition as a gift for Christmas 2003.

Preface to the Original Edition

This study is the revised version of my doctoral thesis under the supervision of Dr P. Maurice Casey at the University of Nottingham, 1983-9. It was undertaken part-time during my ordination training and curacy, being finished after my appointment as Lazenby Chaplain to the University of Exeter. It has affected all my relationships, and everyone I know ought to be thanked. I am grateful for the assistance of staff members and library facilities of St John's College, Nottingham, the Universities of Oxford, Nottingham and Exeter, King's College, London, St George's College, Jerusalem and Bromley Reference Library. Computing assistance was given by Lou Barnard of the Oxford University Computing Service Text Archive and by Project Pallas, University of Exeter. The support and encouragement of the Rt Revd David Say, Lord Bishop of Rochester, the Revd Canon Michael Beek, my vicar at Bromley Parish Church, and the Vice-Chancellor and Lazenby Trust of Exeter University have been vital in ensuring the completion of this work. I wish to thank the Advisory Council for the Church's Ministry, the Dioceses of Rochester and Exeter, the Universities of Nottingham and Exeter, and the Bishop Henry Phillpotts Trust for financial assistance.

Papers about my research were given to the following: the University of Nottingham Theology Department Staff and Postgraduate Seminar, 27 November 1984; the 'Creating Theologians' Conference, St John's College, Nottingham, 19 July 1985; the British New Testament Conference, King's College, London, 20 September 1986; Rochester Diocese Clergy Study Day, 24 March 1987; the University of Exeter Classics Department Staff Research Seminar, 13 May 1988; Tavistock Deanery Chapter, 10 November 1988; the Hooker Group, Exeter, 16 March 1989; Christianity Deanery Chapter, 6 June 1990. I am grateful to all who participated for their comments and questions. In particular, I would like to thank those who have read parts of this study for their helpful comments: Dr Maurice Casey, my supervisor; Dr Stephen Travis and Dr Andrew Lincoln of St John's College for their encouragement, particularly in the initial years, and Professor David Catchpole of the University of Exeter for his support more recently; and Dr Joseph Geiger of the Hebrew University of Jerusalem for his encouragement during my stay there in summer 1984. Particular mention must be made of Dr Christopher Pelling of University College, Oxford who tutored me through my first degree in *Literae Humaniores* and who has been very helpful with the classical side of this thesis. The thesis was examined by Professor Graham Stanton and Dr John Muddiman on 1 November 1989, and I am especially grateful to Professor David Aune of St Xavier College, Chicago for his written comments recommending it for the SNTS Monograph Series; Professor Stanton has been both patient and helpful during the revision.

Finally, my family have suffered the side-effects of postgraduate study. I am grateful to my parents and my mother-in-law for all their love, and to my daughters, Rebecca Siân and Sarah Bethan, who may have delayed the work by being born during its much longer gestation but who have so greatly enriched my life. I owe a debt greater than I can say to my wife, Sue, for all that she has done and has been throughout this entire period, and I dedicate this work to her in thanks on our Wedding Anniversary, 1 September 1990.

Abbreviations

ANRW	*Aufstieg und Niedergang der römischen Welt,* ed. Wolfgang Haase, Berlin: Walter de Gruyter
BJRL	*Bulletin of the John Rylands University Library of Manchester*
CBQ	*Catholic Biblical Quarterly*
CQ	*Classical Quarterly*
CR	*Classical Review*
CUP	Cambridge University Press
ET	English translation
ExpT	*Expository Times*
FGrHist	*Fragmente der griechischen Historiker*
FRLANT	Forschungen zur Religion und Literatur des Alten und Neuen Testaments
GRBS	*Greek, Roman and Byzantine Studies*
HTR	*Harvard Theological Review*
ICC	International Critical Commentary
ICS	*Illinois Classical Studies*
JAAR	*Journal of the American Academy of Religion*
JBL	*Journal of Biblical Literature*
JHS	*Journal of Hellenic Studies*
JR	*Journal of Religion*
JRS	*Journal of Roman Studies*
JSNT	*Journal for the Study of the New Testament*
JSNTSS	*JSNT* Supplement Series
JSOT	*Journal for the Study of the Old Testament*
JTS	*Journal of Theological Studies*
NCBC	New Century Bible Commentary
NICNT	New International Commentary on the New Testament

NovT	*Novum Testamentum*
NTTS	New Testament Tools and Studies
NTS	*New Testament Studies*
OCT	*Oxford Classical Text*
OUP	Oxford University Press
QGFF	*Quaderni del Giornale Filologico Ferrarese*
SAP	Sheffield Academic Press (formerly JSOT Press)
SBL	Society of Biblical Literature
SBLDS	SBL Dissertation Series
SBLMS	SBL Monograph Series
SNTSMS	Society for New Testament Studies Monograph Series
SupNT	Supplement to *Novum Testamentum*
TAPA	*Transactions of the American Philological Association*
TZ	*Theologische Zeitschrift*
USQR	*Union Seminary Quarterly Review*
WBC	Word Bible Commentary
WUNT	Wissenschaftliche Untersuchungen zum Neuen Testament
ZNW	*Zeitschrift für die neutestamentliche Wissenschaft*

PART ONE

THE PROBLEM

CHAPTER 1

Historical Survey

The documents . . . presenting themselves as biographies of the Founder of Christianity (1863)

They cannot be included in the category of biographies (1928)

The gospels are biographies, albeit ancient ones. (1977)[1]

The study of the genre of the gospels appears to have gone round in a full circle over the last century or so of critical scholarship. The nineteenth-century assumption about the gospels as biographies is explicitly denied by the scholarly consensus of most of the twentieth century. In recent years, however, a biographical genre has begun to be assumed once more. The latest position is naturally not exactly the same as the original one: much water has flowed beneath the critical bridge in the intervening century, and all this must be taken into account. However, the circular impression of something being asserted, denied and then coming back into fashion is not all that misleading. This book attempts to provide a good foundation for the reintroduction of the biographical view of the gospels. We begin, therefore, with a brief survey of the progress of the debate, considering the arguments of several key works

---

1. Ernest Renan, *Life of Jesus*, ET (London: Kegan Paul, 1893), p. 7; Rudolf Bultmann, 'Evangelien', in *Die Religion in Geschichte und Gegenwart*, ed. H. Gunkel *et al.*, 2nd edn (Tübingen: J. C. B. Mohr, 1928), vol. 2, cols. 418-22, ET as 'The Gospels (Form)', in *Twentieth Century Theology in the Making*, ed. J. Pelikan (London: Collins, 1969), vol. 1, pp. 86-92, quotation from p. 87; C. H. Talbert, *What Is a Gospel?* (London: SPCK, 1978), p. 135.

from the main important periods: the turn from the nineteenth to the twenti-eth century, the middle of this century and recent decades.[2]

A. From the Nineteenth to the Twentieth Century

1. Ernest Renan (1863)

It was fashionable in the nineteenth century to write 'Lives of Jesus', such as that by Ernest Renan. Renan thought it was possible to write a biography of Jesus, beginning with his birth and infancy, his education and the influence of his time and environment (chapters 1-4), and going on through his ministry to the events of his death, concluding with a summary of the essential character of his work (chapter 28). The book's introduction reveals that Renan's main sources are the four canonical gospels, assumed to be biographies, with the evangelists as the biographers of Jesus. Furthermore, the gospels belong to a subgroup of the wider genre of biography: 'They are neither biographies after the manner of Suetonius, nor fictitious legends in the style of Philostratus; they are legendary biographies.' They are to be compared with Lives of saints, heroes or philoso-phers, in which 'historical truth and the desire to present models of virtue are combined in various degrees'.[3] Further, Renan discussed the differences be-tween the synoptic gospels and the fourth. The relationship of John to Jesus is akin to that between Plato and Socrates: the discourses 'represent to us the ser-mons of Jesus, as the dialogues of Plato render us the conversations of Socrates', and thus John is seen as 'the biographer of Jesus, as Plato was of Socrates'.[4]

2. C. W. Votaw (1915)

Such comparisons of the gospels with contemporary classical biography reached their zenith in Clyde Weber Votaw's article of 1915 in which he set out

2. For brief surveys of the debate, see R. H. Gundry, 'Recent Investigations into the Liter-ary Genre "Gospel"', in *New Dimensions in New Testament Study,* ed. R. N. Longenecker and M. C. Tenney (Grand Rapids: Zondervan, 1974), pp. 97-114; M. J. Suggs, 'Gospel, genre', in *The Interpreter's Dictionary of the Bible,* Supplementary Volume (Nashville: Abingdon Press, 1976), pp. 370-2; Vernon K. Robbins, 'Mark as Genre', *SBL 1980 Seminar Papers* (Chicago: Scholars, 1980), pp. 371-99; R. A. Burridge, 'Gospel', in *A Dictionary of Biblical Interpretation,* ed. R. J. Coggins and J. L. Houlden (London: SCM, 1990), pp. 266-8.

3. Introduction, Renan, *Life of Jesus,* pp. 1-34; quotations from p. 25.

4. *Ibid.,* pp. 19 and 130.

to place the gospels within the literature of the Graeco-Roman period.[5] After a very brief introduction to classical literature and the way in which the gospels were used as 'memorabilia' of Jesus by Christians undertaking the task of evangelizing the Graeco-Roman world, he comes to the crucial question of biography. He subdivides this genre into two groups: historical biography, which presents all the dates and facts in an ordered accurate method, and popular biography, intended to acquaint the reader with the subject in a practical or hortatory way. Although the two groups shade into one another, Votaw is convinced that they can be distinguished by their method: accurate history or disconnected memorabilia. The gospels are of the popular variety because of their method and 'the extreme difficulty of recovering the historical Jesus'.[6] However, to the same group, and for the same reasons, other writings intended to promote the personality and message of three other moral-religious teachers may also be consigned. These are Socrates (469-399 BC), Apollonius of Tyana (*c.* AD 10-97) and Epictetus (*c.* AD 50-130). Votaw, therefore, proceeds to compare such works with the gospels, beginning with a brief description, with extracts, of the works by Arrian on Epictetus and Philostratus on Apollonius of Tyana. The similarities and parallels he discovers are put down to their all 'belonging to the same type of literature, namely, popular biography'.[7]

The closest parallel, however, is that between Socrates and Jesus, and also between the writings of their disciples: the second part of the article compares the gospels with Plato's *Dialogues* and Xenophon's *Memorabilia*. They all share a common motive — to restore the reputation of one executed by the state — and a common core of historical information about their subject, but this is provided by a portrait rather than a photograph, overlaid with reflection and interpretation. Furthermore, the time interval between the death of the subject and the writing of the accounts is approximately the same. The differences — that the Socratic literature is more extensive and that the gospels have been written down in a language different from that spoken by their subject — do not prevent the parallel.

---

5. Originally C. W. Votaw, 'The Gospels and Contemporary Biographies', *American Journal of Theology* 19 (1915), pp. 45-73 and 217-49; reprinted separately as *The Gospels and Contemporary Biographies in the Graeco-Roman World* (with an introduction by John Reumann) by Fortress Press, Facet Books, in 1970. Page references are to the latter edition.

6. Votaw, 'The Gospels and Contemporary Biographies', pp. 5-8.

7. *Ibid.*, p. 27.

3. *Evaluation*

Both authors attempt to relate the gospels to Graeco-Roman biography. Such setting of the gospels within the literary relationships of their day must be applauded. However, apart from the obvious difficulty that Renan and Votaw wrote before the insights of form criticism, there are problems with both their understanding of genre theory and their handling of Graeco-Roman biography.

The literary theory of genre requires careful consideration of how works may be described as belonging to a shared genre. Renan sees his own *Life of Jesus,* nineteenth-century ideas of biography and Graeco-Roman Lives as all being the same thing. Votaw never asks how genre may be defined; parallelism of subject-matter, particularly of Jesus and Socrates, together with a shared purpose is sufficient for these works to belong to the same type of literature. The criteria are thus all to do with content; questions about literary form or analysis of structure are hardly discussed, if at all. The disparity between the length of the gospels and that of the *Apollonius of Tyana* or the Socratic literature does raise questions about these works belonging together. Votaw's concerns are more about overall, general impressions to be gained from the works, rather than generic considerations of a technical nature. If the gospels are to be identified with these biographies, much more attention will need to be given to analysis of form and structure and to what actually constitutes genre.

Graeco-Roman biography includes works of a wide range of types, subjects and dates. Subdivisions within this range need to be accurately defined. Renan's distinction is again in terms of content, particularly the historical veracity or legendary nature of the work. Votaw's historical and popular biographies are identified also in terms of the historical objectivity of the works. Whether any ancient biographies would qualify for inclusion in the first group with its modern stress on critical research is debatable. Further, the stress on content and overall impression of the subject means that works of a clearly different genre, e.g. Plato's *Dialogues,* which are philosophical treatises, can be considered as biographies for the purposes of comparison with the gospels.

Thus, much more consideration needed to be given both to the literary theory of genre and to the nature of Graeco-Roman biography if Renan's and Votaw's comparison of the gospels with such works was to prove profitable. However, developments in German scholarship meant that it would be over fifty years before these comparisons would be considered again within critical orthodoxy.

B. The Rise of Form Criticism

The development of form-critical approaches turned the focus of attention away from the evangelists as authors to the oral transmission of units of gospel tradition. We cannot document here this massive shift in the interpretation of the gospels as a whole, but will consider the two main contributions to the question of gospel genre which established the consensus for the next fifty years, namely, that they are unique, *sui generis* pieces of literature.

1. Urliteratur *and* Kleinliteratur

Unlike Renan and Votaw, Norden (1898) saw no parallels and thought the gospels were something new and different from contemporary literature.[8] Wendland (1912) anticipated Votaw's historical v. popular distinction with a different stress: Graeco-Roman biography depended upon the author's literary personality and intention. However, the process of collecting and assembling units of oral tradition, lying behind the gospels' composition, prevented such literary concerns. The evangelist thus became more of a popular storyteller and collector with no personal individuality, and the parallels for the gospels should be sought among similar products of oral tradition, such as the Homeric literature or the stories in the Pentateuch.[9]

Overbeck (1882) also stressed the preliterary development of the gospels with the term *Urliteratur* for the New Testament books, lying between the oral material of the primitive Christian communities and later, truly literary writings of the patristic period.[10] Dibelius (1919) differentiated between formal 'literary' works, produced by the conscious intention of an author, and the end product of popular tradition and story-telling. The gospels 'are unliterary writings' *(Kleinliteratur)*. 'They should not and cannot be compared with "literary" works' *(Hochliteratur)*.[11] Such a process of oral tradition has a radical effect on the question of the personality of the author(s): because many anonymous individuals are involved, we cannot talk of the work

---

8. E. Norden, *Die antike Kunstprosa* (Stuttgart: Teubner, repr. 1958), vol. 2, pp. 480-1.

9. P. Wendland, *Die urchristlichen Literaturformen,* 2nd edn (Tübingen: J. C. B. Mohr, 1912), pp. 266ff.

10. F. Overbeck, 'Über die Anfänge der patristischen Literatur', *Historische Zeitschrift* NF 12 (48) (1882), pp. 417-72.

11. M. Dibelius, *Die Formgeschichte des Evangeliums,* 2nd edn (Tübingen: J. C. B. Mohr, 1933); ET *From Tradition to Gospel,* trans. B. L. Woolf (London: James Clarke, 1971), pp. 1-2.

as belonging to the personality of any one; rather, it is the development of the tradition itself which is the dominant factor.

2. *Karl Ludwig Schmidt*

In 1919, Schmidt demonstrated that the differences between the synoptic gospel accounts can be seen most clearly in the links or seams by which the various stories are joined. From this he concluded that these units, or pericopae, circulated independently within the oral tradition and were then strung together, like so many pearls on a piece of string, by the evangelist.[12] It is clear that this leaves very little room for any concept of authorial intention, purpose or literary pretensions — and thus the question of the genre of the whole work is replaced by a concern for the particular form of each individual pericope.

However, it was his seminal article in 1923 for the Festschrift for Hermann Gunkel's sixtieth birthday which really set the tracks for the next four decades.[13] Schmidt began by dismissing Votaw's suggestions, drawing upon Wendland's comments about the literary personality of the author, which is present even in Xenophon or Arrian, but absent from the gospels. The parallelism of the gospels with the *Memorabilia*, noted by Votaw, is superficial, nothing other than the similarity of Jesus and Socrates. The difference is clear: the former are *Kleinliteratur*, but Xenophon is *Hochliteratur*. A search of contemporary Greek, Jewish, oriental and Rabbinic literature reinforces the argument that the gospels are a form of folk literature and the evangelist 'a naive folk story-teller' ('ein naiver Volkserzähler').[14]

His own suggestion about the place of the gospels in the history of literature begins with the uncompromisingly ringing declaration that the gospel is basically 'not *Hochliteratur*, but *Kleinliteratur*, not the product of an indi-

---

12. K. L. Schmidt, *Der Rahmen der Geschichte Jesu* (Berlin: Trowitzsch und Sohn, 1919), reprinted (Darmstadt: Wissenschaftliche Buchgesellschaft, 1964).

13. K. L. Schmidt, 'Die Stellung der Evangelien in der allgemeinen Literaturgeschichte', in *EYXAPIΣTHPION: Studien zur Religion und Literatur des Alten und Neuen Testaments*, ed. Hans Schmidt (Göttingen: Vandenhoeck und Ruprecht, 1923), vol. 2, pp. 50-134; ET as Karl Ludwig Schmidt, *The Place of the Gospels in the General History of Literature*, translated by Byron R. McCane (University of South Carolina Press, 2002), with an introduction by John Riches, pp. vii-xxviii — see the discussion of Riches's criticism of my assessment of Schmidt in Chapter 11, pp. 284-5 below.

14. Schmidt, 'Die Stellung der Evangelien', pp. 55-76, quotation from p. 75; ET McCane, p. 24.

vidual author, but a folk-book, not biography, but cult-legend'.[15] On the other hand, Graeco-Roman biographies belong to *Hochliteratur* because of their conscious literary intention; even a book like Philostratus' *Apollonius of Tyana* shows clearly the self-conscious personality of the author.[16] The gospels cannot be compared with such works; instead, other parallels must be sought among examples of *Kleinliteratur*. Those suggested include the German folktales of Dr. Faustus, legends about saints and monks, St Francis, and the great Maggid of the Hasidim. These comparisons lead us a step further, to the 'cultic character' of such traditions, stories passed on within groups or communities, for the sake of their own beliefs and expectations.[17]

Thus Schmidt put forward three important arguments, which militate against any discussion of the gospel genre: the distinction between *Hochliteratur* and *Kleinliteratur*, with the gospels being the latter and finding their parallels among oral folktales, the absence of the literary 'I' on the part of the evangelists, and the stress on setting their production and transmission within a cultic community. On this basis, questions may well be asked about the form of the individual units, but not the genre of the gospel as a whole.

3. Rudolf Bultmann

Bultmann's work ensured that this approach to the genre of the gospels dominated the scholarly consensus. It is seen most clearly in *The History of the Synoptic Tradition* (second edition 1931) and in his article of 1928 on the gospels. He built on these assumptions in *Theology of the New Testament*, and the Supplement of 1962 to *The History of the Synoptic Tradition*, although updating the bibliography, does nothing to alter the view expressed in the vital concluding pages.[18] From such a consistent approach, Bultmann's views on three areas, the analogies to the gospels, the development of their overall form, and its uniqueness, can be documented easily.

First, Bultmann considers the setting of the gospels in their contemporary literary environment and comes to the conclusion that there are no par-

---

15. Schmidt, 'Die Stellung der Evangelien', p. 76: 'nicht Hochliteratur, sondern Kleinliteratur, nicht individuelle Schriftstellerleistung, sondern Volksbuch, nicht Biographie, sondern Kultlegende'; ET McCane, p. 27.

16. *Ibid.*, p. 82; ET McCane, p. 34.

17. *Ibid.*, p. 114; ET McCane, pp. 68ff.

18. R. Bultmann, *The History of the Synoptic Tradition*, revised edition with Supplement, trans. John Marsh (Oxford: Blackwell, 1972); 'The Gospels (Form)'; *Theology of the New Testament*, trans. K. Grobel (London: SCM, 1952), esp. vol. 1, pp. 86ff.

allel works. Against Votaw, he is particularly concerned to rule out any question of a link with the genre of biography, since the gospels have 'no interest in historical or biographical matters' such as Jesus' human personality, origin, education or development, or his appearance and character. Then he follows and reproduces Schmidt's arguments about *Hochliteratur* and *Kleinliteratur*: the lack of cultivated techniques and the absence of the authors' personalities mean that they are not 'major' or 'grand literature'.[19] There is a tenuous link with the genre of memoirs and Lives of the philosophers because of the shared feature of gathering together dialogues and episodes, but the gospels' mythic and cultic background, together with their absence of historical or scientific concerns, means that the parallel is unacceptable. Instead, he turns to *Kleinliteratur* and picks up Schmidt's suggestions about Faust, St Francis and so on. Even these are not true parallels: the gospels' cultic background is one of worship of Jesus as Son of God and Lord, rather than the admiration of the hero as in the other cases.

The second issue concerns the development of the form of the gospels and how this unique literature came to be produced. The overall plan of *The History of the Synoptic Tradition* is clear: part I considers 'The Tradition of the Sayings of Jesus', and then part II discusses 'The Tradition of the Narrative Material'; part III, 'The Editing of the Traditional Material', shows how the two traditions are brought together finally into the gospel form. Thus the overall form of the gospels is an accidental result of the fusion of sayings and narrative by Mark: 'This in fact marks the purpose of the author: *the union of the Hellenistic kerygma about Christ . . .* with the *tradition of the story of Jesus*.'[20] This statement seems to contradict the points above about the absence of any author or authorial purpose. However, although Bultmann says that Mark is responsible for the form of the gospel — 'It is in Mark that *the Gospel type* is first to be met' — it is clear that the real origin is to be found in the kerygma: 'Thus the kerygma of Christ is cultic legend and the *Gospels are expanded cult legends*.'[21] Similarly, in *Theology of the New Testament* he says, 'there develops out of the kerygma *the literary form: Gospel.* Its oldest exemplification is for us the Gospel of Mark.'[22] Bultmann then sets out seven stages in the development of this literary type from the kerygma of the death and resurrection of Jesus to the production of a gospel.

Finally, this all means that the gospels 'are a unique phenomenon in the

---

19. Bultmann, *History*, pp. 371-2; 'Gospels', p. 87. English translations have *Hochliteratur* variously as grand/major and *Kleinliteratur* as minor/lesser literature.

20. Bultmann, *History*, pp. 347-8; Bultmann's italics.

21. *Ibid.*, pp. 369 and 371; Bultmann's italics.

22. Bultmann, *Theology*, p. 86; Bultmann's italics.

history of literature', 'an original creation of Christianity'.[23] This becomes the standard form-critical view that the gospels are *sui generis*. In fact, Bultmann concludes that we cannot even talk in terms of genre for the gospels: in answer to the question, 'Can it be described as a unique literary genus?', he argues that the gospels are so 'completely subordinate to Christian faith and worship' that 'it is hardly possible to speak of the Gospels as a literary genus; the Gospel belongs to the history of dogma and worship'.[24] These sentiments are the last sentences of Bultmann's mighty *The History of the Synoptic Tradition*. They are also the last words on the question of the genre of the gospels for nearly half a century.

4. Evaluation

Crucial to both Schmidt and Bultmann was the distinction between *Hochliteratur* and *Kleinliteratur*. The two types of literature are seen in very rigid terms — and ne'er the twain shall meet. Any attempt to ask literary questions about the gospels, and in particular, their genre, is automatically precluded in advance. However, it is unlikely that such rigid boundaries can be maintained in first-century literature; literary distinctions are more flexible. Votaw's distinction between 'popular' and 'historical' biography, whatever else its difficulties, at least had the merit of allowing for a continuum of development from one to the other. The form critics' distinction merely has the effect of removing the gospels from any discussion of their context within the first century on the grounds that they do not share some predetermined literary aspirations. However, as Suggs has pointed out: 'The alleged lack of literary expertise on the part of the evangelists is not a valid objection . . . books of any genre may be poorly written.'[25] Much more detailed and accurate study of the various genres, types and levels of first-century, and especially Graeco-Roman, literature is needed.

The second question concerns the form of the gospel as a whole: Bultmann concluded that no analogy was necessary for this, since it was merely a by-product of the collecting together of the individual units within the oral tradition. This is a scarcely sufficient explanation. There are many different ways of collecting together units of oral tradition. Study of the Homeric traditions considers not only the development of the different stories as

23. Bultmann, 'Gospels', p. 89; *History*, pp. 373-4.
24. Bultmann, *History*, p. 374.
25. In his *IDB* article, Supplement, p. 371.

individual units, but also the process whereby the whole narrative of the *Iliad* or *Odyssey* came together through deliberate selection. Furthermore, the oral development of the Homeric poems does not prevent discussion of the question of the genre of the whole, i.e. epic. Equally, the oral background of the gospels' material does not obviate the need to consider the selection of the units and their overall genre.

Thirdly, this approach led to the eclipse of the author: if oral tradition is considered responsible for both the individual units themselves and also the form of the whole through the kerygma, then the evangelist is seen as little more than a mere stenographer at the end of the oral tunnel. This emphasis, together with Schmidt's comments on the absence of the literary 'I' in the gospels, precluded discussion of any purpose or intention on the part of the evangelists. In fact, as already noted, even Bultmann himself is forced to use the word 'purpose' to describe Mark's significant step in combining the kerygma with narrative tradition about Jesus. Thus it is clear that the evangelist as author, and all that this implies in terms of intention, must be taken into account, and this leads inevitably in the direction of genre.

Finally, the form-critical view emphasized the unique character of the gospels. This may have had important theological implications for Bultmann and others as befitting the narrative of the unique proclamation of the gospel — but from a literary point of view, it is a nonsense. It is hard to imagine how anyone could invent something which is a literary novelty or unique kind of writing. Even supposing it were possible, no one else would be able to make sense of the work, with no analogy to guide their interpretation: 'One cannot imagine a writer successfully inventing a genre for him or herself; for a genre to exist some form of reader recognition, of social acceptance, is necessary.'[26]

We may conclude, therefore, that much greater attention needs to be given to literary theory, particularly the theory of genre, and to the development of the range and types of first-century literature before credence can be given to form-critical notions that the gospels are *sui generis*.

C. Redaction Criticism and the Return of the Author

The intense scholarly activity about individual gospel pericopae over the following decades meant 'the study of the literary genres employed in early Chris-

---

26. Jeremy Hawthorn, *Unlocking the Text: Fundamental Issues in Literary Theory* (London: Edward Arnold, 1987), p. 45; see also, John S. Kloppenborg, *The Formation of Q: Trajectories in Ancient Wisdom Collections* (Philadelphia: Fortress, 1987), p. 3.

tian writing was for a long period largely ignored'.[27] Even into the 1970s, scholars like Kümmel merely repeated the ritual assertion of the gospels' uniqueness:
'In the Synoptic Gospels we meet for the first time a new and distinctive literary
genus. Viewed as a literary form, the Gospels are a new creation.'[28] However, the
general review of form criticism and the rise of redaction criticism through the
1960s led to the eventual reintroduction of questions about genre.

1. *The Critique of Form Criticism*

The general critique of form criticism came from various sources, putting
several areas in particular under scrutiny.[29] The analogy between the development of the gospel pericopae and folklore needed reconsideration because of
developments in folklore studies: it was less easy to assume steady growth of
an oral tradition in stages; significant steps were sometimes large and sudden;
the length of time needed for the 'laws' of oral transmission to operate, such
as the centuries of Old Testament or Homeric tradition, was greater than that
taken by the gospels; even the existence of such 'laws' was questioned.

Second, the form-critical concentration on the individual parts missed
the significance of the whole. Further, the transition from individual units of
oral tradition into a written document had an important effect on the interpretation of the material; as Kelber put it, 'writing always entails a rewriting
of worlds'.[30] Literary criticism, therefore, which had come to mean little more
than discussion of the sources and units of the gospels, began to include also
artistic intention, ability, purpose and so on. Finally, the form-critical approach had the effect of giving the community the active role in the formation of the gospel material, whereas communities tend to be passive with regard to their traditions; the active innovations come on the part of the story-
tellers — and thus we are back to the person of the author once more.

27. Kloppenborg, *Formation of Q*, p. 1.

28. W. G. Kümmel, *Introduction to the New Testament* (London: SCM, 1975), p. 37.

29. See, for example: W. D. Davies, *Invitation to the New Testament* (London: DLT, 1967);
E. P. Sanders, *The Tendencies of the Synoptic Tradition* (CUP, 1969); E. Güttgemanns, *Candid
Questions concerning Gospel Form Criticism: A Methodological Sketch of the Fundamental
Problematics of Form and Redaction Criticism*, trans. W. G. Doty (Pittsburgh: Pickwick, 1979);
William G. Doty, 'Fundamental Questions about Literary-Critical Methodology: A Review Ar-
ticle', *JAAR* 40 (1972), pp. 521-7; William G. Doty, 'Linguistics and Biblical Criticism', *JAAR* 41
(1973), pp. 114-21.

30. Werner Kelber, *Oral and Written Gospel* (Philadelphia: Fortress, 1983), p. 116; see similarly, E. Best, *Mark: The Gospel as Story* (Edinburgh: T&T Clark, 1983), pp. 16-20.

2. Authors and Readers

The development of redaction criticism paved the way for the study of the evangelists as creative individuals. Norman Perrin defines it as 'studying the theological motivation of an author as this is revealed in the collection, arrangement, editing, and modification of traditional material, and in the composition of new material or the creation of new forms within the traditions of early Christianity'.[31] Whereas form criticism directs attention to the literary forms of individual pericopae, redaction criticism directs us to the author as *redactor* or editor of the traditional material which came down to him.

Bornkamm applied this approach to the gospel of Matthew: first in a famous study in 1948, he analysed 'The Stilling of the Storm' in Matt. 8:23-7 against its source in Mark 4:35-41 and showed how Matthew was concerned to reinterpret the story in terms of Christian discipleship.[32] A few years later, he considered the consequences of such study for Matthew as a whole, and in particular his concern for the church.[33] Conzelmann demonstrated similar creativity in Luke, and his stress on the three periods of *Heilsgeschichte* as the key to Lukan theology has determined much subsequent work on Luke.[34] Finally, Marxsen completed the application of redaction criticism to the synoptic gospels with his work on Mark.[35] Naturally the last is the most difficult of the three; assuming Markan priority, Matthew's and Luke's editing of their source reveals something of their theology, purposes and methods. It is clearly more difficult to apply this discipline to texts whose sources are unknown. However, redaction criticism has been applied not just to Mark, but also to Q and to John as it has become part of the standard equipment of New Testament scholars.

If form criticism concentrated on the text and redaction criticism on the authors, increasing attention has been devoted in recent years to the third party — the reader(s). The terms by which such study is known, reader-

---

31. Norman Perrin, *What Is Redaction Criticism?* (London: SPCK, 1970), p. 1.

32. G. Bornkamm, 'The Stilling of the Storm in Matthew', in *Tradition and Interpretation in Matthew*, ed. G. Bornkamm, G. Barth and H. J. Held (London: SCM, 1963), pp. 52-7.

33. 'End Expectation and Church in Matthew', in *Tradition and Interpretation*, pp. 15-51. Original German version: 'Enderwartung und Kirche im Matthäusevangelium', in *The Background of the New Testament and Its Eschatology. Studies in Honour of C. H. Dodd*, ed. W. D. Davies and D. Daube (CUP, 1956), pp. 222-60.

34. H. Conzelmann, *Theology of St. Luke*, trans. G. Buswell (London: Faber & Faber, 1960).

35. W. Marxsen, *Der Evangelist Markus* (Göttingen: Vandenhoeck & Ruprecht, 1st edn 1956, 2nd edn 1959); ET *Mark the Evangelist* (New York and Nashville: Abingdon Press, 1969).

response criticism or audience criticism, imply a set approach; in fact, it is anything but monolithic and embraces a spectrum of scholars and approaches, pioneered by people like Wolfgang Iser and Stanley Fish. Common to them all is a stress on the person of the reader, who is active in the construction of the meaning of the text. There is debate about the 'ideal' reader who can interpret the text perfectly, the 'real' or actual reader, and the 'implied' reader, a mediating concept of a reader with a certain amount of competence able to recognize the clues to the reading encoded in the text. Thus, the reader may be seen as completely 'in' the text, put there by the author, or 'over' the text and able to impose any reading he wishes upon it; a middle position envisages a dialogue between text and reader.[36] In biblical studies we must also take into account that the audience may have been listening as a group, rather than assuming the modern habit of private reading.[37] Such approaches raise questions about the gospels' possible audience or readers, their background, education and literary knowledge — all of which makes the study of genre and generic expectations even more important.[38]

3. The Implications for Genre Study

These recent developments have many implications for the study of genre. Once redaction critics had demonstrated that the evangelists were not mindless recorders of the oral tradition, but had creative, *theological* purposes in writing their gospels, then questions about their creative *literary* intentions, including genre, could not be far behind. Curiously enough, Perrin, at the end of his survey of redaction criticism, was content to repeat the form-critical view that the gospels are 'the characteristic and unique literary product of early Christianity'.[39] It is perhaps a mark of how secure and well entrenched Bultmann's view of the uniqueness of the gospel genre was that the revival of interest in the authors of the gospels did not immediately and necessarily raise the question of genre. Even into the 1970s scholars like Kümmel

36. For a brief introduction, see James L. Resseguie, 'Reader-Response Criticism and the Synoptic Gospels', *JAAR* 52 (1984), pp. 307-24; also Stephen D. Moore, *Literary Criticism and the Gospels: The Theoretical Challenge* (New Haven: Yale University Press, 1989); and Patrick Grant, *Reading the New Testament* (London: Macmillan, 1989).

37. See Moore, *Literary Criticism and the Gospels*, pp. 84-8.

38. Mary Ann Beavis, *Mark's Audience: The Literary and Social Setting of Mark 4.1-12*, JSNTSS 33 (SAP, 1989), is a good example of its application to such issues.

39. Perrin, *What Is Redaction Criticism?*, pp. 74 and 78-9; see also his article 'The Literary Gattung "Gospel" — Some Observations', *ExpT* 82 (1970), pp. 4-7.

and Lohse continued to assert that the gospels were *sui generis* and not to be compared with other ancient literature.[40] However, by 1978 Petersen was surely right to observe:

> Redaction critics are rarely conscious of the consequences of their conclusions for the historical-critical evolutionary theory. . . . Nevertheless, *the evolutionary theory has collapsed because redaction criticism has pulled the plug on its source of power.* Whereas the theory saw the power of literary formation in a romantic symbiosis of tradition and environment, redaction criticism has relocated this power in authors on the one hand and in genres on the other, with genres now construed as cultural media of communication. Wittingly or not, therefore, redaction criticism has made possible the asking of literary questions about our non-literary writings. Indeed, I suspect that it has made it impossible not to ask them, since outside of biblical studies issues of authorship, composition, and genre are considered to be literary issues.[41]

Not everyone, however, took so long to realize these implications and through the door opened by redaction critics for the return of the author there began to flow a steady trickle of studies by literary critics on the question of the genre of the gospels, which in time became a flood of suggestions. To these, then, we must now turn for the last part of this survey.

D. The Search for a Genre

1. Aretalogy

Fifty years after Votaw, Smith and Hadas' *Heroes and Gods* set the gospel of Luke alongside Porphyry's *Pythagoras*, Philo's *Moses* and Philostratus' *Apollonius of Tyana*. All four works were described as *aretalogy*, 'an ancient type of biographical writing . . . a formal account of the remarkable career of an impressive teacher that was used as a basis for moral instruction'. This often involved the miraculous, at the subject's birth or death or during his life, and included disciples and opponents, often leading to hostility and even martyrdom. Such accounts would be written by disciples or by other teachers

---

40. Kümmel, *Introduction to NT*, p. 37; Eduard Lohse, *The Formation of the New Testament*, trans. M. E. Boring (Nashville: Abingdon, 1981), p. 119.

41. Norman R. Petersen, *Literary Criticism for New Testament Critics* (Philadelphia: Fortress, 1978), p. 18; his italics.

to promote their doctrines.[42] To exemplify such writings, Hadas discussed various heroes from throughout the Greek tradition in part I, and Smith provided translations and summaries of the four works in part II.[43] Hadas is conscious of one major difficulty with their thesis, 'that we have no complete text surviving from the past specifically labelled aretalogy', but does not doubt the genre's existence.[44]

2. Trajectories

Robinson and Koester attempted to get away from more static concepts such as 'background' and to draw 'trajectories' of literary types from periods preceding the New Testament through the gospels and beyond into second-century and non-canonical literature.[45] Robinson began his work in the early 1960s with the relationship of John and Mark, suggesting a 'signs/miracles' source behind Mark, analogous to another behind John, in which Jesus is assimilated to the type of a miracle worker/'divine man' (θεῖος ἀνήρ); in an attempt to redress the balance, the gospels become a kind of 'aretalogy in reverse' or 'aretalogical parody'.[46] Koester also picks up the link with aretalogy and Jesus as θεῖος ἀνήρ in his attempt to place the genre of the gospels.[47] The issue of genre is also applied to Q by Robinson, with the suggestion that it belongs to the genre of λόγοι σοφῶν, the Sayings of the Sages.[48]

3. Evaluation

Here at least gospel genre is being placed within the web of contemporary literary relationships. Even if these attempts were not completely successful,

42. Moses Hadas and Morton Smith, *Heroes and Gods: Spiritual Biographies in Antiquity* (London: Routledge & Kegan Paul, 1965), p. 3.

43. See also Morton Smith, 'Prolegomena to a Discussion of Aretalogies, Divine Men, the Gospels and Jesus', *JBL* 90 (1971), pp. 174-99.

44. Hadas and Smith, *Heroes and Gods*, p. 60; see also the preface, p. xiii.

45. J. M. Robinson and H. Koester, *Trajectories through Early Christianity* (Philadelphia: Fortress, 1971).

46. Robinson, 'Problem of History in Mark, Reconsidered', *USQR* 20 (1965), pp. 131-47; 'The Johannine Trajectory', in *Trajectories*, pp. 232-68; 'On the *Gattung* of Mark (and John)', in *Jesus and Man's Hope*, vol. 1 (Pittsburgh Theological Seminary, 1970), pp. 99-129.

47. Koester, 'One Jesus and Four Primitive Gospels', in *Trajectories*, pp. 158-204, especially 'Jesus as the Divine Man (Aretalogies)', pp. 187-93.

48. Robinson, '*Logoi Sophon*: On the Gattung of Q', in *Trajectories*, pp. 71-113.

they encouraged other work in similar directions, as well as some severe criticisms.[49] The latter have centred around the actual existence of the two major concepts, aretalogy and the 'divine man', and whether the analogies proposed between these concepts and the gospels are actually true. The absence of any examples of the genre of aretalogy was noted by Hadas himself, and this was picked up in the criticisms by Kee and Tiede: Tiede's dissertation begins 'there appears to be no unified picture of what constituted an aretalogy in the ancient world' and questions whether in fact we can talk of it as a literary genre at all.[50] The adjective 'aretalogical' may better describe certain tendencies in ancient literature, rather than using 'aretalogy' as a genre.

Tiede also suggests that the image of the 'divine man' is a composite one, combining elements of the miracle-worker with the philosopher-teacher, but that such a composite is not found in any one person. Holladay goes even further, arguing that the whole concept has become counter-productive: θεῖος ἀνήρ cannot simply be equated with a miracle-worker, nor does it mean someone who is a god; only in the sense of someone who is in a general way 'of God' does it have any usefulness. Finally, Gallagher rejects the links between divine men, aretalogy, biographical texts and religious propaganda, and denies that there was one single, simple Hellenistic conception of θεῖος ἀνήρ — the variety of possible concepts and suggested candidates reflect the diversity of Hellenistic society.[51]

Thus, an inadequate theory of genre has allowed too easily an assertion of the existence of aretalogy as a genre, rather than just a tendency, and an insufficient study of the first-century context led to the transformation of the

49. See among others: P. Achtemeier, 'Toward the Isolation of Pre-Markan Miracle Catenae', *JBL* 89 (1970), pp. 265-91; Achtemeier, 'The Origin and Function of the Pre-Marcan Miracle Catenae', *JBL* 91 (1972), pp. 198-221; Achtemeier, 'Gospel Miracle Tradition and the Divine Man', *Interpretation* 26 (1972), pp. 174-97; H. D. Betz, 'Jesus as Divine Man', in *Jesus and the Historian: Written in Honor of Ernest Cadman Colwell*, ed. F. T. Trotter (Philadelphia: Westminster, 1968), pp. 114-33; O. Betz, 'The Concept of the So-called "Divine Man" in Mark's Christology', in *Studies in New Testament and Early Christian Literature: Essays in Honour of Allen P. Wikgren*, ed. D. E. Aune (Leiden: Brill, 1972), pp. 229-51; J. B. Cobb, 'Trajectories and Historic Routes', *Semeia* 24 (1982), pp. 89-98; D. Georgi, *Die Gegner des Paulus im 2. Korintherbrief* (Neukirchen-Vluyn: Neukirchener, 1964); H. C. Kee, 'Aretalogy and Gospel', *JBL* 92 (1973), pp. 402-22; Kee, *Community of the New Age: Studies in Mark's Gospel* (London: SCM, 1977); M. E. Boring, *Truly Human/Truly Divine: Christological Language and the Gospel Form* (St. Louis: CBP Press, 1984), pp. 19-20.

50. D. L. Tiede, *The Charismatic Figure as Miracle Worker*, SBLDS 1 (Missoula: Scholars, 1972), p. 1.

51. Tiede, *Charismatic Figure*, pp. 244-9; C. R. Holladay, *Theios Aner in Hellenistic-Judaism: A Critique*, SBLDS 40 (Missoula: Scholars, 1977), pp. 241-2; E. V. Gallagher, *Divine Man or Magician?* SBLDS 64 (Scholars, 1982), pp. 173-80.

useful concept of a 'divine man' into an all-embracing paradigm. Attempts to solve the genre of the gospels through aretalogy and trajectory, therefore, have failed to win widespread critical assent.

4. The Jewish Background

Three main areas of Judaism have been investigated for parallels to the gospels: Old Testament literature, midrash and Rabbinic biography. The most common parts of the Old Testament have been the Moses legends and the Pentateuchal traditions: thus Baker compares the sequence of the narrative about Jesus in the gospels with that of Moses, while Hobbs sees Exodus as a source of 'models' for Mark, comparing the 'six days' of Mark 9:2 with those of Exodus 24. Kline notes the similar combination of teaching and narrative material within a covenantal context and sees a structural parallel with Exodus, which he calls 'the Gospel of Moses', whereas for Glasswell it is the idea of fulfilment in history which provides the link between Matthew and the Pentateuchal traditions.[52] For still others, the parallel is to be found within the Elisha legends or patterns of late Old Testament prophecy.[53]

Michael Goulder has picked up earlier suggestions that the gospels are lectionaries, designed to be read in worship,[54] and argued that they were composed according to the principles of midrash: Mark is a midrashic work following Old Testament works, designed to run over half a year, whereas Matthew is a midrash on Mark, and Luke follows on from Matthew.[55] It is difficult to demonstrate the existence of such works within primitive worship, and the narrative itself is not always in suitable blocks. In addition, Philip Al-

52. Dom Aelred Baker, 'Form and the Gospels', *Downside Review* 88 (1970), pp. 14-26; Edward C. Hobbs, 'Norman Perrin on Methodology in the Interpretation of Mark', in *Christology and a Modern Pilgrimage: A Discussion with Norman Perrin*, ed. Hans Dieter Betz (Missoula: SBL/Scholars, 1974), pp. 53-60; Meredith G. Kline, 'The Old Testament Origins of Gospel Genre', *Westminster Theological Journal* 38 (1975), pp. 1-27; M. E. Glasswell, 'St. Matthew's Gospel — History or Book?', *Communio Viatorum* 24 (1981), pp. 41-5.

53. Raymond E. Brown, 'Jesus and Elisha', *Perspective* 12 (1971), pp. 85-104; Heinrich Kraft, 'Die Evangelien und die Geschichte Jesu', *Theologische Zeitschrift* 37 (1981), pp. 321-41.

54. Philip Carrington, *The Primitive Christian Calendar: A Study in the Making of the Marcan Gospel* (CUP, 1952); W. D. Davies, 'Reflections on Archbishop Carrington's "The Primitive Christian Calendar"', in *The Background of the NT*, ed. Davies and Daube, pp. 124-52; Aileen Guilding, *The Fourth Gospel and Jewish Worship* (OUP, 1960).

55. Goulder, *Midrash and Lection in Matthew* (London: SPCK, 1974); *The Evangelist's Calendar: A Lectionary Explanation of the Development of Scripture* (London: SPCK, 1978); *Luke: A New Paradigm* (SAP, 1989).

exander has concluded that Goulder's appeal to midrash as the explanation of Matthew's redaction of Mark is 'highly questionable' and difficult to fit into the usual methods and rules of midrash. Similarly, R. T. France has disputed how widespread midrashic techniques were in the first century AD, while Leon Morris has turned his previous criticisms of lectionary hypotheses by Carrington and Guilding against Goulder also.[56] Graham Stanton's investigation of the Jewish background has produced the concept of Matthew as a creative interpreter or exegete, elucidating or expanding the tradition; similarly David Orton calls him a scribe, both faithful to the old and productive of the new (Matt. 13:52).[57]

Alexander is also responsible for a clear and helpful survey of the evidence for biographical material within the Rabbinic tradition.[58] He examines the classification of the different types, the development and literary aspects of the anecdotes and their function within Rabbinic society, with a cautious underplaying of the kind of 'heroification' rampant in many studies on aretalogy and divine men. After a brief comment on the historicity of the anecdotes, he compares them with the gospels and concludes: 'There are no Rabbinic parallels to the Gospels as such. This is by far the most important single conclusion to emerge from this paper.' This result is surprising, given the biographical precedents within the Old Testament (Moses and David) and the wealth of Rabbinic anecdotal material, but he concludes that no Rabbi held 'the central position that Jesus held in early Christianity'. The benefits from such a comparative study are a renewed stress on the *written* style and nature of the gospels, as opposed to the more oral Rabbinic material, and the raising of various questions about the analytical techniques commonly employed by gospel critics. For the origin of the gospel genre, however, Alexander concludes that we must look else-

---

56. Philip S. Alexander, 'Rabbinic Judaism and the New Testament', *ZNW* 74 (1983), pp. 237-46, and 'Midrash and the Gospels', in *Synoptic Studies: The Ampleforth Conferences of 1982 and 1983*, ed. C. M. Tuckett, JSNTSS 7 (Sheffield: JSOT Press, 1984), pp. 1-18, quotation from p. 13; R. T. France, 'Jewish Historiography, Midrash, and the Gospels', in *Gospel Perspectives III: Studies in Midrash and Historiography*, ed. R. T. France and D. Wenham (Sheffield: JSOT, 1983), pp. 99-127; and Leon Morris, 'The Gospels and the Jewish Lectionaries', *Gospel Perspectives III*, pp. 129-56.

57. G. N. Stanton, 'Matthew as a Creative Interpreter of the Sayings of Jesus', in *Das Evangelium und die Evangelien*, ed. Peter Stuhlmacher (Tübingen: J. C. B. Mohr, 1983), pp. 273-87; ET as *The Gospel and the Gospels*, ed. Peter Stuhlmacher (Grand Rapids: Eerdmans, 1991), pp. 257-72. See also, David E. Orton, *The Understanding Scribe: Matthew and the Apocalyptic Ideal*, JSNTSS 25 (SAP, 1989).

58. Alexander, 'Rabbinic Biography and the Biography of Jesus: A Survey of the Evidence', in *Synoptic Studies*, pp. 19-50; quotation p. 40.

where and suggests the Graeco-Roman world.[59] Therefore, we shall concentrate for the rest of this study upon Graeco-Roman literature arising from that world.[60]

5. *The Graeco-Roman Milieu*

Renewed interest in the Graeco-Roman milieu has appeared in both the USA and Europe. The SBL *Task Force on Gospel Genre* produced several important papers in the early 1970s: Petersen stressed the necessity of genre criticism for literary interpretation; Baird enumerated twelve different genres to be found within the gospels, but claimed that the overall combination of them was unique; Doty saw the definition of genre in relational terms and that a work's genre is to be found in the structure of the whole work; Georgi, writing from within an aretalogical approach, thought that 'Mark consciously presents the record of Jesus in analogy to the philosopher-vita'.[61] Throughout the next decade, many and various attempts were made to find parallels and analogies with Graeco-Roman literary genres: Barr looked at the Socratic Dialogues, Bilezikian at Greek Tragedy, Du Plessis at historical monograph and biographical narrative, Roland Frye at dramatic history (as seen in Plutarch, Shakespeare and Shaw), Praeder at the ancient novel, Standaert at the canons of rhetorical discourse and Via at the concept of tragi-comedy.[62] The issues of

59. *Ibid.*, pp. 40-1; note also: 'The Rabbinic world, however, provides no parallel for the overall work we call Gospel', in *Narrative Parallels to the New Testament*, ed. Francis Martin, SBL Resources for Biblical Study 22 (Atlanta: Scholars, 1988), p. 19; similarly, Rabbi Michael Hilton and Fr. Gordian Marshall OP, *The Gospels and Rabbinic Judaism* (London: SCM, 1988), compare only individual gospel units with Rabbinic material, not the overall form of the gospels.

60. Several reviewers of the original edition criticized me for not comparing the gospels more with Jewish literature. However, at this point we are following Philip Alexander's direction towards Graeco-Roman literature in order to evaluate the major treatments of the genre of the gospels which were comparing them to Greek or Latin works. The question of why there are no Jewish or Rabbinic parallels for the gospels will be discussed further in Chapter 11, pp. 300-304 below and in my article 'Gospel Genre, Christological Controversy and the Absence of Rabbinic Biography', reproduced in Appendix II, pp. 322-41 below.

61. Norman R. Petersen, 'So-called Gnostic Type Gospels and the Question of the Genre "Gospel"', Working Paper for the Task Force on Gospel Genre (SBL, 1970); *SBL Proceedings 1972: Book of Seminar Papers for 108th Annual Meeting*, ed. Lane C. McGaughy, vol. 2, contains: J. Arthur Baird, 'Genre Analysis as a Method of Historical Criticism', pp. 385-411; William G. Doty, 'The Concept of Genre in Literary Analysis', pp. 413-48; Dieter Georgi, 'The Records of Jesus in the Light of Ancient Accounts of Revered Men', pp. 527-42, quotation from p. 541.

62. David Laurence Barr, 'Towards a Definition of the Gospel Genre: A Generic Analysis and Comparison of the Synoptic Gospels and the Socratic Dialogues by means of Aristotle's

the authors and genres of the gospels have clearly returned determined to make up for the neglect of the previous fifty years.

Finally, we come at long last to the point where the critical wheel has turned full circle, to the comparison of the genre of the gospels with Graeco-Roman biography. In all his work, Charles H. Talbert is keen to establish links between the gospels and Graeco-Roman literature, especially biography. The fullest discussion of his view is in *What Is a Gospel?* in which he responds to Bultmann's objection that the gospels cannot be biography and proposes a new classification of the main examples of Graeco-Roman biography and fits the gospels squarely into this.[63] Writing at the same time as Talbert, Philip Shuler also proposed a biographical genre for the gospels; he argued for the existence of a subgroup of biography, encomium or laudatory biography, with examples of this genre, and then suggested how the gospels could be fitted in as well.[64] Although neither Talbert's nor Shuler's work has been accepted in its entirety, they have helped to produce a massive sea change in the interpretation of the gospels. Assumptions that the gospels are biographies or contain some biographical material or features are increasingly common.[65] Gerald Downing agrees with Talbert and Shuler against the Bultmannian *sui generis* view of the gospels, but believes the search for a distinctive genre to be mistaken. Instead, very important analo-

---

Theory of Tragedy', Ph.D. Diss., Florida State University, 1974; Gilbert G. Bilezikian, *The Liberated Gospel: A Comparison of the Gospel of Mark and Greek Tragedy* (Grand Rapids: Baker, 1977); Isak du Plessis, 'Die genre van Lukas se evangelie', *Theol. Evang.* 15.1 (Pretoria: 1982), pp. 19-28; Roland Mushat Frye, 'A Literary Perspective for Criticism of the Gospels', in *Jesus and Man's Hope*, vol. 2 (Pittsburgh Theological Seminary, 1971), pp. 207-19; Susan Marie Praeder, 'Luke-Acts and the Ancient Novel', in *SBL Seminar Papers* (Chico: Scholars Press, 1981), pp. 269-92; B. H. M. G. M. Standaert, *L'Evangile selon Marc: composition et genre littéraire* (Zevenkerken: Brugge, 1984); Dan O. Via, Jr., *Kerygma and Comedy in the New Testament* (Philadelphia: Fortress, 1975).

63. C. H. Talbert, *What Is a Gospel? The Genre of the Canonical Gospels* (Fortress 1977/ SPCK 1978); full details of the rest of the work of Talbert and the other scholars mentioned below will be found in our discussion in Chapter 4 below.

64. P. L. Shuler, *A Genre for the Gospels: The Biographical Character of Matthew* (Philadelphia: Fortress, 1982).

65. See, for example, V. K. Robbins, *Jesus the Teacher* (Philadelphia: Fortress, 1984), pp. 1-5; Kloppenborg, *Formation of Q*, pp. 262 and 327-28; Laurence Cantwell, 'The Gospels as Biographies', *Scottish Journal of Theology* 34 (1981), pp. 193-200; W. S. Vorster, 'Kerygma/History and the Gospel Genre', *NTS* 29 (1983), pp. 87-95; Christopher Tuckett, *Reading the New Testament* (London: SPCK, 1987), pp. 75-6; Mary Ann Beavis, *Mark's Audience*, pp. 37-9; Martin, *Narrative Parallels to the New Testament*, pp. 19-24; B. Lindars, *John* (SAP, 1990), p. 26, and *The Study and Use of the Bible*, ed. John Rogerson, Christopher Rowland and Barnabas Lindars (Basingstoke: Marshall Pickering, 1988), p. 237.

gies between the gospels and Graeco-Roman literature are to be found in a search for shared *motifs*.[66]

Other suggestions about the gospels and Graeco-Roman biography have been coming out of Germany. Berger's discussion of New Testament genres included a section on biography and the same volume of *ANRW* also included relevant articles by Köster, Dormeyer and Frankemölle.[67] The symposium at Tübingen in 1982 had papers on the individual gospels which raised questions of genre — Hengel on Mark, Stanton on Matthew, Marshall on Luke, and Dunn on John — as well as two further contributions specifically on genre and Graeco-Roman biography: Guelich attempted to reintroduce the 'unique' point of view, arguing that the gospels have no real analogies in either Jewish or Graeco-Roman literature. Meanwhile, the classicist, Albrecht Dihle, provided a detailed coverage of the development of Graeco-Roman biography; he is clear about the general biographical character of the gospels, but less prone to classify them with the specific Greek literary genre of biography as seen in the works of Plutarch.[68] Lastly, David Aune's interest in both the general setting of the New Testament within the Graeco-Roman literary world and in the specific issue of the genre of the gospels is clear from all his work. Aune argues for the biographical genre of Mark, Matthew and John, but Luke-Acts is seen as a little different. Relating the genres of New Testament books to their Graeco-Roman counterparts is central for their interpretation.[69]

---

66. F. G. Downing, 'Contemporary Analogies to the Gospels and Acts: "Genres" or "Motifs"?', in *Synoptic Studies*, ed. Tuckett, pp. 51-65.

67. K. Berger, 'Hellenistische Gattungen im Neuen Testament', in *ANRW* II.25.2 (1984), pp. 1031-432 and 1831-85; H. Köster, 'Überlieferung und Geschichte der frühchristlichen Evangelienliteratur', pp. 1463-542; D. Dormeyer and H. Frankemölle, 'Evangelium als literarische Gattung und als theologischer Begriff', pp. 1543-704.

68. Peter Stuhlmacher (ed.), *Das Evangelium und die Evangelien* (Tübingen: J. C. B. Mohr, 1983), ET as *The Gospel and the Gospels*, ed. Peter Stuhlmacher (Grand Rapids: Eerdmans, 1991), containing: R. Guelich, 'The Gospel Genre', pp. 183-219 (ET pp. 173-208); M. Hengel, 'Probleme des Markusevangeliums', pp. 221-65 (ET 'Literary, Theological, and Historical Problems in the Gospel of Mark', pp. 209-51); G. N. Stanton, 'Matthew as a Creative Interpreter of the Sayings of Jesus', pp. 273-87 (ET pp. 257-72); I. H. Marshall, 'Luke and His "Gospel"', pp. 289-308 (ET pp. 273-92); J. D. G. Dunn, 'Let John Be John: A Gospel for Its Time', pp. 309-39 (ET pp. 293-322); A. Dihle, 'Die Evangelien und die griechische Biographie', pp. 383-411 (ET 'The Gospels and Greek Biography', pp. 361-86).

69. David E. Aune, *The New Testament in Its Literary Environment* (Cambridge: James Clarke & Co., 1988).

Conclusion

This historical survey has followed the discussion about the genre of the gospels through some 125 years of critical scholarship. We have gone around in an apparent circle with the same books now being cited as parallels analogous to the gospels as when we started. The conclusion is obvious therefore that, whatever might have been the case during the long reign of hypotheses about the oral kerygma and the uniqueness of the gospels, the more recent situation is that no one theory has really commanded widespread support. However, it is currently coming back into fashion to suggest some form of biographical genre for the gospels, despite the difficulties and criticisms of this view. It is of crucial importance that either the biographical hypothesis be given a proper scholarly footing or else exposed as a false trail.

As this survey has unfolded, we have seen that there have been two major areas of vulnerability affecting most theories: their handling of the literary theory of genre on the one hand and their understanding of the development of the various types of literature and literary relationships contemporary with the gospels on the other. If this is correct, it might explain some of the difficulties, since what is being suggested is a very demanding interdisciplinary study involving three vast and complicated disciplines: gospel studies, literary theory, and the literature of the Jewish and Graeco-Roman worlds. The secondary literature in each of these fields is enormous, and the expert from one discipline who strays into another is prey to any number of potential hazards. Nonetheless, the attempt must be made if an answer is to have any chance of succeeding with a reasonable degree of support. In order to exercise some control on the size of the three disciplines, we shall limit gospel studies here almost exclusively to the four canonical gospels, and contemporary literature to the genre of Graeco-Roman biography, since this is the analogy currently gaining favour. First, however, we must establish a good grasp of the literary theory of genre and the development of biography in the Graeco-Roman world; in the light of these two elements, a critique of the more recent attempts, detailed above but not yet evaluated, can then be undertaken. The second part of this study will offer a methodology whereby selected works of Graeco-Roman biography can be compared with the gospels in order to establish whether the gospels may indeed be included within the genre of biography.

CHAPTER 2

Genre Criticism and Literary Theory

[The New Testament writings] . . . their subject would not fit into any of the known genres.[1]

All literature may in fact be genre-bound, without this being consciously realised.[2]

W hen we cross over into the discipline of literary theory to lay a secure methodological foundation for the exploration of gospel genre, we notice immediately a similarity of scholarly debate and disagreement. On the one hand, some important literary figures such as Auerbach, quoted above, or Northrop Frye,[3] also assert that the gospels are unique. On the other hand, the quotation from Alastair Fowler is typical of much contemporary thinking which denies that anything can be *sui generis*. All are agreed that words like 'literary theory' and 'literature' do not admit of easy or precise definitions.[4] Increasingly, much modern literary theory sees literature and literary works as operating within frameworks of conventions and expectations. Chief

1. Erich Auerbach, *Mimesis: The Representation of Reality in Western Literature* (Princeton: University Press, 1953), p. 45.

2. Alastair Fowler, 'The Life and Death of Literary Forms', in *New Directions in Literary History*, ed. Ralph Cohen (London: Routledge & Kegan Paul, 1974), p. 81.

3. Northrop Frye, *The Great Code: The Bible and Literature* (London: Routledge & Kegan Paul, 1982), pp. 41 and 62.

4. Alastair Fowler, *Kinds of Literature: An Introduction to the Theory of Genres and Modes* (OUP, 1982), p. 1, or Northrop Frye, *Anatomy of Criticism* (Princeton: University Press, 1957), p. 13.

among these is the notion of genre: 'Every work of literature belongs to at least one genre. Indeed, it is sure to have a significant generic element.'[5] Many discussions of gospel genre repeat Hirsch's statement: 'All understanding of verbal meaning is necessarily genre-bound.'[6] If literature itself and verbal meaning are in fact 'genre-bound', then any notion of the gospels as generically unique serves only to confine them never to being understood. Petersen concludes: 'To say that "gospel" is a unique Christian genre only raises the problem of generic code; it does not solve it.'[7] To assist in solving it, this chapter will examine how the concept of genre is handled by literary theorists. After a brief look at the historical background, attention will be given to what genre is, how it may be defined, to its behaviour and how it is used in the interpretation of verbal meaning. Because of the interdisciplinary nature of this study, there will be copious quotation and reference to literary theorists for the benefit of those unfamiliar with this area.[8]

A. Historical Background

1. Classical Criticism[9]

Plato puts his classification of literature on the lips of Socrates; he divides poetry into three groups according to their mode of representation: simple narrative in the person of the author, narrative conveyed by 'imitation' (μίμησις), and that which mixes both sorts.[10] Aristotle's opening words of the *Poetics* describe his subject as 'poetry and its forms' (τῶν εἰδῶν αὐτῆς). These 'forms' or 'kinds' are epic, tragedy, comedy and dithyramb, to be distinguished by three criteria: the media of imitation (rhythm, speech, har-

---

5. Fowler, *Kinds of Literature*, p. 20.

6. E. D. Hirsch, Jr., *Validity in Interpretation* (New Haven: Yale University Press, 1967), p. 76; quoted by Talbert, *What Is a Gospel?*, p. 11; Mary Gerhart, 'Generic Studies: Their Renewed Importance in Religious and Literary Interpretation', *JAAR* 45 (1977), p. 312; Kloppenborg, *Formation of Q*, p. 2.

7. Petersen, *Literary Criticism for NT Critics*, p. 44.

8. For summaries, see Heather Dubrow, *Genre* (London: Methuen, 1982); Fowler, *Kinds of Literature*; *Theories of Literary Genre*, ed. J. P. Strelka (Pennsylvania State University Press, 1978); Hirsch, *Validity in Interpretation*, pp. 68-126; René Wellek and Austin Warren, *Theory of Literature*, 3rd edn (Harmondsworth: Penguin, 1963), pp. 226-37.

9. See further, D. A. Russell, *Criticism in Antiquity* (London: Duckworth, 1981); *Ancient Literary Criticism: The Principal Texts in Translation*, ed. D. A. Russell and M. Winterbottom (OUP, 1972).

10. *Republic*, 392d; trans. *Anc. Lit. Crit.*, p. 61.

mony), the objects of imitation (the people and what they are doing) and the mode of imitation (authorial narrative, or representing someone else, or with those involved actually doing something).[11] That literary genres should be described as 'forms' to be 'imitated' reflects the wider Platonic concept of the 'Ideal Forms' governing all things. For Aristotle, the important principle is that literary works should conform to the form, metre, style, language, and so on, which is *appropriate* or *fitting* to the genre, i.e. τὸ ἁρμόττον.[12] This principle of 'propriety' was crucial in ancient genre theory. Both Cicero, with regard to rhetoric (*Orator* 70-75), and Horace, for poetry, stress the principle of *decorum*. The *Ars Poetica* mocks a painter who might combine unsuitable partners, such as a human head on a horse's neck or a beautiful woman with an ugly fish (lines 1-9); similarly, various metres are fitting for different genres of poetry: 'Everything must keep the appropriate place to which it was allotted' (lines 73-92).[13] The later scholiasts, librarians and grammarians have a similar concern in their various divisions for all the forms of ancient literature. While one must be cautious about reading back from later rhetorical theory to the actual practice of classical poets and prose writers, the general guiding principle of classical genre criticism is clear: 'Each genre has its own rules and proprieties.'[14]

2. Dark and Middle Ages

Such writing as survives from these times tends to follow classical models. In biography, the work of Suetonius has great influence, for instance on Einhard's *Vita Karoli* (c. AD 835) or on the *St Wulfstan* of William of Malmesbury (c. 1093-1143). Meanwhile, William of Poitiers' *Gesta Guillelmi Ducis* (c. 1075) reflects many classical parallels and shows knowledge of Sallust. As regards genre itself, the mediaeval period had an interesting contrast between theory and practice. There is little critical consideration of genre itself, and what there is tends to be only in general terms. On the other hand, it was a period of experimentation and development of new genres and generic labels.[15]

11. *Poetics*, 1447a-1448a; trans. *Anc. Lit. Crit.*, pp. 90-3.

12. See the discussion about metres for genres, *Poetics*, 1459b-1460a: 'nature herself teaches people to choose the metre appropriate to the composition', trans. *Anc. Lit. Crit.*, p. 125.

13. Trans. *Anc. Lit. Crit.*, pp. 279-81; see also, C. O. Brink, *Horace on Poetry* (CUP, 1971).

14. Quintilian, *Institutio Oratoria*, 10.2.21; trans. *Anc. Lit. Crit.*, p. 403; see also, *Menander Rhetor*, ed./trans./comm. by D. A. Russell and N. G. Wilson (OUP, 1981).

15. Fowler, *Kinds of Literature*, pp. 142-7; Dubrow, *Genre*, pp. 52-5.

3. The Renaissance and Neo-classical Periods

The Renaissance rediscovered both classical literature itself and genre criticism and theory, especially Aristotle and Horace. Italian critics such as Julius Caesar Scaliger and Antonio Sebastiano Minturno promoted ideas of genres with their different forms and rules. English critics, such as Sir Philip Sidney, also concentrated on Aristotle and Horace, though with perhaps less stress on the rules.[16] Neo-classical critics also followed classical theory and rules. Ben Jonson translated Horace's *Ars Poetica* in rhyming couplets: 'Each subject should retain/The place allotted it, with decent thews.'[17] Those writing on criticism include Dryden, Goldsmith and, above all, Pope's *An Essay on Criticism*. Once again, however, we find a tension between theory and practice. 'What does engage them above all . . . is repeating and refining the rules for each genre and testing particular works against those norms' — even though often these rules were not followed totally by the writers themselves.[18]

4. The Nineteenth Century

The explosion of literature in the nineteenth century brought many changes and developments of genres. The Romantic critics, with their great stress on the individual, rejected generic rules and norms. Under the pressures of the new situation of wider audiences, rapid publication and cheaper printing, genres could multiply and be short-lived — as can be demonstrated by the different types of the novel.[19] Darwinian evolutionary theory also contributed to this ferment, such that even someone as concerned for Aristotelian principles as Matthew Arnold was prepared to accept change and development of genres.[20]

This brief survey has demonstrated how influential Aristotelian genre theory was up to the beginning of the twentieth century. Despite much experimentation and development of genres themselves, the theory of genre itself did not develop much beyond Aristotelian concepts of separate genres of literature, each with its own rules and appropriate features. All this, however, was about to change.

---

16. Dubrow, *Genre*, pp. 55-63.
17. *Of the Art of Poetry*, lines 124-5, trans. *Ars P.* 1.89; Fowler, *Kinds of Literature*, p. 181.
18. Dubrow, *Genre*, p. 70; see also pp. 63-71, and Fowler, *Kinds of Literature*, pp. 27-8.
19. Wellek and Warren, *Theory*, pp. 232-3.
20. Dubrow, *Genre*, pp. 77-81.

5. The Twentieth Century

Northrop Frye comments that 'the critical theory of genres is stuck precisely where Aristotle left it. The very word "genre" sticks out in an English sentence as the unpronounceable and alien thing it is.'[21] He moves from such classical prescriptivism to a descriptive approach, for a literary critical method of 'classification' or 'schematization' of literature.[22] Such a taxonomy is attempted through four essays: the theory of *Modes*, concentrating on the subject or hero; the theory of *Symbols*, or units of literary structure, classified by different phases of the interpretation; the theory of *Myths*, a broad category linked to ideas of archetypes, related to the four seasons; and the theory of *Genres*. The last is 'an undeveloped subject in criticism'; he adds to the three Greek genres of epic, drama and lyric, a fourth, 'prose' or 'fiction' for the novel and the printed page.[23] Despite the importance and influence of Frye's work, it still remains true that his principal concern is taxonomic; for the development and function of genres we need to look elsewhere.

Benedetto Croce argued that such attempts to classify literature prevent the interpretation of each individual work. Others suggested that every work must be seen as unique, and thus the level of genre is reduced to that of the individual work, interpreted as the reader is able; the intention of the author is irrecoverable and cannot be used as a guide. However, Wellek and Warren's *Theory of Literature* contains a whole chapter on 'Literary Genres', as well as discussion of the development of genres.[24] Following on from this, E. D. Hirsch, Jr. stressed the importance of genre in the proper interpretation of literature and, against the 'intentionalist fallacy', reasserted a defence of author as determinative of the meaning of the text.[25] Finally, Alastair Fowler dedicated his comprehensive survey, *Kinds of Literature*, arguing for the importance of genre for all communication, to 'E. D. Hirsch, Jr.'[26]

Additional interest in genre has come from structuralist critics. This area is complicated by the fact that structuralism as such is a wide-ranging and diverse philosophy or ideology, encompassing much more than literary

21. Frye, *Anatomy of Criticism*, p. 13.

22. *Ibid.*, 'Polemical Introduction', pp. 3-29.

23. *Ibid.*, pp. 246-8.

24. Wellek and Warren, *Theory*, pp. 226-37 and 252-69; see also Eliseo Vivas, 'Literary Classes: Some Problems', *Genre* 1 (1968), pp. 97-105.

25. Hirsch, *Validity*, esp. pp. 68-126; and also, *The Aims of Interpretation* (Chicago: University Press, 1976).

26. Fowler, *Kinds of Literature*, p. viii; see also, 'Life and Death'.

theory. Further, various groups such as the Russian formalists and the French experts on linguistics and semiotics have had major influence upon structuralist approaches to literature at different times. Thus it is probably safer to speak of structuralists rather than structuralism itself.[27] Structuralist approaches are more concerned with a theory of reading than a theory of literature itself. From linguistics, structuralists have borrowed Ferdinand de Saussure's distinction between *langue* — a system of rules and norms, as in a language — and *parole* — an actual utterance manifesting the system. When the *parole* is in written form, it is divorced from the speaker: therefore, the key activities are *écriture* and *lecture,* writing and reading, rather than a writer and his work. The *reader,* in order to understand any particular *parole,* must become *competent* in mastering the *conventions* which make up the underlying structures of the *langue. La langue* is thus seen as a *system* of relations and oppositions. Crucial to the understanding of this system are the *signs* and what they *signify* to the reader, hence the use of *semiotics.* Through these signs and conventions the reader is enabled to *naturalize* a written communication, to bring it within his own culture and understanding — and thus discover the meaning. Such a stress on the reader led Roland Barthes to talk of 'The Death of the Author'[28] and many 'post-structuralists' concentrate solely on reader and text. The study of text-linguistics attempts to apply the insights of linguistics to a whole text, rather than just sentences, through analysis of its discourse; meanwhile, the importance of the reader is stressed in the development of reader-response criticism.[29]

It is thus clear that genre is a major literary element, necessary for writing, reading and valid interpretation. Its importance for hermeneutics can be seen in the work of people like Gadamer, Todorov and Ricoeur.[30] Genre is

27. See Jonathan Culler, *Structuralist Poetics: Structuralism, Linguistics and the Study of Literature* (London: Routledge & Kegan Paul, 1975); Daniel Patte, *What Is Structural Exegesis?* (Philadelphia: Fortress, 1976); Petersen's *Literary Criticism for NT Critics,* pp. 33-48, summarizes important work by Roman Jakobson and Vladimir Propp's *Morphology of the Folktale* (Austin: University of Texas Press, 1968).

28. Roland Barthes, 'La Mort de l'auteur', *Mantéia* 5 (1968), ET 'The Death of the Author', in *Image Music Text,* trans. Stephen Heath (London: Fontana, 1977), pp. 142-8; the final words conclude: 'The birth of the reader must be at the cost of the death of the Author.'

29. Klaus W. Hempfer, *Gattungstheorie: Information und Synthese* (Munich: Fink, 1973); for reader-response criticism, see Chapter 1, notes 36-8 above.

30. Hans-Georg Gadamer, *Truth and Method* (London: Sheed and Ward, 1975); Tzvetán Todorov, *The Fantastic: A Structural Approach to Literary Genre* (Ithaca, N.Y.: Cornell University Press, 1975); Paul Ricoeur, 'The Hermeneutical Function of Distanciation', *Philosophy Today* 17 (1973), pp. 129-41; Ricoeur, *Hermeneutics and the Human Sciences: Essays on Language, Action and Interpretation,* ed./trans. John B. Thompson (CUP, 1981); see also Mary Gerhart, 'Generic

part of the structure operative in the distance between a reader and a text which needs to be mastered in order for understanding and interpretation to take place.

6. Summary

The critical theory of genres was dominated by classical notions of Ideal Form and the need for appropriate methods and styles for each genre. Despite such theory, however, these ideas were often ignored in actual literary practice. After classical prescriptivism was replaced by descriptive approaches, in recent years genre has assumed renewed importance as a guide to the proper understanding of any verbal communication.

B. Purposes and Functions

1. Nominalism and Classification

According to Juliet, 'a rose by any other name would smell as sweet' (*Romeo and Juliet* II.2.43). Thus names have no power in themselves, but are merely useful labels or descriptions, so that everybody understands what is being described. What constitutes the group or genre is that they all share the same name. Such a *nominalistic* view of genres has been adopted by various theorists, most notably Croce.[31] The purpose of naming objects is an aid to communication, but has no effect on the properties of the object — hence the smell of the rose remains unchanged. If, however, this notion is transferred to less concrete objects such as literary genres, then the name begins to have a purpose: at first it may be a passive one in mere classification, as with types of roses, but soon it goes on to have an influence or control on the writing so named: 'Classification is a mode of naming, and I have enough empathy with the elementary principle of naming to desire that names acquired in classifying do their jobs — the exerting of a certain amount of linguistic control over entities.'[32] However, this notion soon runs into difficulties: literary genres are not so easily classifiable as different sets of flowers. So, whereas Hough can re-

---

Studies', *JAAR* 45 (1977), pp. 309-25, and 'Generic Competence in Biblical Hermeneutics', *Semeia* 43 (1988), pp. 29-44; Anthony C. Thistleton, *The Two Horizons* (Exeter: Paternoster, 1980).

31. Benedetto Croce, *Aesthetic: As Science of Expression and General Linguistic* (London: Peter Owen, 1953), esp. pp. 67-73 and 111-17.

32. W. G. Doty, 'The Concept of Genre', 1972, p. 413; Wellek and Warren, *Theory*, p. 226.

fer to genres as 'pigeon-holes', Fowler replies that 'in reality genre is much less of a pigeon hole than a pigeon'.[33] Even Northrop Frye is aware of the need to go beyond mere classification: 'The purpose of criticism by genres is not so much to classify as to clarify such traditions and affinities'.[34] None the less, clarification does not take us much further and so Frye's account is criticized by many as being merely a taxonomy.[35] Genre, therefore, is not merely a name, nor just a method of classification.

2. Descriptive or Prescriptive?

Such nominalistic or descriptive approaches to genre are a reaction against classical and neo-classical theory which was prescriptive: genres were fixed, clearly distinguished one from another and each with their own appropriate elements to be included and rules to be obeyed. In fact, literary works and genres cannot be directed in this mechanistic fashion, and both classical and neo-classical authors broke their rules regularly. However, the retreat into descriptivism will not succeed either; taxonomy on its own is insufficient. Therefore some form of middle ground must be sought between these two extremes which allows for more direction and operation than mere descriptive classification, yet which avoids the legalistic prescriptive system of much classical theory. Doty was quoted above as wanting genres to exert 'a certain amount of linguistic control over entities'. Wellek and Warren argue similarly that genres do have an effect; they are not just principles of order, but act as 'institutions', even 'institutional imperatives'. They find this middle ground, therefore, in a notion of *regulation:* 'We must conceive of genre as a "regulative" concept, some underlying pattern, a convention which is real, i.e. effective because it actually moulds the writing of concrete works'.[36]

3. Conventions

If classical theory involved rules, contemporary debate prefers conventions. As Frye said in 1957, 'the study of genres has to be founded on the study of

33. Graham Hough, *An Essay on Criticism* (London: Duckworth, 1966), p. 84; Fowler, *Kinds of Literature*, p. 37; see also Gerhart, 'Generic Studies', p. 312.

34. Frye, *Anatomy of Criticism*, p. 247.

35. Todorov, *The Fantastic*, p. 18; chapter 1, *passim*, criticizes Frye; see also, Culler, *Structuralist Poetics*, p. 136.

36. Doty, see n. 32 above; Wellek and Warren, *Theory*, pp. 226 and 261-2.

convention'.[37] Since then, structuralist critics have made convention one of their key concepts. The whole of speaking and writing is itself a system of conventions — and this includes genre: 'A genre, one might say, is a conventional function of language.'[38] Genre is one of the conventions in a *langue* which we must master to understand a *parole*. Hirsch also sees language as a system of conventions: 'There is probably no better single word than "convention" to embrace the entire system of usage traits, rules, customs, formal necessities and proprieties which constitute a type of verbal meaning.'[39] If language is made up of conventions, this is even more true of literature, which has not only the conventions of the language in which it is written, but also all the literary conventions relevant to that type of writing. Thus, in order to master a specific piece of literature (the *parole*), we need to know the *langue* of the language and the *langue* of that piece of literature. Chief among such conventions is genre: 'Of all the codes of our literary *langue*, I have no hesitation in proposing genre as the most important, not least because it incorporates and organizes many others. . . . It is an instrument not of classification or prescription, but of meaning.'[40] In this way, therefore, meaning becomes the middle ground sought between prescription and description.

4. A Set of Expectations

Next we must consider how this convention functions. Hirsch sees genre as 'a system of expectations': 'These expectations could have arisen only from a genre idea: "in this type of utterance, we expect these types of traits".'[41] Such expectations arise out of our previous experience of other, similar types of utterance. This idea of generic expectations is of crucial importance in much structuralist criticism in understanding both how language itself functions as well as the use of genre. Thus Culler says that genres are 'sets of expectations which allow sentences of a language to become signs of different kinds in a second-order literary system. The same sentence can have a different meaning depending on the genre in which it appears.' Genre functions as a 'norm or expectation to guide the reader in his encounter with the text'. He goes on to quote the French structuralist, Marcelin Pleynet: 'It is indeed this word (novel, poem) placed on the cover of the book which (by convention) geneti-

---

37. Frye, *Anatomy of Criticism*, p. 96.
38. Culler, *Structuralist Poetics*, p. 136.
39. Hirsch, *Validity*, p. 92.
40. Fowler, *Kinds of Literature*, p. 22.
41. Hirsch, *Validity*, pp. 83 and 73.

cally programmes or "originates" our reading. We have here (with the genre "novel", "poem") a *master word* which from the outset reduces complexity.'[42]

Such an understanding of genre does occupy the middle ground between descriptivism and prescriptivism. It is clearly much more than a nominal description of the work, for it is influencing the author's actual writing as well as forming the reader's expectations in advance. On the other hand, we are not talking about prescriptive rules, which must be obeyed, but rather a conventional set of expectations, which allows scope for the expectations to be fulfilled and occasionally for the unexpected. Dubrow uses the notion of 'contract' to describe this:

> The way genre establishes a relationship between author and reader might fruitfully be termed a generic contract. Through such signals as the title, the metre and the incorporation of familiar topoi into his opening lines, the poet sets up such a contract with us. He in effect agrees that he will follow at least some of the patterns and conventions we associate with the genre or genres in which he is writing, and we in turn agree that we will pay close attention to certain aspects of his work while realizing that others, because of the nature of the genres, are likely to be far less important.[43]

Thus, not only can the same sentence have different meanings within different generic contexts, but so can larger units. Exactly the same footage of a typical film motif, such as a spy fighting with a soldier on top of a railway carriage, will produce very different audience reactions, depending on whether it forms part of a spy thriller (tension) or a comic parody (laughter). 'Without helpful orientations like titles and attributions, readers are likely to gain widely different generic conceptions of a text, and these conceptions will be constitutive of their subsequent understanding.'[44] If we apply this insight to the gospels for a moment, it is clear that very different expectations will arise from considering their genre as lectionary or aretalogy. Furthermore, we can have no idea of what to expect from a *sui generis* work!

---

42. Culler, *Structuralist Poetics*, pp. 129 and 136, quoting Pleynet, *Théorie d'ensemble* (Paris: Editions du Seuil, 1968), pp. 95-6.

43. Dubrow, *Genre*, p. 31; see also, Culler: 'The function of genre conventions is essentially to establish a contract between writer and reader', *Structuralist Poetics*, p. 147.

44. Hirsch, *Validity*, p. 75; Dubrow, *Genre*, pp. 1-7, makes a similar point by exploring the different reactions and expectations arising from considering a brief paragraph as the opening sentences of works of differing genres, such as a murder novel or *Bildungsroman*.

5. Mistaken Expectations

This idea of genre as a set of expectations is most clearly grasped, argues Hirsch, when a mistake is made in our expectations. Thus communication may proceed quite happily until problems occur, especially something totally *un*expected. At this point, we may experience a flash of insight which radically alters our expectations and revises our understanding of the communication to date: 'Oh! you've been talking about a book all the time. I thought it was about a restaurant.'[45] A true understanding of the genre may be hidden in the text at the start, therefore; perhaps useful master-words like the title are missing, or misunderstood. However, as reading or communication proceeds, the revision of our mistaken expectations leads us to a proper understanding of genre. Hirsch develops this in his later work, *The Aims of Interpretation*, with the concept of 'Corrigible Schemata' — a phrase taken from Piaget's research in child development. Developmental psychologists start out with a schema in the same way that scientists begin with a hypothesis, or art historians with a genre: 'A schema sets up a range of predictions or expectations which, if fulfilled confirms the schema, but if not fulfilled causes us to revise it . . . the process of understanding is itself a process of validation.'[46] This all helps to clarify still further the concept of genre as a set of expectations; we approach a work with certain generic expectations which are then constantly checked and revised in the light of what we actually find. Dubrow describes the process of reading a work with changing expectations and points out that we often go back to earlier passages to check something, or even re-read the entire work.[47]

The confounding of generic expectations plays an important part in much comedy. Speaking of the operation of genre at the level of intelligibility or *vraisemblance*, Culler says: 'We know, for example, that it would be totally inappropriate for one of Corneille's heroes to say, "I'm fed up with all these problems and shall go and be a silversmith in a provincial town".'[48] Of course, that is precisely what *does* happen in much comedy, whether it be the Aristophanic παρὰ προσδοκίαν joke, where 'contrary to expectation' we get a sudden insertion of comic bathos in a passage of pseudo-high-flown language, or the deliberate mixing of genres for comic effect typical of modern television comedy, such as *Monty Python's Flying Circus*.

45. Hirsch, *Validity*, p. 71.
46. Hirsch, *The Aims of Interpretation*, pp. 32-3.
47. Dubrow, *Genre*, pp. 107-8.
48. Culler, *Structuralist Poetics*, p. 145.

Fowler also considers possible mistakes and imports a concept from information theory: 'In information theory, oral and written conventions work as signal systems, by which communications are constructed from series of signals.' In direct speech one can check back with the speaker to ensure that one has 'heard' the intended message. In literary works this is impossible, and when these works are old or unfamiliar, the possibilities for mistakes are increased. To counter this, information theory uses redundancy, defined as 'an additional set of rules, whereby it becomes increasingly difficult to make an undetectable mistake.' Redundancy is thus a superfluity or overabundance of rules and conventions to ensure that the message gets through all the 'noise' of extraneous signals which may mislead. Such superfluity means that even old or unfamiliar works whose conventions have been somewhat forgotten may be able to be reconstructed successfully. Redundancy in literature is expressed by literary conventions and 'of all literary forms the class whose continuance probably matters most is genre.'[49] So Fowler concludes his massive study of genres in *Kinds of Literature* with the statement: 'Genre is an organizing principle of the redundancies by which it is possible to break the hermeneutical circle and to reconstruct old or difficult works'.[50] So when dealing with documents like the gospels which are not part of our contemporary literature and whose conventions are unclear it is through genres that we may enter into the hermeneutical circle and comprehend their meaning.

6. Summary

Genres operate in a middle ground between the two extremes of classical prescriptivism and nineteenth-century descriptivism. They are conventions which assist the reader by providing a set of expectations to guide his or her understanding. Such expectations are corrected and further refined in the light of actual reading. Through genre we are enabled to understand even old or unfamiliar works, like the gospels.

---

49. Fowler, 'Life and Death', pp. 78-80, definition of redundancy quoted from Colin Cherry, *On Human Communication* (New York, 1961), p. 185; see also *Kinds of Literature*, pp. 21-2.
50. Fowler, *Kinds of Literature*, p. 278.

C. Definitions and Levels

1. *Terminology*

In discussions of genre theory and criticism, there are a large number of terms at hand: genre, form, type, kind and so on. This situation is especially complicated for biblical scholars because of the range of the word 'form', from the wider meaning of the 'form of a book as a whole' through to the technical use of 'forms' in form criticism. Translation from German muddies the water still further: both *Gattung* and *Formen* are often used untranslated in English.[51] Doty comments that German Old Testament scholars use *Gattung* for a preliterary type, which the New Testament scholars call *Formen*, reserving *Gattung* for the whole literary type, which we call 'genre'. For Doty, 'form' does not equal *Gattung*, but rather form and content together make up *Gattung*.[52] To prevent this confusion, the word *Gattung* will be avoided here. As for 'form', the range of possible meanings requires careful attention to its context. If it is intended to refer to technical form-critical 'forms' — of the various pericopae — this will be made explicit. 'Form' on its own is taken to include notions of shape or structure — as in 'the form of the book'. The plural use of 'literary forms' refers to specific literary conventional types which may range from forms as small as phrases to forms of complete works. Thus the qualifying context of the word must always be observed.

The main problem is the absence of a suitable English term. We will avoid the German *Gattung*, but 'genre' is French. Some early criticism preferred Latin or Greek words such as γένος, εἶδος, or *species*. Some dictionary definitions of 'genre' do not even include literary types or kinds.[53] Therefore some writers have tried to avoid 'genre' and use other terms. Shuler uses 'pattern' from time to time,[54] though whether this is any clearer is debatable. Hirsch prefers 'type', but this too has a wide range and he has to return to 'genre': 'It will be convenient to call that type which embraces the whole meaning of an utterance by the traditional term "genre".'[55] The gloss 'class' is equally problematic, particularly in the light of the discussion on classifica-

---

51. See J. M. Robinson's article, 'On the *Gattung* of Mark (and John)', where *Gattung* means the genre of the whole.

52. Doty, 'The Concept of Genre', pp. 418 and 434; see also Ernest Stahl's discussion of *Gattung, Art, genus, species* and genre in *Theories of Literary Genre*, ed. Strelka, p. 80.

53. Absent in the *Shorter Oxford English Dictionary* (OUP, 1973), but defined by *Chambers Twentieth Century Dictionary* as 'a literary species'.

54. Shuler, *A Genre for the Gospels*, p. 25.

55. Hirsch, *Validity*, p. 71.

tion above. Wittgenstein's term 'family resemblance' identifies the resemblance which several examples have in common. The attraction of 'family resemblance' is that it is sufficiently vague to cope with the blurred edges of genre (unlike 'class'), yet still sharp enough to have some meaning. 'Family resemblance theory seems to hold out the best hope to the genre critic.'[56] For our purposes, while 'family resemblance' will provide a useful analogue for genre, it is rather cumbersome without being much clearer. Thus, whereas such terms as pattern, class, type or family may help to expand the meaning of genre at any one time, none of them are sufficiently satisfactory to replace it for our circumstances, and therefore genre will continue to be the principal term for this study.

2. Levels of Genre

Classical literary theory sees genres at the level of *Universals,* especially Aristotle's genres of epic, lyric and drama. Frye follows this notion of large universal genres, while adding his fourth, 'prose'. These genres become so large and unwieldy that they cease to be of any use. Levels are polarized between Aristotelians — who think genres are very limited in number — and Croceans — who say there are as many genres as there are literary works.[57] Culler argues that certain post-structuralist interpretations, such as those of the *Tel Quel* group, similarly end up with as many groups as there are works, each with its own unique system.[58] Similarly, some gospel critics think each of the gospels to be unique, providing four different genres. However, if the universal genres are too big, calling every work its own genre is to make the concept so small that it has no use; the idea of a group or family of one does not yield much assistance for comparison. So we would argue that genre cannot operate truly at either extreme, but at several intervening levels.

3. Broad and Intrinsic Genres

Hirsch's idea that the true genre of a work may lie hidden at the start and emerge precisely as reading goes on has already been met. Thus, at the beginning genre is a vague and imprecise idea — which he calls *broad genre.* At the

---

56. Fowler, *Kinds of Literature,* p. 42.
57. See Hirsch, *The Aims of Interpretation,* pp. 67-71.
58. Culler, *Structuralist Poetics,* pp. 241-54.

end of the process of reading is the final understanding of the actual meaning as expressed precisely in the specifically chosen words — and so we may talk of unique meanings rather than unique genres. Between these extremes lies the work's *intrinsic genre,* which is the controlling conception, the shared set of expectations or contract, common to both author and reader; this is not as precise as the exact words, but yet a lot more precise than the vague, broad genre with which one commenced reading. In this way, Hirsch's intrinsic genre is similar to our 'set of expectations' concept: 'Understanding can occur only if the interpreter proceeds under the same system of expectations, and this shared generic conception, constitutive both of meaning and of understanding, is the intrinsic genre of the utterance.'[59]

So, genre starts at the broad, heuristic level, open to correction; becomes defined more exactly at the intrinsic level where reading confirms or corrects our initial expectations; and proceeds on to the actual, unique meaning of this particular text. We may represent the process as follows:

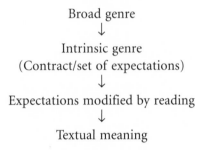

Broad genre
↓
Intrinsic genre
(Contract/set of expectations)
↓
Expectations modified by reading
↓
Textual meaning

This is rarely a simple, linear process; the developing encounter with the text involves the need for checking and redefining our expectations, and so we may move back through one or two stages several times before finally arriving at the meaning. The process is, therefore, one of narrowing and closer focus.

4. Mode, Genre and Subgenre

Fowler also has three levels at which generic conceptions operate, but they are levels of function, not meaning, affecting both composition and interpretation. We begin with the central level, for this is what we have been calling genre: this is explained as 'historical genre', a group about which there is general agreement in terms of historical origins and shared features of both form

59. Hirsch, *Validity,* pp. 80-1.

and content, even allowing for variety and change.[60] Operating at a higher or broader level above this is the concept of *mode*. Whereas a genre can be described in terms of a noun, mode is better seen adjectivally. Thus, a tragedy is an example of that genre and we would have certain expectations arising from the appropriate conventions of tragedy; however, things may occur in a tragic mode in all sorts of different writings and genres without those conventions. So mode is more wide-ranging and vague; it never implies a particular external form or structure and includes only a selection of the genre's features.[61] Thirdly, there is the lower or narrower level of subtypes or *subgenres*. Most genres can be subdivided, usually according to specific details such as subject-matter or motifs. In fact, whereas genre itself is a mix of many features of both form and content, subgenre is often determined by a particular subject or content. Such subgenres, Fowler suggests, are akin to what are termed genres in the classical rhetorical manner, such as *propemptikon* or *renuntiatio amoris*.[62] A representation of these levels of genre must show movement outwards, with genre in the centre:

Mode
(motifs and styles)
↑
Genre
(form and content)
↓
Subgenre
(subject and material)

While Hirsch's levels of genre help to ascertain the meaning of texts through increasing awareness of their genre, Fowler's levels of generic function illuminate both the understanding of the development of a group of texts and the genre to which they belong.

5. Constituent Features of Genre

Genre is thus a group of literary works sharing certain 'family resemblances' operating at a level between Universals and actual texts and between modes

---

60. Fowler, *Kinds of Literature*, pp. 56-7.
61. *Ibid.*, pp. 106-11.
62. Fowler, *Kinds of Literature*, pp. 111-18: see pp. 59-61 below.

and specific subgroups, and functioning as a set of expectations to guide interpretation. Next we must consider how genre is constituted and recognized, i.e. what sort of features help to make up a genre: 'If a theory of genres is to be more than a taxonomy it must attempt to explain what features are constitutive of functional categories which have governed the reading and writing of literature.'[63] The temptation to think of genre as defined by *one* particular feature, or even a couple, should be avoided because any one feature can appear in a number of different sorts of works. Therefore, one should look for many features; it is the combination of them which constitutes the genre. Thus genre is described by Doty as a 'congeries' or 'cluster of features', and Hirsch agrees: 'The best way to define a genre — if one decides that he wants to — is to describe the common elements in a narrow group of texts which have direct historical relationships.'[64] These common elements include those of both form and content: 'Genre should be conceived, we think, as a grouping of literary works based, theoretically, upon both outer form (specific metre or structure) and also upon inner form (attitude, tone, purpose — more crudely, subject and audience).'[65] This mixture of many different generic features makes up the cluster which we call a genre. These features are not in themselves definitive, but they contribute to the overall picture of the genre. So Fowler concludes: 'A kind is a type of literary work of a definite size, marked by a complex of substantive and formal features that always include a distinctive (though not usually unique) external structure.'[66]

6. Signalling the Whole

We cannot wait until the reading of the text is complete, and all the features have been noted, before deciding about the genre, since genre is a set of expectations to guide the reading. Therefore we need certain features to indicate or suggest the broad genre, and then closer reading of all the text in the light of those expectations will enable the intrinsic genre to be grasped more clearly. As Dubrow reminds us, this is not a legalistic process — if this is an example of genre *x*, then we must find *a, b, c* — but rather 'what if/then probably': 'What if the genre of this work is the *Bildungsroman?* Then probably the hero will. . . .'[67] Certain features give immediate generic clues, such as Pley-

---

63. Culler, *Structuralist Poetics*, p. 137.
64. Doty, 'The Concept of Genre', p. 440; Hirsch, *Validity*, p. 110.
65. Wellek and Warren, *Theory*, p. 231.
66. Fowler, *Kinds of Literature*, p. 74.
67. Dubrow, *Genre*, pp. 106-7.

net's 'master-word', the description on the book's cover which programmes our reading. Other elements can direct our generic expectations right at the beginning, such as the title of the work; allusion to other writers or examples, possibly in a prologue; the opening phrase or sentence may signal the genre;[68] certain names may indicate genre, such as heroes in epic, shepherds in pastoral or characters such as Pilgrim and Hopeful in allegory.[69] In this way we break into the hermeneutical circle: once we have picked up an initial vague or broad genre from one or more such indicators or signals, this genre programmes our expectations for certain other features also to occur. Whether or how they do so helps refine generic understanding down through intrinsic genre to the actual meaning of the specific utterance.

However, not every feature should be expected to occur in every example of the genre. Todorov says that genre is 'a principle operative in a number of texts, rather than what is specific about each of them'.[70] This prevents such an approach becoming the prescriptive rules of classical theory. It does not matter if a particular work does not have all the features or fit the genre exactly. What is important is that it has *sufficient* features for the family resemblance to be recognized: 'Recognition of genre depends on associating a complex of elements which need not all appear in one work. . . . Usually there are so many indicators, organized into so familiar a unity, that we recognize the generic complex instantly.'[71]

The final issue here concerns how all these features and conventions are learned. In structuralist terms this is described as the *acquisition of literary competence,* learning the 'grammar' of literature. While such grammar can be learned by explicit study, like the grammar of language itself, many generic conventions are acquired by authors and reader alike in *unconscious* ways, as we acquire the grammar of our native language: 'Codes often come to a writer indirectly, deviously, remotely, at haphazard. . . . So much of genre's operation is unconscious.'[72] This point may help to explain how the evangelists acquired the ideas of their chosen genre(s) and how their first readers understood their meaning immediately, whereas we, like foreigners, must undertake a deliberate process of learning and interpretation because of the great distance between us and the writers' culture and conventions.

---

68. Compare how the phrases 'Once upon a time . . .' and 'Good evening, here is the news . . .' function as immediate indicators of genre and provide the listeners with quite different expectations about how to interpret what follows.

69. See Fowler, *Kinds of Literature,* chapters 5 and 6 on Names and Signals.

70. Todorov, *The Fantastic,* p. 3.

71. Fowler, 'Life and Death', pp. 80-1.

72. Fowler, *Kinds of Literature,* pp. 43 and 52.

7. Summary

The term 'genre' includes ideas of pattern, class, type and family resemblance. Genre operates at an intermediate level between that of Universals and that of specific verbal meaning. From the point of view of function, mode is a broader concept than genre, which itself can be divided into subgenres. For the purposes of understanding, genre often begins as a vague, broad concept and is then refined by reading. Genre is made up of a wide range of features, comprising both form and content, several of which play an important part in signalling the genre at the start. Acquisition of such features and genres by authors and readers is often largely unconscious.

D. Development and Relationships

1. Generic Shifts

Genres do not resemble some kind of eternally immutable Platonic Ideal Forms, but are in a constant state of flux, shifting and regrouping as features alter and as new works are written. Consider for example the development of epic from Homer to Vergil and on through Spenser and Milton: there is still a family resemblance, but many of the specific *features* have altered immensely. Both genres themselves and the boundaries between them shift from age to age and according to locality.[73] Their names also change: 'Not only do generic labels change with time, but also (and this is far more confusing) the same labels come to be used in different ways.'[74] Thus, if we follow the term 'epic' still further to the film industry and the kinds of productions called either 'epic' in general (mode) or 'an epic' (genre), the point is clear. Given that genres, their boundaries and labels all shift, discussion of genre must always take account of such flexibility. Also, we must discuss the concept of genre appropriate to the time and place of writing, rather than confuse the issue by bringing in later, particularly twentieth-first-century, understandings of the genre as we may know it today.

---

73. Culler, *Structuralist Poetics*, p. 129.
74. Fowler, *Kinds of Literature*, p. 130; see further, chapter 8 'Generic Labels'.

43

2. *Generic Development*

An obvious model for generic development is some form of evolutionary process. Wellek is unhappy with this idea, since it is possible that a writer may reverse the development consciously and use archaic conventions. On the other hand, it is clear that there is development, and so the literary critic needs to establish literary relationships between the various authors and works.[75] Fowler, however, rejects Wellek's dismissal of evolutionary concepts. Genre evolves in the way a species evolves, or an institution. Like an institution, it is circumscribed by the confines of period and locality; as cultures change, so genres reflect that change. Thus it is appropriate to use biological analogies and talk in terms of 'the Life and Death of Literary Forms'.[76] Fowler's three-stage model for the development of genres will be followed below.

First, we need to appreciate the genre's *origins,* including both the sociological setting within which it arises and the literary setting within which it is placed.[77] As with the gospels, this may be an oral stage. Genre analysis of the whole literary form, however, really begins once the oral tradition assumes a literary shape and is written down. This is the genre's *primary stage,* the assembling of the various features into a recognizable group, so that these originally independent motifs become linked together. Often this phase may be unconscious: the writer may just see it as some fresh ideas. However, from a subsequent perspective, the new genre is realized.[78] An early practitioner can come to have enormous influence on subsequent writers — for example Aeschylus on tragedy or Theocritus on pastoral. Hans-Georg Gadamer stresses that genre is history-bound and is influenced by its classic expression or representation. Such classics affect both the composition and interpretation of subsequent examples of the genre.[79]

The *secondary stage* is when other writers begin to produce literature based consciously on the primary model. The classical stress on μίμησις/ *imitatio* assisted with this process. This stage is marked by conscious modification or sophistication of the genre. Thus Vergil draws on the primary Homer for his secondary *Aeneid,* or the primary Theocritus for his secondary *Eclogues,* but with each he takes the genre further on to a new stage.[80] The *tertiary stage* occurs when there is a quite new reinterpretation in a different di-

---

75. Wellek and Warren, *Theory,* pp. 255-60.
76. Fowler, 'Life and Death', pp. 83-8; *Kinds of Literature,* pp. 164-7.
77. See Doty, 'The Concept of Genre', pp. 422-8 on sociological settings.
78. Fowler, *Kinds of Literature,* pp. 156-9; 'Life and Death', p. 90.
79. Gadamer, *Truth and Method,* pp. 257-8.
80. Fowler, *Kinds of Literature,* pp. 160-2; 'Life and Death', p. 90.

rection. Often this may mean importing new features, or include burlesque or satire. The secondary stage can never be quite the same again.[81]

These stages may interpenetrate chronologically — so Vergil, as well as being secondary to Theocritus, acts as a primary stage for Milton, Spenser and Drayton. Further, he is quite capable of tertiary reinterpretation within his own work. So Fowler concludes that we must 'think in terms of continuous generic development. "Primary", "secondary" and "tertiary" then become relative to an observer interested in particular generic forms.'[82]

3. Generic Mixtures and Flexibility

Most literary critics are agreed that nothing literary comes about 'in a special act of creation *ex nihilo*. Human beings do not create in that way.'[83] All work is dependent on what precedes it; anything completely new would be incommunicable: 'The totally familiar and repetitive pattern is boring; the totally novel form will be unintelligible — is indeed unthinkable.'[84] Such comments undermine the form-critical view of the gospels' *sui generis* character: the totally new cannot even be thought, let alone communicated. In fact, the creation of new types arises from old types: a new vessel made by a craftsman involves somehow the old shapes known previously, argues Hirsch. The new depends on a 'leap of the imagination' from the known into the unknown, to assimilate it and make it known, either through an amalgamation of two old types, or an extension of an existing type.[85] Similarly, Wellek and Warren say 'the good writer partly conforms to the genre as it exists, partly stretches it . . . by and large, great writers are rarely inventors of genres; they enter into other men's labours and make them great.'[86] Of course, the new work is not merely the same as that from which it came. What is made by the amalgamation or extension of previously known forms is something new: a genre transcends its source. Thus, when Theocritus assembles his sources, ideas and inspirations for his poetry, he puts together the primary stage of the literary genre of pastoral. So new genres do not spring into being fully formed, like Athena from the head of Zeus, but they emerge and develop through the mixing and extending of previous forms.

---

81. Fowler, *Kinds of Literature*, pp. 162-4; 'Life and Death', p. 91.
82. Fowler, *Kinds of Literature*, p. 164.
83. Northrop Frye, *Anatomy of Criticism*, p. 97.
84. Wellek and Warren, *Theory*, p. 235; see also Hirsch, *Validity*, p. 103.
85. Hirsch, *Validity*, pp. 104-5.
86. Wellek and Warren, *Theory*, p. 235.

Genres continue to mix in their development. Despite the strict theoretical rules about purity of genres, both classical and neo-classical authors mixed their genres. Genres are as susceptible to change as all literary conventions. Fowler argues that they can be transformed in various ways: topical invention; combination of generic repertoire; aggregation of short works; changes of scale; changes of function, especially of speaker; counterstatement or generic inversion; inclusion of one genre within another; and mixtures and hybrids. Cairns has a not dissimilar list for the changes of classical genres by topical invention or rearrangement; generic inversion; inclusion; reaction; and speaker/addressee variation.[87]

Even more flexible than the genres themselves are generic modes. Generic 'modulation' is a major feature of literary development and the method whereby one genre frequently influences another. So Fowler concludes: 'In short, the whole developing tissue of literature is made up of multifarious extensions and interactions of genre.'[88] Further, this flexibility allows for variations in genre both synchronically and diachronically. The development is not simply one of a linear nature along the temporal axis. Genres may vary at the same time in different places, authors or even within the same author's works.

4. Generic Relationships

Genre involves literary relationships; as Doty says, 'generic definitions are best understood as relational terms — they demonstrate how some literary works are similar'.[89] If genre involves 'family resemblances', then the key to correct generic understanding will be to relate literary works to other works to ascertain points of contact and divergence. Indeed, Dubrow so likens genres to human personalities that she can refer to generic relationships in terms of rebellion, hostility or hospitality.[90]

Such comparisons must be contemporary with the period when the work was composed. Therefore, arguing that the gospels are not biographies because they do not compare with modern biography is pointless. We need to know the original genre and its predecessors: 'A work's genre is the genre at composition, which relates to an antecedent genre, itself the cumulation of a

---

87. Fowler, *Kinds of Literature*, pp. 170-90; F. Cairns, *Generic Composition in Greek and Roman Poetry* (Edinburgh: University Press, 1972), pp. 98-245.
88. Fowler, *Kinds of Literature*, p. 212.
89. Doty, 'The Concept of Genre', p. 439.
90. Dubrow, *Genre*, pp. 116-8.

series of earlier forms.'[91] So genre must always be set in its historical context. Study of the historical context will include analysis of which genres were actually available at the time. Although there is a great variety of genres possible, the dictates of literary fashion and canon mean that 'each age has a fairly small repertoire of genres that its readers and critics can respond to with enthusiasm. And the repertoire easily available to its writers is smaller still.'[92] Therefore, it is no use censuring Mark for not writing in the conventions and genre of, for example, modern investigative journalism; this was just not available to him. He could develop a new genre by extending those available perhaps, but a leap of that magnitude into the unknown is not possible.

Fitting genres into their literary network is sometimes represented by drawing genre maps. While this can occasionally have some illustrative use, as in the next chapter, such maps do have their limitations: 'Genres are better understood . . . through a study of their mutual relations. . . . These relations are partly diachronic or dynamic (formation, combination, mixture), partly static (similarities, contrasts).'[93] Hierarchies of genres were important for classical prescriptivism, as in the hierarchies proposed by Aristotle, Cicero, Horace or Quintilian. However, generic hierarchies are just as susceptible to change and literary fashion as everything else generic.[94]

5. Summary

Genres are dynamic and flexible groupings whose boundaries and labels shift. Generic development moves from initial origins through three main stages. No genres develop *ex nihilo*: instead, they extend or amalgamate other existing genres. Developed genres are open to further mixture and modulation. Therefore it is vital that genres are studied in terms of their literary relationships to the works of their own day and age.

91. Fowler, 'Life and Death', p. 86.
92. Fowler, *Kinds of Literature*, pp. 226-7.
93. *Ibid.*, p. 255; pp. 239-55 discuss genre maps.
94. Fowler discusses hierarchies in *ibid.*, chap. 12.

E. Interpretation and Evaluation

1. *The Use of Genre*

Genre is at the heart of all attempts to communicate, a crucial component of the *filter* through which a writer's idea passes between its conception and its expression as a written word. Similarly, it is part of the filter through which written words must pass to reach the reader's understanding. However, if the writer's filter is that of a first-century Hellenized Jew and the reader's filter is that of a twentieth-first-century western biblical critic, it is hardly surprising if some distortion occurs in the act of communication. Thus, in the same way that one must learn the evangelist's language to read the actual words written, so too one must learn his literary language, *langue,* to appreciate the concepts being communicated, *parole.* Chief in literary language is genre: 'A speaker and an interpreter must master not only the variable and unstable norms of language but also the particular norms of a particular genre.'[95] Genre is used in the construction, interpretation and evaluation of meaning, and each requires a final brief consideration.

2. *Construction of Meaning*

The first activity a reader undertakes is to reconstruct the communication written down by the author. Your mind is currently reconstructing thoughts which originated in my mind from these squiggles of ink printed on the page. If I communicated my thought via the symbols ⊕•⧷◊⊥″√♠⌐°∇, you could not reconstruct it, since you do not know the code or genre in which it is written. Construction of meaning works its way up different levels — from the actual printed ink marks to the language itself and on to the literary context and conventions under which I write, and genre is integral to the process: 'Genre can be a powerful instrument in construction, since its conventions organize most other constituents, in a subtly expressive way.'[96] Here the structuralist observation that we are '*homo significans:* a creature who gives sense to things'[97] helps to explain why things like ⊕•⧷◊⊥″√♠⌐°∇ are so frustrating: we simply cannot make sense of them and derive meaning from them. This process of making sense is *vraisemblablisation,* often translated as

---

95. Hirsch, *Validity,* p. 71.
96. Fowler, *Kinds of Literature,* p. 259.
97. Culler, *Structuralist Poetics,* p. 264.

'naturalization', to bring the text into our world of understanding: 'to naturalize at these various levels is to make the text intelligible by relating it to various models of coherence'[98] — in other words, by deciphering the conventions, by translating the codes within which the message has been sent. Here genre recognition and interpretation are vital.

Ricoeur sees genre at this level as 'work': 'To master a genre is to master a "competence" which offers practical guidelines for "performing" an individual work.'[99] Another way of describing this activity is *re-cognition* of what the author has communicated. However, one can only recognize what the author has actually sent, the meaning which his signals transmit, rather than his own private intentions. If he did not manage to encode them into the work, or we have lost the means to decode them from the text, then they are lost. So it is not always possible to be sure that one has arrived back at the author's original meaning, even after all this process of genre recognition and reconstruction.

3. Interpretation of Meaning

Much recent debate has concerned *valid or invalid interpretations;* whether the author determines the interpretation or whether any interpretation the reader can find in the text is valid. Seeing genre as a 'contract' or 'code' between author and reader assumes that the author's intentions can be reconstructed. Some critics believe that it is impossible to recover the author's intention, the 'intentionalist fallacy'. Such views are put forward by various 'post-structuralist' critics, including Roland Barthes' 'Death of the Author' and the *Tel Quel* school.[100] *Reader-response criticism* has also put the stress on the reader, rather than the author. Any contract or dialogue is solely between the reader and the text: 'Meaning is a product of the interaction between text and reader.'[101]

Hirsch's 'Defence of the author' (the title of chapter 1 of *Validity in Interpretation*) reasserts the importance of genre: 'Understanding can occur only if the interpreter proceeds under the same system of expectations [as the speaker/author used], and this shared generic conception, constitutive both of meaning and of understanding, is the intrinsic genre of the utterance.'[102]

98. *Ibid.*, p. 159.

99. Paul Ricoeur, 'The Hermeneutical Function of Distanciation', *Philosophy Today* 17 (1973), pp. 129-41; quotation from p. 135.

100. See note 28 above and Culler, *Structuralist Poetics*, pp. 241-54.

101. Resseguie, 'Reader-Response Criticism', *JAAR* 52 (1984), p. 322.

102. Hirsch, *Validity*, pp. 80-1.

Valid interpretation depends on the 'if/then' implication of the utterance: 'If the meaning is of *this* type, then it carries this implication . . . valid interpretation depends on a valid inference about the proprieties of the intrinsic genre.'[103] This is a control on the subjectivity of the reader's response: 'The unifying and controlling idea in any type of utterance, any genre, is the idea of purpose'; that is, the author's purpose: 'All valid interpretation of every sort is founded on the re-cognition of what an author meant.'[104]

If we apply this to the gospels, it is clear that their genre needs to be known in order for valid interpretation of their meaning to take place. However, Hirsch does allow that in certain sorts of literature the author may have intended the text to mean more than he himself knew at the time, or intended the text to be used and pondered by future generations of readers. Such texts might be legal or biblical texts intended to have a wider meaning.[105] In such cases, a wider interpretation is valid because the author intended to make the text wide-ranging. Usually, however, we cannot know more of the author's purpose and intention than the text reveals — and this is primarily through genre.

4. Evaluation of Meaning

Finally, genre plays an important role in the evaluation of meaning — assessing how good or bad the meaning is, and how well or badly it has been expressed. Because there is no extrinsic, agreed system of values, evaluation is very hard. An intrinsic mode of evaluation could be to consider how well the work fulfils its genre. However, is a work which fulfils a silly purpose excellent simply because it has fulfilled its generic purpose?[106] Furthermore, fashions change in what is valued about genres: classical theory praised the need to keep to the rules of the genre and what is appropriate, whereas in much modern theory, originality — which often involves breaking the rules — is valued highly. In both cases, generic considerations play an important role.[107]

---

103. *Ibid.*, pp. 91 and 121; see also, Dubrow, *Genre*, p. 106.
104. Hirsch, *Validity*, pp. 99 and 126.
105. *Ibid.*, pp. 121-6.
106. See Jasper Griffin, 'Genre and Real Life in Latin Poetry', *JRS* 71 (1981), pp. 39-49.
107. For further discussion, see Hirsch, *The Aims of Interpretation*, esp. pp. 114-23, and Fowler, *Kinds of Literature*, chapter 14.

5. Summary

Genre is a system of communication of *meaning*. Before we can understand the meaning of a text, we must master its genre. Genre will then be our guide to help us re-construct the original meaning, to check our interpretation to see if it is valid and to assist in evaluating the worth of the text and communication.

Conclusion

Dubrow concludes: 'Generic categories and principles rarely provide simple answers to problems about literature — but they regularly offer us one of the surest and most suggestive means of seeking those answers.'[108] This study of genre has demonstrated that it functions as a set of expectations, a kind of contract between author and reader to guide interpretation of the text. The behaviour of genres has been examined at various levels, as well as the models proposed for the development and growth of genres. What has emerged is that genre is a concept absolutely basic to the study of texts and one which involves the attempt to set them within the web of literary relationships of their own day. There are several implications of all this for gospel genre.

First, *the gospels cannot be described as unique in terms of genre.* The form-critical view of them as *sui generis* betrays a fundamental flaw in its understanding of literary theory. As Vivas says, likening genre to a plan followed by artist, critic and reader alike:

> Let me iterate the point: the plan is not *sui generis*. No artist, however talented, can make objects each of which is in a class by itself. If he could, his work would be totally idiotic, utterly private, each job would be a monad without windows or pre-established harmony. His work would say nothing to anyone but himself, the maker — if it did that much.[109]

Second, *the gospels must be compared with literature of their own day.* They should not be castigated for lacking features of modern works, such as investigative journalism, psychological study or modern biography, nor compared with later concepts of genre or literature, such as Shakespearian tragedy or whatever, without great caution and awareness of possible anachronism.

Third, *the bewildering array of genres proposed in recent years for the gos-*

108. Dubrow, *Genre,* p. 118.
109. Vivas, 'Literary Classes: Some Problems', *Genre* 1 (1968), p. 103.

pels arises from a failure to appreciate the proper definition of genre and the lev-els at which it functions. Many of the proposed analogies are *modal* rather than *generic* descriptions, e.g. whereas Mark could well have many dramatic characteristics (modes), its form and content will not allow it actually to be described as drama (genre). The gospels do contain many features and char-acteristics from a wide range of *generic modes,* identification of which can prove very helpful. This does not alter the fact their actual *genre itself* has still to be clearly established.

With this understanding of genre as our background and framework, the next step in this study must be to establish a similarly clear understanding of classical literature and in particular the forms and genre of Graeco-Roman biography.

CHAPTER 3

Genre Criticism and Graeco-Roman Biography

Much, perhaps too much, has been written on ancient biography as a literary genre with formal origins and fixed rules.[1]

In order to define the genre of Graeco-Roman biography, we must abandon the notion that an intricate, standard biographical form was developed and passed on through the centuries.[2]

O ur study of literary theory has demonstrated that genre is a crucial tool for the study and interpretation of a text in that it provides a form of contract between author and reader, giving a set of expectations for both composition and interpretation. Now we turn to another discipline, that of classical literature, to provide us with the second area of expertise needed for our study. We shall begin with the use made of genre criticism among classicists to discover if similar ideas about genre may be found to be important here also. Then we will turn to the genre of Graeco-Roman biography itself to consider its genre and development. Only after all this has been done will we be in position to assess the relationship of the gospels with Graeco-Roman biography.

---

1. Opening words of B. Baldwin, 'Biography at Rome', in *Studies in Latin Literature and Roman History,* vol. 1, ed. Carl Deroux (Collection Latomus, vol. 164, Brussels, 1979), pp. 100-18; = chapter 2 of his *Suetonius* (Amsterdam: Hakkert, 1983), pp. 66-100.

2. Patricia Cox, *Biography in Late Antiquity: A Quest for the Holy Man* (University of California Press, 1983), p. 54.

A. Genre Use and Theory

1. Theory and Practice

The innocent New Testament scholar who crosses over into study of classical literature may be tempted to read off concepts of ancient literary theory either from the various authors' prefaces to their works or from the rules of the later grammarians and rhetoricians, such as Quintilian or Menander Rhetor. These concepts and rules can then be projected back on to the particular work in question and seen as determinative. Such an approach is adopted by Shuler.[3] However, all that we have discovered about genre as a flexible set of expectations rather than prescriptive rules raises theoretical questions about this. Further, some classicists themselves are sceptical about the use of prefaces and rhetoricians in this way.

There was much interest at the beginning of the twentieth century in the study of genres, called εἴδη or γένη, with Latin literature studied as a further development from Greek.[4] This resulted in a source-critical approach to ascertain how much the writer had imitated from previous authors and how much was original. R. K. Hack, however, argued strongly against such notions of the evolution of genres, using an analysis of Horace's *Ars Poetica* as an example of how this 'doctrine of literary forms' was misleading.[5] He identified and described two contrasting approaches over generations of critics to the *Ars Poetica*: to treat the work as an εἰσαγωγή, written according to a fixed rhetorical scheme, or as an *epistula* and therefore written in a loose conversational style. Both schools then judge the work on its success or failure according to how it fulfils the predetermined outline and rules of the proposed genre — and, in the case of failure, some going so far as to rearrange the work to suit the outline as it 'should' be. The basic error of both approaches to Horace, argued Hack, is to place the primary emphasis on the *form* of a work as determining its structure and content, even to the extent of the actual text being chopped about in a cavalier fashion to fit the supposed form.

To illuminate the problem, Hack turned his attention to ancient literary theory. As we have seen, the guiding principle of theorists such as Horace and Cicero was 'propriety', where everything such as content and metre must fit

3. Shuler, *A Genre for the Gospels*, pp. 36-56.

4. E. Norden, *Einleitung in die Altertumswissenschaft* (Leipzig: Teubner, 1905), vol. 1, p. 324.

5. R. K. Hack, 'The Doctrine of Literary Forms', *Harvard Studies in Classical Philology* 27 (1916), pp. 1-65.

the Ideal Form, εἶδος or γένος.[6] However, Hack showed that Horace does not keep his own rules: only nine out of seventeen *Epodes* are truly satirical (as they 'should' be) whereas the other eight are lyric, indistinguishable from the *Odes*. The *Odes* themselves are a mixture of genres, or even new creations: 'Horace, the perfect artist, was a desperate mixer of genres.' Furthermore, the best of his poems are the very ones which break the rules; the validity of the laws 'is in inverse ratio to the originality and personal merit of the poems'. So a contradiction emerges where 'the laws of the lyric genre upheld by Horace the critic are definitely annulled by Horace the poet'.[7] The notion of poems conforming to some generic Ideal which is universally valid is Platonic in character, with similarities to the 'laws' of science. Literature, however, does not work like that. Instead of deciding the genre in advance, and then criticizing a work for how well or badly it fits the genre, the critic should recognize the role played by creative poetic genius which takes basic rules, but bends or breaks them in the attempt to produce literature.[8] Hack thus sounds a warning not to take the theoretical writings and prefaces of classical authors too strictly as a rigid guide to their work.

A similar conclusion is reached by L. E. Rossi.[9] Instead of determining a work's genre from external considerations, such as formal laws and theory, it must be discovered by internal examination of various features ('elementi') such as themes, structure, language, metre, music and dance.[10] Also important is the relationship of author to audience, the social contexts and historical situations which produced both the literature and the generic expectations affecting it. Thus Rossi sets out to produce not a history of genres themselves, but an account of the development of the 'laws' governing them. However, he does not have a fixed or rigid concept of genre. Such ideas might have been around in rhetorical works of late antiquity, but this was because they saw genre as a means of *classifying* literature. Rossi identifies three main periods, beginning with the *archaic period*, when the laws were not actually written down in a manual of literary theory, but were observed by artists passing them on one to another. In the *classical period* the laws start to be written down and codified; reflection upon them is passing from the poets themselves to theorists and philosophers, particularly Aristotle and his fol-

6. Hack, 'Doctrine', pp. 15-27 on Horace, pp. 37-43 on Cicero and others; see pp. 26-7 above.

7. Hack, 'Doctrine', pp. 27-32; quotations from pp. 30, 32 and 31.

8. *Ibid.*, pp. 63-5.

9. L. E. Rossi, 'I Generi Letterari e Le Loro Leggi Scritte e Non Scritte Nelle Letterature Classiche', *Bulletin of the Institute of Classical Studies* 18, University of London (1971), pp. 69-94.

10. *Ibid.*, p. 71.

lowers. However, the laws are observed to a large degree. It is the third period, the time of the *Alexandrians,* where a divergence appears: the laws are increasingly codified and written down, with various classificatory works being produced. Yet at the same time, this period is one of great literary innovation. The very act of codifying generic laws gave scope for experimentation and change.[11] The period of the last centuries BC and the first century AD is a time of flexible genres. Latin writers continue this fluid mix of theory and practice. Generic laws are not rigid, but norms and practice are in creative tension, 'costante dialettica'.[12] The gospels are written, therefore, during this period of flexibility and innovation.

Thus we have a warning about slavish use of ancient theory in the analysis of genre. Prefaces and the like may be helpful, but they are no substitute for analysis of the text itself.

2. The Mixing of Genres

Next we need to consider how new genres are developed in a period of creative experimentation and innovation. Kroll used the concept of the 'crossings' of genres; throughout ancient literature, genres were being mixed and crossbred to achieve new results, particularly in the shift from the countryside to the towns. Genres tend to originate in real life in various settings, especially in the countryside. However, once literature became separated from this, together with the rise of towns and literary centres, the old boundaries between genres were weakened. Poets took old genres as a starting-point to produce new ones ('in die alten Gattungen und Stoffe neue Variationen zu bringen').[13] Thus in Theocritus, bucolic poetry, different metres and dialects, various other generic types of poems, are all included. Poetic forms such as epigram and elegy are closely linked, for generic boundaries are fluid.[14] Such crossings are the key to Horatian lyric: both odes and epodes are a mixture of their forbears, plus Hellenistic influence, rhetorical figures and much else besides. Other genres show similar crossings: epyllion and epic tend to affect each other's development; epistle has a tendency to mix with other genres, such as moral philosophy (e.g. Seneca) or elegy (Ovid's *Heroides*); direct speech gets mixed with forms such

11. Rossi, 'I Generi Letterari', p. 83: 'questa terza epoca scrive le leggi, sì, ma per violarle'.

12. *Ibid.*, p. 86.

13. Wilhelm Kroll, 'Die Kreuzung der Gattungen', chapter 9 of *Studien zum Verständnis der römischen Literatur* (Stuttgart: J. B. Metzler, 1964 reprint of 1924 edn), pp. 202-24, quotation from p. 202.

14. *Ibid.*, p. 208: 'die Grenzen sind fließend'.

as hymns, lyrics, mime or elegy. Finally, Kroll turns his attention to Petronius' *Satyricon*, which he sees as a mixture of many genres, and so finds its unity in the author's talent rather than in a classification.

Thus we must conceive of literature as a network of relationships with flexible boundaries. Genre experimentation and overlap, Kroll's 'Kreuzung' or Rossi's 'mistione dei generi',[15] is a key concept for study of both ancient biography and the gospels themselves.

3. Genre in Composition and Evaluation

Francis Cairns stresses that until one knows the generic make-up of any poem, its quality and the ability of the poet cannot be assessed. His argument may be summarized as follows: first, although many poems may seem incomplete or inconsistent, we must accept the text as we have it, rather than chop it about to fit a prior notion of genre. Instead, the solution to the difficulties is to be found in the fact that ancient poems and speeches 'are members of classes of literature known in antiquity as γένη or εἴδη, which will be described in this book as *genres*'. Genres are to be defined, not in terms of *form* (e.g. epic, lyric, epistle), but in terms of *content* and can be identified by two sets of elements: the primary elements, which are the persons, situations or functions which are logically necessary for the genre, and the secondary elements, which are the *topoi*, the 'smallest divisions of the material' which appear in many different genres. The knowledge of the genres and their primary and secondary elements constitutes an agreed body of knowledge between the poet and his audience: 'These writings assume in the reader a knowledge of the circumstances and content of the particular genre to which they belong, and they exploit this knowledge.' Thus writer and audience share a 'common background'.[16] Such generic expectation was 'part of the cultural and social heritage of all educated men in antiquity', and because the genres were used in primary school exercises, 'they can be considered as the minimum formal rhetorical equipment of any literate person from the Hellenistic period on'.[17] Only against such expectation can originality and sophistication be judged. We are to expect, therefore, an early initial announcement of the poem's genre to alert us to the expected primary elements and *topoi*. In the light of these expectations, the poet may then proceed to generic sophistica-

15. Rossi, 'I Generi Letterari', p. 84.
16. Cairns, *Generic Composition*, 1972, pp. 6-7.
17. *Ibid.*, pp. 37 and 75.

tion using many different techniques, such as the introduction of new *topoi* or the selection and rearrangement of the standard *topoi;* alteration, expansion or contraction of *topoi;* the inversion of the genre, providing the opposite from that which the audience is expecting; reaction of speaker or addressee with new material, or variation of speaker and addressee; and the inclusion of new genres within the one dominant genre of the poem.

Cairns is convinced of the value of such generic studies for two reasons: first, that they help the modern reader to understand poems or works which may seem confused initially because of the lack of the assumed shared background, and secondly that they help the appreciation of the artist's originality and skill, by permitting observation of how he works within his chosen genre. Once again, genre is seen as an 'agreed contract' between author and reader, assisting with correct interpretation and proper evaluation.

However, it has been argued that in his attempt to demonstrate the importance of genre, Cairns has overplayed his hand. Jasper Griffin has questioned the basic assumption that ancient literature existed in 'a time-free zone', in which the theoretical writings of later rhetoricians may be used to assess the poetry of earlier generations. In fact, the rhetoricians derived their material and generic names originally from the poets themselves, and so they cannot be used as the judges over the poets: 'Many of the alleged "genres" do not exist in the ancient texts and have to be invented and named by the contemporary scholar.'[18] Furthermore, Cairns' method of evaluating poems, according to how well they fit their genre, seems to turn poetic appreciation upside down: poems like Theocritus' *Idylls* 12 and 17, not normally considered to be of high merit, are to be esteemed because they exemplify their genre so well.[19] One is reminded of Hack's assessment that the best poems of Horace are the very ones which break the rules. Griffin concludes his critique of Cairns by pleading that the poems must be considered as primary, and that the poets derived their forms not from the rhetoricians, but from real life experiences of saying farewell to friends, or being shut out at night by a lover.

Griffin's critique is at its strongest in the attack on Cairns for making the later rhetoricians dominant in generic analysis. On the other hand, Cairns' stress on the importance of genre in literary appreciation as a kind of agreement between author and reader does fit in well with our study of the literary theory of genres in Chapter 2 above. Where his case is perhaps vulnerable is in his use of the term 'genre' at a much 'lower' level — to denote

---

18. Griffin, 'Genre and Real Life in Latin Poetry', *JRS* 71 (1981), pp. 39-49, quotation from p. 40; 'time-free zone' idea in Cairns, *Generic Composition,* p. 32.

19. Griffin, 'Genre and Real Life in Latin Poetry', p. 41.

different types of poem or units within them, defined totally in terms of content alone. It would seem better, using Fowler's terminology, to see this as the level of subtype, or subgenre, or literary unit — and to keep genre for the description of a whole work, defined in terms of both form and content.

Thus we may conclude that classicists also view genre not as something rigid or static, defined by a predetermined set of laws or rhetorical rules, but as something dynamic and flexible, encompassing both form and content. Secondly, the boundaries of genre are flexible and hard to delineate precisely. Consciously and unconsciously, authors import new material across these boundaries to alter and develop the genres, mixing them as part of their artistic sophistication; therefore, models of genre with an element of spectrum or continuum about them will be more helpful than concepts of pigeon-holes or strict classifications. Finally, a correct understanding of the genre of a work will enable the modern reader to share in the common background of an ancient author and his audience, and thus to be able to interpret and evaluate the work more accurately. We may now turn, therefore, from this general study of the use of genre by classicists to the particular genre in which we are interested, namely Graeco-Roman biography.

B. The Genre of Graeco-Roman Biography

1. Terminology and Definitions

The immediate problem to be faced in discussing Graeco-Roman biography is that it was never strongly delineated as a genre by the ancients. Indeed, the word *biographia* does not appear until Damascius' *Life of Isidorus,* written in the fifth century AD, but only preserved by the ninth-century writer, Photius. Momigliano points out that the description used from the Hellenistic age onwards was simply 'Lives', βίοι, or *vitae*.[20] This nomenclature is clear from its use on manuscripts (Satyrus' Βίων Ἀναγραφή) and in ancient references to such works, e.g. Eunapius' comment that Lucian Δημῶνακτος φιλοσόφου . . . βίον ἀνέγραψεν (Eun. *VS* 454). In addition, it is the word used by Plutarch to describe his own work: γράφομεν . . . βίους (*Alex.* 1.2) or τῇ περὶ τοὺς βίους ἀναγραφῇ (*Per.* 2.4; see also *Comparison Lys./Sulla* 1.1).

The ancient literary theory of the genre is no clearer than the nomencla-

---

20. Photius, *Bibliotheca* 181 and 242; see Arnaldo Momigliano, *The Development of Greek Biography* (Cambridge, Mass.: Harvard University Press, 1971), p. 12.

ture. As Geiger has pointed out, the genres of prose were never as clearly fixed as those of poetry; he considers it a 'futile path that led to the reconstruction of ancient literary theory' about biography and suggests that it may be more profitable to use modern conceptions.[21] Momigliano has a simple definition: 'An account of the life of a man from birth to death is what I call biography.' This, he says, is not profound but it has the merit at least of excluding from the definition precisely how biography is to be written.[22] Both the definitions offered by C. H. Talbert and David Aune have such limitations, asserting that biography must be prose narrative and including comments about its purpose and supposed historicity.[23] While not going as far as these, Geiger criticizes Momigliano for defining the genre solely in terms of content; accordingly, he prefers the definition offered by the *Oxford English Dictionary*: 'the history of the lives of individual men, as a branch of literature'. Thus a line is drawn between 'biographical elements in various literary forms' and 'a literary form devoted to biography'[24] — our distinction of mode and genre.

However, it is precisely the use of modern concepts of 'biography' which led Bultmann and the form critics to deny that the gospels are biographies: Marxsen refers to 'the absence of everything required for a biography (sequence of events, development, Jesus' appearance, etc.)'.[25] Here the implications of using the modern word 'biography' are clear: if such things are 'required', as Marxsen put it, then many Graeco-Roman βίοι are not biography either. All of these definitions have the problem of defining in advance what this genre will look like. Some βίοι will relate to history, but not all; some will give 'an account from birth to death', but not all include the subject's death (especially autobiography!). In this study, therefore, we shall use simply 'Lives' — βίοι — and see what sort of texts are described as that within the ancient world.

2. Theory and Practice

This lack of a clear theory of the genre of βίος is evident in some of the authors' prefaces to their works. We have already warned against over-reliance

---

21. Joseph Geiger, *Cornelius Nepos and Ancient Political Biography* (Stuttgart: Franz Steiner, 1985), pp. 12-14.

22. Momigliano, *Development*, p. 11.

23. Talbert, *What Is a Gospel?*, p. 17; Aune, *The New Testament in Its Literary Environment*, p. 29.

24. Geiger, *Cornelius Nepos*, pp. 14-15.

25. Willi Marxsen, *Introduction to the New Testament* (Oxford: Blackwell, 1968), p. 125; see also p. 10 above.

on such prefaces, preferring to examine the authors' actual practice in the texts themselves. Shuler seems convinced that his study of the authors' statements in Polybius, *Histories* X.21.8, Cicero's Letter to Lucceius (*Ad Fam.* V.12.3), Lucian's *How to Write History* 7, Nepos' *De viris illustribus* XVI: *Pelopidas* 1 and Plutarch's *Alexander* 1.1-3 demonstrates a clear 'dichotomy' or 'distinction between history and biography' in ancient thought over four centuries.[26] In fact, Polybius and Lucian are distinguishing not biography, but *encomium* from history, and Cicero is merely asking for more eulogy of himself in Lucceius' history than would normally be allowed by the canons of history. Although Nepos and Plutarch are contrasting βίοι with history, these passages demonstrate the difficulty they are having with their accounts rather than a clear 'dichotomy' in their minds. Nepos is unsure how to proceed, how much to put in or to leave out: 'dubito quem ad modum exponam'.

Plutarch's famous introduction to the *Alexander* is often quoted and worth detailed attention. He attempts to distinguish ἱστορία from βίοι, which he is writing. History, says Plutarch, is concerned for the famous actions and illustrious deeds of men and for great events like sieges or battles; βίος is interested in men's character, which may be revealed by 'little things' (πρᾶγμα βραχὺ) like the odd phrase or jest. First we must note that Plutarch is cautious in his choice of words: illustrious deeds do not *always* (πάντως) reveal virtue or vice — but they may do so quite often, whereas the little things show character *often* (πολλάκις) rather than always. Thus the distinction Plutarch is drawing is certainly not to be construed as a hard and fast rule.

Secondly, we need to ask why Plutarch felt the need to discuss the difference between history and βίος at this point, about a third of the way through the whole corpus of the *Lives*.[27] Geiger has pointed out that we get such apologies and protests only in ancient *political* biography because there is 'a clear danger of transcending the limits of the literary genre and slipping into history'. Intellectual biography, lives of philosophers or literary men, does not have this problem, and therefore we do not find similar statements in their prefaces.[28] In fact, Plutarch does include much historical material, great events, battles and politics in his *Lives*, and like other ancient historians feels the need to apologize about digressions; as Wardman concludes, 'it can only be that he is, so to say, genre-conscious; and the genre by which he is still constrained is historiography'.[29]

26. Shuler, *A Genre for the Gospels*, pp. 36-40.

27. A. E. Wardman, 'Plutarch's Methods in the *Lives*', *CQ* 21 (1971), pp. 254-61, see p. 257; and also, C. P. Jones, 'Towards a Chronology of Plutarch's Works', *JRS* 56 (1966), pp. 66-70.

28. Geiger, *Cornelius Nepos*, pp. 20-3 and 113-15; quotation from p. 114.

29. A. E. Wardman, *Plutarch's Lives* (London: Paul Elek, 1974), p. 9.

Given all this, the reason for his explanation here is quite straightforward: 'It was simply that his current subjects were too vast to admit every detail.'[30] Plutarch has too much material about Alexander and therefore this introduction is an apology to readers who notice the omissions. The same difficulty occurred with the *Pompey*, which, like *Alexander*, is one of the longest of Plutarch's *Lives;* here also we find similar apologies for omissions, see *Pompey* 8.6. In other *Lives*, he has the reverse problem: thus the *Marcellus* requires padding to approximate to the length of its partner, *Pelopidas*, and even with several digressions it still only manages to be half the length of the *Alexander* or *Pompey*. Plutarch is similarly selective when discussing a person whose life will be well known to his readers from their prior knowledge of the great historians; e.g., about Nicias because of Thucydides' account of the Sicilian expedition, or about Cyrus' death in the *Artaxerxes*, known from Xenophon's account.[31] Thus the omissions, and the explanations for them found in the prefaces, are less to do with biographical theory than with constraints of space and material available.

Thus, important though this introduction to the *Alexander* is as an insight into Plutarch's concept of what he is writing, once again we have seen that a theoretical comment in a preface must be approached with caution. The *Alexander* remarks 'are not to be taken in isolation' for they do not apply across the board to all his biographies.[32] We may conclude, therefore, that these prefaces and programmatic statements do *not* show that all the ancient writers had a clear literary theory of βίος distinguished from other genres; on the contrary, they show their embarrassment at the mixing of the genres and the possibility of confusion with neighbouring genres.

3. The Mixing of Genres — genera proxima

The concept of flexible generic boundaries with 'crossings' fits better with models in terms of a spectrum or continuum than with rigid pigeonholes. Thus we may imagine βίος as a spectrum or band of literature positioned between history at one extreme and encomium at the other, as follows:

$$\text{History} \equiv = - - = \equiv \; \text{βίος} \; \equiv = - - = \equiv \; \text{Encomium}$$

---

30. Baldwin, 'Biography at Rome', p. 103; see also D. A. Russell, *Plutarch* (London: Duckworth, 1972), pp. 115-6, for the same point.

31. Wardman, 'Plutarch's Methods', *CQ* (1971), pp. 258-9.

32. Wardman, *Plutarch's Lives*, p. 160; see also, *CQ* (1971), p. 261.

Certain works may be close to the boundary at one end — such as obvious encomia like Isocrates' *Evagoras* or Xenophon's *Agesilaus* with their close links with rhetoric; while at the other extreme the border with history is unclear — and hence the struggles of Nepos or Plutarch. Even the historian has a tendency to straddle the boundary from time to time, and we find elements of biography in Tacitus' *Annals,* for instance.[33] McQueen suggests that the work of Quintus Curtius Rufus also might be seen as 'a fusion of the two genres'. There is, however, a third element in Curtius, his literary and moralizing tendencies, which display his rhetorical abilities. In such passages, says McQueen, 'the biographer and historian is overcome by the rhetorician'.[34] At this point, then, we discover that even the spectrum is an unhelpful model — because Curtius cannot be overlapping at both ends simultaneously. What is needed is a concept where βίος can relate to a number of different *genera proxima* at the same time, including, as mentioned, history, encomium, rhetoric and moralizing — but also other genres such as the entertaining story or early novel and a link with the didactic genres of philosophical and political beliefs, teachings and polemic. The boundaries between βίος and any of the *genera proxima* are flexible, and so borrowing or sharing of generic features across the border is to be expected. As we have already noted, genre maps are notoriously difficult and misleading if taken to have some fixed or absolute worth. However, the kind of picture we are trying to describe may be represented as in the figure on page 64. It must, of course, be borne in mind that such a representation applies from the point of view of βίος only. Here we are trying to represent the relationships of the *genera proxima* to βίος, and not necessarily to each other. A different picture could be drawn by placing another genre at the centre, such as history, and seeing which genres relate to that. However, such a diagram helps us to see where the different levels of genre operate, in that the actual genre of βίος itself is the central circle, which may contain any number of *subgenres,* whereas the biographical *mode* may be found operating in any of the *genera proxima* beyond βίος proper.

If we try to apply this model to Plutarch, it is clear that the most obvious generic neighbour is history, as Wardman emphasizes. He is less convinced about a link with encomium: 'The eulogy or encomium is to be regarded as a distant forbear of Plutarchian biography.'[35] Pelling disagrees and

---

33. Baldwin, 'Biography at Rome', p. 114; Ronald Syme, 'History or Biography. The Case of Tiberius Caesar', *Historia* 23 (1974), pp. 481-96.

34. E. I. McQueen, 'Quintus Curtius Rufus', in *Latin Biography,* ed. T. A. Dorey (London: Routledge & Kegan Paul, 1967), pp. 17-43. quotations from pp. 20 and 32.

35. Wardman, *Plutarch's Lives,* pp. 1-18, quotation from p. 10; see also, Geiger, *Cornelius Nepos,* p. 23.

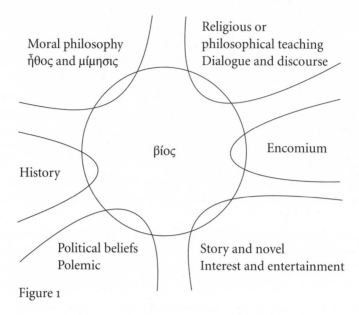

Figure 1

criticizes Wardman's treatment of encomium as 'uneasy and narrow'.[36] The amount of overlap from history or encomium can vary from *Life* to *Life:* some have only the sketchiest historical background (e.g. *Alcibiades, Cato Minor, Crassus* or *Antony*), whereas others, such as *Caesar,* have detailed historical analysis: 'Plutarch's biography is a very flexible genre, and his interest in historical background is one of the things which vary.'[37]

The other generic border which Plutarch tends to straddle is with moral philosophy, through his interest in character. Plutarch's concern for moral philosophy is evident by his other writings, notably the *Moralia,* and he is concerned that the readers of the *Lives* should learn from his description of these characters how to live their lives, through imitation, μίμησις (see the opening sections of the *Pericles, Aemilius, Demosthenes*). Most of the characters depicted are good, for our emulation — though some are weak, displaying κακία, such as Antony or Demetrius. So here we have another crossing of the genres: 'The *Lives* therefore are, for Plutarch, moral philosophy in another genre.'[38] It is important to note that this mixing of the genres takes place simultaneously;

36. In his review of Wardman's *Plutarch's Lives* in *JHS* 1976, pp. 189-90.

37. C. B. R. Pelling, 'Plutarch and Roman Politics', in *Studies in the Ancient Historians,* ed. Woodman, Moxon and Smart (CUP, 1985), p. 159.

38. Wardman, *Plutarch's Lives,* p. 37; see also, A. J. Gossage, 'Plutarch', in *Latin Biography,* ed. Dorey, p. 49.

it is not the case that Plutarch is being a historian one minute and moralizing another. 'Plutarch is as much a moralist as an historian even where he is relating rather commonplace historical matter. His major interest is in illuminating the virtues or vices of a hero through the type of "insignificant" detail which he felt was often overlooked by the major historians.'[39] In fact, his moralistic and literary interests could even assist the difficult historical choice of which heroes to include in his *Parallel Lives:* Geiger argues that Aemilius Paulus and Timoleon found their way into the series because of their common denominator of τύχη, with lives being lived with courage in the face of Fate.[40]

4. A Flexible Genre

The picture has now emerged of the genre of βίος nestling between history, encomium and moral philosophy, with overlaps and relationships in all directions. Plutarch has been used as an example to illustrate these last sections, and we can now conclude with some observations on the flexibility of the genre, also taken from Plutarch. By careful study of some of the Roman *Lives*, Christopher Pelling concluded that six of them were written together at the same time, drawing on the same sources and information: the *Crassus, Pompey, Caesar, Cato Minor, Brutus* and *Antony*.[41] Any differences between them must be due to Plutarch's literary methods, therefore, and so we can study how he went about his writing and how much licence he allowed himself. For our study, the significant conclusions concern the relationship between Plutarch's biographical theory and practice. We have already seen how the introduction to *Alexander* (paired with *Caesar*) differentiates history and βίος. Pelling cites other similar passages in Plutarch, such as *Nic.* 1 and *Aem.* 1.1, and concludes: 'The theory is clear and consistent. Biography will often concentrate on personal details, and may abbreviate its historical narrative; its concern will be the portrayal of character, and its ultimate purpose will be protreptic and moral.'[42]

39. F. E. Brenk, *In Mist Apparelled: Religious Themes in Plutarch's Moralia and Lives,* *Mnemosyne* Supplementum 48 (Leiden: Brill, 1977), p. 184; see also, Russell, *Plutarch,* pp. 115-6.

40. J. Geiger, 'Plutarch's Parallel Lives: The Choice of Heroes', *Hermes* 109 (1981), pp. 85-104, see the conclusion on p. 104; see also, Gossage, 'Plutarch', pp. 60-1; C. P. Jones, *Plutarch and Rome* (OUP, 1971), p. 105; J. R. Hamilton, *Plutarch: Alexander, A Commentary* (OUP, 1969), pp. xxxiii-xxxiv.

41. C. B. R. Pelling, 'Plutarch's Method of Work in the Roman Lives', *JHS* 99 (1979), pp. 74-96.

42. C. B. R. Pelling, 'Plutarch's Adaptation of His Source Material', *JHS* 100 (1980), pp. 127-40; quotation from p. 135.

When this theory is tested against the actual texts, some *Lives* fit it very well: both *Pompey* and *Cato* stress the central character, with lessons being pointed out and morals drawn, often by means of the 'little things' mentioned in *Alex.* 1.2. These two examples are personal, moralistic and non-historical. However, others of the *Lives* written at the same time are quite different. *Caesar* has more historical material and very few 'little things'; there is little moralizing or concern for Caesar's ἦθος — instead the work is dominated by the notion of Caesar as tyrant of the people, the δῆμος/τυραννίς motif. *Antony* is different again; here there is little history, but great depiction of character. While there may be some moralizing, the interest in character is much more dramatic, even tragic, especially towards the end. Thus works written simultaneously from the same sources end up with quite different configurations and relationships to the *genera proxima* — while all the time remaining βίοι. So Pelling concludes: 'A writer's programmatic statements can sometimes be a poor guide to his work, and some Lives fit Plutarch's theory better than others. . . . This biographical genre is an extremely flexible one, and admits works of very different patterns.'[43]

5. Summary

The use of genre theory among classicists is similar to that seen in modern literary theory. Genre is an important convention, which sets up certain expectations for the reader by way of an agreed, though sometimes unconscious, contract. An awareness of genre and its conventions was widespread in the ancient world through elementary schooling, particularly in its use of rhetorical exercises and moralistic stories of the heroes. Genre criticism has a role to play, therefore, in both the interpretation and evaluation of ancient texts. However, we have also seen a divergence between ancient theory and practice. Theoretical statements, particularly those in authors' prefaces and in the later rhetoricians and grammarians, must always be tested against the actual practice of the writers themselves in their texts. Often this will reveal a failure to apply the theory strictly, and sometimes the greater the divergence from theory, the greater the literary creativity of the author.

Ancient genres were flexible and existed within the whole web of literary relationships of their day. There was plenty of scope for mixing and overlap at the boundaries of the genres, with a resulting rich mix of other features

---

43. Pelling, 'Plutarch's Adaptation', *JHS* 1980, p. 139; see further, Pelling, 'Plutarch and Roman Politics', pp. 159-87; Gossage, 'Plutarch', pp. 53-60.

within the genre itself. This is true of Graeco-Roman biography in general and Plutarch's βίοι in particular. Ancient βίος was a flexible genre having strong relationships with history, encomium and rhetoric, moral philosophy and the concern for character.

C. Greek and Hellenistic Biography

1. The Origins of Greek Biography

A tight definition of biography will allow us to begin our survey only in the fourth century BC with the writings produced by the philosophical schools, which is where Leo and Dihle commence their studies.[44] On the other hand, interest in the lives of others clearly goes back a lot further. Stuart sees various factors behind βίος: an interest in epic heroes; individual poetry, such as lyric or elegiac; tragedy; and the funeral dirge over the dead, starting with Andromache's for Hector, *Iliad* 24.720ff., and going on to prose encomium, or eulogy over the dead.[45] Momigliano prefers to see anecdotes, sayings, letters and apologetic speeches as the true antecedents. Several factors combine to produce biography in the fifth century: an interest in literary antiquity, in the lives of both the heroes and the bards themselves, and also in the lives of the Seven Sages. The specific catalyst was perhaps Persian in origin, in that the first Greek biographical works are written by those in the service of the Great King, at the same time as biographical writing is appearing in the Jewish tradition through Nehemiah and possibly Ezra, as well as the Aḥiqar traditions among the Elephantine Jews.[46] The interest in individuals can also be seen in the development of historiography: Homeyer sees many mini-biographies in Herodotus, particularly the stories about Cyrus or Cambyses, which issue forth in both Thucydides' interest in people like Themistocles and the work of Isocrates and Xenophon.[47]

---

44. Friedrich Leo, *Die griechisch-römische Biographie nach ihrer literarischen Form* (Leipzig: Teubner, 1901); A. Dihle, *Studien zur griechischen Biographie* (Göttingen: Vandenhoeck & Ruprecht, 1st edn 1956, 2nd edn 1970); the best list of βίοι from the fifth century BC to the fourth century AD is probably to be found on pp. 1231-6 of Klaus Berger's article, 'Hellenistische Gattungen im NT', in *ANRW*, II.25.2.

45. D. R. Stuart, *Epochs of Greek and Roman Biography* (Berkeley: University of California Press, 1928), pp. 9-29, 38-9.

46. Momigliano, *Development*, pp. 23-8, 35-6.

47. Helene Homeyer, 'Zu den Anfängen der griechischen Biographie', *Philologus* 106 (1962), pp. 75-85.

2. The First Writers

The first biographical writings, if not yet βίοι proper, are found in the fifth century BC, often known to us from fragments or references in later authors. Skylax of Caryanda, *c.* 480 BC, wrote an autobiographical prose account of his voyaging for Darius, and also a work about Heraclides, king of Mylasa, according to the *Suda*. Ion of Chios, *c.* 440, wrote of his travels and *Visits* to interesting people; the fragments include anecdotal mentions of Cimon, Pericles and Sophocles. Stesimbrotus, *c.* 420?, produced a pamphlet 'Concerning Themistocles, Thucydides and Pericles' which seems to have had biographical interest as well as political motives. Xanthus of Lydia, *c.* 421/410, wrote about Empedocles the philosopher (according to Diogenes Laertius, *Emped.* VIII.63).[48]

Geiger is reluctant to claim such works as 'biographies'; however, such 'biographical elements' do help to illuminate the roots of biography itself.[49] From such works, and from the developing interest in individuals, the various elements which will form βίος eventually begin to come together from the neighbouring genres. Biographical writings certainly existed during the fifth century BC, and the first actual βίοι may have been written during this time, but are no longer preserved today.

3. The Fourth Century

Three main factors are usually adduced to explain why βίοι start to be written in the fourth century: a new political mood, in which the individual is more prominent than in fifth-century collectivism, philosophical concerns and interest in the individual philosophers, and rhetorical interest through the use of encomiastic speeches. Isocrates claims to be the first to write prose encomium in the *Evagoras, c.* 370 BC, and Xenophon probably followed this as a model for his *Agesilaus, c.* 360 BC; both of these works will be considered in more detail in Chapter 6 below.

Biographical interests occur in much other material during this period.

48. For more details of these generally, see Stuart, *Epochs*, pp. 30-59; Momigliano, *Development*, pp. 23-42; and Cox, *Biography in Late Antiquity*, pp. 5-6. On Ion, see K. J. Dover, 'Ion of Chios: His Place in the History of Greek Literature', in *Chios: A Conference at the Homereion in Chios, 1984*, ed. John Boardman and C. E. Vaphopoulou-Richardson (OUP, 1986), pp. 27-37; for Stesimbrotus, see C. B. R. Pelling, 'Childhood and Personality in Greek Biography', in *Characterization and Individuality in Greek Literature,* ed. Pelling (OUP, 1990), p. 214, and note 8.

49. Geiger, *Cornelius Nepos*, pp. 14-15.

Crucial as a stimulus to βίος was the production of material about Socrates, notably Plato's *Dialogues* and *Apology*, and Xenophon's *Memorabilia* which combines anecdote and memoir to illustrate the character of Socrates as a defence against his detractors. Geiger sees the urge to write about philosophers, especially Socrates, as an important factor in the development of the 'new literary genre'; politicians and statesmen could be dealt with by historiography. Dihle likewise stresses the role of Socrates.[50] Isocrates also included some biographical material in many speeches, including on Alcibiades in *Concerning the Team of Horses,* a speech composed for Alcibiades' son in *c.* 397, and some autobiographical material in *About the Exchange, c.* 354. As well as *Evagoras,* he also wrote prose encomia of *Helen, c.* 370, and *Busiris, c.* 385, although since both have mythical subjects, these are in the tradition of epideictic ('for display') rhetoric rather than βίοι proper. Xenophon included detailed character sketches of the generals in his *Anabasis, c.* 385. His *Cyropaedia* is described by Momigliano as 'the most accomplished biography we have in classical Greek literature', although its mainly fictitious character means that the description of 'paedagogical novel' is more accurate.[51] Cyrus was also the subject of writings by Antisthenes. Autobiographical material appears in the *Anabasis,* and in Plato's *Epistle* 7 (if considered genuine).

From these examples we can see how βίος literature is taking shape in relation to its neighbouring genres of history, rhetoric, encomium and entertainment — and in one or two cases, the description of βίος itself might not be inappropriate, even if we have not yet reached a full genre.

4. Aristotle and the Philosophical Schools

Aristotle and his school, with their great interest in research, analysis and definition, take the crucial step. Although Aristotle wrote no biography himself, biographical material abounds in his writings in the form of anecdotes, sayings and apt remarks (ἀποφθέγματα, γνῶμαι, χρεῖαι) and examples (παραδείγματα). Work develops on individual writers and poets, as well as particular philosophers and the different schools and approaches. Aristoxenus is often seen as the 'founder' of biography.[52] According to the story, Aristoxenus, annoyed because Theopompus was preferred over him as Aristotle's

50. Geiger, *Cornelius Nepos,* pp. 19-20; Dihle, *Studien,* pp. 13-34.

51. Momigliano, *Development,* p. 55.

52. Leo, *Die griechisch-römische Biographie,* p. 102; Momigliano considers philosophical influence to be less important for the development of βίοι in *Second Thoughts on Greek Biography* (Amsterdam: North-Holland, 1971), see esp. pp. 14-15.

successor, went off in a huff to write a βίος of Socrates which would show all his faults. In this, Aristoxenus, who was a Pythagorean before coming to the Peripatos, attacks Socrates for plagiarizing Pythagoreanism. He also wrote other βίοι of philosophers.

References, quotations and fragments of the work of other writers are known, although, since none of these works have survived, it is not always clear which are writers of true βίος and which just collectors of stories or encomiasts;[53] given our picture of the flexible nature of βίος evolving from its neighbouring genres, this border confusion is only to be expected at this stage. These philosophical writers include Clearchus who wrote on Plato. Phainias of Eresus wrote *On the Socratics, On the Sicilian Tyrants and On Poets,* and also a monograph on his home town. Demetrius of Phalerum may have written about Demosthenes; Diogenes Laertius and Plutarch quote from a work by him on Socrates, possibly a rejoinder to Aristoxenus. Diogenes also makes use of material from Dicaearchus of Messene; his work, Περὶ βίων, may have been a collection of βίοι, and there is an interesting use of the word βίος in his account of the development of Greek civilization entitled Περὶ τοῦ τῆς Ἑλλάδος βίου.[54]

Two types of function seem to have been in mind for these early βίοι: interest and information about previous philosophers or writers, but also a clear tradition of their use for polemical ends in the continuing philosophical debate between the different schools.

5. Hellenistic Biography and Alexandria

During the third century BC, the house of Macedon influenced literature as everything else. Biographical literature and encomia are produced, including Theopompus' *Philippica* (c. 345) and Ephorus' work on Alexander and the Diadochi — all unfortunately now lost; from such works the tradition of Alexander literature begins. The interest in philosophers continues: Antigonus of Carystus wrote Lives of philosophers, possibly at Pergamum, c. 250. At Al-

53. See Fritz Wehrli, *Die Schule des Aristoteles,* 10 vols. (Basel: Schwabe & Co, 1967-9) for the fragments; for further discussion see Momigliano, *Development,* pp. 66-79, who is cautious about how many are true biographers, other than Aristoxenus; Stuart, *Epochs,* pp. 119-54, who believes Aristoxenus is not unique or alone; and Geiger, *Cornelius Nepos,* pp. 51-5.

54. For the influence of Dicaearchus upon the late Republic at Rome, especially on Atticus, Nepos and Varro (who followed the idea of βίοι of a people with his *De vita populi Romani*), see Elizabeth Rawson, *Intellectual Life in the Late Republic* (London: Duckworth, 1985), pp. 101-3.

exandria, Callimachus and his circle amassed vast quantities of data and information for the libraries; to supplement ancient texts, anecdotes and stories
about the authors were sought — produced as small βίοι. Hermippus, *c.* 200,
used this material for his βίοι of the Seven Sages, Pythagoras, Gorgias, Aristotle and others — what Momigliano calls 'learned sensationalism',[55] so typical of the Alexandrian style. Aristo of Ceos, *c.* 200, wrote on Epicurus, Socrates and Heraclitus. Sotion, *c.* 180, used Callimachus' files to produce his
Succession of the Philosophers, later to influence Diogenes Laertius. Satyrus
wrote about men of letters and was not above indulging in the old habit of
deducing 'facts' about their lives from authors' works. His *Life of Euripides,*
from Book VI of his βίων ἀναγραφή, is in dialogue form with a dramatic atmosphere. Since this is the earliest work to survive, albeit fragmentary, with
the actual name of βίος, we shall study it in Chapter 6.

Thus, this period continues the broad mix, enriched by Callimachean
interest in general information. βίος can be used for propaganda, for philosophical debate and polemic, or just for descriptive and informative purposes, revealing a person's character through anecdotes and stories. There are
various *topoi* basic to them all, such as nationality, parentage, early pursuits,
education, death and burial, as well as specific areas related to each individual, morals, virtues, deeds and so on. The manner or tone is not often neutral,
but argues for praise or blame of the subject. Here the overlap between βίος
and encomium easily occurs, as well as that with history. Exact delineation of
where each text belongs would not be easy; with only references and quotations in later digests, such as Diogenes Laertius', precision is impossible.

6. Classification

Leo's great analysis of Graeco-Roman biography distinguished two main
strands: the *Plutarchian* with Peripatetic origins and arranged around a chronological structure, used for men of action and politics, and the *Suetonian,*
more systematically or topically ordered from Alexandrian origins, for literary men. Such a neat division is appealing, but not easy to prove with the lack
of evidence from this time. Indeed, more recent study of ancient biography
shows that topically based studies of philosophers and writers were around
long before the Alexandrian period. Any distinction of approach probably reflects the fact that men of action require their deeds to be dealt with chrono-

---

55. Momigliano, *Development,* p. 79; see pp. 79-89 for this period, and also Stuart, *Epochs,*
pp. 155-88.

logically whereas it is easier to handle someone's literary output or philosophical ideas by a topical arrangement. Momigliano says that Leo's brilliant analysis cannot be sustained since 'Hellenistic literary biography was far more elegant and sophisticated than Leo had thought'.[56]

Furthermore, Geiger has disputed whether the Plutarchian, political biography does go back to the Peripatetics; the use of Jerome's introduction to *De viris illustribus* in the search for Hellenistic political biography has been a 'blind avenue'.[57] Against Leo and Steidle's arguments, he suggests that no real examples of this form of βίος are known; two genres are well attested at this time, namely the historical monograph and the intellectual biography of writers and philosophers. The deeds of generals and politicians could be recorded in historical writings, but philosophical and literary figures like Socrates needed the new form; political biography proper is a child of Roman times. Once again, therefore, we are back to the flexible nature of this genre and its hazy boundaries with neighbours like history and encomium.

D. Roman Biography

1. The Origins of Roman Biography

Leo sought the origins of Plutarch and Suetonius in Peripatetic and Alexandrian biography, but Stuart is not convinced: the systematic arrangement of Suetonius is basic to the logical Roman mind, and he was 'a compiler extraordinary, a chronic lexicographer'.[58] Furthermore, many elements within the Roman tradition were predisposed to produce biography: concern for details, respect for one's ancestors and family tradition, the need for public honour, all led to an indigenous tradition of biographical material. Specific antecedents can be found in epitaphs and inscriptions; in the dirge and the funeral laudation; in the *Tabularium* in the Forum (the state archives) and in family records and the *imagines* of the ancestors. Many basic features of these records are biographical: lineage; career, honours or offices gained; salient incidents; domestic life. Behind all this is the exemplary motive so descendants can emulate the *exempla maiorum*. An exemplary purpose in writing was important in much Roman historiography as well as later biography.

---

56. Momigliano, *Second Thoughts*, pp. 10-11.

57. Geiger, *Cornelius Nepos*, p. 32; Moles' review suggested that Geiger's overall argument is itself 'too clear-cut' for the complexity and flexibility of the material, *CR* 39 (1989), pp. 229-33.

58. Stuart, *Epochs*, p. 230; see further pp. 189-220; also Momigliano, *Development*, pp. 94-5, and Geiger, *Cornelius Nepos*, pp. 78-84.

2. *The Republic*

Biographical literature starts to appear at the end of the Republic. In *c.* 44 BC, Varro published his *Imagines,* 700 portraits of famous kings, leaders, poets, philosophers and writers, each accompanied with an epigram. Roman biography gets properly under way with Cornelius Nepos: born *c.* 99 BC in the Po valley, he moved to Rome *c.* 65 to live a quiet life writing. It is possible that he was influenced by Varro, although this is debated.[59] In his main work, *De viris illustribus,* the distinction of 'Plutarchian' and 'Suetonian' biography again breaks down for some Lives do have a clear chronology, while others are more topically arranged and anecdotal. The work is dedicated to the Roman knight and patron Atticus — and in his apologetic opening, Nepos is not unaware that he is starting something new: 'non dubito fore plerosque, Attice, qui hoc genus scripturae leve et non satis dignum summorum virorum personis iudicent' (Praefatio 1.1). Nepos' *Life of Atticus,* his only extant contemporary biography, will be included in our detailed study in Chapter 6.

Part of the Roman tradition tending naturally towards biography was the custom of publishing autobiographical memoirs — *Commentarii.* Often a trusted slave-secretary would produce an 'authorized version' of letters or memoirs, as Tiro did for Cicero. In the Civil Wars at the end of the Republic the different sides sought to put their views across, as in Caesar's *Commentaries,* for example. A whole range of material was produced concerning Cato, the last great Republican leader, who committed suicide at Utica in 46 BC rather than fall into the hands of Caesar. Again biography is used for polemic and propaganda purposes as Cato became 'the focal point of a vivid literary polemic with scarcely hidden political overtones'.[60] Plutarch's biography of him will be studied in Chapter 7.

3. *The Early Empire*

During the early Empire, the use of biography for political purposes continues with the propaganda of the imperial house, begun by Augustus' *Res Gestae* — a list of his great deeds for the nation and the honours he received in return. The surviving fragments of Nicolas of Damascus' *Life of Augustus* describe the rise of the young Octavian to become heir to Caesar, in an enco-

---

59. See Geiger, *Cornelius Nepos,* pp. 81-2.

60. Joseph Geiger, 'Munatius Rufus and Thrasea Paetus on Cato the Younger', *Athenaeum* 57 (1979), pp. 48-72; quotation from p. 48.

miastic way with analysis of his virtues.[61] On the other side, biography becomes a vehicle for unorthodox political or philosophical ideas. The focus
around Cato continued: when Thrasea Paetus retired from active politics under Nero, he wrote a *Life of Cato*, probably as a statement of his own position
— and this may have contributed to his death: 'The composition of the *Cato*
was a political act and a declaration of faith.'[62] Thrasea himself became the
subject of a political biography by Arulenus Rusticus, while Herennius
Senecio wrote one about Helvidius Priscus. Both authors and their texts per-
ished as subversive under Domitian in AD 93. These texts probably focussed
on the ideal of the hero and his patient suffering and death under the tyrant.
The genre of *exitus illustrium virorum* became fashionable under oppression
by Tiberius, Nero and Domitian.[63] Such a focus on the subject's death is an
important parallel for the Passion narratives in the gospels, as well as a major
influence on later martyrologies, such as the *Acta Alexandrinorum*.

This brings us neatly to the *Agricola* of Tacitus. The genre of this work
has long been in dispute. Various models have been suggested for it, from
Hübner's *laudatio* (1866) and Gudeman's comparison with panegyric (1902)
to Shuler's 'encomium biography'. Plutarch brings together in his own person
the fusion of the Greek and Roman traditions of biography in his *Parallel
Lives*, setting a Greek and a Roman side by side for comparison. He writes in
Greek, conscious of all the Greek biographical tradition, and yet he had travelled to Rome and was widely read there. Twenty-two pairs of *Parallel Lives*
survive today, together with four single examples. Suetonius, born *c.* 70 AD,
wrote several series of *Lives*, including *On Illustrious Men*, *Rhetoricians* and
Poets. His most famous work is the *Lives of the Caesars*, dedicated about AD
120. The structure of Suetonius' *Vitae* is interesting for, instead of a strictly
chronological approach, he deals with the main material of the reign on a
topical basis in an attempt to assess the real character, virtues and vices of the
subject; there is a return to chronology for the account of the end of the reign
and death. These stories, highly readable and full of anecdotes and scandal,
show a form of Graeco-Roman biography which has affinities, not with history or encomium, but with the novel and the entertaining story. Momigliano
considers Tacitus, Plutarch and Suetonius to be responsible for keeping biography from becoming merely a tool for imperial propaganda.[64] Again, therefore, we shall return to these authors in Chapter 7.

61. See Momigliano, *Second Thoughts*, pp. 8 and 13.

62. Geiger, 'Munatius Rufus', p. 71.

63. Pliny, *Epistles* V.5.3 and VIII.12.4; see Geiger, 'Munatius Rufus', pp. 61-2; for *exitus* and
the gospels, see Berger, 'Hellenistische Gattungen im NT', *ANRW* II.25.2, pp. 1257-9.

64. Momigliano, *Development*, p. 100.

4. The Later Empire

Although this final period takes us beyond the time of the gospels, it is worth mentioning some of the features of βίος as it developed. Perhaps the most important second-century writer in this field was the philosophical satirist, Lucian: among his surviving works are various items displaying biographical features, such as the *Encomium of Demosthenes* and pieces entitled simply by the subject's name, such as the *Nigrinus* or *Alexander the False Prophet*. There is also the Δημώνακτος βίος, to be studied in Chapter 7.

Philosophical biography becomes very important in the third century. Diogenes Laertius' compendium of βίοι of philosophers extracted many earlier, yet now lost, writers. Philostratus wrote the *Life of Apollonius of Tyana*, a wandering philosopher-cum-miracle worker, describing his travels, teaching and great deeds. Since some have compared this with the gospels, we shall return to it in Chapter 7. Further interest was aroused in Pythagoras, with βίοι of him written by both Iamblichus and Porphyry; again, the use of biography in philosophical debate is to be noted. This becomes even more apparent in the pagan-Christian debates of the end of the third and early fourth centuries with Porphyry's *Plotinus* and Eusebius' *Origen*. As Cox has put it, 'biography was from its inception a genre that found its home in controversy' with the twin aims of apologetic and polemic, attack and defence, hence its use in the 'holy war' between the pagan schools and Christianity.[65]

Imperial biography also continues, with the *Scriptores Historiae Augustae*, some thirty accounts of different Caesars, both those who became emperor and also their heirs and usurpers. Following Suetonius, these Lives are topically based with a mix of biography and annals, official documents and anecdotes. The use and interpretation of the *SHA* is problematic because of the multiple authorship and large amounts of fictitious material.[66]

This mixture of the strands of political and philosophical biography continued beyond the Empire itself. In the former category, we have Einhard's *Vita Karoli*, published *c.* AD 835. In this account of Charlemagne, the influence of Suetonius can be seen in the topical arrangement. However, the *Gesta Guillelmi Ducis* by William of Poitiers is the reverse with its chronological structure and few anecdotes; the influence of historiography as the neighbouring genre is stronger here, although this panegyric account of William the Conqueror by his one-time chaplain has more than a hint of encomium too.[67]

---

65. Cox, *Biography in Late Antiquity*, p. 135.
66. A. R. Birley, 'The Augustan History', in *Latin Biography*, pp. 113-38.
67. For Einhard, see *Latin Biography*, pp. 96-108; for William, see pp. 139-55.

Philosophical biography seems to have given way to hagiography, or 'sacred biography' as Heffernan prefers to call it, Lives of the saints, 'written by a member of a community of belief' for exemplary purposes of imitation.[68] Many were collections of anecdotes and miracle stories, though others show the influence of Graeco-Roman biography upon them. In the Norman period, William of Malmesbury wrote *Lives* of recent saints such as Dunstan and Wulfstan, as well as a major history of England.[69] The great figure for mediaeval hagiography, St Francis, inspired many writings, including two *Vitae* by Thomas of Celano, the first in 1228 as part of the canonization process and the later version in 1246. These and other pieces like *The Legend of the Three Companions* were officially suppressed in 1266 in favour of the *Life* written by the then Minister General, St Bonaventura.[70]

Conclusion

It is perhaps fitting that this survey of a possible genre for the gospels should have begun with the writings of adherents of philosophical schools and ended with the works of members of a religious Order. The first conclusion is therefore obvious: *biography is a type of writing which occurs naturally among groups of people who have formed around a certain charismatic teacher or leader, seeking to follow after him.* If it was true of Socrates, Cato and St Francis that their followers sought to keep their memory alive by writing βίοι and *vitae* of them, then βίος literature is a sensible place to begin a search for the genre of the gospels, written about Jesus by his followers.

Secondly, we have seen that *a major purpose and function of βίοι is in a context of didactic or philosophical polemic and conflict.* The main impetus forming the first true βίοι out of an amalgam of history and encomium was the debate about Socrates, as different schools competed to be seen as his true followers. Similarly, βίοι of Cato were used by both sides in the Civil War which brought the late Roman Republic to a close, and as a method of political and philosophical opposition to the Principate in the early Empire. In the debate between pagans and Christians for the control of the intellectual world of the late Empire, βίοι of saints and philosophers were pressed into service. The propaganda value of βίοι was recognized by politicians from the

68. Thomas J. Heffernan, *Sacred Biography: Saints and Their Biographers in the Middle Ages* (OUP, 1988), pp. 15-16 and 28-30.

69. See D. H. Farmer, 'Two Biographies by William of Malmesbury', in *Latin Biography*, pp. 157-76.

70. See R. Brooke. 'The Lives of St. Francis of Assisi', in *Latin Biography*, pp. 177-98.

time of Augustus' *Res Gestae* to the *Scriptores Historiae Augustae*. Finally, the debate about the future of the Franciscans after the saint's death was also conducted partly by composing *Vitae* of the master. If the gospels were composed and used in a setting of the early Christian communities struggling to interpret the significance of Jesus for themselves and to resist other interpretations as erroneous, then another possible link with βίοι might be made.

Thirdly, we have followed the development of this genre over the course of a thousand years of Graeco-Roman history and beyond into the Dark Ages and Mediaeval period, across the known world from ancient Persia to Norman England. Thus, *βίος is a genre capable of flexibility, adaptation and growth,* and we should avoid facile and simplistic definitions. Furthermore, βίος nestles among neighbouring genres such as historiography, rhetoric, encomium, moral philosophy, polemic and the novel or story, with some examples tending towards overlap with one or more neighbouring borders and yet still remaining recognizably within the genre of βίος. Subgenres within βίος literature may be defined in terms of content (political v. philosophical-literary βίοι) or structure (chronological v. topical) or the influence of neighbouring genres (historical v. encomiastic).

Finally, this survey has demonstrated various possible analogies between the gospels and Graeco-Roman βίοι. Therefore, it is eminently sensible to begin a search for the genre of the gospels within the sphere of βίος, *but such an attempt to consider the gospels as βίοι must always take account of this wider picture of its flexible and developing nature.*

CHAPTER 4

▬▬▬▬▬▬▬▬▬▬

Evaluation of Recent Debate

The Gospels do stand without adequate parallel in form and content in the literary world.[1]

The Gospels are a subtype of Greco-Roman biography.[2]

The historical survey in Chapter 1 concluded with various recent attempts comparing the gospels with Graeco-Roman biography. We suggested that either this hypothesis should be put on a sound scholarly footing or exposed as a false trail. In order to undertake proper evaluation of these theories, a thorough study of both the literary theory of genre and of the development of Graeco-Roman biography was necessary. Now that this has been done, we can return to the recent debate better equipped to assess the various contributions. Close analysis of the last thirty years reveals three main periods: the first phase occurred during the 1970s, when the dominant consensus that the gospels are not biography began to be challenged; the second, during the early 1980s, was a response, with some wishing to re-establish the old consensus and others to take it into new pastures; the third phase, towards the end of the decade, gradually increased pressure for the gospels to be seen as some type of biography. We shall examine some leading examples from each phase to evaluate how successful these seem in the light of our study so far.

---

1. R. Guelich, 'The Gospel Genre', *Das Evangelium und die Evangelien*, p. 216; ET as *The Gospel and the Gospels*, p. 205.
2. David E. Aune, *The New Testament in Its Literary Environment*, p. 64.

A. The First Protests

1. Graham Stanton

The first real voice of protest against the traditional critical consensus against the gospels as biographies came through Stanton's 1969 Ph.D. thesis, revised for publication as *Jesus of Nazareth in New Testament Preaching*. Stanton is clearly aware at many points that he is challenging critical orthodoxy. He discusses pre-Lukan traditions about Jesus (in the speeches in Acts), Luke's own presentation of Jesus, and Paul's preaching and teaching, and argues that all of them demonstrate an interest in Jesus' earthly life, character and activity, reflecting a concern in early Christian preaching 'from a period well before the appearance of Mark'.[3] From a comparison of the gospels with contemporary literature, he concludes that they are closest to Graeco-Roman biographical writings and quite distinct from Jewish writings such as the *Pirqe Aboth* or Rabbinic material and from later second-century gospels and gnostic writings. They tell us a 'surprisingly large amount' about the life and character of Jesus of Nazareth.[4] The early church intended to include such material in missionary preaching, for who Jesus is, is shown by his actions as well as by his words. We cannot escape such biographical material in the New Testament — and it should form part of our preaching today.

Chapter 5, the comparison with ancient biographical writing, is crucial for our concern. Bultmann's position is rejected by demonstrating that many Graeco-Roman βίοι also lack modern presuppositions such as chronology and psychological character development. Stanton's coverage of contemporary literature is very good, referring to the whole range of βίοι from earliest origins, through Satyrus and Plutarch to later authors like Philostratus. Unfortunately he does not follow the argument through to its logical conclusion. Having demonstrated the similarities with Graeco-Roman biographies, he concludes that the gospels must have been considered 'biographical'.[5] However, on the same page he refers to the 'wholly justifiable insistence that the gospels are not biographies' — while in fact he has removed the justification for this view earlier in the chapter. Throughout the book he is careful to use the adjective 'biographical' of the Jesus tra-

---

3. G. N. Stanton, *Jesus of Nazareth in New Testament Preaching*, SNTSMS 27 (CUP, 1974), p. 116.

4. *Ibid.*, p. 136.

5. *Ibid.*, p. 135.

ditions, rather than the generic noun 'biography', and he is aware of the difficulties of the modern connotations attaching to the term.[6] In addition, the book's concern is with the Jesus traditions and their place in New Testament preaching rather than the genre of the gospels themselves. However, to conclude that the gospels are biographical was a major step forward and it would not be long before others would draw the conclusion about biography itself.

Stanton continued his interest in literary theory and gospel studies in his other work such as his 1978 Inaugural Lecture and his work on Matthew.[7] His book on the person of Jesus and the gospels includes a section on 'the gospels as biographies'. This provides a brief survey of the question, from Votaw and Bultmann to Talbert and Shuler, and argues once again that the gospels must not be judged by the criteria of *modern* biography.[8] More recently, Stanton has moved the discussion on to the fourfold nature of the gospels and the implications of this for the development of the codex.[9] In addition, now that the biographical hypothesis he first espoused has become widely accepted, he has directed his fire against another scholarly consensus — namely that the early manuscripts of the gospels were written by workaday 'documentary hands' in a downmarket utilitarian context, unlike ancient biography; his analysis of papyri challenges this view and therefore makes another link between the gospels and βίοι.[10]

2. Charles H. Talbert

C. H. Talbert has been engaged in research into the Graeco-Roman parallels and links with the gospels over an extended period of time, from a discussion of the literary patterns in Luke-Acts, through analysis of the concepts of the 'immortals' and the 'descending-ascending redeemer myth' to his classic

---

6. *Ibid.*, p. 170.

7. Stanton, *Interpreting the New Testament Today: An Inaugural Lecture in the Chair of New Testament Studies,* King's College, London, 14th November 1978, pp. 4, 7 and 13; 'Matthew as a Creative Interpreter of the Sayings of Jesus', *Das Evangelium und die Evangelien,* pp. 273-87.

8. G. N. Stanton, *The Gospels and Jesus* (OUP, 1989), pp. 15-20; this has now been updated and revised as *The Gospels and Jesus,* second edition (OUP, 2002), see pp. 13-18; also in his *A Gospel for a New People: Studies in Matthew* (Edinburgh: T&T Clark, 1992), p. 64, n. 3, Stanton suggests that he was 'too cautious' in his assessment of the gospels as biographies in the first edition of *The Gospels and Jesus* in 1989.

9. Graham N. Stanton, 'The Fourfold Gospel', *NTS* 43 (1997), pp. 347-66.

10. Graham N. Stanton, *Jesus and Gospel* (Cambridge University Press, 2004); see especially chapter 9, pp. 192ff.

work, *What Is a Gospel?* Subsequent work has shown a continuing interest in examining such Graeco-Roman links.[11]

Here we shall consider the flagship for his ideas, *What Is a Gospel?*, which received widespread attention and major reviews. It begins with a brief survey of 'The Problem' of the genre of the gospels and previous attempts to solve it. Bultmann's three objections that the gospels cannot be biography because of their mythical and cultic setting and their world-denying eschatological outlook are dealt with in turn, by pointing out the presence of similar features in much Graeco-Roman biography. Thus, the 'myth' of Jesus is compared with ideas of the 'immortals' and the 'descending-ascending redeemer myth'. The cultic function of the gospels is linked to the social use of Lives of philosophers and rulers within various groups in Graeco-Roman society; Talbert proposes a new classification of Graeco-Roman biography into five types, rejecting Leo's twofold division, and then fits the gospels squarely into this. Finally, Overbeck's suggestion that the early Christians were so eschatologically minded that they could not use worldly literary forms is rejected; the gospels are constructed on a 'compositional principle' of 'inclusive reinterpretation', also used in the production of ancient biography. Thus the form-critical denial of the gospels as biographies rests on insecure foundations; Mark and John are biographies designed to defend the subject against misunderstanding (Type B), Luke-Acts is a 'life of the founder', plus narrative of his successors (Type D), and Matthew is a Life designed to provide the hermeneutical key for the legitimate interpretation of the subject's teaching (Type E).

Despite the probability that Talbert is responsible for the paradigm shift away from form-critical notions of the gospels' uniqueness, *What Is a Gospel?* is full of difficulties in both of our key areas. First, Talbert's use of classical material is rather suspect, with some idiosyncratic interpretation of the primary texts to which he refers and little use of secondary literature ei-

11. Charles H. Talbert, *Literary Patterns, Theological Themes and the Genre of Luke-Acts*, SBLMS 20 (Missoula: Scholars, 1974); 'The Concept of Immortals in Mediterranean Antiquity', *JBL* 94 (1975), pp. 419-36; 'The Myth of a Descending-Ascending Redeemer in Mediterranean Antiquity', *NTS* 22 (1976), pp. 418-40; *What Is a Gospel? The Genre of the Canonical Gospels* (Fortress 1977/SPCK 1978); 'Biographies of Philosophers and Rulers as Instruments of Religious Propaganda in Mediterranean Antiquity', in *ANRW* I.16.2 (1978), pp. 1619-51 — essentially a repeat of much of *What Is a Gospel?*; 'The Gospel and the Gospels', *Interpretation* 33 (1979), pp. 351-62; 'Prophecies of Future Greatness: The Contribution of Greco-Roman Biographies to an Understanding of Luke 1.5–4.15', in *The Divine Helmsman: Studies on God's Control of Human Events, Presented to Lou H. Silberman*, ed. James L. Crenshaw and Samuel Sandmel (New York: Ktav, 1980), pp. 129-41; 'Once Again: Gospel Genre', *Semeia* 43 (1988), pp. 53-73, with a response by D. P. Moessner, pp. 75-84.

ther on the texts or on the field in general. Thus Aune describes him as a 'blindfolded man staggering across a mine-field'.[12] This illustrates the problems of interdisciplinary study: some of Talbert's 'parallels' are dubious on closer study.

However, his classification of Graeco-Roman biography is a welcome new approach to the problem of how to distinguish suitable subgenres of βίος. Although he divides βίοι on the grounds of 'cultic' or 'social' functions, in fact, the differences are more those of *purpose* — and this rigid approach does not allow for the fact that many βίοι had several purposes, and would thus fit in several of his category types. This problem manifests itself when Mark and John turn out to be of the same type, while Luke and Matthew end up as something different. If some other generic features were taken into account, rather than just purpose and social function, this strange result would not occur. This brings us to his handling of genre theory: there is insufficient attention given to how genres and 'types' are determined. Page 11 has a few sentences on Hirsch, Fowler, and on Wellek and Warren, and Chapter 1 concludes with a brief excursus attempting to distinguish biography from history and romance (pp. 16-17), but there is little use of this theoretical background to control the rest of the book.

Finally, *What is a Gospel?* is essentially a negative argument: Bultmann's rejection of the biographical genre of the gospels is dismissed because other ancient βίοι were equally mythic, cultic and world-denying. This does not positively establish the biographical genre of the gospels. In the end, *What Is a Gospel?* does not tell us what a gospel *is;* it just destroys the arguments of earlier critics who thought it is *not* biography. Thus, *What Is a Gospel?* is unsatisfactory on several grounds, especially its handling of the classical material and its use of literary theory. However, it would be unjust to end on these negative comments. In Talbert's favour it must be said that here we have a real attempt to relate the gospels to the world of classical literature. If, in the end, it fails because of flaws in methodology and understanding, at least the attack on the old view of the genre of the gospels and the consideration of the world of Graeco-Roman literature opened a way for others to pursue. Furthermore, Talbert himself has continued to debate the arguments for the biographical genre of the gospels, especially with regard to

12. David E. Aune, 'The Problem of the Genre of the Gospels: A Critique of C. H. Talbert's *What is a Gospel?' in Gospel Perspectives II: Studies of History and Tradition in the Four Gospels,* ed. R. T. France and David Wenham (Sheffield: JSOT Press, 1981), pp. 9-60; quotation from p. 17. Talbert has replied to Aune in 'Reading Chance, Moessner, and Parsons' in *Cadbury, Knox, and Talbert: American Contributions to the Study of Acts,* ed. M. C. Parsons and J. B. Tyson (Atlanta: Scholars Press, 1992), pp. 229-40.

the implications of his ideas about biographical succession narratives for the genre of the Acts of the Apostles.[13]

3. Philip L. Shuler

Shuler's Ph.D. thesis about the genre of all three synoptic gospels was published as a book on the genre of Matthew;[14] the later sections on Mark and Luke were omitted, though the reason for this is not made clear. Whereas Talbert's work was essentially negative, dismissing Bultmann's objections, Shuler tried to mount a positive case to establish the genre of the gospels as being a subgroup of biography, which he calls encomium or laudatory biography. He too begins with a useful survey of previous work, looking at C. W. Votaw, K. L. Schmidt, M. Hadas and M. Smith, and C. H. Talbert. The second chapter is in two parts: first he has some discussion of the theory of genre, and then he sets out to demonstrate the existence of his chosen genre of 'encomium/laudatory biography'. From various classical writers' prefaces and statements he argues for a clear distinction between encomium and history, which is then fleshed out by reference to later rhetorical writers' discussion of the rules and techniques of encomium. The genre can be recognized by three features: the *aim* of praising the subject, the *techniques* of amplification and comparison, and the use of various set *topoi*, such as period, ancestry, character, virtues and so on. Chapter 3 provides various examples of the genre: Isocrates' *Helen, Busiris* and *Evagoras;* Xenophon's *Agesilaus;* Philo's *De vita Mosis;* Tacitus' *Agricola;* Lucian's *Demonax;* Josephus' autobiographical *Life;* and the *Apollonius of Tyana* by Philostratus. From this collection, he argues for a common pattern of shared purposes, techniques and *topoi*.

Then he turns to Matthew and considers the birth and death *topoi*, and the techniques of a lack of concern for geography, thematic arrangement, am-

13. Charles H. Talbert, 'Ancient Biography' in *The Anchor Bible Dictionary*, ed. D. N. Freedman (New York: Doubleday, 1992), vol. I, pp. 745-9; Talbert, review of R. A. Burridge, *What Are the Gospels?* in *JBL* 112 (1993), pp. 714-5; Talbert, 'The Acts of the Apostles: Monograph or Bios?' in *History, Literature, and Society in the Book of Acts,* ed. Ben Witherington III (Cambridge University Press, 1996), pp. 58-72.

14. P. L. Shuler, 'The Synoptic Gospels and the Problem of Genre', Ph.D. Dissertation, McMaster University, 1975; revised for publication as *A Genre for the Gospels: The Biographical Character of Matthew* (Philadelphia: Fortress. 1982); his paper 'The Genre(s) of the Gospels' for the 1984 Jerusalem symposium *The Interrelations of the Gospels,* ed. D. L. Dungan (Leuven: University Press. 1990), pp. 459-83, with a response from Peter Stuhlmacher, pp. 484-96, summarizes the Ph.D. material on all three synoptic gospels and adds a brief look at John.

plification of the *topoi* and the comparison of Jesus with those around him; Matthew's purpose is to state the identity of Jesus as Son of God, to elicit praise and to provide a paradigm for the disciples' emulation. Thus the book concludes that Matthew reveals 'a striking number of affinities with the encomium biographical genre and its shared conventions — enough to justify Matthew's classification within this genre'; Matthew has 'consciously or unconsciously appropriated a ubiquitous literary type'. The thesis has further detailed discussion in a similar vein of Mark and Luke and reaches the same conclusion.[15] This a good example of how to demonstrate a positive case for the relationship of the gospels with Graeco-Roman literature. Unfortunately, there are various difficulties which mean that the final result is less than compelling.

First, although Shuler's treatment of genre theory (pp. 24-34) is a significant advance on Talbert's, it has its limitations and does not have sufficient effect on the rest of the book. For instance, although in the theory section he suggests that genre is a dynamic pattern, his generic proposal of a fixed written form is far too rigid, especially when he tries to suggest that a wide range of diverse works dating over half a millennium apart are all members of the same narrow genre. Genre is better understood as a developing and flexible cluster of features, all of which need to be taken into account. Shuler considers only *topoi*, certain techniques, and purpose — and these are hardly determinative on their own. The techniques of amplification and comparison are used throughout classical literature, so their appearance in encomium biography and in the gospels does not show that they belong to the same genre. Other features are ignored, whereas consideration of size would have pointed out the significant difference between the short works of Isocrates and the extremely long *Apollonius of Tyana,* while the mode of representation would have raised the relationship of Isocrates' oral speeches being in the same tight genre as a carefully written biography.

Secondly, although at first his handling of classical material seems much more satisfactory than Talbert's, the ample quotation from primary texts is all from Loeb translations, and there is little use of secondary literature, commentaries and articles. It is doubtful whether this genre of 'encomium biography' can be said to exist at all. Shuler quotes five authors' prefaces and statements to demonstrate their awareness of the 'dichotomy between history and biography', but closer analysis shows some confusion of the terms 'encomium', 'βίος' and 'history'. Shuler wriggles on the hook somewhat, declaring that 'it is unlikely that this different terminology indicates

---

15. Shuler, *A Genre for the Gospels,* pp. 108-9; 'The Synoptic Gospels', pp. 317-20.

separate genres'.[16] Furthermore, we demonstrated in the last chapter, with respect to Shuler's choice, that authors' prefaces and programmatic statements are notoriously unreliable in determining exact genre. In fact, few classicists would agree with the identification of these works as 'encomium biography', if indeed the genre exists in the first place. Even when Shuler makes use of classicists' work, he can be very selective: in his attempt to argue that Tacitus' *Agricola* is 'epideictic oratory' within this genre of encomium biography, he claims the support of the Oxford commentary: 'generally speaking . . . we are in agreement with the assessment of R. M. Ogilvie and Ian Richmond'; there then follows a composite quotation made up from pages 11, 12, 14 and 20 of Ogilvie's Introduction. In fact, in the sections Shuler left out, Ogilvie specifically denies what Shuler is trying to prove: 'Still less should we be misled into seeing the *Agricola* as a special kind of "biographical encomium" or as a literary variant of the funeral laudation'.[17] Such mishandling of the secondary literature by Shuler does not inspire confidence.

Thirdly, the attempt to fit Matthew, or all three synoptics, into this genre just reveals the differences between them. It rests on demonstrating that they too exhibit the same features. Shuler equates the *purpose* of rhetorical praise of an individual with Matthew's intention to elicit a response of faith — but these are not really the same. He concentrates on Matthew's birth and death/resurrection *topoi,* but the full range of Jesus' life and ministry must be included. The shared *techniques* of a lack of concern for geography and thematic arrangement of material are common to most other ancient genres; Matthew's use of 'amplification' is also different from the rhetorical technique, and Jesus is not explicitly 'compared' with John the Baptist or the Pharisees, in the manner of Plutarch's σύγκρισεις.[18] Similar comments might also be made about his handling of Mark and Luke in his Ph.D. thesis. A larger range of generic features, especially those predominantly linked with biography, needs to be considered before the gospels can be identified with βίοι.

Sadly, therefore, we cannot accept Shuler's identification of Matthew and the synoptics as 'encomium biography'. If Shuler had managed to demonstrate both the existence of this genre and that the gospels belonged to it, then we would indeed have derived great hermeneutical benefit from his

---

16. Shuler, *A Genre for the Gospels,* p. 42.

17. Shuler, *A Genre for the Gospels,* p. 75; Ogilvie and Richmond, *Agricola* (OUP, 1967), pp. 12-13.

18. For fuller discussion of Plutarch's use of comparison, see C. B. R. Pelling, 'Synkrisis in Plutarch's Lives', in *Miscellanea Plutarchea,* ed. Frederick E. Brenk and Italo Gallo, *Quaderni del Giornale Filologico Ferrarese* 8 (1986), pp. 83-96.

work. Unfortunately, however, his brave attempt to grapple with literary theory and the classical material fails because of his over-rigid understanding of the genre and his highly selective approach to both ancient biography and to the gospels. One is reminded of Procrustes' hospitality arrangements for his guests: once Shuler has finished chopping Matthew to fit into encomium biography, I no longer recognize the victim — and I am none too sure of the existence of the bed!

Thus, throughout the 1970s a lot of useful work was done to establish links between the gospels and Graeco-Roman literature, and the idea began to gain ground. However, weak literary theory and poor handling of the classical material meant that none of these attempts succeeded.

B. The Response

By the start of the 1980s, there was building up a frequently, if not always cogently, argued case for a biographical genre of the gospels. The 1982 Tübingen Symposium, *Das Evangelium und die Evangelien,* gave detailed attention to the matter. Papers on the individual gospels raised some questions of genre: Martin Hengel asked whether Mark was a collector or theologian, looking at the influence of accounts of Moses on Mark; the shift in the use of the term εὐαγγέλιον from Paul's understanding to describe the whole story of Jesus may be derived from Peter. Graham Stanton saw Matthew as a creative interpreter who was not trying to create a new genre; if Mark is an εὐαγγέλιον, so is Matthew. Howard Marshall suggested that Luke wrote Luke-Acts as a two-volume historical account, drawing on his predecessors for the first half and contributing the additional concept of the story of salvation in the church. Finally, James Dunn compared John and the synoptics: it is striking that he 'felt it necessary to retain the format of a *Gospel*.'[19] Thus all four contributions stressed the intimate connection of the four canonical gospels, but we must consider in detail two further contributions specifically on genre and Graeco-Roman biography.

---

19. Peter Stuhlmacher (ed.), *Das Evangelium und die Evangelien,* WUNT 28 (Tübingen: J. C. B. Mohr, 1983), ET as *The Gospel and the Gospels,* ed. Peter Stuhlmacher (Grand Rapids: Eerdmans, 1991), containing *inter alia:* M. Hengel, 'Probleme des Markusevangeliums', pp. 221-65 (ET 'Literary, Theological, and Historical Problems in the Gospel of Mark', pp. 209-51); G. N. Stanton, 'Matthew as a Creative Interpreter of the Sayings of Jesus', pp. 273-87 (ET pp. 257-72); I. H. Marshall, 'Luke and His "Gospel"', pp. 289-308 (ET pp. 273-92); J. D. G. Dunn, 'Let John Be John: A Gospel for Its Time', pp. 309-39 (ET pp. 293-322), quotation from p. 338 (ET p. 322).

1. Robert Guelich

Guelich's article begins with a brief discussion of genre and whether the gospels are *sui generis*. The various theories about their genre are either analogical — those which provide parallels, or derivational — that the gospels are unique and derive their genre from how they came into being. The many and varied analogies in both Jewish and Graeco-Roman literature, including Talbert's and Shuler's suggestions, are unconvincing. Next he considers the unique school, Dibelius' evolutionary hypothesis and Güttgemann's critique, and then Dodd's kerygmatic solution; Dodd is vulnerable on the existence of the basic outline of the kerygma. Since the written kerygma idea is the most promising, Guelich tries to provide a more adequate version. Mark applies εὐαγγέλιον to the whole work (1.1) as well as to Jesus' own preaching (1.15). This shift from the more usual Pauline use of εὐαγγέλιον as just the death-resurrection-return nexus to equate the conceptual eschatological gospel with the narrative gospel is actually very Jewish; it lies not in Mark's creativity, but in the tradition itself. Acts 10.34-43, which he believes to be pre-Lukan, possesses exactly the same framework and material. *Formally,* the framework of the gospels is the narrative of Jesus' ministry and Passion, and they contain the *material* of the kerygma — that God has acted in Jesus Christ. Thus, 'the literary gospel ultimately represents the Church's gospel in narrative form'.[20] This approach is restated briefly in Guelich's recent *Commentary,* where he is prepared to use the word 'biographical' of the gospels; however, he concludes: 'Formally, then, these gospels belong to the broad category of hellenistic biography . . . materially, they are *sui generis*.'[21]

Thus Guelich suggests that searching for generic parallels and literary relations in the ancient world, Jewish or Greek, is not helpful; preferring the kerygmatic hypothesis, he argues that not only do the individual units and pericopae come from the oral tradition, but so do the actual framework and generic identity. Sensitive to the theoretical point that unique genre is a contradiction in terms, he says that 'the gospels are unique' only means that they form their own literary genre of four or so. However, this pushing of the origins of the genre back into the oral tradition itself, like the old form-critical approaches, runs into problems. The idea that sermons such as Acts 10.34-43 'formally' provide the framework of the narrative account is difficult: form is much more than just framework, and a written document of prose narrative

---

20. Guelich, 'The Gospel Genre', *Das Evangelium und die Evangelien*, pp. 183-219 (ET pp. 173-208); quotation from p. 213 (ET p. 202).

21. Robert Guelich, *Mark 1–8.26*, WBC 34A (Dallas: Word, 1989), pp. xix-xxii.

of some 10,000-20,000 words is quite different from an oral sermon of a few verses — and thus we have a different genre. As for such sermons also providing the 'material', the idea that 'God was at work in Jesus' life, death and resurrection' is also central to the Pauline epistles — but that does not make them of the same genre as the gospels. So, much more thought about the theory and nature of genres is required.

Secondly, Guelich's *sui generis* concept depends on his conclusion that there were no adequate parallels for the gospels in either the Jewish or Graeco-Roman literary worlds. To move deftly from pointing out the shortcomings of Talbert and Shuler to a total dismissal of βίος as a parallel is not a logically compelling step. The fact that their unsatisfactory grasp of classical biography and literary theory does not make a persuasive case does not mean that a case cannot be made. It is very unlikely that the gospels have no relations with contemporary literature, and Guelich's modified acceptance of 'broad biography' in his *Commentary* demonstrates this.

2. Albrecht Dihle

There is also some interdisciplinary input from Albrecht Dihle, whose work on classical biography has already been mentioned.[22] He begins by observing that concepts of literary genre apply only to a small fraction of what is written, and that the gospels have been read in a biographical manner for centuries, despite warnings to all those beginning New Testament study *not* to do so. Since they contain a narrative framework unlike the Jewish traditions of, for example, *Pirqe Aboth* or the Qumran material on the Teacher of Righteousness, he considers whether Greek biography may have provided a model. Dihle's account of Greek biography suggests that the basic determining factor is an interest in individuals for moral purposes. Plutarch is the best example of this moral biographical interest. The apparent similarities in the gospels are not enough for them to belong to such a clearly defined genre. They lack the basic anthropological presupposition of a shared human nature between hero and reader out of which the hero's ascent to moral perfection is a spur to the reader's own life; this is not applicable to the incarnate Son, perfect from the start. There is some literary contact with Greek ideas of history,

---

22. Dihle, 'Die Evangelien und die griechische Biographie', in *Das Evangelium und die Evangelien*, pp. 383-411 (ET 'The Gospels and Greek Biography', pp. 361-86); there is also a shortened version in *Zeit. Theol. Kirche* 80 (1983), pp. 33-49. For his other work on biography, see Dihle, *Studien,* and his *Die Entstehung der historischen Biographie*, Sitzungsberichte der Heidelberger Akademie der Wissenschaften 3 (Heidelberg: Universitätsverlag, 1987), pp. 1-90.

especially in Luke, and the gospels may be termed biography, but not the specific Greek literary genre.[23] Eventually, therefore, this contribution from a classical scholar with a background in biography yields a negative result.

Once again, we will consider this argument from the two aspects of literary theory and the understanding of Graeco-Roman biography. First, Dihle's analysis is lacking any discussion of genre theory. Instead, we get assertions which demonstrate that Dihle sees genre in very strict terms: for a text to be ordered within a genre, certain prerequisites *must* be met ('müssen sehr viele Voraussetzungen erfüllt sein'). This means that only a small fraction ('einen kleinen Bruchteil') of what is written can be put into literary genres. The word 'biography' can be used in two ways, 'terminologisch und unterminologisch', and biographical accounts can be written without using the strict genre.[24] Such an understanding of genre reflects the old *Hochliteratur* v. *Kleinliteratur* debate. However, our previous analysis has demonstrated how difficult it is to distinguish levels of literature and written texts from one another in this fashion. The inability to produce a sharp and clear distinction reflects rather a spectrum of written communication from the sublime to the ridiculous, and questions of genre can and need to be raised at all levels. One can ask about the genre of the text on a sauce bottle label, for instance.

The second criticism follows from the first; this tight, rigid concept of genre affects all of Dihle's understanding of Graeco-Roman biography. The biggest difficulty with this is that Plutarch seems to end up as the sole example of the literary genre of biography. Biography, for Dihle, is more than just an account of a life; there has to be a moral purpose as with Plutarch, and this link goes back to the Peripatetic tradition itself. Unfortunately, the embarrassing lack or fragmentary nature of other examples leads Dihle to the pessimistic conclusion that Plutarch has to be the only complete model left standing.[25] Not only will the gospels not conform to this genre, but neither will most of the other examples of ancient βίοι.[26] So here we have an argument which is both perverse and circular. Biography is defined by Plutarch's βίοι, and then all other βίοι are tested against this narrow concept and found not to be the same as Plutarch, and thus they are not biography. In fact, it is doubtful

23. Dihle, 'Die Evangelien', 'die spezifisch griechische Kunst der Biographie', p. 406 (ET 'we must keep the idea of the specific Greek art of biography at a distance', p. 383).

24. Dihle, 'Die Evangelien', pp. 383-4 (ET p. 361).

25. 'eines einzigen großen Trümmerfeldes, aus dem nur Plutarchs Biographien als vollständige Denkmäler herausragen', *ibid.*, p. 394; ET 'unfortunately the tradition of biographical literature of the Hellenistic and imperial periods resembles a huge expanse of ruins in which only Plutarch's biographies stand out as complete monuments', p. 371.

26. *Ibid.*, p. 399 (ET p. 376).

whether even all Plutarch's βίοι would pass the test, since not all of them are dominated by his moral concerns. At this point, therefore, the whole of Dihle's argument collapses. The gospels are *not* being compared with Greek biography; the gospels and the rest of Greek biography are being compared with one understanding of Plutarch — and found to be different. That they belong together with these other βίοι as some form of biography other than the strict genre is accepted by Dihle on several occasions (e.g. p. 406). Given our understanding of genre as applying right across written communication and our understanding of Graeco-Roman biography as an ill-defined genre nestling between history, moral philosophy, encomium, politics, story-telling and the rest, then the genre is reopened both for the rest of Graeco-Roman biography and the gospels.

3. F. Gerald Downing

Although he agrees with Talbert and Shuler against the form-critical *sui generis* view of the gospels, Downing nonetheless believes the search for a distinctive genre for the gospels to be mistaken. Instead, he has suggested frequently that important analogies between the gospels and Graeco-Roman literature are to be found in a search for shared *motifs*.[27] In rejecting the 'unique' hypothesis, he has a marvellous picture of a small group of early Christians gathered to listen to Mark being read for the first time, never having heard such an extended string of stories before and saying: 'This is *sui generis*.'[28] However, no parallel genre has been found, nor is one likely to be found: the attempt is 'mistaken and misleading'.[29] Instead, the search for recurrent patterns of shared *motifs* is likely to prove more fruitful.[30] These motifs include such things as the subject's birth, precocity, calling, great deeds and death. From this analysis, he concludes that the selection of motifs made by the evan-

---

27. F. G. Downing, 'Contemporary Analogies to the Gospels and Acts: "Genres" or "Motifs"?', in *Synoptic Studies*, JSNTSS 7, pp. 51-65; 'Cynics and Christians', *NTS*, 30 (1984), pp. 584-93; 'Ears to Hear', in *Alternative Approaches to New Testament Study*, ed. A. E. Harvey (London: SPCK, 1985), pp. 97-121; 'The Social Contexts of Jesus the Teacher: Construction or Reconstruction', *NTS* 33 (1987), pp. 439-51; *Christ and the Cynics: Jesus and Other Radical Preachers in First-Century Tradition*, JSOT Manuals 4 (SAP, 1988); see also his work *Strangely Familiar* (published by the author privately, 44 Cleveland Rd., Crumpsall, Manchester, M8 6QU) for full analysis of these shared features.

28. Downing, 'Ears to Hear', p. 97; see also, 'Contemporary Analogies', pp. 51-2.

29. Downing, 'Contemporary Analogies', p. 51.

30. *Ibid.*, pp. 52-4; 'Ears to Hear', p. 108.

gelists follows a pattern common in the first-century world; similarly, early Christian preaching would have seemed similar to that of the Cynics.[31]

Downing is well read in the classical material, and his common motifs and analogies are most illuminating. However, such motifs are all to do with *content;* he has little to say about the overall *form* of the whole, or genre of a work. Also, his list has a certain natural obviousness about it; one may come up with a similar pattern because that is the natural way to describe a person's life and significance, rather than to fulfil a literary pattern. Downing has not accounted for the genre of the whole; the same list of motifs could occur in a speech, or letter, or biography, all of which could be used to describe someone. The fact remains that these are all different genres, using the same material. Once again, our concept of genre as derived from many features is important. A common pattern of motifs is certainly one feature we shall be looking for; but used as a sole control, it is incapable of distinguishing different genres.

4. Mary Ann Tolbert

Finally among those who have responded to the biographical proposal without agreeing with it, mention should be made of Tolbert's work on Mark. Her goal is 'to articulate an interpretation of the whole Gospel of Mark using the perspectives of literary criticism'.[32] She does this in two parts: a general consideration of the text and its setting, followed by a sequential analysis of the gospel itself. It is a stimulating attempt to consider Mark both in a framework of modern literary criticism and also within its original historical and cultural context, and is thus akin to the present study. Her section on the genre of Mark is particularly relevant: she begins with a brief discussion of genre as a 'set of shared expectations' between author and audience; both the attempts to rule out genres for the gospels because of a lack of generic fit and proposals of precise genres for them fail because they 'misconstrue the nature of genre'. There can be no unique genres by definition, but genres are 'fluid patterns'.[33] Turning to the genre of Mark itself, she asserts that 'no extant ancient texts, written *prior* to the composition of the Gospels, display any obvious overall

---

31. For Jesus and Cynics, see also Burton L. Mack, *A Myth of Innocence: Mark and Christian Origins* (Philadelphia: Fortress, 1988), pp. 67-9; C. M. Tuckett, 'A Cynic Q?', *Biblica* 70 (1989), pp. 349-76, dissents.

32. Mary Ann Tolbert, *Sowing the Gospel: Mark's World in Literary-Historical Perspective* (Minneapolis: Fortress, 1989), p. 21.

33. *Ibid.*, pp. 49-50.

resemblance', although she is prepared to allow for similarity of later works such as Philostratus' *Apollonius of Tyana*.[34] While βίος is most often proposed as Mark's genre, 'it generally charts the entire course of life from birth to death' and Mark does not. Mark is a mix of aretalogy, biography and memorabilia, but much less sophisticated. It belongs to the category of *popular literature* open to a wide spectrum of society (as in Votaw's distinction rather than Schmidt's *Kleinliteratur*) with similarities to the ancient novel, such as the *Alexander Romance* and the work of Xenophon of Ephesus.[35]

From the perspective of our two-pronged critique of genre theory and ancient literature, all credit must be given to Tolbert for her material on genre: her analysis of how it functions and why previous attempts to solve gospel genre have failed is very similar to the conclusions we have already drawn. However, more is needed on ancient literature: the similarities between Mark and ancient novels are to do with language, style and plot, but genre involves more than these. Indeed, she accepts that Mark is not an ancient novel, but rather belongs in popular literature with the novel. 'Popular literature', however, is not a genre, but a level which includes works from many genres. Nor is it true that nothing resembling Mark predates him, or that βίος covers the 'entire course of life', as we shall show in due course. Thus, despite some excellent analysis, Tolbert's conclusion that Mark is popular literature does not solve the problem of the genre of the gospels.

Thus the response to the suggestion that the gospels are in the genre of Graeco-Roman biography has criticized correctly the shortcomings in the work of Talbert and Shuler. However, here too problems of methodology, literary theory and treatment of the classical texts abound. The way is still open for the biographical hypothesis, if it can be securely established.

C. The New Orthodoxy?

Our historical survey concluded that assumptions that the gospels are or contain biographical material are increasingly common.[36] This is despite the fact

---

34. *Ibid.*, p. 55.

35. Tolbert, *Sowing the Gospel*, pp. 59-79; see also, Marius Reiser, 'Der Alexanderroman und das Markusevangelium', in *Markus-Philologie*, ed. H. Cancik, WUNT 33 (Tübingen: J. C. B. Mohr, 1984), pp. 131-63.

36. See Chapter 1, note 65 above; and for similar assumptions by a classicist, 'What Is Early Christian Literature? An Outsider's View', unpublished paper delivered at King's College, London, 19 November 1985, by Prof. Averil Cameron.

that none of the proposed arguments of scholars like Talbert and Shuler have found widespread acceptance, We need to consider, finally, some major contributions, mostly from Germany and America, which appeared at different points in the 1980s proposing a biographical genre for the gospels.

1. Hubert Cancik

Cancik's articles make no mention of Talbert, Shuler or any other attempt to consider the problem later than Stanton's *Jesus of Nazareth*;[37] if they were produced in isolation from the debate, their conclusion is all the more interesting. The first essay, 'Die Gattung Evangelium', is an attempt to place the gospels within the framework of ancient literature. Mark is written with a clear historiographical structure, with references to places, times and people, and contains narrative and teaching; thus, the obvious genre is βίος. The form critics pointed out the lack of full treatment, childhood stories, psychological development and so on in the gospels; however, these aspects are also missing from other ancient βίοι. Cancik concludes, therefore, that Hellenistic and Roman readers would have seen Mark as 'Biographie Jesu', if somewhat exotic ('eine ziemlich exotische').[38] However, Jews, God-fearers and proselytes would recognize another link, to the Old Testament prophetic writings: 'Jesus was also a prophet. Mark is also a prophetic book.' The gospel, and indeed the New Testament itself, is a book between two worlds, but the non-Jews, for whom Mark was writing, would have understood it as *'Leben Jesu'*.[39] Because of the importance of the Passion story in Mark, Cancik spends the rest of the article looking at martyrology and at the death of Nero according to Pliny's and Suetonius' accounts. The second essay, 'Bios und Logos', consists mainly of an analysis of Lucian's *Demonax* and concludes with a list of the similarities and differences between Lucian and Mark. All the features required by the form critics for biography, yet lacking in Mark, are also lacking in the *Demonax*, which nonetheless bears the title of a βίος.

These two articles clearly bear out much that we have said so far. It is a pity that they do not engage with the rest of the debate beyond the early

37. H. Cancik (ed.), *Markus-Philologie*, WUNT 33 (Tübingen: J. C. B. Mohr, 1984), containing *inter alia*: 'Die Gattung Evangelium. Markus im Rahmen der antiken Historiographie', pp. 85-113; 'Bios und Logos. Formengeschichtliche Untersuchungen zu Lukians "Leben des Demonax"', pp. 115-30; also, Marius Reiser, 'Der Alexanderroman und das Markusevangelium', pp. 131-63.

38. Cancik, 'Die Gattung Evangelium', p. 96.

39. *Ibid.,* p. 98.

1970s; as it is, Cancik's comparison of the gospels with βίοι does not take us much beyond Stanton, nor is there any real treatment of genre theory. However, they are another support for the βίος theory.[40]

2. *Klaus Berger*

The most comprehensive recent treatment of genre and the New Testament is Berger's massive contribution to *ANRW,* complete with a huge bibliography.[41] Berger considers all the possible genres in New Testament literature, as well as an introductory section on methodology and genre theory. The section on 'Biographie' begins with a useful table listing the whole range of Graeco-Roman βίοι from the fifth century BC (Skylax) to the fourth AD (Iamblichus and the *SHA*). From all this analysis, Berger draws various conclusions: that there are various ways of classifying ancient biography; nearly all biography has some relationship with encomium; the use of sayings is common in Hellenistic biography; the 'typical' is more important than the individual; biography has a strong element of fiction; the beginning and end of a βίος are chronological, but not necessarily the rest; 'call' narratives are common; lives of politicians, poets and philosophers were well known; biography often had an apologetic character and was related to the depiction of leaders; and that its relationship to history varied during the period. After all this comes a brief summary of Talbert's critique of Bultmann. Berger concludes that the gospels are to be explained from the ancient genre of biography, itself dependent on encomium; the gospels are closest to Lives of philosophers, with Matthew and Luke having an additional tendency towards that of a king. This conclusion is also borne out in his study of other related genres, aretalogy, *exitus illustrium virorum* and *ultima verba,* and evangelium.[42]

This brief analysis of Graeco-Roman βίοι provides an excellent survey for those unfamiliar with classical literature, and Berger derives many helpful observations from it. Unfortunately, the final conclusions are little more than a summary of Talbert, with all his shortcomings. However, Berger firmed up

40. Cancik takes his work further in his 'The History of Culture, Religion and Institutions in Ancient Historiography: Philological Observations concerning Luke's History', *JBL* 116 (1997), pp. 673-95, discussed in Chapter 11 below.

41. Berger, 'Hellenistische Gattungen im NT', *ANRW,* II.25.2 (1984), pp. 1031-432, indexes pp. 1831-85.

42. *Ibid.:* 'Aretalogie', pp. 1218-31; 'Biographie', pp. 1231-45; *'Exitus illustrium virorum* und *ultima verba',* pp. 1257-9; 'Evangelium', pp. 1259-64.

his conclusions a little in his later work; after discussing Shuler, Dihle and Guelich, and other various possible links with Graeco-Roman biography and Jewish traditions, Berger suggests a biographical genre for the gospels, although without a full demonstration of his case.[43]

3. Dormeyer and Frankemölle

The same volume of *ANRW* also contains a major article by Detlev Dormeyer and Hubert Frankemölle, both of whom published books subsequently which repeated large amounts of the article, with some further expansion.[44] Frankemölle concentrates on the concept of 'gospel', looking at the use of εὐαγγέλιον in both the New Testament and later writings, as well as at its Jewish and Hellenistic-Roman usage. It is the development of the word from the kerygmatic concept of the good news about Jesus to the narrative gospel which concerns him; Dormeyer also discusses this and sees εὐαγγέλιον as belonging to the epideictic genre, *Prunkrede,* as a subgenre of ancient biography.[45] Dormeyer's major contribution is his exhaustive analysis of the study of the genre of the gospels from patristic times to the Enlightenment and then on through form and redaction criticism to the current debates. Here he considers both literary approaches of text-linguistics and structuralist understandings and also the various attempts to place the gospels within differing genres. Aretalogy, drama and the novel are all included, followed by more detailed treatment of biography; in addition to the work of people like Talbert, Shuler and Berger on Hellenistic biography, Dormeyer draws attention to Old Testament 'Idealbiographie' and the work of Baltzer on biographical material

43. Klaus Berger, *Formgeschichte des Neuen Testaments* (Heidelberg: Quelle & Meyer, 1984); esp. 'Evangelium und Biographie', pp. 346-57.

44. D. Dormeyer and H. Frankemölle, 'Evangelium als literarische Gattung und als theologischer Begriff. Tendenzen und Aufgaben der Evangelienforschung im 20. Jahrhundert, mit einer Untersuchung des Markusevangeliums in seinem Verhältnis zur antiken Biographie', *ANRW* II.25.2, pp. 1543-1704; D. Dormeyer, *Evangelium als literarische und theologische Gattung* (Darmstadt: Wissenschaftliche Buchgesellschaft, 1989); H. Frankemölle, *Evangelium — Begriff und Gattung: ein Forschungsbericht* (Stuttgart: Katholisches Bibelwerk, 1988); *ANRW* II.25.2 also contains H. Köster, 'Überlieferung und Geschichte der frühchristlichen Evangelienliteratur', pp. 1463-1542, and D. L. Tiede, 'Religious Propaganda and the Gospel Literature of the Early Christian Mission', pp. 1705-29.

45. Dormeyer, 'Die Kompositionsmetapher "Evangelium Jesu Christi, des Sohnes Gottes" Mk. 1.1. Ihre theologische und literarische Aufgabe in der Jesus-Biographie des Markus', *NTS* 33 (1987), pp. 452-68; see also, Helmut Koester, 'From the Kerygma-Gospel to Written Gospels', *NTS* 35 (1989), pp. 361-81.

about the prophets.[46] Markan Christology, as seen in the titles Son of God, Christ, Son of Man, and Teacher, displays this biographical tendency. The gospels are not new or unique works ('eine unabhängige Neubildung'); the combination of faith and preaching about Jesus with narrative of his earthly life (form and content of the gospel) is the great accomplishment of the evangelists, which makes their work into a new biographical subgenre ('die neugeschaffene biographische Untergattung "Evangelium"').[47]

These are substantial pieces of work which have made important contributions to the debate through the full analysis of all the relevant scholars and approaches. However, they have no treatment of literary theory of genre and very little handling of examples of ancient literature and βίοι. While their conclusions may well be correct, therefore, they cannot be viewed as conclusively established until this work has been done.

4. Barr and Wenting

The collection of papers from the SBL Seminar on Luke-Acts 1979-83 contains a comparison of Luke-Acts with classical biography.[48] Barr and Wenting's paper consisted of three main sections: it began with some brief discussion of genre theory, including a rejection of the concept of *sui generis* works and evaluation of Talbert's critique of Bultmann. The middle section analysed the 'Conventions of Classical Biography', including the type of hero, the purpose of the work, its literary manner, the external pattern, the internal organization, the focus on the subject's character, and the presentation of the material in the third person; within these conventions, there was wide scope for diversity. Thirdly, these criteria were applied to Luke-Acts, and similarities and differences were discovered: the hero is not a noble person; the addition of Acts takes the focus beyond the subject, and the scale is larger; the use of appropriate language has links with classical writers; the external pattern does not fit with the classical

---

46. Dormeyer, *ANRW* II.25.2, pp. 1574-8, and *Evangelium*, pp. 168-73; K. Baltzer, *Die Biographie der Propheten* (Neukirchen: Neukirchener Verlag, 1975).

47. Dormeyer, *Evangelium*, p. 194; *ANRW* II.25.2, p. 1601.

48. David L. Barr and Judith L. Wentling, 'The Conventions of Classical Biography and the Genre of Luke-Acts: A Preliminary Study', in *Luke-Acts: New Perspectives from the SBL Seminar*, ed. Charles H. Talbert (New York: Crossroad, 1984), pp. 63-88; a pre-1982 date is implied by the footnote on p. 80 that Shuler's *A Genre for the Gospels* 'appeared too late to be considered in this essay' — though they should have considered his Ph.D. thesis. Interestingly, Barr's own 1974 Florida Ph.D. Dissertation compared the synoptic gospels with Socratic Dialogue; see Chapter 1, n. 62 above.

conventions of series or pairs of βίοι; the internal organization is similar; the apologetic purpose is in some tension with historical concerns. Despite the differences, the authors conclude ancient audiences 'would have heard it with some of the same expectations with which they heard biographies'.[49] The paper concludes with some tables analysing Plato's *Apology, Crito* and *Phaedo,* Xenophon's *Memorabilia,* Nepos' *Great Generals,* Philo's *Moses,* Plutarch's *Demosthenes* and *Cicero,* Tacitus' *Agricola,* Suetonius' *Augustus,* Lucian's *Demonax* and, of course, Luke-Acts. The following criteria are used for the analysis: title, language, date, length, sources, point of view, type of hero, characterization, divine traits, technique, pattern, purpose and aesthetic intent.

This paper is an interesting addition to the biographical hypothesis. Its general approach and methodology (similar to that upon which this present study was already proceeding) seem to be correct. However, it has several difficulties which make it less compelling, quite apart from the preliminary nature of the study and its brevity — thirteen pages of text, plus tables, will not overturn half a century of scholarly consensus. The first problem is caused by the study being done on Luke-Acts as an entity. Many of the differences with Graeco-Roman biography, such as the external organization, the wider focus and scale beyond the subject, follow from including Acts in the analysis. If Luke alone were compared, these differences would fall away.

Second, the categories chosen for analysis are rather mixed: formal or structural features, such as language, date or 'pattern', are placed with content-based features, such as 'type of hero' or 'divine traits' without any attempt to distinguish the different levels at which these operate. Further, some of the categories, e.g. 'technique', are very vague and need fuller discussion before they can yield clear results. Finally, the analysis has not made it clear that some of the works do *not* belong to the genre of classical biography: the *Apology* is a speech, the *Crito* and *Phaedo* are philosophical dialogues, and the exact genres of the *Memorabilia* and *Agricola* are disputed among classicists. That these can appear in the table with no generic *dissimilarities* being noted does not give confidence that Luke-Acts is also in the genre of classical biography. This unease about the handling of the classical material is compounded further by the paucity of reference to classical scholarship. The analysis of the 'Conventions of Classical Biography' needs proper earthing in the literature to make it secure. The sense of insecurity is not helped by the blatant error contained in the 'language' column of the tables: Plutarch did *not* write in Latin, but Greek!

As a preliminary study, this paper has much to commend it. Within a short space, a lot of ground is covered and a sensible methodology for com-

---

49. Barr and Wenting, 'The Conventions of Classical Biography', p. 76.

paring the gospels with Graeco-Roman βίοι is undertaken. However, a fuller and much more accurate treatment is necessary if the attempt is to be successful.

5. David E. Aune

David Aune's interest in both the relationship of the New Testament to the world of classical literature and also in the specific area of gospel genre has been clear for many years.[50] We will consider here *The New Testament in Its Literary Environment* as the fullest statement of his views. Aune's general approach is twofold: he analyses a genre within both Graeco-Roman and Jewish literary traditions and then he applies this to the biblical books. The genre of the gospels is considered with respect to literary and non-literary parallels; he analyses and dismisses kerygmatic and lectionary hypotheses, and discusses ancient biography, both Graeco-Roman and Israelite-Jewish. From a study of the form, content and function of the gospels, especially Mark, he concludes that they are 'a type of ancient biography'. Luke-Acts is thought to be different, because of the two-volume nature of the work; so this is compared with ancient historiography and declared to be 'general history'. Finally, the same approach is applied to the epistles and Revelation.

As always, we will consider our two main areas. Aune's knowledge of ancient literature is very good, but his useful little survey of Graeco-Roman biography (pp. 29-36) is rather lost in all the other material of Chapter 1; it needs much fuller treatment, taking account of some of the work on biography cited in our discussion above, especially that by Geiger and Pelling, and a wider setting within its own literary environment of historiography and encomium. The definition of biography as 'a discrete prose narrative devoted exclusively to the portrayal of the whole life of a particular individual perceived as historical' is asserted rather than proven.[51] The stress on 'the whole life' would rule out both the gospels and many ancient biographies.

---

50. D. E. Aune, 'Septem sapientium convivium (Moralia 146B-164D)', in *Plutarch's Ethical Writings and Early Christian Literature*, ed. H. D. Betz (Leiden: Brill, 1978), pp. 51-105; 'Magic in Early Christianity', *ANRW*, II.23.2 (1980), pp. 1507-57; 'The Problem of the Genre of the Gospels: A Critique of C. H. Talbert's *What Is a Gospel?*', in *Gospel Perspectives II* (SAP, 1981); 'The Gospels as Hellenistic Biography', *Mosaic* 20 (1987), pp. 1-10; *Greco-Roman Literature and the New Testament*, ed. Aune, SBL Sources for Biblical Study 21 (Atlanta: Scholars Press, 1988), esp. pp. 107-26 on Secundus; *The New Testament in Its Literary Environment* (Cambridge: James Clarke & Co., 1988).

51. Aune, *The New Testament in Its Literary Environment*, p. 29.

Secondly, a more detailed coverage of genre theory would help. He defines a genre as 'a group of texts that exhibit a coherent and recurring configuration of literary features involving form (including structure and style), content, and function'.[52] New Testament literature is then compared with examples of the relevant genre, analysed by form, content and purpose. This represents a significant advance on anything previously studied and goes some way along the lines suggested by our study of genre theory earlier. However, there are still other important generic features which Aune does not consider, both structural features, such as size, scale, prose or metre, and content-based features, such as titles, opening sentences or prologues, settings and occasions. These would help to identify genre more accurately.

Finally, whereas Barr and Wentling concluded that Luke-Acts could be fitted into the genre of biography, Aune believes quite the opposite; Mark, Matthew and John are all 'a subtype of Graeco-Roman biography', but 'Luke does not belong to a type of ancient biography for it belongs with Acts, and Acts cannot be forced into a biographical mold.'[53] As we noted with Talbert, this is an odd result; some other way of dealing with the problem of the two-volume nature of Luke-Acts needs to be found: perhaps Luke itself could be one genre, and Acts another, related genre. Furthermore, given the usual view of the difference between John and the synoptics, more attention should be devoted to the genre of the fourth gospel if Aune wishes to group it with the others.

This book is an excellent introduction to the literary world of the New Testament, written in an approachable style without footnotes and likely to become essential reading for all beginning New Testament study. However, the lack of full annotated documentation and the necessary brevity of treatment of some key areas will not establish the case positively and finally for the biographical genre of the gospels to become the new scholarly consensus and orthodoxy. That task still remains to be done.

6. E. P. Sanders and Margaret Davies

Sanders' and Davies' general introduction to *Studying the Synoptic Gospels* includes several chapters concerned with genre. Chapter 2, 'Genre and Purposes', shows how the gospels do not conform to modern notions of biogra-

---

52. *Ibid.*, p. 13; there is also some helpful consideration of the methodological problems in genre criticism of the gospels on pp. 22-3.

53. *Ibid.*, p. 77.

phy, but points out the different criteria of accuracy used by ancient writers, as well as the difficulties writers like Luke had and their effect on chronology and geography. Chapters 17, 18 and 19 consider the genre of the synoptics in turn. Matthew is compared with both Hellenistic and Jewish biographies (e.g. *Apollonius of Tyana* and Philo's *Moses*) and some similarities and differences are noted; they conclude 'the most satisfactory definition of the genre is "a theodicy about creation and re-creation"'.[54] Mark and Luke are then found to be of the same genre, despite Luke's greater links with Hellenistic biography and historiography.[55]

It is good to see genre and Graeco-Roman literature given extensive attention; however, there are problems in the treatment of both. To conclude that the genre of the gospels is 'theodicy' without any indication of what its generic features might be or whether this is a recognizable genre to ancient or modern readers is not really very helpful. Most of the similarities noted with Graeco-Roman literature are to do with content: the parallels between the activities of Jesus and Apollonius without regard to the works' differences of size or presentation (let alone the later date) will not establish a shared genre. 'Theodicy' is not a genre, but can be expressed in many genres, from prophecy to apocalyptic, from hymns to drama. Once again, much greater attention to genre theory and to Graeco-Roman literature is needed.

Conclusion

We have now come to the end of the first part of our study, the survey of the problem of the genre of the gospels and the attempts to solve it. It may be helpful at this point, therefore, just to draw a few threads together. In Chapter 1 the historical survey ranged from nineteenth-century ideas about the link of the gospels with Graeco-Roman biography, through the dominance of the form-critical consensus that they were *sui generis* works, to the more recent suggestions made about the gospels' genre. It became apparent that only an interdisciplinary study involving gospel studies, literary theory of genre and proper understanding of literature which was contemporary with the gospels could provide a satisfactory answer. In Chapter 2, therefore, we attempted to provide an adequate coverage of the literary theory of genre. This showed that genre functions as a flexible set of expectations affecting both

---

54. E. P. Sanders and Margaret Davies, *Studying the Synoptic Gospels* (London: SCM, 1989), p. 265.

55. *Ibid.*, pp. 275 and 296.

author and reader; the proper recognition of genre is absolutely basic to the interpretation and appreciation of written communications. This means that the gospels cannot be *sui generis,* but must be set within the web of literary relationships of their own day. Accordingly, Chapter 3 considered the use of genre within classical scholarship, particularly as it relates to the genre of βίος (as it is better termed than 'biography' with all its modern connotations). βίος nestles between various neighbouring genres such as history and encomium; its development was traced from its origins in early travelogue and speeches, through the Alexandrian and Roman periods, to its late imperial shift into mediaeval biography and hagiography. Finally, in this Chapter 4 some evaluation of recent debate about the gospels as biography has been attempted. Although the idea has become increasingly common that the genre of the gospels may indeed have a link with Graeco-Roman biography, most proposals have failed because of problems in methodology or genre theory, as well as lack of a proper understanding of classical literature.

I undertook this study initially because, as someone with a classical background, I was unimpressed with the arguments put forward by New Testament scholars, especially in America, to demonstrate the biographical genre of the gospels. Therefore a negative result was expected, exposing the biographical hypothesis as untenable. However, as the work has developed, I have become increasingly convinced that, despite the poor quality of many of the arguments for this hypothesis, it is indeed the right one and that the gospels are part of the genre of ancient βίος literature. Therefore, we must now turn our attention away from the negative task of assessing the work of others and background considerations, to the positive need to establish a case for this hypothesis which rests on the firm foundations of literary theory and classical biography which have been laid down so far.

PART TWO

THE PROPOSED SOLUTION

CHAPTER 5

Generic Features

*The best way to define a genre . . . is to describe the common elements
in a narrow group of texts.*[1]

Recognition of genre depends on associating a complex of elements.[2]

We have seen that genre functions by providing a set of expectations as
a sort of contract between author and reader. It is constituted and
mediated through a variety of different generic features, none of which
need be peculiar to the genre; however, when they are taken all together,
they reveal a particular pattern, which enables us to recognize the genre.
Now we need to identify these 'generic features' as a list against which we
can compare the gospels and Graeco-Roman βίοι, to see whether they exhibit the same pattern and family resemblance. There is good reason for
making the list as comprehensive as possible.[3] As we have just shown, failure to recognize the diversity of the range of generic features has been a
consistent problem of most treatments of the genre of the gospels, leading
to their ultimate failure. Literary critics, however, tend to have much longer
lists. Although there are differences, a recognizable overall grouping is clear,
with many critics including some or most of the following: representation,
structure, metre, size, scale, subject, values, mood, occasion, attitude, setting, characterization, purpose, formal units, use of sources, motifs and the

---

1. Hirsch, *Validity,* p. 110.
2. Fowler, 'Life and Death', p. 80.
3. See Hawthorn, *Unlocking the Text,* p. 47.

like.[4] We will use all these features in our analysis, in order to be as wide-ranging and comprehensive as possible.

These features then have to be organized. They need to include elements concerned with the text's structure and form as well as its content and material — Wellek and Warren's 'outer form' and 'inner form'.[5] Often analogies in one or another of these areas are taken to establish a clear link on their own: thus Downing's identification of analogies of motifs did not take into account how these elements of similar content can appear in works of different formal structures.[6] Therefore, the following study must include both groups of features; as Strelka says: 'Outer *and* inner form of the literary work, its aesthetic literary (not merely linguistic) structure, and its thematics will provide elements for its special genre-form and genre-unity.'[7] However, the distinction is not always easy to maintain: thus 'characterization' is an 'outer form' in terms of the methods used by the author, whereas the quality of the characters seems more to do with content, i.e. 'inner form'.

David Hellholm and the SBL Apocalypse Group prefer a threefold division into form, content and function, which is used by Collins, Hellholm and Aune to solve problems of apocalyptic genres.[8] Furthermore, Aune uses the same tripartite scheme for his generic analysis of the gospels and Acts in their literary environment.[9] However, the distinction does not always work; Hellholm notes that some 'characteristics could show up in one or even two more groups as well, depending on the perspective': thus a vision could be seen as a formal characteristic and also have to do with content.[10] The third division of 'function' may be a separate group when we have other evidence about the purpose of the work and its audience or social setting. However, with these works Aune has to 'attempt to infer function from the text', as Collins points out; indeed Aune quotes Collins saying 'our knowledge of function and setting is often extremely hypothetical and cannot provide a firm basis for generic classification'.[11] This must mean, therefore, that this category

---

4. See for instance, Wellek and Warren, *Theory*, p. 231; Fowler, *Kinds of Literature*, chapter 4, pp. 55-74; Hawthorn, *Unlocking the Text*, p. 47; Doty, 'The Concept of Genre', p. 440; Cox, *Biography in Late Antiquity*, pp. 54-65.

5. Wellek and Warren, *Theory*, p. 231.

6. Downing, 'Contemporary Analogies', see pp. 90-91 above.

7. Strelka, *Theories of Literary Genre*, p. viii; his italics.

8. *Early Christian Apocalypticism: Genre and Social Setting*, Semeia 36 (1986); see pp. 2-7 (Collins), pp. 17-18 (Hellholm) and pp. 65-96 (Aune).

9. Aune, *The New Testament in Its Literary Environment*; see esp. pp. 32-6, 47-63, 84-96 and 116-38.

10. *Semeia* 36 (1986), p. 25.

11. *Ibid.*, pp. 6-7 and 68-9.

of function remains closely linked with content, and so one could be justified in continuing to consider it as an internal feature. Interestingly, Aune himself does not use form, content and function for his analysis of Graeco-Roman epistles and their New Testament counterparts, preferring a more traditional form-critical analysis by formulas and types.[12]

Thus our study must include the whole list of generic features, beyond the limited range of Shuler's, Guelich's and Dihle's approaches to something wider than Aune's form, content and function. The problems of classifying the features into outer/inner or content/function could be avoided by analysing them as a whole, without any grouping; this is probably how genre is grasped by a reader encountering the text. For the convenience of a more clearly ordered analysis, however, we intend to consider them in the following sequence:

(i) **Opening Features:** The title, opening words, prologue or preface are considered first as the initial features to strike the reader and to begin conveying the genre of the work.

(ii) **Subject:** This is taken next since, as we shall see, it is determinative for βίοι.

(iii) **External Features:** The mode of representation, metre, size or length, the structure or sequence, and scale all help to convey the formal, external appearance of the text. The use made of literary units, sources and methods of characterization communicate how the text was formed or composed.

(iv) **Internal Features:** In addition to the subject and the opening features, the setting and topics describe the content of the work. The style, tone, mood, attitude, values and quality of the characterization all help to convey this content. Finally, we shall consider what the content reveals of the text's function within its social setting and occasion of writing, and of the author's intention or purpose.

How all these features are used and combined forms a conventional set of expectations — the contract, albeit unwritten or even unconscious, between author and reader. Thus, authorial intention and audience expectancy may be seen as a connection between internal and external features, as well as being the instrument whereby the author 'encodes' and the reader 'decodes' the communication, to use the language of Information Theory. These features will not all occur in exactly the same way in every example of the genre,

---

12. Aune, *The New Testament in Its Literary Environment*, pp. 158-225.

but there must be enough similarity to communicate the family resemblance. Some features will be primary and necessary for the genre, whereas others may be secondary or optional.[13] Furthermore, some features may be very immediate and assist in 'signalling' the genre straightaway, whereas others play their part in confirming or correcting that initial impression.

A. Opening Features

1. Title

The first feature to signal genre is often the title itself. This may contain the name of a genre itself, e.g. *The Tragedy of King Richard the Second,* or *A History of England,* or as a subtitle, e.g. *Which One's Cliff? — The Autobiography.* Conventions may operate, such as using the name of a chief character for Greek Tragedy, the *Agamemnon* or *Antigone,* or the name of the Chorus in Aristophanic Comedy, e.g. the *Frogs, Birds* or *Clouds.* In this way the title provides us immediately with a first impression about its genre, acting as the 'master word' to guide later interpretation, which will confirm or refute the genre.[14] As Fowler points out, conventions and fashions about titles vary in time; some ancient works were even known by their opening words, as are the books of the Pentateuch in Hebrew, e.g. $b^e re'shith$ 'in the beginning' for Genesis — compare the custom of calling sacred choral anthems by their opening words. The sixteenth to the eighteenth centuries saw widespread use of subtitles with clear generic clues, whereas often today this function is achieved by the publisher's 'blurb' on the cover.[15]

As Oliver has shown, the title of an ancient scroll was usually written on the outside, sometimes as a parchment label, to facilitate identification. In addition, the title might appear at the start of the text itself, as well as in a colophon at the end. Usually such headings or labels were 'of the simplest possible form', the author's name and a brief title.[16] One problem is that the titles of

13. See Cairns, *Generic Composition,* p. 6.

14. So called by Pleynet; for full quotation, see p. 34 (n. 42) above. Similarly, Peter Hellwig describes titles as a key *(Schlüssel* or *Interpretationshilfe)* for the reader; see his article, 'Titulus oder Über den Zusammenhang von Titeln und Texten', *Zeitschrift für Germanistische Linguistik* 12 (1984), pp. 1-20.

15. See Fowler, *Kinds of Literature,* pp. 92-8.

16. Revilo P. Oliver, 'The First Medicean MS of Tacitus and the Titulature of Ancient Books', *TAPA* 82 (1951), pp. 232-61, see p. 243; for further discussion of ancient titles, see Henrik Zilliacus, 'Boktiteln i antik litteratur', *Eranos* 36 (1938), pp. 1-41.

many ancient works are not original, given by their authors; instead, they were added by librarians or grammarians. However, this need not mean that they are worthless as generic indicators, since they still tell us, in our literary milieu, how literary people in the ancient world saw these works, in their literary milieu.

2. *Opening Formulae/Prologue/Preface*

The opening words also signal the genre: 'History, epideictic oratory, philosophical dialogue, political treatise or whatever, your first sentence had to announce what you were writing.'[17] *Arma virumque cano* alerts us to the epic nature of Vergil's *Aeneid* (I.1), whereas the formulaic opening 'Paul, an apostle, to the church (or saints) at . . . grace to you and peace' leads us to expect epistolary features. The lack of an expected opening questions the presumed genre of a work, e.g. the lack of any epistolary greeting at the beginning of the 'Letter' to the Hebrews causes some to see it as a treatise or sermon.[18] The opening sentence may open the work itself, or begin a formal preface by the author, in the first person, explaining his reason and purpose in writing and giving a clear indication of genre; this is particularly common in ancient historiography.[19] Alternatively, there may be a prologue, as in tragedy or comedy, setting the scene and explaining the background; again, clear generic expectations flow from this, which are then confirmed or corrected as the work proceeds and more features appear.

B. Subject

Although genre is not determined by subject alone, subject and content are important generic features not to be underestimated. Within classical literary theory, the stress on 'appropriateness' (τὸ πρέπον, 'decorum') meant that certain subjects 'fitted' certain genres — and conversely, other subjects were *not*

---

17. Donald Earl, 'Prologue-Form in Ancient Historiography' in *ANRW* I.2 (1972), p. 856.

18. See, e.g., Hugh Montefiore, *The Epistle to the Hebrews* (London: A. & C. Black, 1964), p. 33; F. F. Bruce, *The Epistle to the Hebrews*, NICNT Series (Grand Rapids: Eerdmans, 1964), p. xxiii.

19. For examples of historiographical prefaces, see Thucydides, *History of the Peloponnesian War,* I.1-23, esp. 21-22, or Livy's *Praefatio* to *Ab urbe condita;* see Earl's discussion 'Prologue-Form in Ancient Historiography', *ANRW* I.2, pp. 842-56, and Fowler, *Kinds of Literature,* pp. 98-105, for further discussion.

appropriate. Thus Aristophanes, in his comic literary contest between the two great Athenian tragedians, makes Aeschylus criticize Euripides for bringing onto the stage people and subjects quite inappropriate for tragedy, so lowering the tone.[20] Similarly, we expect epic to have great heroic figures, philosophical dialogues to be full of questions about truth, justice and beauty, and love elegy to have graphic descriptions of the poet's emotional state. There is, however, the problem of how the subject is to be defined. The following tools may assist us.

1. Analysis of the Verbs' Subjects

A first step in simple linguistic analysis of a sentence or clause is to consider the function and structure of the various parts of speech, to see what is the subject or object, how the verb is being used and so on. Louw argues that semantics is about more than the meaning of individual words or phrases, but includes the meaning of the sentence, paragraph, or even the whole work itself.[21] Since the subject of the verb dominates a sentence's surface structure, it ought to be possible to analyse all the verbs to ascertain the overall subject of the work. From the allocation of verbal subjects, it may be argued that if someone or something dominates the results, then the subject of the whole is clear. If, however, two or more subjects share the distribution, then we may talk of multiple subjects.

Since the subject dominates the surface structure of the sentence, some linguists prefer 'agent': thus Rudanko uses the terms 'Agent', 'Experiencer', 'Benefactive' and 'Object' in his analysis of case grammar.[22] The advantage of 'Agent' is clear in active/passive transformations, e.g. 'I hit the dog' and 'the dog is hit by me'; in both, 'I' am the agent, the subject of the deep structure, even though the grammatical subject of the surface structure changes between active and passive. However, there are problems with this nomenclature: Rudanko's study and terms relate to 'present-day English', a non-inflected language, and he admits to less uniformity of terminological practice among case grammarians.[23] Since we are concerned with the inflected

---

20. Aristophanes, *Frogs* 1010-98 — see Stanford's commentary (London: Macmillan, 1971) *ad loc.*, pp. 161-7.

21. J. P. Louw, *Semantics of New Testament Greek* (Philadelphia: Fortress/SBL, 1982).

22. Juhani Rudanko, *Complementation and Case Grammar: A Syntactic and Semantic Study of Selected Patterns of Complementation in Present-Day English* (Albany: State University of New York Press, 1989), pp. 51-5.

23. Rudanko, *Complementation and Case Grammar*, p. 54.

ancient languages of Latin and Greek, where cases are clearly marked by case endings and where terminology and usage are agreed by grammarians, we will remain with the traditional analysis by verbs and subjects, and the case endings of Nominatives, Accusatives, etc. Furthermore, the active/passive transformation does affect our concern for the overall subject of the work. As Louw says, 'the only thing changed is the focus. In the active construction the focus is on the agent, while in the passive construction it is on the experiencer.'[24] There may be no difference between the deep structure of the sentences 'The Pharisees approached Jesus' and 'Jesus was approached by the Pharisees', but the change of subject in the surface structure is significant both for the focus of the sentence and ultimately for the overall subject of the still deeper structure of the work's total meaning and concern.

We intend, therefore, to analyse the verbal subjects in various works to see whether there is any similarity between the results obtained from Graeco-Roman βίοι and from the gospels themselves. This can be done in one of two ways. By far the more accurate is to undertake an individual analysis by hand of all the verbs and work out their subjects. This manual analysis has been done for the gospels and some of our important βίοι. However, since it is very time-consuming, it is not suitable for larger texts, such as Homer. The second method takes advantage of the inflected nature of Latin and Greek. Computer word searches can be undertaken on the frequency of various proper names in different case endings; in particular, the frequency of the name's occurrence in the *nominative case* indicates that the named person is the subject of a verb, clause or sentence. Clearly, this is a very blunt instrument which can pick up only a certain proportion of the verbal subjects — those expressed by a noun in the nominative. The computer will miss verbs where the subject is contained within the verb, or is understood from the previous verb or sentence. Nonetheless, after due allowances are made for these shortcomings, it is hoped that the computer method as well as the manual method may demonstrate its usefulness in our analysis in the following chapters.

At this point, a brief look at the results obtained in other narrative genres will provide some 'control' with which to compare our results. In such works, two or three subjects, at least, tend to share the limelight. In Homer's *Iliad,* for instance, Achilles and Hector, as the main characters, share the honours, but with very small percentages: the name 'Achilles' features in 4.3% of the sentences or major clauses of the whole *Iliad* and occurs in the nominative in 2.0%, whereas his foe scores 5.4% and 2.4%, with the other heroes and gods close behind (see Figure 2, Appendix I, p. 308). The *Odyssey,* however,

---

24. Louw, *Semantics of New Testament Greek*, p. 67.

shows the effect of a pseudo-biographical concentration on one figure, as Odysseus has almost twice the score of anyone else (8.8% and 4.8%) (see Figure 3, Appendix I, p. 309). This same technique may help us to distinguish between a work of historiography (a book of Thucydides for example, or a monograph) and a βίος of a general or statesman. Thus, in two books of Herodotus' *Histories* dealing with Darius' subjugation of Ionia and Xerxes' invasion of Greece down to his victory at Thermopylae (Books VI and VII), the Persian kings can manage to be in only a few of the sentences, 3.5% and 6.6% respectively, with 0.9% and 3.7% in the nominative, while all the other individual subjects are spread out behind. Even if one attempts to analyse 'corporate' subjects, such as a town or race and all its members, none of them score highly: a computer search for all words beginning with 'Athen-' reveals that all the mentions of Athens and Athenians occur in only 8.4% of the sentences, with Persia and the Persians in 7.6%; the other collective subjects feature even less significantly (see Figure 4, Appendix I, p. 310). On a slightly larger scale, analysis of the whole of Xerxes' campaign (Books VI-IX) shows Xerxes to be in 6% of the sentences, with 2.9% in the nominative; these figures are similar to those for Xerxes in Books VI and VII alone. Over all nine books of the *Histories,* Xerxes occurs in 2.4% and Darius in 2.9%; both of them are the subject of just 1% of the sentences, revealing little overall control of the entire work.

It is against such figures that the results for Graeco-Roman βίοι and the gospels will be compared. All the computer analysis figures are derived from computer searches of texts from the *Thesaurus Linguae Graecae,* originally undertaken at the Oxford University Computing Service and repeated on an IBYCUS computer for a check.[25] The results are fully displayed in Appendix I.

2. Allocation of Space

If analysis of verb subjects can tell us about the overall subject of the work, analysis of the allocation of space will make it clear how this subject is being

25. This area has changed enormously over the last two decades. The original research in the mid 1980s was the first attempt at Oxford to use computer search methods on humanities texts, and involved flying computer tape in from California and setting up large mainframe computers with no Greek fonts or accents! The same experiments were then redone in 1990 on an IBYCUS desktop and confirmed similar results. Today, it is easy to undertake this kind of analysis across the whole of Greek literature. Results may differ slightly from the original experiments because of different texts and improved computer methods, but not significantly. Therefore, for continuity with the first edition of the book, we have retained the original results here and in the Appendix.

treated. All aspects of the subject may be given similar amounts of attention, or one particular element may occupy the greater part of the text. In this case, we have more evidence for deciding what the real subject of the work actually is.

C. External Features

By now, a reasonably clear initial picture of a work's genre should have emerged, to be confirmed or corrected by other features.

1. Mode of Representation

The work can be mediated to us in various ways, each of which leads on to other alternatives. Thus we need to ask whether the work was designed for oral presentation, such as a speech, or as a written text, even allowing for the fact that written texts were often received by being read aloud in the ancient world. Next, we notice whether it is in prose or verse and how it is constructed — through dialogue, drama, disconnected units, or continuous narrative. Finally, the speaker must be considered: whether the work is all in one voice, in the first or third person, or through several voices or participants, as in drama.

2. Metre

For the wide range of ancient genres in verse, the type of metre chosen is also an important generic feature. The ancient theorists and critics were clear that certain metres were fitting for certain genres. Even if it is the case that such theories were not always observed in practice, nonetheless, metre did play a role in indicating genre: thus Aristophanes will often make comic capital out of using high-flown tragic metre and rhythms in his plays, only to undercut them with a joke, indicated by suddenly changing the metre, or using a variation of metre allowed only in comedy.[26]

26. See A. M. Dale, 'Old Comedy: The "Acharnians" of Aristophanes' in *Collected Papers* (CUP, 1969), p. 284; see also Horace on proper metres for genres in *Ars Poetica*, lines 73-92, p. 27 above.

3. Size and Length

Aristotle refers to size as a generic feature for tragedy, with each subject ἐχούσης τι μέγεθος.[27] Often this feature has been ignored by scholars, with the consequence that works of quite differing sizes, and therefore possibly different genres, are grouped together with the gospels. Fowler, however, is quite unequivocal about the importance of this feature: 'A genre not characterized by any definite size is not a kind.'[28] We can distinguish size by the very approximate groupings of long, medium-length and short, defined by scrolls and 'sittings'. Much classical literature was read aloud at a social gathering, perhaps after dinner. Longer genres tend to be in several books, requiring several scrolls, and not intended to be read at one sitting. Shorter genres, on the other hand, fit several complete works to a scroll, and several could be read at one time. Medium-length genres are those in between, i.e. works to be read at one sitting and usually one to a scroll, or with one or at the most two partners.[29] The average length of a scroll may be gauged by the divisions of the major works into 'Books': thus the average length of a book of Herodotus is 21,000 words, and of Thucydides, 19,150. After the Alexandrian Library reforms, an average scroll's contents would be about 10,000-25,000 words, allowing for different sizes of handwriting.[30] Thus we might define shorter genres as those below 10,000 words, medium-length as those between 10,000 and 25,000, and longer ones as above 25,000; obviously there is overlap at the boundaries, such as an unusually long example of a short genre, or a shorter version of a long genre, both appearing, therefore, in the medium category.

There are three main types of longer genres: historiography ranges from the enormous length of Herodotus (189,489 words), Thucydides (153,260), and Pausanias (224,602) to the relatively smaller *Anabasis* of Xenophon (58,285). Epic is also large, e.g. Homer's *Iliad* (115,478) and *Odyssey* (87,824). Thirdly, we have Plato's major philosophical works (*Republic*, 89,358 and *Laws*, 106,297) and Aristotle (*Physics*, 57,056 and *Nicomachean Ethics*, 58,063). All these large works require several scrolls or books. However, smaller genres will fit several to a scroll: the orations of Demosthenes and Isaeus range from

---

27. Aristotle, *Poetics* VI.1450b.25.

28. Fowler, *Kinds of Literature*, p. 64; see also Geiger, *Cornelius Nepos*, pp. 26-9 for Aristotle's μέγεθος applied to political biography.

29. See Fowler, *Kinds of Literature*, p. 63 on 'sittings', and Oliver, 'The First Medicean MS of Tacitus', *TAPA* (1951), pp. 246-8 on books and scrolls.

30. Scrolls tended to be 8-12 inches high and 30-35 feet long; columns were 2-4 inches wide, with 18-25 letters per line and 25-45 lines per column; see F. G. Kenyon and C. H. Roberts, 'Books, Greek and Latin', in the *Oxford Classical Dictionary*, 2nd edn (OUP, 1970), pp. 172-5.

1,000 to 5,000 words; most ancient hymns and epigrams are below 100; the Idylls of Theocritus average below 1,000. At the longer end, ancient tragedy and comedy usually fit two or three plays of 5,000-10,000 words to one scroll; the latter may also be seen as shorter medium-length.

Works in the medium-range category include historical monographs and romance, e.g. Longus' *Daphnis and Chloe* (20,929) and some longer speeches, e.g. Demosthenes' *De corona* (22,893), *In Aristocratem* (15,704), *In Timocratem* (14,896). Some philosophical treatises may be included, e.g. Aristotle's *De generatione et corruptione* (16,836) or *Athenaion Politeia* (16,830), although most treatises are below 10,000 and thus 'smaller', whereas the major philosophical works are in the longer category. Plato's *Dialogues* tend to be between 5,000 and 25,000 and thus also of medium length; his *Apology for Socrates* is 8,854. Xenophon's *Apology* is smaller (2,027), but he did write medium-length works such as the *Symposium* (9,655) and *Oeconomicus* (18,123). Significantly, the other genre of medium length is βίος, as we will see.

For this generic feature, therefore, we need to measure the length of the gospels. The search for their genre should then be conducted among works of a similar size — and this raises questions about notions such as Kelber's 'extended parable' or Guelich's comparison with a brief sermon in Acts 10.[31]

4. Structure or Sequence

This concerns how the work develops and is organized. For instance, the structure may be a sequence of scenes, interspersed with passages of choral lyric, as in classical drama; it may follow the flow of a conversation or argument, with questions and answers, speeches and replies, as in philosophical dialogue. Various rhetorical genres, speeches and letters follow a conventional sequence of elements. The material may be organized chronologically, topically, geographically, etc., and the text in a continuously unfolding sequence, or a series of disparate, unconnected elements. If it is narrative, this may be continuous or disjointed, following the passage of time, or a certain person, event or place. From this variety, it is clear that some structures indicate specific genres, such as the conventional structure of Greek Tragedy. Other structures may be common to various genres, e.g. continuous chronological narrative features in epic, historiography and story. Thus structure does not determine genre, but works of the same genre will exhibit similar structures.

---

31. See above, p. 13 (Kelber) and pp. 87-8 (Guelich), and p. 194 below for a discussion of these related to the size of the gospels.

5. Scale

Scale is the feature which assesses how broad a canvas the author feels free to paint on. The scale may be wide, as in some historiography, particularly Annals, when all the various events of a year are recorded. Alternatively, it may be narrow, with a particular focus on one individual subject, place or event. Thus we need to consider that which is *omitted* as well as that which is included, and whether the reason for the omission was merely for economy of size, or rather because of limitations of scale and focus.

6. Literary Units

A text is made up from various literary units, including prologue, preface, speeches, dialogue, anecdotes, maxims, discourses, catalogues, stories, songs, choral interludes, physical or geographical descriptions and the like. These units may be carefully linked together and interwoven so much that it is difficult to distinguish them; other works may be little more than a stringing together of unconnected units. Obviously, the same units will appear in various different genres and cannot be determinative; nonetheless, we may expect to find similar selections and patterns of units in works of similar genres.

7. Use of Sources

Many possible sources were used by ancient writers in composing their works, as we know from their own descriptions of their work, as well as from direct source analysis and criticism. Written sources include historical documents, archives, letters, treatises, histories, biographies, inscriptions, collections of sayings or anecdotes, philosophical writings, dialogues, discourses, speeches, memoirs and so on. Oral traditions were highly respected within a less literate society and could include family memories and precedents, stories, eyewitness accounts, personal memories, the tradition of a school or group, anecdotes and so on. Sources cannot be determinative for genre, for the same source may be used by different writers (or even the same writer) to write totally different genres. However, within a genre we may expect to find similar sorts of sources being used in a similar sort of way; thus the bard's use of oral formulae and units previously composed is a typical feature of Homeric epic and quite different from the balance of sources found in some forms of historiography.

8. *Methods of Characterization*

Characterization is an important feature for our study, if only because the absence of character analysis was one reason why form critics denied the link of the gospels with biography.[32] Here we are concerned with the external feature of the formal techniques whereby the author builds up his picture of the characters in his work, rather than the quality of that picture, which is an internal feature relating to content. The methods of ancient characterization were much more indirect than their modern counterparts. Detailed character analysis and psychological assessment are lacking, not just in the gospels, but in the bulk of ancient literature. Instead, character is revealed by the person's words and deeds, especially the latter: as Aristotle put it, 'actions are signs of character' (*Rhetoric* I.ix.33, 1367b). So we find anecdotes revealing how the person behaved in a difficult situation, facing a certain decision or responding to a crisis. Sometimes direct analysis is given after or alongside the story, to make the point clear in case anyone missed it. These techniques of characterization are not confined to any one genre, but the methods selected and used within any one genre should be similar.

9. *Summary*

Through the analysis of all these external features, a clear pattern will emerge. Some features may be required by convention, such as mode of representation, metre and size. Other features may be common to a number of genres, but help to put together a family resemblance between works of the same genre, confirming the initial generic indication gained from the opening features. Similar works of the same genre exhibit a certain structure, on a broad or narrow scale, using certain sorts of literary units and sources, and displaying character by certain methods.

D. Internal Features

1. *Setting*

Setting can be a clear mediator of genre; for example, if at the start we find ourselves under a shady tree, with a hot sun, a gently lapping brook and some

---

32. Bultmann, *History,* p. 372; see pp. 9-10 above.

flocks for company, as with many of Theocritus' *Idylls* or Vergil's *Eclogues*, this indicates the pastoral genre, leading us to expect a bucolic singing contest to follow. However, if the backdrop is a burning city, with armed men on the rampage, we are probably in epic or perhaps tragedy, e.g. Euripides' *Trojan Women*. Other genres do not have such clear geographical settings; historiography tends to range widely, for instance. Questions about the dramatic setting, such as how the scenes are structured, who is centre stage or in the spotlight, what kind of action takes place, all apply more widely than drama itself and can be asked about any narrative sequence.

2. *Topics/τόποι/Motifs*

Certain *topoi* or motifs occur in, and indicate, specific genres. For instance, the motif of the child, usually from a rich family, abandoned at birth but preserved by a kindly yokel along with various tokens which later help him or her to discover their true identity in the nick of time and marry their noble lover, or enter into their inheritance, is fairly standard in much New Comedy, such as Menander, e.g. *Epitrepontes,* or even the later Euripides, e.g. *Ion.* Within various poetic genres, several set *topoi* feature: the excluded lover late at night at the beloved's door in the *paraclausithyron* (or *komos*), or the farewell speech to someone departing for foreign parts in the *propemptikon.* Cairns argues that the use of a standard *topos* at the start is intended as 'a clear generic announcement'. However, he warns about making *topoi* determinative of genre, because 'the ability of many topoi to move from one genre to another is central to generic originality'; they are secondary elements and 'no quantity of secondary elements makes an example of a genre, although their presence is a welcome confirmation of an assignment based on primary elements.'[33] This is a warning to those like Shuler and Downing[34] not to overemphasize *topoi*, especially in isolation. However, within our approach using a wide range of generic features, *topoi* can be very helpful in confirming a generic link between works, if they all make use of similar examples.

33. Cairns, *Generic Composition,* pp. 6, 25, 99-100; see pp. 57-9 above.
34. Shuler, *A Genre for the Gospels,* pp. 52-7, see pp. 83-6 above; Downing, 'Contemporary Analogies', see pp. 90-1 above.

3. Style

Style often appears to be subjective, but may be divided into three rough categories, high, middle and low, or by using terms like high-brow, moderately educated and popular.[35] The level of style may be shown by vocabulary: compare Aeschylus' haughty language with Aristophanes' use of slang, and notice all the comic possibilities caused by mixing the two. Alternatively, characters can be indicators of differing levels, such as the tragic hero and the comic buffoon. This feature may vary within genres: much of the debate in the literary contest of the *Frogs* between Aeschylus and Euripides turns on the question of what is or is not the appropriate level, style, vocabulary, language, heroes, and subjects for tragedy.[36] Thus style, taken with other features, does have a part to play in determining genre.

4. Tone/Mood/Attitude/Values

These four features taken together combine to give a distinctive atmosphere to a work. Although appreciation and analysis of these features can be subjective, the overall impression of the atmosphere of satire, history and encomium, mediated through them, will be quite different. Tone refers to the impression or importance suggested; for instance, the tone may be serious or light-hearted, sarcastic or marvelling. The mood may vary according to the action, joyful or sorrowful, triumphant or depressive; often it will be connected with the subject and reflect his or her mood, or perhaps the mood of the author. The attitude to the subject may be reverential, mocking, (dis)approving or despairing, while the attitude towards the reader or audience is hectoring, pleading, disdaining, informing or just plain neutral. Values are connected with the world-view being described or mediated; this may be one shared by the author and which he wishes to impart to the reader or audience, or it may be one internal to the work, which is merely being described. As a generic feature, however, it can be useful: compare the moral world of the heroes of Homeric epic with Tacitus' view of Nero's court, or the values of pastoral.[37] Works of the same genre will often breathe a similar atmosphere.

35. See Fowler, *Kinds of Literature*, pp. 70-2.
36. Aristophanes, *Frogs* ll. 905-1481.
37. See Thomas G. Rosenmeyer, *The Green Cabinet: Theocritus and the European Pastoral Lyric* (University of California Press, 1969), for the values and qualities of the pastoral genre.

5. *Quality of Characterization*

If the method of characterization is an external feature, its quality is clearly internal, including the sort of picture which emerges of the characters, the types chosen and how well or thinly drawn they are. Modern scholars, especially non-specialists in classical literature, must avoid confusing modern notions of character and development with ancient concepts of ἦθος. Within modern literature, especially biography, there is great interest in the psychological development of character and personality. Such ideas cannot be transferred wholesale into ancient literature.[38] It used to be argued that the ancients viewed character as fixed from birth and immutable, with no notion of development.[39] If there seems to be a character change, as with Tiberius in his later years for instance, this is explained as the revelation of his true nature concealed by his hypocrisy in earlier years; see Tacitus' *Annals*, 1.4.3 or 6.51.3. Recently, classical scholars have been reassessing the whole question of character in ancient literature.[40] Thucydides asserts that his history has lasting value, κτῆμά ἐς αἰεὶ, because the same sorts of characters will recur and do the same sorts of actions, and therefore future generations should be able to learn something from the cataclysms of the past.[41] Equally, the great emphasis on the exemplary and moral purpose of much ancient historiography and biography does not fit in with the supposed lack of interest in the development of character. Gill makes use of a distinction between 'character' and 'personality'. Interest in personality is an attempt to understand or explain a person psychologically, and this is the predominantly modern concept, brought in with Lytton Strachey and Erikson. On the other hand, the ancients were often concerned about a person's character from the moral point of view, for praise or blame.[42] There is some evidence of an interest in personality in ancient biography; however, as Pelling argues, often any development which appears is actually for literary purposes, rather than true psychological development. Furthermore, characterization is

38. Momigliano, *Development*, p. 17.

39. Dihle, *Studien*, pp. 76ff.

40. See *Characterization and Individuality in Greek Literature*, ed. C. B. R. Pelling (OUP, 1990), for discussion across many Greek genres.

41. *History of the Peloponnesian War*, I.22.4; see the way Gomme writing in 1945 relates this to the recent experience of world war in his commentary, *ad. loc.* (OUP, 1945).

42. Christopher Gill, 'The Character-Personality Distinction', in *Characterization and Individuality*, pp. 1-31; also 'The Question of Character-Development: Plutarch and Tacitus', *CQ* 33 (1983), pp. 469-87.

genre-related in that different genres have slightly different expectations about characterization.[43]

Thus, the generic feature of characterization and, in particular, the types and quality of characterization in ancient literature are quite complex. Rather than dismissing the gospels' characterization because of modern expectations, we must compare them with ancient βίοι to ascertain whether they exhibit similar approaches and attitudes to characterization.

6. Social Setting and Occasion

This feature concerns what the text may reveal about its function and production. Thus classical drama shows that the plays took place at Athenian religious festivals, and much Latin poetry appears suitable for readings after dinner at parties. Other genres were produced for a specific occasion, such as a funeral laudation or a panegyric on a new emperor. Therefore, the text must be examined for internal clues to its social setting, the kinds of social grouping presumed for the audience, and the situation or occasion within which it was read. Similar hints about setting and occasion may be found within works of one genre.

7. Authorial Intention and Purpose

Although we must be cautious in the reconstruction of an author's intention(s) and not make this as determinative for genre as Shuler and Dihle did, nonetheless, the purpose of the author is essential to any concept of genre as a set of expectations or contract between the author and the reader or audience. The author may choose his genre specifically to suit his purpose; some genres have a single purpose, such as the intent to praise in encomium. The purpose may be expressed explicitly in a preface or prologue; however, textual analysis is still necessary, since the author's expressed desires and purposes are not always a reliable guide to his actual practice. In other genres, however, it may be the case that there is no one purpose which is essential to the nature of the genre and its examples. Often, the author may have a number of different purposes, some applying to various members of his envisaged audience, while others reflect his purely literary concerns. However, we

---

43. Pelling, *Characterization and Individuality,* pp. vi-vii, 226-36 and 261-2; see also his 'Aspects of Plutarch's Characterisation', *Illinois Classical Studies* 13.2 (1988), pp. 257-74.

may expect that there will be a similarity of purposes between similar works of the same genre.

8. Summary

Few of these internal features determine the genre of a work. Many occur in a similar fashion in a number of differing genres, and so caution must be exercised in deducing generic relationships between works on the grounds of such shared features. However, in our wide-ranging approach, these features can play a part in helping identify genre if considered all together. Thus, no one or two features establish the genre, but the content of the work and its internal features play their part in building up and confirming the genre indicated by all the other features.

Conclusion

We have now set out a clear methodology of genre analysis to study Graeco-Roman βίοι and the gospels. Genre is identified through a wide-ranging variety of different internal and external features, including both content and structure. The first suggestion of genre will be recognized through the opening features of a text and its title. The subject will be identified by analysis of verb subjects, as well as through the allocation of space. An initial expectation of genre will then begin to emerge, which is confirmed or corrected by further analysis, first of the external features of representation, size, structure and so forth, and finally by the internal features of further aspects of content.

This is a formidable list and contrasts with the limited range of generic features used in previous attempts to discover the genre of the gospels. However, the list must not be used mechanically, as Fowler says: 'Recognition of genre depends on associating a complex of elements, which need not all appear in one work. . . . Usually, there are so many indicators, organized into so familiar a unity, that we recognize the generic complex instantly.'[44] Thus we do not expect total congruity for works to belong together, but rather an overall pattern which emerges when a text is analysed by these features. There are bound to be differences and divergences arising from the flexible nature of genres. To ascertain whether the gospels belong to a certain genre, we need to analyse a number of works belonging to that genre in order to build up this

44. Fowler, 'Life and Death', pp. 80-1; see also Todorov, p. 42 above.

common pattern and to ascertain how far texts may diverge from it, yet still remain within the genre. Then, and only then, can we analyse the gospels against the same list of features; if they display a similar pattern and diverge from it no more than any other examples, then we are justified in claiming that they belong to the same genre. If, on the other hand, they diverge significantly from the established pattern, then they may not be considered members of the genre. We turn now therefore to our analysis of Graeco-Roman βίοι and the gospels.

CHAPTER 6

The Generic Features of Early Graeco-Roman βίοι

The ancient biographers can always claim the credit for having established biography as a major form of literature.[1]

The discovery of Satyrus' life of Euripides . . . indicated that Hellenistic literary biography was far more elegant and sophisticated.[2]

In the next two chapters the model we have outlined for generic analysis will be used on ten examples of Graeco-Roman biography, of which five predate the gospels and five are later. They are a diverse group, reflecting the overall character and development of this genre. We start with the origins of βίος in Greek rhetorical encomia by Isocrates and Xenophon in the fourth century BC. Next, we enter the Hellenistic and Alexandrian phases with Satyrus' *Euripides*, the first extant work clearly identified as a βίος and 'our only first-hand survival of a Peripatetic biography'.[3] Finally, we come to two βίοι influenced by other cultures: the Roman strand with Nepos' *Atticus* and a βίος emerging from the Jewish world, Philo's *Moses*. If these diverse works show a similar pattern when analysed by our sequence of opening features, subject, external and internal features, then βίος is indeed a diverse and flexible genre.

1. From Dorey's introduction to *Latin Biography*, p. xi.
2. Arnaldo Momigliano, *Second Thoughts on Greek Biography*, p. 11.
3. D. R. Stuart, *Epochs of Greek and Roman Biography*, p. 179.

A. Introducing the Examples

1. *Isocrates'* Evagoras[4]

Isocrates (436-338 BC) lived during the Peloponnesian War and the turbulent years when fourth-century Athens was challenged by Philip of Macedon. Influenced by both Gorgias and Socrates, he was a speech-writer and teacher of rhetoric, interested in philosophy. One of his pupils may have been Nicocles, king of Cyprus from 374, for Isocrates wrote three orations in the period 374-365 BC: *To Nicocles*, an exhortation to the new king, *The Cyprians*, on the duties of his subjects, and the *Evagoras*, about Nicocles' murdered father, born *c.* 435 and ruler of Cyprus *c.* 411-374 BC. Isocrates claims to be the first to write prose encomium (ἀνδρὸς ἀρετὴν διὰ λόγων ἐγκωμιάζειν), which no one has attempted previously (*Evag.* 8). Stuart is not convinced and argues that this is a mere literary rhetorical boast; praise of a contemporary individual can be seen in Plato's *Symposium*.[5] As regards genre, *Evagoras* may be seen as crossing over from rhetoric to βίος: it takes the form of a funeral eulogy praising the king, rather than a full biography. The embarrassing fact that Evagoras has just been murdered is not described at all; instead, we have praise of him as the ideal king, enumerating his virtues.

2. *Xenophon's* Agesilaus[6]

Xenophon (428/7–*c.* 354 BC) probably followed *Evagoras* as a model for his *Agesilaus*, composed *c.* 360 BC. Agesilaus was born in 444 BC and became king of Sparta in 398; a great soldier, he led a major expedition in Asia Minor against Persia in 396-394, and many other campaigns both in Greece and abroad before dying in 360, still on active service. Xenophon served under him in Asia and included discussion of Agesilaus in his history, the *Hellenica*.

---

4. See Momigliano, *Development*, pp. 46-9; Stuart, *Epochs*, pp. 77-118; *Isokrates*, ed. Friedrich Seck (Darmstadt: Wissenschaftliche Buchgesellschaft, 1976), esp. pp. 74-121; Christoph Eucken, *Isokrates* (Berlin: Walter de Gruyter, 1983), esp. pp. 264-9; Paul Cloché, *Isocrate et son Temps* (Paris: Les Belles Lettres, 1963); *Isocrates: Cyprian Orations*, ed. E. S. Forster (OUP, 1912); Stephen Halliwell, 'Traditional Greek Conceptions of Character', in *Characterization and Individuality* (OUP, 1990), pp. 32-59.

5. Stuart, *Epochs*, chapter 4: 'A Question of Priority: The Pretensions of Isocrates', pp. 91-118.

6. See Momigliano, *Development*, pp. 49-57; Stuart, *Epochs*, pp. 69-90; J. K. Anderson, *Xenophon* (London: Duckworth, 1974), chapters 12 and 13.

This material also occurs in the *Agesilaus* itself, but here we have encomium; nonetheless, it contains more historical material than *Evagoras*. It is constructed in two parts, the first being a factual account of Agesilaus' life and the second a systematic review of his virtues.

3. *Satyrus'* Euripides

Satyrus the Peripatetic was known during the nineteenth century as an important author of βίοι,[7] but his work was preserved only in very fragmentary form in quotations from Athenaeus. However, the discovery and publication of *Papyrus Oxyrhynchus* 1176 early in the twentieth century allowed the first study of some actual text.[8] The fragments, dating from the second century AD, come from the end of the scroll, concluding with the title of the sixth book of Satyrus' βίων ἀναγραφή. This contained the Lives of the Tragedians, Aeschylus, Sophocles and Euripides, and it is from the βίος of the last that the fragments come. Fragments 37-39 are closely associated and contain the upper parts of some thirty columns. Fragments 40-57 are small scraps found with the larger items, whereas 1-36 are miscellaneous fragments found previously. Although such partial preservation makes a definitive study of the work impossible, sufficient remains to reveal a number of generic features.

The author came from Callatis Pontica (on the Black Sea)[9] and wrote various βίοι; the Περὶ χαρακτήρων is also widely attributed to him. He certainly lived earlier than the reign of Ptolemy VI Philometer (181-146 BC), when the βίοι were epitomized by Heraclides Lembus.[10] Some scholars place him in Alexandria in the third century BC;[11] others prefer to take Athenaeus' description of Satyrus as ὁ Περιπατητικός (vi.248d; xii.541c; xiii.556a) at its face value, i.e. that he was connected with the Peripatos and perhaps even a contemporary of Aristotle.[12] For our purposes, it is sufficient that Satyrus

7. See U. von Wilamowitz-Möllendorff, 'Lesefrüchte, § LI', *Hermes* 34 (1899), pp. 633-6; Leo, *Die griechisch-römische Biographie,* pp. 118ff.

8. *Oxyrhynchus Papyri* IX, ed. A. S. Hunt (London: Egypt Exploration Fund, 1912), pp. 124-82.

9. This is known from *P.Herc.* 558; see Stephanie West, 'Satyrus: Peripatetic or Alexandrian?', *GRBS* 15 (1974), p. 285, n. 19.

10. *FGrHist* iii. p. 169; see Hunt, *Oxy. Pap.,* IX, p. 125, and West, 'Satyrus', *GRBS* 1974, p. 284.

11. Wilamowitz, 'Lesefrüchte', *Hermes,* 1899, p. 635; Leo, *Die griechisch-römische Biographie,* p. 118; Dihle, *Studien,* p. 104; Momigliano, *Development,* p. 80, but see also *Second Thoughts,* pp. 4 and 7.

12. West, 'Satyrus', *GRBS* (1974), pp. 279-87; Adrian Tronson, 'Satyrus the Peripatetic and the Marriages of Philip II', *JHS* 104 (1984), pp. 116-26.

was an influential early writer of βίοι in the Peripatetic tradition, popular enough to be epitomized two centuries before, and still being copied and circulated a century after, the gospels.

The fragments come from the *βίων ἀναγραφή*, Satyrus' best-known work, frequently cited by Athenaeus and Diogenes Laertius. The βίοι are wide-ranging: philosophers (the Seven Sages, Pythagoras, Empedocles, Zeno of Elea, Anaxagoras, Socrates, Diogenes, Anaxarchus, Stilpo), poets (the tragedians), statesmen and generals (Alcibiades), monarchs (Dionysius the Younger, Philip) and orators (Demosthenes).[13] The *Life of Euripides* was an important source for other accounts, such as the *Γένος Εὐριπίδου*, the Life often attached to ancient manuscripts of Euripides' plays.[14] In addition to confirming Satyrus as the source of stories already known, the fragments provide some new information about Euripides, about his prosecution by Cleon for impiety (Frag. 39.x.15-20), the reasons for his retirement from Athens (39.xv.26ff.) and his involvement in Timotheos' *Persae* (39.xxii.27-30).

4. Nepos' Atticus[15]

Cornelius Nepos, born *c.* 99 BC in Cisalpine Gaul around Milan and the Po valley, moved to Rome *c.* 65 BC and spent his life writing; he died in 24 BC. His patron was Titus Pomponius Atticus (109-32 BC), a Roman knight not involved in political life, despite his very close acquaintance with Cicero. Although he too knew many key figures of the disturbed end of the Republic, such as Cicero, Nepos similarly avoided participation in politics. Instead, he concentrated on his literary production, which included history, geography, moral *exempla,* love poetry and biography. He wrote separate βίοι, such as the Lives of Cicero and Cato (now lost), and the *De viris illustribus* in at least six-

13. The fragments are collected and annotated in *De Satyro Peripatetico,* ed. C. F. Kumaniecki, Polska Akademja Umiejętności Archiwum Filologiczne Nr. 8 (Cracow: Gebethner et Wolff, 1929).

14. Full text in Graziano Arrighetti (ed.), *Satiro, Vita di Euripide,* Studi Classici e Orientali, vol. 13 (Pisa: Libreria Goliardica Editrice, 1964), Appendice, pp. 93-5; an English version is in Mary R. Lefkowitz, *The Lives of the Greek Poets* (London: Duckworth, 1981), Appendix 5, pp. 163-9; see her discussion on p. 99.

15. See Edna Jenkinson, 'Nepos — An Introduction to Latin Biography', in Dorey, *Latin Biography,* pp. 1-15, and 'Genus scripturae leve: Cornelius Nepos and the Early History of Biography at Rome', *ANRW* I.3 (1973), pp. 703-19; Geiger, *Cornelius Nepos and Ancient Political Biography,* and 'Cornelius Nepos, *De Regibus Exterarum Gentium', Latomus* 38 (1979), pp. 662-9; Nicholas Horsfall, *Cornelius Nepos: A Selection, including the Lives of Cato and Atticus* (OUP, 1989).

teen books, of which *Foreign Generals, Cato* and *Atticus* survive. It was first published *c.* 34 BC, with a second edition after Atticus' death in 32, probably by 27 BC (*Att.* 19). Nepos is often derided for his plain, simple style. He is important for our study, since his work is the first surviving example of Roman biography. He had clearly read the *Evagoras* and *Agesilaus,* and wrote a Life of the latter in *De viris illustribus* XVII. However, the influence of Roman funeral laudations and the *exempla* and *imagines* of the ancestors is also apparent. Geiger argues that Nepos is the real originator of ancient political biography with his combination of βίος and Roman political concern.[16] If not himself a great literary artist, Nepos inspired and influenced his successors, Plutarch, Tacitus and Suetonius.

5. Philo's Moses[17]

Like Nepos, Philo shows the development of βίος in another culture, Alexandrian Judaism. His dates are unclear, but he probably lived *c.* 30/25 BC to AD 45; a leading member of the Jewish community in Alexandria, he was part in the delegation to Gaius Caligula in AD 39/40. He has a clear intention in most of his work: to (re-)interpret Jewish beliefs via Greek, especially Platonic, philosophy, often using allegorical methods. He manages this so successfully that many commentators see him as more Greek than Jewish.[18] The *Life of Moses* is a little different, with less allegory, as he seeks to make Moses known to a wider Gentile audience. The influence of Greek models may be seen in the systematic treatment of Moses as king, lawgiver, priest and prophet; such a topical analysis is not unlike that of Isocrates and Xenophon. With this mixture of Greek βίος and a Jewish background, the *Moses* makes an interesting comparison with the gospels.

---

16. See especially Geiger, *Cornelius Nepos,* pp. 66-116.

17. See E. R. Goodenough, *An Introduction to Philo Judaeus* (Oxford: Basil Blackwell, 1962); and *ANRW,* vol. II.21.1 (1984), esp. S. Sandmel, 'Philo Judaeus: An Introduction to the Man, His Writings, and His Significance', pp. 3-46, and P. Borgen, 'Philo of Alexandria. A Critical and Synthetical Survey of Research since World War II', pp. 98-154; for a full bibliography, see E. Hilgert, 'Bibliographia Philoniana 1935-1981', pp. 47-97.

18. See Goodenough, *An Introduction to Philo Judaeus,* pp. 75-90, and Sandmel, 'Philo Judaeus', *ANRW* II.21.1, pp. 31-6.

B. Opening Features

1. *Titles*

The titles of these works are essentially just the subject's name, although in some the genre is stressed by terms like βίος. The first two examples are known solely by name: the *Evagoras* and the *Agesilaus*. Fortunately, the Satyrus fragments contain the end of the scroll (Frag. 39, column xxiii) with the title as follows:[19]

Σατύρου
Βίων Ἀναγ[ρ]αφῆς
ς·
Αἰσχύλου,
Σοφοκλέους,
Εὐριπίδου.

Thus the full title of the work, *βίων ἀναγραφή*, is a clear generic indicator: Satyrus' *Euripides* is called a βίος, even though it has some odd characteristics. Further, after the title of the whole work, scroll/volume number and the colon, the name of the subjects come in the genitive case, dependent on the understood βίοι, denoting the specific Lives in this scroll. Even if this title is not original to Satyrus himself, it shows that the work was interpreted by ancient literary scholiasts or librarians as βίος. The *Atticus* is also known by the subject's name, although it too is part of a larger work entitled *De viris illustribus*, another clear indicator of βίος. Both the word 'Life' and the name in the genitive case are in *περὶ τοῦ βίου Μωυσέως*, but in addition, Philo uses a formula often found in the titles of philosophical and other treatises, namely *περὶ τοῦ . . .* ; this may suggest that the *Moses* also has elements of the philosophical treatise about it.

2. *Opening Formulae/Prologue/Preface*

Some begin with a formal prologue: as is proper for oratory, Isocrates begins with a prologue, addressed to Evagoras' son, Nicocles, explaining his intention in the innovative, if difficult, task of praising a man's virtue in words

---

19. There is a good photograph of the manuscript of Frag. 39, columns xvii-xxiii including the title, in Hunt, *Oxy. Pap.* IX, Plate V; see also, Oliver, 'The First Medicean MS of Tacitus', *TAPA* (1951), p. 245.

(*Evag.* 1-11). This theme of difficulty in doing the task properly is also found in Xenophon's brief prologue/opening sentence in the *Agesilaus* I.1. Unfortunately the start of Satyrus' *Euripides* is missing, while Nepos launches straight in. Philo, however, follows his Greek models with a preface on his intention to write a Life of Moses (Μωυσέως . . . τὸν βίον ἀναγράψαι διενοήθην, I.1). In addition to the feature of a prologue, we note that often the first word(s) is or includes the subject's name. Isocrates mentions Evagoras' name within his first periodic sentence. Xenophon's fifth word is Ἀγησιλάου. Nepos, with no prologue, begins 'T. Pomponius Atticus . . .'. So too Philo, but in the genitive, Μωυσέως. . . . Thus our works all display the feature of the subject's name right at the start of the work.

C. Subject

1. Analysis of Verb Subjects

We have suggested that in βίος one person will dominate as the focus and subject. Computer analysis of Xenophon's *Agesilaus* reveals that the subject's name occurs in 69 of the 370 sentences or major phrases (18.7%) and is in the nominative in 35 (9.5%). No other individual scores significantly; corporate proper names appear in the sentences — 10% contain Gree-k/ce, ('Ελλ-) and 4% Persia/ns (Περσ-) — but few as subjects in the nominative (see Figure 5, Appendix I, p. 311). The domination by Agesilaus is clear. The larger fragments of Satyrus' *Euripides* were submitted to manual analysis: Frags. 8, 37, 38 and 39 gave a moderately sized sample of 252 verbs in total.[20] The results show a heavy bias: Euripides himself is the subject of sixty-five (25.8%) of the verbs, with a further forty-four (17.5%) occurring within quotations from his plays. There are few other individual subjects: eleven first person singular and plural verbs (4.4%), referring to the main participants in the text, and four occurrences of the comic playwright, Aristophanes, who often mentioned Euripides in his works. Thus despite the limitations of the fragmentary state of the manuscript, verbal analysis shows a very significant dominance by Euripides, both as the subject of a quarter of the verbs and with nearly a further sixth within quotations from his works (see Figure 6, Appendix I, p. 312).

Of course, such a concentration on one person does not automatically

---

20. As compared with 1,113 in Tacitus' *Agricola*, 628 in Lucian's *Demonax* and 2,500-4,300 in the gospels; see analyses below.

make a work a βίος. A similar 'skewing effect' was noted in the *Odyssey* compared with the *Iliad,* but it is still epic because of its other features. Similarly, computer analysis of two other semi-biographical works of Xenophon also show this skewing effect: the *Cyropaedia* and the *Memorabilia.* The *Cyropaedia,* a long legendary account of the childhood of Cyrus in some 80,000 words, is dominated by Cyrus, whose name occurs in 16.3% of the sentences, including 9.5% where he is in the nominative (see Figure 7, Appendix I, p. 313). Since the *Memorabilia* is the sayings of Socrates, it is not surprising that his name occurs in a tenth (9.9%) of the sentences, with just under half (4.8%) having him in the nominative (see Figure 8, Appendix I, p. 314). Despite such pseudo-biographical concentration, other βίος features are missing. So Momigliano describes the *Cyropaedia* as a 'pedagogical novel . . . not, and probably never claimed to be, a true account of the life of a real person' and the *Memorabilia* as a 'biographical form' for 'what amounted to fiction', a collection purporting to be sayings of Socrates.[21]

If we compare these figures with the 'control' results from Homer and Herodotus in the previous chapter, the point is clear. In other forms of literature, the subjects of the verbs are wide and varied. However, a distinguishing feature of βίος is the concentration on one person as subject, reflected even in the verbal syntax.

2. Allocation of Space

It is often claimed that biography, unlike the gospels, covers the whole of the subject's life from birth to death.[22] We need to consider the allocation of space to see if it is even-handed. The *Evagoras* contains eight major sections of roughly equal length. This may reflect its rhetorical nature, rather than βίος: later rhetorical theory and school exercises emphasize covering various topics about the subject in a set order. Here, at the beginning, the overlap with neighbouring genres, such as rhetoric and encomium, is bound to be greater.[23]

---

21. Momigliano, *Development,* pp. 52-7.

22. See above, pp. 60 (Momigliano), 92 (Tolbert) and 98 (Aune).

23. Theon, *Rhet. Gr.,* II.109ff., has no less than thirty-six definite stages for encomium — see H. I. Marrou, *A History of Education in Antiquity* (London: Sheed and Ward, 1956), pp. 197-205; for *Evagoras* and Platonic philosophy, see Eucken, *Isokrates,* pp. 267-9.

I: Content analysis of Isocrates' *Evagoras*

Chapters	Date (BC)	Topic	Percentage of work
1-11		Introduction	14.5
12-20		Background	9.8
21-32	435-411	Early years and rise	13.0
33-39		Formal comparison	8.7
40-50		Deeds and virtues	14.5
51-64	411-374	War deeds	17.5
65-72		Evaluation	11.0
73-81		Conclusion	11.0

In the *Agesilaus,* however, *one* major campaign (396-394 BC) dominates, occupying well over a third, whereas the next thirty-four years and all the other campaigns are squeezed into just an eighth. This may be because Xenophon considers this campaign to show Agesilaus' character best,[24] or because Xenophon served under him in this campaign and thus knew it best. Clearly, even coverage is not a prerequisite for Xenophon; the first forty years of Agesilaus' life, his race and ancestry, and everything before he became king, are all covered in one opening paragraph (1-4). Another third of the work is an analysis of Agesilaus' virtues, tackled in turn: piety, justice, self-control, courage, wisdom, patriotism, graciousness, foresight and simplicity of life all having fairly similar coverage.

II: Content analysis of Xenophon's *Agesilaus*

Chapters	Date (BC)	Topic	Percentage of work
I.1-5	444-397	Introduction and early years	4.0
I.6–II.16	396-394	Persian campaign	37.4
II.17-31	394-360	Other campaigns and deeds	12.7
III–X		Individual virtues	35.2
XI		Summary	10.7

Frags. 1-7, 12-34 and 42-57 of Satyrus are too small for their content to be reconstructed; Frag. 8 appears to be the end of a discussion of Euripides' style, whereas Frags. 37-39 cover his views on philosophy, religion, politics and women, concluding with his withdrawal to Macedonia and eventual death

---

24. See J. K. Anderson, *Xenophon*, pp. 146-71.

there, attacked by King Archelaus' dogs. What percentage of the total these sections are cannot be known.

Nepos has a twofold approach, like Xenophon: while over half is devoted to Atticus' life, much of this is an account of the part Atticus played in the troubled last years of the Republic; then a quarter of the work discusses his character, before finally returning to chronology for the death.

III: Content analysis of Nepos' *Atticus*

Chapters	Date (BC)	Topic	Percentage of work
1–6	99-49	Early years, education, Rome	26
7–12	49-40	Civil War years	32
13–18		Character and anecdotes	25
19–22	39-32	Later years, death, conclusion	17

Philo also has a twofold pattern: Book I describes Moses' life in the manner of a king and Book II considers Moses topically as lawgiver, priest and prophet, before returning to chronology for the death and conclusion. Within the first section, there is fairly even coverage of the main events described in the Pentateuch, although curiously the Sinai theophany and consequent events are merely mentioned (e.g. I.158, II.70) rather than described in full.

IV: Content analysis of Philo's *Moses*

Chapters	Topic	Percentage of work
I.1-4	Preface	0.6
I.5-334	Life, as king	53.4
II.1-8	Preface	2.0
II.8-65	Lawgiver	8.0
II.66-180	Priest	18.8
II.187-287	Prophet	16.3
II.288-292	Death and conclusion	0.6

These analyses show that the author may order and allocate the interior structure of a βίος as he wishes, with material in a chronological sequence, or mixed up with topical analysis. There may be a generally even coverage of the subject's life, as in the *Evagoras,* or the author may choose to emphasize one small period at the expense of others (e.g., *Agesilaus* and *Atticus*).

D. External Features

1. *Mode of Representation*

These works are all in the mode of prose narrative, but with some notable differences. First, whatever its later influence upon written βίος, *Evagoras* is in an essentially oral mode: it is a speech, ostensibly intended for a festival in honour of the deceased subject and addressed to his son. In addition to βίος features, therefore, rhetorical ones may be expected. Xenophon has rhetorical features also, but *Agesilaus* was probably always intended as a written document. Continuous prose narrative is the mode of *Atticus* and *Moses*.

Given that Satyrus' *Euripides* is called a βίος, its mode of representation is rather a shock, as it is written in dialogue, including some verse. There are at least three speakers: the main speaker, unnamed; a man, Diodoros (addressed by name in Frag. 39.iii.19, xv.13) and a woman, Eukleia (said to be 'well-named', Frag. 39.xiv.31). Scholars were surprised: as Hunt says, 'the method is a singular one to apply to biography'.[25] Perhaps other Lives of Satyrus were in dialogue mode also. The various metres are in the passages quoted from the tragedian himself (e.g. iambic in Frag. 38.iii.8ff. and an Anacreontic verse in 38.ii.12-14) and from comic poets (e.g. 39.xii.1-16 which is Aristophanes' *Thesmo.* 374-5, 335-7, and Frag. 39.ix.25-8, in trochaic metre). Since these metres reflect their originals, they indicate nothing about the genre of *Euripides* except to caution us against dogmatic assertions about exactly *how* βίοι must be written. The fact that an indubitably identified βίος is in such an unusual mode of representation shows that the genre is very flexible and does not always fit predetermined rigid rules; the text rather than the rules must be allowed to determine the genre. With this one exception, however, we may conclude that βίοι are normally written documents in prose narrative, often continuous in form.

2. *Size*

The lengths of the four complete works are:

Isocrates' *Evagoras:*	about	5,000 words
Xenophon's *Agesilaus:*		7,558 words (computer count)
Nepos' *Atticus:*	about	3,500 words
Philo's *Moses:*	about	32,000 words

---

25. Hunt, *Oxy. Pap.* IX, p. 126; see also Dihle, *Studien,* p. 105; Momigliano, *Second Thoughts,* p. 11; and Stuart, *Epochs,* p. 179.

Obviously, we cannot know the precise length of the *Euripides*. However, if Hunt is right that the title was normally placed in the centre of the papyrus (whereas it is at the bottom of the fragment), then each column had approaching sixty lines;[26] the thirty columns of Frags. 37-39, averaging two words to a line, would then contain about 3,600 words, although we do not know what proportion this is of the whole. However, Book VI of the βίων ἀναγραφή contained three Lives; on one papyrus roll with roughly similar treatment, the length of the *Euripides* would be about a third of a scroll, i.e. 7,000-8,000 words with the closely packed writing — about the same length as the *Agesilaus*.

Thus βίοι tend to be 'medium length': Isocrates, Xenophon and Satyrus will fit two or three to a scroll, whereas Philo is longer and would require two scrolls — one for each part of the work. Although Nepos' *Atticus* is the shortest of our examples, it is part of a larger work, the *De viris illustribus*. Therefore, βίοι belong with medium-length works, alongside monographs and treatises of historical, philosophical or scientific concern.

3. Structure

The structure of these works usually has a chronological framework. After the prologue (if such exists), the subject's ancestry and birth are mentioned, with Nepos and Philo including an element about education also. However, all this may be extremely brief: Nepos covers it in one chapter, then carries straight on to when Atticus entered adult public life at the age of twenty-three, going to Athens to avoid Cinna. Equally, Xenophon covers Agesilaus' background and over forty years in barely a page to begin the narrative proper when he becomes king (I.5). After this early material, information about the subject's public life tends to come in a chronological fashion, especially in accounts of leaders and statesmen like *Evagoras, Agesilaus* and *Atticus,* where the sections can even be dated. This is more difficult to do for literary or philosophical subjects: Philo attempts a chronological account of Moses' activity, based upon the Pentateuch, describing Moses as king — as though recognizing the chronological necessity of public life.

This *chronological approach* is interrupted by the insertion of *topical material*. Xenophon and Philo have a carefully structured analysis by topics (Agesilaus' virtues and Moses as lawgiver, priest and prophet) after their chronology. Nepos inserts a section arranged topically to display Atticus'

---

26. Hunt, *Oxy. Pap.* IX, p. 125.

character (13-18). Isocrates, however, inserts his topical material as he goes along. Careful study of the *Euripides* reveals topical sections, identified by structural markers. Thus Frags. 1-8 appear to be concerned with Euripides' style, followed by consideration of his character, identified by the statement, 'such was his artistic skill . . . and he was nearly as great of soul' (Frag. 8.9-12, 20-24). Frags. 37.i.22ff., 38, and 39.i-vi deal with Euripides' opinions. After this, another comment marks the shift from his attitude to women to the poet's withdrawal from Athens, 'let us return again to Euripides' (Frag. 39.xv.14-20), leading to the account of his sojourn in Macedonia and eventual death. However, βίοι do have some outer chronological structure into which the topical material is inserted: the absence of such a structure is one reason why Xenophon's *Memorabilia,* despite its high concentration on Socrates shown by our verbal analysis above, is not a βίος.[27]

After this, all our examples except one return to chronology to describe the last years or days and death, closing with the funeral or honours given or an evaluation of their subject. Even Satyrus has a summing-up phrase to introduce the death: 'These were the things which happened to Euripides while he was alive; as for his death . . .' (Frag. 39.xx.22-26). Momigliano sees this as a definite indicator of genre: 'The text of the papyrus, with its clear transition from a section dealing with the life to a section dealing with the death of the poet, seems to make the biographical intention unmistakable.'[28] The death of Euripides occurs in column xxi of Frag. 39, with a story about Timotheos who composed the epigrammatic epitaph, 'All Greece is Euripides' monument, though Macedon holds his bones' (Γένος Εὐριπίδου, 40),[29] in xxii; finally, xxiii has the title, indicating the end. The one exception is Isocrates, who concludes with an evaluation of Evagoras, exhorting Nicocles to follow his father, but with no mention of his death. Aristotle tells us that Evagoras was murdered (*Pol.* 1311b) and in a rhetorical encomium such embarrassing, non-laudatory material was often omitted; thus we have a clear reason for our one exception of a βίος ending without the death.

Thus, βίοι usually have a basic chronological framework, which may be just the birth or public arrival as a starting point and the death as the end, together with topical inserts.

---

27. 'Einen Bios des Sokrates erhalten wir nicht, nur isolierte, letztlich anekdotische Einzelheiten, die vom geschichtlichen Augenblick grundsätzlich ablösbar sind', *Kommentar zu Xenophons Memorabilien,* ed. Olof Gigon, in 2 vols. (Basel: Friedrich Reinhardt, 1953, 1956); quotation from vol. 2, p. 191.

28. Momigliano, *Development,* p. 80; see also, Stuart, *Epochs,* pp. 181-3.

29. Stuart, *Epochs,* pp. 184-5; see also Kumaniecki's note, *De Satyro Peripatetico,* p. 63.

4. Scale

The scale is limited to the subject's life, deeds and character; as Cox says, 'biography was unique in concentrating on the life of a single personality'.[30] This is particularly notable in the *Atticus,* since here we have an account of the last half-century of the Roman Republic. Most of the great characters, Cinna, Sulla, Caesar, Cicero, Antony, are mentioned only in passing, while the momentous five years of the Civil War and Caesar's rule are covered in one chapter (7), since Atticus himself was neutral. A similar concentration on the subject occurs in the *Evagoras, Agesilaus* and *Euripides.* A slightly broader scale creeps into the *Moses,* since important events and customs of the Jews are recounted, but still all tied into the life of Moses. With this last exception, this feature is clear: βίοι are written on a narrow scale, limiting the focus upon the individual subject.

5. Literary Units

A mixture of literary units make up βίοι, including anecdotes, sayings, stories, discourses and speeches. Cox is clear which is vital: 'One of the most important of these forms is the anecdote, a brief biographical narrative that relates a striking or unusual feature of the hero's character. Anecdotes are the major vehicles of biographical characterizations.'[31] A clearly structured chronological narrative, e.g. *Atticus,* betrays the units less well; on the other hand, the dialogue structure of the *Euripides* shows two main units, quotations and anecdotes. The former are varied, taken widely from both Euripides and the comic poets. Anecdotes form the major part: Hunt refers to his 'fondness for anecdote, which Satyrus shares with his kind, and which was a product of the prevailing interest in individual character and personal traits and details'.[32] Such anecdotes include Euripides being a recluse in the cave, 39.ix; Cephisiphon's seduction of his wife, 39.xiii; whether a mouth which produced such sweet poetry could have bad breath, 39.xx; and his killing by Archelaus' hunting dogs which ends with the punchline of the Macedonian saying: 'Justice even for a dog' (Frag. 39.xxi.33-5). Satyrus has been criticized for this predilection: 'Evidently anecdotes amused Satyrus and facts, as such, did not. He cared about literary style, but he neither cared nor knew about

---

30. Cox, *Biography in Late Antiquity,* p. xiii.
31. *Ibid.,* p. 58.
32. Hunt, *Oxy. Pap.* IX, p. 127.

history.'[33] Other fragments of Satyrus preserved in Athenaeus also show this liking for anecdote, particularly if sensational or outrageous.[34]

Close examination reveals that these literary forms are present in all the βίοι, forming the stuff of their narrative. *Evagoras* betrays its rhetorical influence through units of formal oratory: prooimion, comparison, exordium, apostrophe. On the other hand, units which might be classed as 'legends' or 'miracle-stories' are found in the *Moses*. Thus we conclude that the literary units of stories, anecdotes and sayings are the primary building blocks of all βίοι, although in some they are linked into a more continuous whole than in others.

6. Use of Sources

Writers of βίοι drew material from a wide range of oral and written sources. Philo refers to both the scriptures and oral tradition in his Preface: κἀκ βίβλων τῶν ἱερῶν . . . καὶ παρά τινων ἀπὸ τοῦ ἔθνους πρεσβυτέρων (*Moses* I.4). Our other writers refer to sources in passing: personal knowledge of the subject is claimed by Nepos (saepe . . . domesticis rebus interfuimus, *Att.* 13.7). Xenophon also knew Agesilaus personally, having served under him in the Asian campaign of 396-394 to which he devotes so much space. Satyrus draws on the works of Euripides, as well as other poets, for his extensive quotations; for other details, he had Philochoros.[35] West sees the suggestion of 'fieldwork on the spot' — ὡς οἱ λόγιοί τε καὶ γεραίτατοι μυθολο[γ]οῦσι Μακεδ[ό]νων, 39.xx.29-33 — as 'surely bogus'.[36] In fact, as Mary Lefkowitz points out: 'Ancient biographers took most of their information about poets from the poets' own works.' With respect to the Γένος or *Vita*, often prefaced to ancient manuscripts of Euripides, which is heavily dependent on Satyrus, she says: 'Close analysis again shows that virtually all the information in the *Vita* derives from comedy or Euripides' own dramas.'[37] For example, it is inferred from his depiction of adulterous women that he had his own marriage difficulties, in Frag. 39.xiii.

All these writers select from their sources to display the subject and his character as they see him. Different criteria applied to βίος, and greater selectivity was allowed: 'The author who came to devote a Life, instead of a His-

---

33. G. Murray, *Euripides and His Age*, 2nd edn (OUP, 1965), p. 10.
34. See Tronson, 'Satyrus the Peripatetic', *JHS* (1984), p. 118.
35. Hunt, *Oxy. Pap.* IX, p. 127.
36. West, 'Satyrus', *GRBS* (1974), p. 282.
37. Lefkowitz, *Lives of the Greek Poets*, p. viii and p. 88.

tory, to a great man had to emphasize the difference in genre which allowed a different choice of material.'[38] Thus Isocrates chooses to omit Evagoras' ignominious death. In the *Hellenica*, Xenophon shows that he knows, and disapproves, of certain aspects of Agesilaus' conduct (such as his dealings with Pharnabazus or Sphodrias); these are absent in *Agesilaus* itself: 'He was clearly aware of failings which he felt it his duty, as a biographer, to suppress.'[39]

As in his allocation of space, the βίος writer has a certain freedom and licence, greater than that of the historiographer, to select and edit his oral and written sources, to deal with episodes in greater or lesser detail, or even to include or omit them when composing his portrait of the subject.

7. Methods of Characterization

We have seen that character was usually depicted indirectly through words and deeds rather than by direct analysis, and this applies equally to βίοι: as Xenophon says, it is from Agesilaus' deeds (ἀπὸ γὰρ τῶν ἔργων) that his character's qualities (τοὺς τρόπους αὐτοῦ) will appear (*Ages.* I.6). However, Nepos suggests that mere recitation of deeds belongs more to history ('historiam scribere') than to biography ('vitam enarrare'); the subject's virtues should also be included (*De viris illustribus* XVI: *Pelop.* 1.1). If character traits (τρόποι) and virtues are to be deduced from deeds (ἔργα), then it is not surprising that much of βίος is devoted to describing the subject's words and deeds, unlike modern predilections for psychological analysis. Even direct analysis still tends to be through anecdote: Nepos displays Atticus' character as a careful, economical, loyal friend and *pater familias*, with illustrations of these traits (13-18). Xenophon will point out the character trait to be admired in an incident lest an inattentive reader miss it; e.g. Agesilaus' courage at the battle of Coronea: Ἐνταῦθα δὴ Ἀγησίλαον ἀνδρεῖον μὲν ἔξεστιν εἰπεῖν ἀναμφιλόγως (II.12; see also I.20, 27, 36; II.8 for similar comments). Isocrates praises his subject's deeds and, since this is encomium, uses other formal methods such as comparison with other great men (e.g. Cyrus) to reveal the character of Evagoras (see 33-39). Nonetheless, as Halliwell makes clear, the *Evagoras* is typical of much Greek literature in relying 'primarily on descriptive and narrative means of characterization'.[40]

---

38. Geiger, 'Cornelius Nepos, *De Regibus Exterarum Gentium*', *Latomus* (1979), p. 667; see also, Momigliano, *Development*, p. 56, and *Second Thoughts*, pp. 6-7, 14-5; and G. Anderson, *Philostratus* (London: Croom Helm, 1986), pp. 227-36.

39. J. K. Anderson, *Xenophon*, p. 168; for full details, see pp. 167-71.

40. Halliwell, 'Traditional Greek Conceptions of Character', p. 58.

Satyrus' interest in character is demonstrated by his other work, the Περὶ χαρακτήρων (Athenaeus, iv.168e). Here, Frag. 8.20ff. introduces a section on Euripides' character, and it may continue through Frags. 9 and 10. Anecdotes, particularly the more sensational ones, also help to form an impression of the subject's character. Tronson concludes that he 'gives a general indication of his character through word and action'.[41] This, then, is the typical method employed in all our βίοι.

8. Summary

The external, structural similarities between these works have now emerged. There are occasional differences as is expected with this flexible genre, particularly at the beginnings of the genre with Isocrates' *Evagoras* and its rhetorical features. Nonetheless, a clear family resemblance from this external, structural point of view is as follows:

βίοι are works mostly in prose narrative and of medium length; their structure is a bare chronological framework of birth/arrival and death with topical material inserted; the scale is always limited to the subject; a mixture of literary units, notably anecdotes, stories, speeches and sayings, selected from a wide range of oral and written sources, displays the subject's character indirectly through words and deeds rather than by direct analysis.

E. Internal Features

1. Setting

The geographical settings take us all over the ancient world: to Egypt and the wilderness with *Moses*, to Cyprus with *Evagoras*, to Athens, Sicily and Macedonia with *Euripides*, and to Rome, the heart of the dying Republic, for the *Atticus*. However, all of these settings are chosen because this is where the subject was active. Additionally, the subject is always the focus of the dramatic settings. The *Life of Euripides* is unusual, being a dialogue between three people. Such a setting is more akin to philosophical debate, or indeed to tragedy itself: three speakers are the same number as actors allowed by tragic convention to Euripides in his plays. The three speakers are always discussing Euripides himself. Even when other material does appear, it is linked to the

---

41. Tronson, 'Satyrus the Peripatetic', *JHS* (1984), p. 118.

subject: for instance, the religious material in the *Moses* — the laws, the details of the tabernacle and so forth — still focusses on Moses, for he introduced it all. Equally, topical material, like the analysis of virtues in the *Agesilaus,* still directs our attention onto the man himself since they are *his* virtues. This constant internal focus on the subject affects the settings of the individual scenes and also of their overall content.

2. *Topics*

A number of standard, typical biographical topics or motifs recur throughout these works. Nepos conveniently lists some at the start of *Epamonidas:* 'We shall talk first about his ancestry, next of his education and his teachers, then about his habits and traits of character and anything else which is worth remembering; then finally about his deeds, which many place before the virtues of his mind' (*De viris illustribus* XV: *Epam.* 1.4). Some of these occur in all or most of our works; of the others, a selection is made according to the sort of βίος.

(a) Ancestry

Most βίοι begin with a mention of the subject's ancestry and heritage, his family, or his land or city. Isocrates has a long section on the nobility of Evagoras' ancestry, tracing it back to Zeus and down through the Trojan War hero, Teucer (chapters 12-20). Xenophon also praises Agesilaus' ancestry (back to Heracles), his royal family and the greatness of his country, Sparta (I.2-4). Nepos' opening sentence tells us that Atticus was born of the most ancient Roman stock ('ab origine ultima stirpis Romanae generatus'), whereas Philo comments that Moses was a Chaldean by ancestry (Μωυσῆς γένος μέν ἐστι Χαλδαῖος), but born and raised in Egypt (*Moses* I.5).

(b) Birth

Isocrates refers to Evagoras' birth, but in true rhetorical style mentions omens and portents only to say he will ignore them (21). *Moses* has the familiar story of the baby's birth and the bulrushes (1.8-17). The other three works do not include the birth.

(c) Boyhood and education

These are often used to prefigure the qualities of the later adult: so Isocrates refers to manly virtues and excellence in the boy Evagoras (22-24).

(d) Great deeds

These form the bulk of the narrative, but vary according to the subject. Thus, for a statesman like Evagoras, great deeds include government in peace (40-50) and direction of war (51-64). Xenophon recounts the deeds of Agesilaus on campaign in I.7–II.31. Atticus' greatness consists of avoiding public office and war, continuing his financial transactions and still managing to be a friend to everyone (6-12). Philo depicts Moses' great deeds as a king leading the Israelites out of slavery through the wilderness in Book I, but also his greatness as lawgiver, priest and prophet in Book II. Perhaps Satyrus recorded Euripides' great successes in the dramatic contests in the missing sections.

(e) Virtues

Virtues can be seen in the subject's great deeds (*Ages.* I.6), but also as another separate topic, e.g. Xenophon's treatment of Agesilaus' virtues in III-XI or Nepos' analysis of Atticus' character in 13-18. Other works do not tackle virtues separately, but in the narrative itself.

(f) Death and consequences

Except for *Evagoras,* all these works conclude with the subject's death. This can be in some detail concerning its cause, as in *Atticus* 22 or *Euripides* Frag. 39.xxi, or a briefer reference, as in *Agesilaus* X.3-4 and XI.16 or *Moses* II.291. The subsequent events often include the funeral or burial: *Ages.* XI.16; *Att.* 22; *Moses* II.291.

Thus we have here a set of standard topics used in βίοι, yet without forcing any particular work into a constrictive mould. Each author selects topics from his sources or reinterprets them to suit his subject; but they are all engaged in a similar exercise.

3. Style

The style and level of βίοι can vary; some are formal and highbrow, e.g. Isocrates and Xenophon both write in a high literary manner using formal rhetorical style, following Gorgias: Isocrates uses a long list of antitheses in 43-46,[42] whereas Xenophon probably derived his idea of the succession of virtues in III-IX from Gorgias and occasionally betrays his influence in his style. Nepos and Philo are capable of high style and rhetorical forms, but their βίοι attempt to reach a wider audience; Nepos writes quite plainly in short, simple sentences with a limited vocabulary,[43] and the *Moses* is less allegorical and more accessible than the rest of Philo. Satyrus also has elements of the popular: Hunt describes him as 'a writer with considerable pretensions to literary style' and the fragments as 'smooth and pleasant', avoiding hiatus.[44] Yet this style is not 'high-brow', but rather at a popular anecdotal level.

Thus βίος literature is *not* limited to any one formal or high-brow style and level. Many surviving examples do reflect that approach, but others indicate that the genre stretched much further down the scale; even if many popular βίοι were in circulation, unfortunately, they were less likely to be preserved for posterity.

4. Atmosphere

The four features of tone, mood, attitude and values are taken together to form an impression of the atmosphere. Four of the works *(Evagoras, Agesilaus, Atticus, Moses)* are similar: their tone is respectful and serious, and the mood is generally steady, with undercurrents of thankfulness. The attitude to the subject is respectful and admiring, and often openly encomiastic, causing a didactic or hortative attitude to the reader to encourage emulation. The values come from different situations: the stress on power and honour for the ruler of a Greek city state *(Evagoras);* the virtues important in Greek philosophy *(Agesilaus);* the social approach of the Roman *equites (Atticus);* and a mixture of Jewish religious values with Greek philosophy *(Moses).* However, all four reflect the established values of their respective place and periods. Thus a common atmosphere emerges which is fairly serious and respectful to the point of eulogy.

The atmosphere of *Euripides* reflects its mixture of literary pretensions and the popular level. It is more light-hearted in tone than the others: Euripi-

---

42. Forster considers Isocrates' style to be 'the purest Attic' with the careful rhythm and balance of the clauses, with smoothness resulting from the avoidance of hiatus; here, too, the influence of Gorgias is noted, *Cyprian Orations,* pp. 21-4.

43. See Jenkinson in *Latin Biography,* pp. 11-14 or *ANRW* I.3, pp. 715-7, for Nepos' style; Horsfall is uncomplimentary about his literary abilities, *Cornelius Nepos,* pp. xviii-xix.

44. Hunt, *Oxy. Pap.* IX, pp. 126-7.

des' marital problems are fair game (Frag. 39.xii-xiii) and the story of his death ends with the saying 'Justice even for a dog' (39.xxi.33-5). The mood of the dialogue is like friends conversing rather than the intensity of a Socratic dialogue. Nonetheless, Lefkowitz believes that it still 'preserves a sense of debate over the application of quotations from plays', and Satyrus 'has discussions of Socratic notions in Euripides', whereas in the *Vita* attached to later manuscripts 'all sense of debate has disappeared'.[45] The attitude towards the subject is mixed: there is respect for his skill, yet also fun to be had at the expense of his more unusual habits or sayings. The values of Satyrus are those of a 'moralist and gossip-monger'.[46] All together, these features provide a light atmosphere here. This is a further reminder of the flexibility of βίος, with the contrast between this lighter atmosphere and the more serious tone of the others.

5. Quality of Characterization

The selective use of sources to provide a particular picture, together with the encomiastic elements within some of these works, predisposes them to a stereotypic element in the quality of their characterization. Isocrates is clear: 'everyone knows that those wishing to praise someone must depict him with more good qualities than he really has, while his attackers must do the opposite' (*Busiris* 4). This stereotypic element is there also in *Evagoras*. Halliwell argues that the influence of encomium on the development of βίος led to a lack of individuality: 'Interest in the individual, without which we would have no biographical form at all, is qualified and coloured by the tendency to see him as an exemplar of general, ethical qualities — qualities, that is, which are not uniquely his.'[47] Stereotype is common in character analysis: Nepos' account of Atticus' loyalty and economical attitudes (e.g. *Att.* 13) is too good to be true; on the other hand, the stories about him give the impression of a fairly shrewd financier at work, rather than merely a philanthropic stereotype.

45. Lefkowitz, *Lives of the Greek Poets*, p. 99.
46. Tronson, 'Satyrus the Peripatetic', *JHS* (1984), p. 118.
47. Halliwell, 'Traditional Greek Conceptions of Character', p. 56; see also, 'er ist die Schilderung eines Idealkönigs. Diese sittlich-idealistische Darstellungsweise ist in der ganzen Erzählung zu verfolgen'. Johannes Sykutris, 'Isokrates' "Euagoras"', in *Isokrates*, ed. F. Seck, p. 81; for rhetoric and character, see D. A. Russell, '*Ēthos* in Oratory and Rhetoric', in *Characterization and Individuality*, pp. 197-212.

6. Social Setting and Occasion

All the examples reveal a setting within the educated and ruling classes. The occasion for the delivery of the *Evagoras* is a public festival, as the final chapters of direct address to the dead ruler's son show; the *Agesilaus* was probably occasioned soon after his death, perhaps as an apologetic. There are hints in some texts that a wider audience is sought: Philo wants to inform those ignorant of Moses (I.1-4), and Nepos hoped to reach more with his *De viris illustribus* (see *Praefatio* 1-7). The *Euripides* reveals a social environment interested in stories about important figures, so there is an element of the popular about its setting. For Satyrus and Nepos, the occasion of writing was producing a larger work. Satyrus, for example, is writing a comprehensive collection of βίοι: Euripides must be included in the section on the tragic poets. So these examples contain evidence of a social setting within the upper or educated classes, but with hints that βίοι can have a variety of settings and occasions further down the social scale.

7. Authorial Intention and Purpose

These βίοι display many possible purposes, which we shall consider separately to aid clarity, but several intentions may be combined in one particular work.

(a) Encomiastic

This is the most obvious purpose of βίοι which are also rhetorical encomia, or works in the overlap of the genres. Isocrates describes his intention as both encomium (ἐγκωμιάζειν, *Evag.* 8) and eulogy (εὐλογεῖν, *Evag.* 11). Xenophon has a eulogistic purpose in mind when he says that it is difficult to write worthily of Agesilaus' ἀρετή (I.1). The others do not state an explicit encomiastic intent, though in some it may be implicit.

(b) Exemplary

The other purpose of encomium was to provide an example for others to emulate, and this is common too in many other forms of ancient literature. Isocrates ends with a section explicitly telling Nicocles to emulate his father's greatness (73-81); the speech is intended as the best exhortation (πολὺ καλλίστην . . . ταύτην παράκλησιν) for him and for his children (76). Xenophon's picture of Agesilaus is an example (παράδειγμα) for others to follow to become better people (ἀνδραγαθίαν ἀσκεῖν, X.2).[48] This intention can become almost evangelistic in calling the readers to follow the hero — and there may be an element of this in Philo's attempt to commend Moses to a larger audience as the 'supreme law-giver whose laws they are to accept and honour'.[49] Conversely, an exemplary motive may be discerned in the moralising criticism of Satyrus about Euripides' haughtiness (Frag. 39.ix.16-18) or his aloofness (39.x.5-6). Tronson points out from his other works that 'Satyrus thus had a propensity for relating not only bizarre deaths but also *exempla* of moral excess or extravagance.'[50]

(c) Informative

This was important for 'Satyrus' work, which, like that of other biographers of the Peripatetic school, was essentially popular in its aim, and endeavoured to supply interesting information in an attractive shape'.[51] Philo writes similarly about people's ignorance concerning Moses and his desire to inform them (*Moses* I.1). Nepos says that he wishes to provide a portrait of his subjects' life and character from their deeds ('de rebus gestis', *De viris illustribus* XV: *Epam.* 1.3-4) or virtues ('de virtutibus', XVL: *Pelop.* 1.1), which has an informative approach. Such statements bear out the truth of Momigliano's comment that not all biography was for great debate: 'The educated man of the Hellenistic world was curious about the lives of famous people. He wanted to know what a king or a poet or a philosopher was like and how he behaved in his off-duty moments.'[52]

(d) Entertainment value

Like the last aim, this was part of Satyrus' intent. Certainly, in the fragments of his other Lives, cited in Athenaeus, we hear of 'the outrageous lifestyle of Alcibiades, the bigamy of Socrates, the dining couches of Dionysius II and the gross flattery of Philip's courtier Cleisophus'.[53] The *Euripides* has its own share, such as the sensationalized account of his death or the gossip about his wife's affair.

---

48. 'In the *Agesilaus*, Xenophon represents the King as setting an example of all virtues', J. K. Anderson, *Xenophon*, p. 168.
49. Borgen, 'Philo of Alexandria', p. 118; see also p. 151.
50. Tronson, 'Satyrus the Peripatetic', *JHS* (1984), p. 118.
51. Hunt, *Oxy. Pap.* IX, p. 126.
52. Momigliano, *Second Thoughts*, p. 15.
53. Tronson, 'Satyrus the Peripatetic', *JHS* (1984), p. 118.

(e) To preserve memory

Another informative purpose arises from the desire to preserve the memory of the deceased. Isocrates suggests that his praise of Evagoras' deeds and character (τῶν πράξεων καὶ τῆς διανοίας) is a far better memorial than any statue in its ability to capture his character more truly and in its worldwide fame (*Evag.* 73-74). As personal acquaintances of their subjects, Xenophon and Nepos may be fulfilling this intention also.

(f) Didactic

In philosophical or religious βίοι the desire to teach is natural, about both the subject himself and his teachings. Philo wants to teach what sort of person Moses was (τοιοῦτος μὲν ὁ βίος, II.292), and he also includes discussion of his subject's teachings.

(g) Apologetic and polemic

The use of βίοι in debate was a common intention in early philosophical βίοι. As Cox says:

> Biography was from its inception a genre that found its home in controversy. Biographers like Aristoxenus were self-conscious mediators of specific traditions, and their works had both apologetic and polemical aims, apologetic in defending, affirming, and sometimes correcting opinion about a hero; polemical in suggesting by the strength of the defense, and sometimes by outright attack, the unworthiness of other traditions by comparison.[54]

In the *Agesilaus* Xenophon seems to be defending his hero against criticisms, e.g. 'some may blame him for this' (II.21; see also IV.4; V.6; VIII.7 — the latter stressing Agesilaus' simple lifestyle). Goodenough sees similar aims in Philo: the '*Life of Moses* has always been taken as another apology for the Jews'.[55]

Thus, any attempt to prescribe a single aim for βίος misses out on a rich variety of possible purposes. These include encomiastic intent, to preserve memory, for exemplary, moral, philosophical purposes, polemic, apologetic, entertainment, didactic or informative aims, or to correct false ideas.

---

54. Cox, *Biography in Late Antiquity,* p. 135; see also Berger, 'Hellenistische Gattungen im NT', *ANRW,* II.25.2, p. 1242.

55. Goodenough, *An Introduction to Philo Judaeus,* p. 33; see also Borgen, 'Philo of Alexandria', p. 118.

8. Summary

Internal features are concerned with areas of content, and so it is not surprising that similarities of these features emerge from works all concerned with one person. Of course, there are divergences, especially between the different sorts of subject, but overall a clear family resemblance may be seen:

βίοι are works with a setting focussed upon a person, about whom the writer selects topics from a group of standard motifs. The style and level of extant works are fairly literary, but there is evidence for a wider range which has not been preserved. Likewise, the texts reveal educated social settings and occasions, with popular tendencies. The atmosphere is mostly respectful and serious, although it can be more light-hearted. The quality of characterization may be good, but there is a tendency to stereotype. Finally, we have discovered a wide range of possible purposes, and many works have several intentions simultaneously.

Conclusion

We have now examined five works predating the gospels: two early rhetorical works, a Hellenistic literary βίος and two examples from other cultures, Republican Rome and Alexandrian Judaism. Despite this variety of date and setting, they exhibit a similar range of generic features within a flexible pattern. The primary similarity derives from their subject — an account of a person. This is usually first signalled by the title, the subject's name, sometimes with the word βίος itself (in Satyrus and Philo). Verbal analysis of Xenophon and Satyrus demonstrated the dominance of the subject. Allocation of space need not be even-handed; some concentrate on one particular period. Similar content produces other similar internal features, such as a concentration of the geographical and dramatic setting upon the person and a tendency towards the typical in characterization as the authors make selections from a similar range of topics and motifs. The style and atmosphere of the works are mostly respectful and serious, revealing a social setting within the educated classes; however, Satyrus shows that βίος can be written in a light style and easy atmosphere conducive to a more popular setting. There are a large number of possible purposes and intentions, any of which can be combined within one of our examples. As regards external features, the works tend to be in prose narrative, although *Evagoras* is a speech and *Euripides* is in dialogue. They are of medium length, about 7,000 words long, although Nepos is shorter and Philo longer. All have a basic chronological structure with topical inserts, drawn on

148

a fairly narrow scale. Each author selects common literary units, such as anecdotes, stories, speeches and quotations, drawn from a variety of oral and written sources to portray the subject's character through the indirect means of narrating his deeds and words.

There are boundaries to this flexible genre, however: *Evagoras* often seems the odd one out, as it contains many features typical of rhetoric. Equally, mere concentration on an individual is not sufficient for admission: thus the *Memorabilia* displays some features of βίος, such as the concentration on Socrates, but its other features, such as excessive length, philosophical dialogue and lack of chronology, place it more naturally within philosophical genres, while the *Cyropaedia* is more of a romance or novel.

By the first century AD there was a clear generic grouping of βίος literature, which was widespread from Rome to Alexandria, across the social classes from the high-brow to the popular levels. As a flexible genre, it continued to develop, but within a recognizable family resemblance. Before we consider how the gospels compare with these examples, we shall analyse a further five examples dating from later times to obtain a full picture of how the genre developed.

CHAPTER 7

The Generic Features of Later Graeco-Roman βίοι

Plutarch's Lives *are an outstanding achievement in the field of biographical writing.*[1]

The historical development of Graeco-Roman biography provides a more suitable framework within which to consider these works.[2]

N ow we have studied five βίοι predating the gospels, five further works will show us how the genre develops: three date from the creative period around AD 100, and then we move to the later imperial forerunners of hagiography and the novel. Beyond this point, the genre begins to develop into new forms and new cultures outside our scope. All together, we have a sample of ten different βίοι across some eight centuries within which to place the gospels.

We have seen already that the subjects of βίοι include a wide range of people; eventually, 'the wise man, the martyr, and the saint became central subjects of biography in addition to the king, the writer, and the philosopher'.[3] Within Graeco-Roman biography as a whole, each category could be seen as its own subgroup, some of which may be closer to some neighbouring genres than others. Thus the border between historiography and political βίοι is blurred: some history shows biographical features (for example the concen-

---

1. Alan Wardman, *Plutarch's Lives* (London: Paul Elek, 1974), p. 2.
2. Cox, *Biography in Late Antiquity*, p. 4, referring to attempts to use aretalogy to explain the gospels and later biographies of holy men.
3. Momigliano, *Development*, p. 104.

tration on the emperor in Roman historiography), whereas βίοι of generals or statesmen will show some historical features. As Wallace-Hadrill says: 'History or not history? The problem faces every biographer in varying degree. Biography occupies an ambivalent position on the outskirts of proper historical writing.'[4] Equally, βίοι of philosophers may be closer to the genres of philosophical works or, in the case of one as well-travelled as Apollonius of Tyana, to travelogue or even novel. Considering all their generic features will help us to understand such works.

A. Introducing the Examples

1. *Tacitus'* Agricola

The *Agricola* is probably Tacitus' earliest work, written in AD 98[5] when confidence was reviving after the terror of Domitian. Cornelius Tacitus was born of equestrian stock *c.* AD 56, probably in Narbonese Gaul; elevated by Vespasian, he pursued a senatorial career, becoming consul in 97 and governor of Asia in 112-13; he died in the reign of Hadrian. The *Agricola* and *Germania* were completed around his consulship; his great historical works came later, the *Histories* (dealing with AD 69-96) and *Annals,* covering from Augustus to Nero, AD 14-68. In AD 77 he married the daughter of the consul at the time, Gn. Julius Agricola (*Agricola* 9.6). The subject of Tacitus' first work was, therefore, his father-in-law: Agricola, also born in Narbonese Gaul, at Forum Iulii (modern Fréjus) in AD 40, had a typical senatorial career, mixing military and political posts, tribune of the plebs in 66, praetor in 68 and consul in 77. His military career was spent in Britain, as military tribune under Suetonius Paulinus in 58-61, then commander of the XXth Legion in 70-73, and returning finally as governor in 77 until his retirement in 84 to peace and quiet at Rome, where he died in 93.

The genre of the *Agricola* has been disputed among classical scholars,[6]

---

4. Andrew Wallace-Hadrill, *Suetonius: The Scholar and His Caesars* (London: Duckworth, 1983), p. 8.

5. See *De Vita Agricolae,* ed. R. M. Ogilvie and I. Richmond (OUP, 1967), pp. 10-11, and pp. 854-5 of M. M. Sage, 'Tacitus' Historical Works: A Survey and Appraisal', *ANRW* II.33.2 (1990), pp. 851-1030; see also, T. A. Dorey, '"Agricola" and "Germania"', in his *Tacitus* (London: Routledge & Kegan Paul, 1969), pp. 1-18, and 'Agricola and Domitian', *Greece and Rome* 7 (1960), pp. 66-71; F. R. D. Goodyear, *Tacitus,* Greece and Rome New Surveys in the Classics 4 (OUP, 1970); Ronald Martin, *Tacitus* (London: Batsford, 1981), pp. 39-49.

6. Forni lists many suggested options including *laudatio funebris* (Hübner), political

and we have already noted that Shuler claims it for his genre of 'encomium biography'.[7] It differs from the gospels in many ways, such as its social and literary levels and settings. If some kind of generic relationship can be demonstrated, this will be very significant in placing the gospels within the web of literary relationships of their day.

2. *Plutarch's* Cato Minor

Plutarch was born *c.* AD 45/6 and lived until the early 120s. His family came from Chaeronea in northern Boeotia, and he spent most of his life there, although he travelled to Rome where he became friends with several leading citizens and won his citizenship. He was among the most prolific of ancient writers, writing philosophy, morality, rhetoric, biography and antiquarian history; about half of it still survives. His philosophical tastes tended towards the Platonic, and he was also a priest of the shrine at Delphi. This philosophical interest is clear in works like the *Moralia* but also shines through the *Lives*.[8] Like Tacitus' work, Plutarch's βίοι probably belong to the period after AD 96 when it was safer to publish.[9] He wrote individual Lives, of which four survive, and others in parallel pairs, comparing Greeks with Romans; twenty-two pairs remain, with nineteen having formal comparisons, σύγκρισεις.[10] He distinguishes βίος from history in the famous passage from *Alex.* 1.1-3 but, as

---

pamphlet (Boissier), biographical encomium (Leo), laudatory biography (Andersen), panegyric (Giarratano), prose encomium (Gudeman), idealistic biography and moderate panegyric (Stuart), *monumentum pietatis* in biographical character (Hosius), *laudatio* following rhetorical canons of Quintilian (Cousin) *et al.* — see his edition, *Agricola* (Rome: Athenaeum, 1962), p. 13; see also, Ogilvie's introduction to his commentary, pp. 11-20, and Sage, 'Tacitus' Historical Works', *ANRW* II.33.2, pp. 855-6. The new volume II.33.3 (1991) also contains several helpful articles on the *Agricola*, pp. 1714-1857.

7. Shuler, *A Genre for the Gospels*, p. 75, see pp. 83-6 above; for similar views, see Alfred Gudeman, ed., *Agricola* (Berlin: Weidmann, 1902), pp. 1-13, and J. Cousin, 'Histoire et rhétorique dans l'*Agricola*', *Revue des Etudes Latines* 14 (1936), pp. 31 and 326-36.

8. For his life, see C. P. Jones, *Plutarch and Rome* (OUP, 1971), pp. 3-64; also J. R. Hamilton, *Alexander* (OUP, 1969), pp. xiii-xxiii, and C. B. R. Pelling (ed.), *Plutarch: Life of Antony* (CUP, 1988), pp. 1-10.

9. For dating, see C. P. Jones, 'Towards a Chronology of Plutarch's Works', *JRS* 56 (1966), pp. 60-74; Hamilton, *Alexander*, pp. xxxiv-xxxvii; Pelling, *Antony*, pp. 3-4, and 'Plutarch's Method', *JHS* (1979), pp. 74-96.

10. For pairings and comparisons, see Pelling, 'Synkrisis in Plutarch's Lives', *QGFF* 8 (1986), pp. 83-96, and *Antony*, pp. 18-26; Geiger, 'Plutarch's Parallel Lives', *Hermes* (1981), pp. 85-104; Jones, *Plutarch and Rome*, pp. 105-6; Gossage, 'Plutarch', in *Latin Biography*, ed. Dorey, pp. 60-2.

we have seen, this distinction can be overemphasized, particularly if taken without reference to Plutarch's actual practice. Plutarch's *βίοι* exemplify the flexible nature of this genre, nestling between history, rhetoric and moral philosophy, with a variety of literary and artistic purposes.

Although the *Cato Minor* is roughly contemporary with the *Agricola,* there are many differences. It was written in Greek and in Greece; it is part of a much larger work, the *Parallel Lives,* and it is paired with the *Phocion.* Cato is an interesting subject as a political and public figure, but one with a strong moral and philosophical side. Marcus Porcius Cato (the Younger) was a politician and philosopher active over the last decades of the Republic. Born in 95 BC, he was the great-grandson of Cato the Elder. He was an uncompromising Republican and fought hard against the changes in Roman politics; elected praetor in 54, he failed to obtain the consulship in 51. He consistently opposed the First Triumvirate and their associates, such as Clodius. When the break finally came, he persuaded Pompey to become the senate's champion and served under him in the Civil War. He committed suicide at Utica in 46 BC when he saw that the Republican cause was lost.[11] Cato espoused a mixture of traditional Roman values and Stoicism, having studied with Antipater the Tyrian (*Cat. Min.* 4.1) and later under Athenodorus while serving in the East (10). Plutarch describes his last hours spent in philosophical discussion and reading (67-69). After his death, Cato became a symbol of Republicanism: Cicero wrote a panegyric, the *Cato,* and Caesar a reply, the *Anti-Cato.* Later others, including Cato's nephew Brutus, who was one of Caesar's murderers, Caesar's lieutenant Hirtius, and even Augustus himself, expressed their philosophical and political ideas through writing about him, as 'Catonism' became 'an ideological hallmark of the Early Principate'.[12] Thrasea Paetus' account, composed in his retirement from active politics after upsetting Nero, is described by Geiger as using the genre of 'full-fledged biography, describing the life of the hero from childhood to death' to set out his own beliefs.[13] Not long afterwards, Paetus was himself also to commit suicide having lost to the imperial tyrant. Interestingly, Plutarch can write about Cato, using these polemical *βίοι* as his sources, but without participating in the ideological debate; instead, Cato is just one of his great figures for the *Parallel Lives.*

11. For an introduction to Cato, see *LACTOR* 14, *Plutarch: Cato the Younger* (London: Association of Classical Teachers, 1984); for full discussion, see Rudolf Fehrle, *Cato Uticensis* (Darmstadt: Wissenschaftliche Buchgesellschaft, 1983).

12. Geiger, 'Munatius Rufus', *Athenaeum* (1979), pp. 48-72, quotation from p. 48: see also Wardman, *Plutarch's Lives,* p. 220: 'The cult of the philosophical Romans, Brutus and Cato, was at times a gesture of defiance against an autocracy.'

13. Geiger, 'Munatius Rufus', p. 71.

3. *Suetonius'* Lives of the Caesars[14]

Gaius Tranquillus Suetonius was slightly younger than Tacitus and Plutarch, born *c.* 69, the year of the four emperors. A professional scholar and writer, he held secretarial posts under both Trajan and Hadrian. Little is known about his life, apart from personal references in his work and correspondence with his friend and patron, Pliny the Younger. The letters, covering AD 96-112, mention Pliny's assistance, such as gaining Suetonius the *ius trium liberorum* — the political advantages of parenthood — even though he was childless. He appears to have been dismissed by Hadrian in AD 121/2, but the date of his death is unknown.

Much of his work was biographical, including the large *De viris illustribus* (echoing Nepos' title), now lost. The *De vita Caesarum* has twelve βίοι, beginning with the *Julius Caesar,* which has some chapters missing, and continuing down to *Domitian.* As we have seen, Suetonius differs from Plutarch in his topical analysis of the emperors' reign, with chronology used only for their early years and death. He is interested in the lively story, often to the point of being seen as a scandal-monger, and this, together with his simple, easy to read style, ensured him lasting popularity. The accounts of Julius Caesar and Augustus are the most detailed; the quality of the others deteriorates down through the sequence, probably as a result of his dismissal from the imperial service and its archives and libraries. We shall concentrate, therefore, on these first two *Lives.*

4. *Lucian's* Demonax[15]

Lucian was born about the time Suetonius' official career ended, *c.* AD 120, in Samosata, formerly capital of Commagene but then in the Roman province of Syria. He often calls himself a Syrian and may have had Aramaic as his first language (*Double Indictment* 27). He lived through the 'golden years' of the mid-second century under Hadrian, Antoninus Pius and Marcus Aurelius, and died after AD 180. After an unsuccessful start in the family sculpting busi-

---

14. Wallace-Hadrill, *Suetonius;* Baldwin, *Suetonius;* Wolf Steidle, *Sueton und die antike Biographie,* 2nd edn (Munich: C. H. Beck, 1963).

15. Barry Baldwin, *Studies in Lucian* (Toronto: Hakkert, 1973); Graham Anderson, *Studies in Lucian's Comic Fiction,* Mnemosyne Supplementum 43 (Leiden: Brill, 1976); C. P. Jones, *Culture and Society in Lucian* (Cambridge, Mass.: Harvard University Press, 1986), especially pp. 90-8; Christopher Robinson, *Lucian: And His Influence in Europe* (London: Duckworth, 1979); for a comparison with Mark, see H. Cancik, 'Bios und Logos'.

ness, he trained in rhetoric; as a travelling sophist, he visited much of the ancient world, including Rome, Greece and Egypt. Although philosophy is the main subject of much of his work, he was more an entertainer than a sage, developing his 'dialogues' with a rich vein of satire and comedy: in *Philosophers for Sale* the range of ideas and beliefs available in his pluralistic society is described and examined as though they were slaves up for auction in a mock slave-market.

The eighty or so extant works display a range of literary genres and a capacity for mixture and experiment. Some are little more than formal rhetorical exercises, in which the orator has to accuse or defend a person in a given situation (e.g. *The Tyrannicide*). Others are προλαλίαι, short, warm-up orations for the start of a public performance. He used the genre of philosophical dialogue for his more substantial works, and infused them with a strong whiff of satire (*Dialogues of the Gods, Dialogues of the Dead,* etc.). Other books are concerned with a particular individual: 'biographies, favourable and hostile, were well suited to sophistic practice'.[16] The *Demonax* concerns a philosopher with Cynical tendencies from Cyprus, but resident in Athens, under whom Lucian studied. Little else is known about him outside Lucian's account, except for some apophthegms preserved in other writers.

5. *Philostratus'* Apollonius of Tyana[17]

Flavius Philostratus was born in the later years of Lucian's life, *c.* AD 170. He studied rhetoric at Athens, and then came to Rome and became part of the circle of Julia Domna, wife of the emperor Septimius Severus. He survived the turbulent end of the Severan dynasty, continuing to write and publish, and died *c.* AD 250. His interest in βίοι is demonstrated by his *Lives of the Sophists,* βίοι σοφιστῶν, a picture of the professional sophists and their craft. Philostratus received from the Empress Julia the 'memoirs of Damis', with a request that he should write an account of Apollonius, a first-century philosopher and mystic from Tyana in Cappadocia. An active teacher and religious reformer, Apollonius travelled all over the known world, and Philostratus uses

16. Baldwin, *Studies in Lucian*, p. 79.

17. Eduard Meyer, 'Apollonius von Tyana und die Biographie des Philostratos', *Hermes* 52 (1917), pp. 371-424; G. Petzke, *Die Traditionen über Apollonius von Tyana und das Neue Testament*, Studia ad Corpus Hellenisticum Novi Testamenti, vol. 1 (Leiden: Brill, 1970); E. L. Bowie, 'Apollonius of Tyana: Tradition and Reality', in *ANRW* II.16.2 (1978), pp. 1652-99; Graham Anderson, *Philostratus: Biography and Belles Lettres in the Third Century A.D.* (London: Croom Helm, 1986).

these travels as a backdrop for his words and mighty deeds. The historical authenticity of all this, of Damis and even of Apollonius himself, is much disputed and too complex a distraction to our task to go into here.[18] This work is often compared with the gospels.[19] In fact, its precise genre is disputed: although it is called the *Vita Apollonii,* Bowie says that 'the work is not properly a Vita'. The overlap with both philosophy and *Reiseroman* is noted by Meyer, and Anderson points out links with historiography, dialogue, the novel and romance, concluding that 'it is futile in the end to try to "explain" *Apollonius* in terms of any single genre'.[20] Here too then, generic analysis may help.

B. Opening Features

1. Titles

The full title of the *Agricola* in the *Aesinas Codex* is: 'Cornelii Taciti de Vita Iulii Agricolae liber incipit'. As Martin says: 'The title of the work . . . promises the reader . . . a biography of Tacitus' father-in-law, Gnaeus Julius Agricola.'[21] Plutarch's work is known by the name of the subject, Κάτων, but is also part of the much larger work, the *Parallel Lives.* Similarly Suetonius' overall title is *De vita Caesarum,* with individual books named after their emperors. Although Lucian's work is often called the *Demonax,* its fuller Greek title is βίος Δημώνακτος.[22] Finally, something similar to Philo's περὶ τοῦ . . . formula hap-

---

18. Meyer suggested that Damis was 'lediglich eine Fiktion des Philostratos' for his own ideas against Moiragenes, 'Apollonius von Tyana', *Hermes,* 1917, pp. 393ff; for a modern version, see Bowie, 'Apollonius of Tyana', *ANRW,* II.16.2, who accepts the existence of Apollonius, but is sceptical about the stories and Damis; the opposing view is taken by Graham Anderson, *Philostratus,* pp. 155-97; see also, Petzke's excursus, 'Das Damisproblem', in *Die Traditionen,* pp. 67-72. For fiction in βίοι, see Momigliano, *Development,* p. 56; Berger, 'Hellenistische Gattungen im NT', *ANRW* II.25.2, p. 1239; and Pelling, 'Truth and Fiction in Plutarch's *Lives*' in *Antonine Literature,* ed. D. A. Russell (OUP, 1990), pp. 19-52.

19. See, for example, Petzke, *Die Traditionen,* pp. 51-62; Stanton, *Jesus of Nazareth,* p. 120; Talbert, *What Is a Gospel?,* pp. 36-7, 94-5, 101, 125; Shuler, *A Genre for the Gospels,* pp. 82-5; Boring, *Truly Human/Truly Divine,* pp. 20-1.

20. Bowie, 'Apollonius of Tyana', *ANRW* II.16.2, p. 1652, n. 1; Meyer, 'Apollonius von Tyana', *Hermes,* 1917; G. Anderson, *Philostratus,* p. 235.

21. Martin, *Tacitus,* p. 39. At the end of this manuscript the title has *et Moribus* after *Vita* and this is the title in other MSS — A (Vatican 3429), B (Vatican 4498) and T(Toletanus 49,2): see Forni's commentary, p. 75, and Heinz Heubner, *Kommentar zum Agricola des Tacitus* (Göttingen: Vandenhoeck and Ruprecht, 1984), p. 143.

22. See Eunapios *VS* 454, quoted on p. 59 above; also Jones, *Culture and Society,* p. 22; and Baldwin, *Studies in Lucian,* p. 98.

pens with Philostratus: the title is τὰ ἐς τὸν Τυανέα Ἀπολλώνιον. Bowie notes that this 'is not of the normal biographic form τοῦ δεῖνος βίος' but suggests a 'novelistic formula'[23] — an indication perhaps that this work is on the border between βίος and novel or travel-romance. Anderson translates it as 'in honour of Apollonius of Tyana' or 'a monument to Apollonius'.[24] We conclude from all our examples, therefore, that the titles given to βίοι are based around the subject's name and often, but not always, include the word βίος or *vita*.

2. Opening Formulae/Prologue/Preface

Tacitus begins with a formal prologue, following common literary practice and rhetorical canons, with a strong personal theme about previous biographies and how such works were impossible while Domitian was emperor.[25] In the first chapter, Tacitus uses 'vitam narrare' of his predecessors (1.3), and then for his own work, 'at nunc narraturo vitam' (1.4); the verb reappears in the final words: 'Agricola posteritati narratus et traditus superstes erit' (46.4). 'Narrare vitam' is used by Nepos to distinguish his Lives from more historical works (*De viris illustribus* XVI: *Pelop.* 1.1), so Tacitus is giving us a clear indicator of the genre of βίος here. There is no prologue at the start of the *Cato Minor,* since there is the prologue and initial comparison in its partner, the *Phocion;* see especially chapter 3. Unfortunately the beginning of the *Divus Julius,* the first of Suetonius' *Caesars,* is not preserved, so we cannot tell if the sequence began with a prologue; the other Lives begin immediately with the emperor's ancestry. Both Lucian and Philostratus do have prologues (*Dem.* 1-2; *Apoll.* I.1-3), in which they explain the purpose of their writing, as well as refer to other philosophers.

In these examples, too, we find the subject's name at the beginning. After its prologue, the *Agricola* begins with the opening words: 'Gnaeus Iulius Agricola' (4.1). According to Ogilvie, this is the only certain occasion where Tacitus gives all three of a person's names in the official manner: 'this formal, and perhaps unique, introduction signals that Agricola is the subject of the work'.[26] The *Cato Minor,* with no prologue, begins with the subject's name as the first word, even though it is not the grammatical subject, Κάτωνι δὲ τὸ μὲν γένος . . . , and then we move straight into his ancestry (1.1). This is also

23. Bowie, 'Apollonius of Tyana', *ANRW* II.16.2, p. 1665.

24. G. Anderson, *Philostratus,* pp. 121 and 235.

25. For the prologue, see Karl Büchner, 'Das Proömium zum Agricola des Tacitus', in his *Tacitus und Ausklang* (Wiesbaden: Franz Steiner, 1964), pp. 23-42.

26. Ogilvie, *Agricola,* p. 140; Heubner, *Kommentar,* p. 14.

the case in many of Plutarch's *Lives:* see for example, *Antony* 1.1, Ἀντωνίου πάππος μὲν ἦν . . . , or *Eumenes* 1.1, Εὐμένη δὲ τὸν Καρδιανὸν. . . . Similarly in Suetonius, the family name is often mentioned immediately, leading into the ancestry section, while the subject's actual name begins the main body of the work. Lucian refers to Demonax by name several times in his opening sentences, whereas Philostratus has an opening chapter on Pythagoras, but begins the second chapter with Apollonius' name, repeated again after the preface, Ἀπολλωνίῳ τοίνυν πατρὶς (1.4).

It is now clear that some of our examples begin with a formal prologue or preface, but that all of them mention the subject's name at the very start, or immediately after the prologue.

C. Subject

1. Analysis of Verb Subjects

The large section on the geography, ethnography and history of Britain (chapters 10-17) is sometimes cited as an argument against the *Agricola* being biography. Manual analysis of verb subjects reflects this ambivalence of focus. Agricola clearly dominates, the subject of some 18% of the verbs with a further 4% occurring in his speech (chapters 33-34). All the other named Romans, including Domitian, taken together barely make 8%, with a similar figure for all the soldiers and sailors. However, the *Agricola* has, like a symphony, a second subject: Britain and various Britons, having some 14%, plus a further 7% appearing in Calgacus' speech (chapters 30-32) (see Figure 9, Appendix I, p. 315). Some scholars suggest that chapters 10-17 were originally a separate piece, a monograph or a section for a history, which Tacitus has incorporated into his narrative.[27] However, the reason for all this material on Britain is very simple, as Ogilvie points out: 'Agricola's claim to fame was that he was the conqueror of Britain and, therefore, the life of Agricola was to a large extent the history of the conquest of Britain.'[28]

Computer analysis of the *Cato Minor* reveals that Cato's name occurs in a huge 42.5% of the sentences, and that it appears in the nominative in 14.9% of them. His two political rivals, Pompey and Caesar, score significantly lower

27. See, for instance, the commentaries by Furneaux, 1898, p. 8; Furneaux-Anderson, 1922, p. xxiii; and Goodyear, *Tacitus*, p. 4.

28. *Agricola*, p. 15; for an account of Agricola's activity, see R. Syme, *Tacitus* (OUP, 1958), vol. 1, pp. 19-26.

results, appearing in about an eighth of the sentences (13.4% and 12.6%) and being in the nominative in 3%. After them, no one else has a significant score (see Figure 10, Appendix I, p. 316). Similar results occur in others of Plutarch's *Lives;* the fact that the leaders of the Civil War factions appear in each other's *Lives* produces particularly interesting results. In the *Caesar,* Caesar himself appears in 34.4%, with 11% in the nominative, while Pompey occurs in 13.9%, with 2.5% nominative. The position is completely reversed in the *Pompey,* however: Pompey occurs in 35.8% with 12.1% nominatives, while Caesar appears in 10.9% with 2.4% nominatives. Something very similar happens with Marius and Sulla: in the *Marius,* Marius scores 32% and 9.2%, while Sulla can only manage 5.5% and 2.4%; in the *Sulla,* however, Sulla scores 32.4% and 11.2%, with Marius getting 9.1% and 2.1%. Thus we may conclude that the subject of one of Plutarch's *Lives* is likely to appear in about a third of the sentences and to be the subject of at least a tenth; however, his nearest rival will appear in only a tenth, and be the subject of very few indeed (2 to 3%).

Much of the *Demonax* consists of conversations between Demonax and someone else, leading up to a witty saying or clever pronouncement by the sage himself. This is reflected in manual analysis of the verbs: Demonax is the subject of a third of them (33.6%) and speaks a further fifth (19.7%), whereas all those with whom he converses make up only another fifth when taken all together (20.9%) (see Figure 11, Appendix I, p. 317).

Despite the potential problems of precision which were anticipated for this method of analysis, these results, plus those in the previous chapter, reveal a clear and consistent picture: βίος literature is characterized by a strong concentration and focus on *one* person, and this is reflected even in the verbal syntax.

2. Allocation of Space

The *Agricola* does give a bare outline of Agricola's life — but this is only sketchy. Birth, parentage, boyhood and education are all covered swiftly in one chapter (4). The first thirty-eight years of Agricola's life have not quite 13% of the text and the last ten years just over 9%. Remarkably, one year, AD 84, has huge coverage — over a quarter of the work; closer inspection reveals that chapters 30-38 in fact cover only one day, the battle of Mons Graupius. So Tacitus chooses one period — the one which best displays his subject — for disproportionate treatment: 'That Tacitus should give to Agricola's final campaign more space than he gives to the whole of the narrative of the six preceding years is a clear indication that he regards the battle as the climax of

Agricola's career.'[29] Finally, Agricola's death and its aftermath also receive attention: chapters 43-46 have almost 10% of the whole — more than all the previous ten years.

V: Content analysis of Tacitus' *Agricola*

Chapters	Date (AD)	Lines	Percentage of work
1-3	–	50	5.6
4-9	40-78	113	12.6
10-17	–	164	18.3
18-24	78-82	120	13.4
25-28	83	65	7.2
29-39	84	234	26.1
40-43	84-93	83	9.3
44-46	–	67	7.5

Plutarch covers Cato's early years briefly and then describes the central period of his political career fairly evenly. However, the end of his life gets the greatest attention, over a sixth (17.3%) of the total work.

VI: Content analysis of Plutarch's *Cato Minor*

Chapters	Date (BC)	Topic	Percentage of work
1-7	95-73	Birth, childhood and education	15.0
8-15	72-66	Slave wars, military tribune in Asia	9.2
16-21	66-65	Quaestor	10.3
22-29	64-63	Cicero consul; Catilinarian conspiracy	11.5
30-49	62-56	Pompey and Caesar; Cato in Cyprus	13.8
40-46	55-53	Praetorship	10.3
47-51	52-50	Growing tension	6.9
52-55	49-48	Civil War, Pharsalus	5.7
56-73	47/46	Last days in Africa, death	17.3

Death scenes are a standard feature of biography: 'the final moments of personages and their last words have through the centuries been a common motive in biographical composition' for such scenes are 'always fraught with possibilities, dramatic and melodramatic, for portraying the character of the

29. Martin, *Tacitus*, p. 43.

departed'.[30] The character of Cato is revealed in his final meal and discussion with his friends about philosophy (on Stoic paradoxes and the good man, 67), and in his reading and re-reading of Plato's *Phaedo* (68.2, 70.1). Murrell sees a literary purpose also: 'The last chapters (66-73) provide a charming and memorable close . . . to the energetic and turbulent life of one whose character can provoke the most diverse re-action — admiration and respect, hostility and contempt.'[31] However, in addition to his literary purpose, Plutarch has a moral problem: the principle of divine retribution dictates that bad men's lives and deaths show that crime does not pay and good men's the reverse. An ignominious death after Cato's apparent failure to stop the evil against which he has fought all his life has to be balanced: 'His attempt to prove that the good are rewarded, by relating elaborate funerals for the unjustly afflicted, also seems contrived.'[32] So Cato is declared to be 'Saviour' (σωτῆρα) by the immediate gathering at his door of 300 senators and the people of Utica (71.1). Great honours, decoration and a procession are given to the body, and it is buried near the sea 'where a statue now stands, sword in hand' — a romantic, yet victorious image (71.2). Even his enemy, Caesar, is brought on to speak well of him (72.2). All of this contrives to give a triumphant end to the βίος.

This disproportionate attention to Cato's death may also relate to the genre of *exitus illustrium virorum,* as composed by Capito and Fannius.[33] The tradition of the deaths of philosophers is seen in the *Acts of the Pagan Martyrs.* Geiger demonstrates the similar pattern in the deaths of Cato here and of Thrasea Paetus in Tacitus' *Annals:* both deaths are consciously modelled on the death of Socrates, as is shown by Cato's last reading of Socrates' final dialogue *(Phaedo).*[34] Another extended death scene occurs in Plutarch's *Antony* where we have a 'Last Supper' with friends, with discourse and instruction, on the night before the subject's death (*Ant.* 75), followed by detailed treatment of subsequent events, including Cleopatra's death.[35]

The allocation of space in Suetonius' *Caesars* is arranged topically. Clearly, Suetonius is not trying to provide an even-handed chronological coverage. Instead, the whole of the period up to Augustus' Principate is summarized in a few chapters (5-8), and then we have three main sections on his military, political and personal affairs, before returning to a chronological account of his death and connected events.

---

30. Stuart, *Epochs of Greek and Roman Biography,* p. 245.
31. In his introduction to *LACTOR* 14, p. v.
32. F. E. Brenk, S.J., *In Mist Apparelled,* p. 270.
33. Pliny, *Epistles* VIII.12.4; V.5.3; see p. 74 above.
34. Geiger, 'Munatius Rufus', *Athenaeum,* 1979. pp. 61-5.
35. See Pelling, *Antony,* pp. 16-18, 293-4 and 302-3.

VII: Content analysis of Suetonius' *Divus Augustus*

Chapters	Topic	Percentage of work
1-4	Ancestry and family	3.0
5-8	Birth, early years to accession	3.5
9-25	Wars and military affairs	16.0
26-60	Administration and rule of empire	35.0
61-96	Personal and family matters	36.0
97-101	Death, omens, funeral, will	6.5

Something similar may be observed with Lucian's *Demonax:* the brief section about his life merely mentions his birth and education (3-11), and then we move into portrayal of his character. The main section (12-62) is made up of many stories and anecdotes, each leading up to a pronouncement or saying of the sage.[36] Of course, since the focus of interest in a philosopher is his teaching, this is to be expected.

VIII: Content analysis of Lucian's *Demonax*

Chapters	Topic	Percentage of work
1-2	Preface	6
3-11	Life and character	25
12-62	Anecdotes and sayings	60
63-67	Later years, death, conclusion	9

Philostratus has a brief introduction and account of the early years, but devotes the bulk of his work to the travels of Apollonius and the many philosophical dialogues which he had during them. What sort of period this is supposed to represent and how the years are allocated is impossible to say. Significantly, however, Apollonius' imprisonment, trial and death comprises over a quarter of the work. (See the content analysis on p. 163.)

Clearly, therefore, an even-handed allocation of space is *not* required in βίος literature: one period of the subject's life can dominate, e.g. the Mons Graupius campaign in the *Agricola*. Furthermore, a tenth of the *Agricola*, over a sixth of the *Cato Minor* and a quarter of the *Apollonius of Tyana* are taken up with the person's final days and the events surrounding the death. This makes for very interesting parallels with the last meal and death of Jesus in the gospels and the corresponding disproportionate allocation of space there.

36. See Cancik, 'Bios und Logos', pp. 121-2.

IX: Content analysis of Philostratus' *Apollonius of Tyana*

Chapters	Topic	Percentage of work
I.1-3	Introduction	0.9
I.4-17	Early years	4.0
I.18–VI.43	Travels and dialogues	68.8
VII.1–VIII.7	Imprisonment and trial	21.0
VIII.8-31	Later events, death, appearances, honours	5.3

Our ten examples together show that the allocation of space in βίοι may involve a generally even coverage of the subject's life *(Evagoras)*, but the author may choose instead to emphasize one small period at the expense of others *(Agesilaus, Agricola, Cato Minor)*; he may combine chronological and topical material in roughly equal proportions *(Agesilaus)*, or stress the subject's deeds in a chronological sequence (usually for statesmen, e.g. *Agricola, Atticus*) or put the emphasis on his character and sayings (usually for philosophers, e.g. *Demonax, Apollonius of Tyana*).

D. External Features

1. Mode of Representation

The *Agricola* is in continuous prose narrative, mostly in the third person. It includes two set speeches by Agricola and Calgacus before the crucial battle; Ogilvie notes rhetorical influences in the opening and closing sections (in the style of Cicero), and historical influence in the middle of the work (following Sallust and Livy).[37] The *Cato Minor*, like all of Plutarch's *Lives*, is presented in continuous prose narrative and ordered chronologically. It is designed as a whole and flows smoothly. It too contains many sayings and speeches, mainly reported, with notable exceptions like the final speech (68-9) which lends emphasis to the death scene. Suetonius presents his material in continuous prose also, but differs in the non-chronological sequence of the narrative, preferring to order it by topical sections. Although Lucian's *Demonax* is still prose narrative, the bulk is not continuous, but rather a string of unconnected anecdotes and stories. The *Apollonius of Tyana* is in continuous prose narrative, including blocks of formal dialogue in the manner of philosophical works: e.g., the dialogue on kingship and the Republic with Vespasian (V.32-40) or

37. Ogilvie, introduction to *Agricola*, p. 22.

the discussion with the Egyptian sages (VI.10-21). This is a further indication of the mixed genre of this work. Thus we may conclude that the normal mode of representation for βίοι is prose narrative, often continuous and chronological, but allowing for other modes, especially those of rhetoric, to be inserted.

2. Size

The *Agricola* contains about 7,000 words (896 lines in the *OCT*), too long for a short work, and too short for a long one. As Dorey says: 'The *Agricola* is the right length: short enough for its contents to be assimilated easily and rapidly, but long enough to contain solid material and a wealth of detail.'[38] It thus falls into our category of medium length, if at the shortish end, and it is comparable with the *Agesilaus* and the estimated length of Satyrus' *Euripides*. The *Cato Minor* is about 16,500 words, while its pair, the *Phocion*, is considerably shorter at about 10,000; together they would fill one scroll. The *Cato Minor* is one of Plutarch's longer examples, with only *Antony, Alexander* and *Pompey* being longer, about 19,000-20,000 words. The mismatch in length between the *Cato Minor* and its pair is unusual; Plutarch normally prefers to have both *Lives* of similar length, even if it means padding one to fit the other — for instance, *Fabius* is extended to the length of *Pericles,* and *Publicola* similarly to match its pair, *Solon*. However, all the *Parallel Lives* of Plutarch are of medium length, averaging around 10,000 or 11,000 words each; the shortest pairs are *Sertorius/Eumenes* (about 14,000 words in total) and *Philopoemen/Titus* (about 12,000), with each Life making up about half the total. Suetonius' *Lives of the Caesars* also average about 10,000 words; the longest are *Divus Julius* (12,000 words still existing despite the loss of the opening chapters) and *Augustus* (16,000), while the shortest are the two groups of the Three Emperors of AD 69 and the three Flavians, each group being 10,000 words in total. Our final two examples are rather different, since one is much shorter and the other longer: *Demonax* is just over 3,000 words, whereas Philostratus' *Apollonius of Tyana* is a massive 82,000 words.

We take 'medium length' to mean about a scroll's length for the maximum and two or three works to a scroll for a minimum — about 5,000 to 25,000 words at the very extremes. Lucian's *Demonax* is the shortest of these examples, comparable to the length of Nepos' *Atticus*. In an interesting discussion of the length of βίοι, Geiger suggests that 'political biography in its fully developed form was as a rule a much lengthier literary genre than intel-

---

38. Dorey, '"Agricola" and "Germania"', p. 8.

lectual biography'.[39] This is certainly true of writers like Plutarch, compared with the short *vitae* attached to poets' and writers' manuscripts. The odd one out here is clearly Philostratus, who has given his *Apollonius of Tyana* a length beyond the medium range; significantly, it falls within the range of both longer philosophical works (e.g. Plato's *Republic*, 89,358) and also pseudo-historical/fictional works, like Xenophon's *Cyropaedia* (80,684). Once again, there is a problem in describing the *Apollonius of Tyana* as a βίος.

3. Structure

The *Agricola* has a chronological structure following the main events of Agricola's life, finishing with his death and a laudatory conclusion. Within this basic framework, specific items are given space — such as the disproportionate consideration of the battle of Mons Graupius and the background section on Britain (10-17) inserted into the chronological sequence when Agricola commences his governorship. Similarly, *Cato Minor* begins with the subject's birth, family and childhood, and closes with his death and burial. Unlike many βίοι, chronology is followed very closely here, almost on a year by year basis. This is easier to do for the Life of a politician than for a poet or philosopher; as Hamilton says:

> In general, in composing his biographies, Plutarch relates his hero's career from birth to death in chronological order. But he allows himself a good deal of scope, and the precise arrangement and the amount of space allotted to each topic depends on whether the hero is predominantly an orator, a politician, or a military man, and on the amount of material available to him.[40]

Plutarch even apologizes for inserting a topical item on Cato's relationships with women out of chronological sequence: 'even though this happened later, I decided to anticipate it while recording the topic of his women' (25.5). Geiger believes that such departures from the chronological sequence occur in passages derived from Munatius' ἀπομνημονεύματα or *Memorabilia* about Cato, modelled upon Xenophon and thus less chronologically ordered.[41]

Suetonius, on the other hand, has only the barest chronological frame-

---

39. Geiger, *Cornelius Nepos*, pp. 26-9 and 34-5; quotation from p. 28.

40. Hamilton, *Alexander*, p. xxxix; see also, Russell, 'On Reading Plutarch's *Lives*', *Greece and Rome* 13 (1966), p. 149.

41. Geiger, 'Munatius Rufus', *Athenaeum*, 1979, pp. 56-7.

work, beginning with the emperor's ancestry and family and his accession at the start, and his death and related events at the end; the bulk comprises topical sections on his virtues and vices, foreign campaigns and policy, administration at home and so on.[42] Lucian is even less chronological: we move straight from Demonax' birth and education (chapters 3-5) into anecdotes about his character (5-10) and a loosely connected sequence of stories and sayings (12-62). As Cancik notes, the *Demonax* is more loosely structured with less integration of teaching and activity than even Mark's gospel.[43] Philostratus provides a seemingly chronological account of his hero's travels, but there is little dating: any story of a set of journeys will appear chronological. Meyer sees the chronology of the account as 'das Werk des Philostratos'.[44] All these authors return to chronology to describe the subject's last days and death, closing with the funeral or honours given, or with an evaluation of their subject. Cox sees a similar pattern in later biography:

> The only structural statement one can make to characterize the genre as a whole is a very simple one: the Graeco-Roman biography of the holy man is a narrative that relates incidents in the life of its subject from birth or youth to death. The hero's activities provide points of reference for the insertion of material not always related in an obvious way to the narrative's presumed biographical purpose.[45]

Thus, βίοι have a basic chronological framework, possibly little more than the birth or public arrival as a start, and death as the end, with topical material inserted; βίοι of statesmen or generals (Agricola, Cato, Evagoras, Agesilaus, Atticus) tend to be more chronological, whereas philosophical (Demonax, Apollonius) or literary (Euripides) βίοι are more likely to be topically arranged.

4. Scale

The scale of the *Agricola* is quite broad in that it includes some of the history, geography and ethnography of Britain. Although some classicists cite this as

---

42. See Wallace-Hadrill, *Suetonius*, pp. 10-15.

43. Cancik, 'Bios und Logos', p. 128; also, Jones, *Culture and Society*, pp. 91-3.

44. Meyer, 'Apollonius von Tyana', *Hermes*, 1917, p. 405; see also, Petzke, *Die Traditionen*, pp. 51-62.

45. Cox, *Biography in Late Antiquity*, p. 55; also, Berger, 'Hellenistische Gattungen im NT', *ANRW* II.25.2, p. 1239.

an argument against its being βίος,[46] the scale is narrower than that of a true historical monograph or geographical treatise like Tacitus' *Germania*. Therefore, suggestions that the *Agricola*, or the Britain section (10-17), was originally intended for a historical work are not convincing.[47] The scale is still focussed upon Agricola, and any departure from this is best explained as furthering understanding of the subject himself. The limitation of scale is particularly marked in the *Cato Minor,* where the focus is concentrated on the subject, despite all the major events of the end of the Republic which were happening around him. For instance, at the battle of Dyrrachium, we are told about Cato's speech encouraging the men and about his weeping over the mutual slaughter of Romans (54.5-7), but nothing about this very significant battle itself, for which Plutarch refers us to his *Pompey* (54.6). He often gives cross references to other *Lives* for events not concerning Cato himself (e.g. to the *Elder Cato* in 1.1, or 73.4 for the death of Cato's daughter related in *Brutus* 13 and 53). Suetonius' topical arrangement of his works naturally limits the scale to the subject, because it is his virtues or vices and military or administrative skills which are being described. Lucian's anecdotal approach entails a limited scope with each story being about Demonax himself.

The work with more extraneous material and a wider scale is the *Apollonius of Tyana* again. Philostratus includes geographical, historical or ethnographical background at various points. As Anderson says, 'where the *Life* differs most . . . is in its sheer scale: here it stands side by side with the largest of sophistic novels'.[48] This is clearly somewhat different from the generic feature noted in our other βίοι, that the scale is limited to the subject and his concerns.

5. Literary Units

The *Agricola* is a carefully written coherent whole, without obviously separate literary units. However, there are several different structural units: personal anecdote (e.g. his mother's response to his early passion for philosophy, chapter 4); units of geographical description (10), speeches (Calgacus, 30-32; Agricola, 33-34);[49] stories (e.g. the desertion of the cohort of Usipi, 28) — all

46. See commentaries by Furneaux, pp. 8f.; Furneaux-Anderson, pp. xxiii-xxviii; Ogilvie, pp. 14-16; and Goodyear, *Tacitus,* pp. 4-5.

47. Andresen's theory, *Festschrift d. Gymn. zum grauen Kloster,* Berlin, 1874; see Furneaux-Anderson, p. xxiii; and Ogilvie, p. 15, n. 1.

48. G. Anderson, *Philostratus,* p. 229.

49. See Martin, *Tacitus,* pp. 43-5 on speeches in *Agricola.*

of which are typical of both historical writing and βίος. The *Cato Minor* is also written as a continuous whole; the early years do use anecdotes, with some of them leading up to a notable saying of Cato (e.g. his desire as a boy of fourteen to slay Sulla, chapter 3; or about his habit of silence, 4). Other units include direct and indirect speeches, larger anecdotes and separate stories. However, the *Lives* differ in the type of literary units used according to Plutarch's desired emphasis or sources available. Thus the *Phocion* and *Cato Maior* have many apophthegms, the *Alcibiades* and *Alexander* more personal details, and the *Caesar* historical and tragic elements.[50]

Lucian and Philostratus betray their units more clearly, and are often compared with the gospels. The main unit of the *Demonax* is termed by Lucian 'λελεγμένων' (chapter 12): such 'sayings' comprise units of about fifty words, beginning with a vague phrase to introduce or place the story, e.g. 'when . . . ', introducing a character who says or does something which leads to the actual saying of Demonax. Such units are basic to biographical writing from Aristotle onwards: variously termed ἀποφθέγματα, γνῶμαι, παραδείγματα and χρεῖαι, they have excited the interest of biblical scholars as possible parallels to synoptic 'pronouncement-story' forms, and much work has been done on their analysis and classification.[51] In addition, units which may be seen as 'legends' or 'miracle-stories' are found in *Apollonius of Tyana*.

It is clear, therefore, that all our examples are formed from a similar range of literary units of stories and anecdotes, sayings and speeches, with some being rather carefully composed while others are more of a loose connection of units.

6. Use of Sources

Tacitus had access to several types of sources: oral family tradition and personal memory, Agricola's own notes, senatorial records and letters, and other writers for geographical and historical background (such as Strabo, Pliny, Varro, Caesar, Livy).[52] Like other authors of βίοι, he makes a selection from

50. See Gossage, 'Plutarch', pp. 58-9; and Pelling, 'Plutarch's Adaptation', *JHS* 1980, pp. 136-8.

51. For Aristotle, see pp. 69-70 above, and Momigliano, *Development*, pp. 72-3; for chreia and *Demonax*, see Cancik, 'Bios und Logos', p. 122, and Jones, *Culture and Society*, pp. 91-3; on chreia generally, see R. C. Tannehill (ed.), *Pronouncement Stories*, *Semeia* 20 (1981), and *The Chreia in Ancient Rhetoric*, ed. R. F. Hock and E. N. O'Neil (Atlanta: Scholars Press, 1986).

52. For personal memory, see 'saepe ex eo audivi', *Agricola* 24.3; for other sources, see Forni's commentary, pp. 51-5.

these for his desired portrait of his subject. Thus Dorey argues that Tacitus' portrayal of Domitian's hatred for Agricola is historically false: Tacitus is keen to prevent his father-in-law being seen as a friend of the tyrant, and so 'to make good his case he would naturally ignore anything that might interfere with his chosen interpretation of the facts'.[53] Whether or not one agrees with Dorey's interpretation, the latitude allowed to the writer of a βίος in his use of sources is clear.

Plutarch also uses a wide range of oral and written sources. He read widely in Greek literature, but less so in Latin, since he states that he learned it later in life and was never completely fluent (*Demosth.* 2.2-4). Hamilton has counted 150 historians (including forty in Latin) cited by Plutarch in the *Moralia* and *Lives*.[54] Likewise, Pelling considers that there are some twenty-five sources behind the seven late Republican Lives *(Lucullus, Pompey, Crassus, Cicero, Cato Minor, Brutus, Antony),* including historical authors (especially Pollio), other βίοι, memoirs, contemporary primary sources, letters and documents, and oral sources.[55] To these, Geiger adds Plutarch's use of Thrasea Paetus' and Munatius' *Lives* of Cato.[56] Such a wide range is striking, and, as a writer of βίοι, Plutarch had greater latitude in use of sources than was often the case for historians.[57] This would have caused difficulties: as Pelling points out, a modern scholar can work with many books and papers strewn all over the study floor, constantly checking and comparing different authorities; papyrus scrolls without chapter headings and indexes are a different matter.[58] Like the Elder Pliny (as described by his nephew in *Epist.* III.5), Plutarch would have read widely first, with some note-taking, and then followed one main source when writing, supplemented by notes and memory. Such a method allows for great selectivity of material, and an account of an incident in one *Life* is sometimes contradicted by another. Although this can be explained by poor memory, more often it is because he wants to tell the story this way this time to illustrate this particular person's character. While Plutarch did not allow himself wholesale fabrication (as happened in enco-

53. Dorey, 'Agricola and Domitian', pp. 66-71, quotation from p. 71; see also, '"Agricola" and "Germania"', pp. 5ff.

54. Hamilton, *Alexander*, p. xliii; on Plutarch's sources, see Jones, *Plutarch and Rome*, pp. 81-7; and Gossage, 'Plutarch', pp. 51-7.

55. Pelling, 'Plutarch's Method', *JHS* 1979, pp. 83-90; for *Antony*, see his commentary, pp. 26-31.

56. Geiger, 'Munatius Rufus', *Athenaeum*, 1979, pp. 48-72.

57. See Pelling, 'Truth and Fiction in Plutarch's *Lives*', esp. pp. 28-9; also, Momigliano, *Development*, pp. 56-7.

58. See Pelling, 'Plutarch's Method', *JHS*, 1979, esp. pp. 91-6, and *Antony*, pp. 31-3.

mium or invective), he does have an element of imaginative 'creative recon-struction' of the truth as he saw it, in order to illustrate the way 'it must have been'.[59]

Suetonius had access to many sources, including documents in the im-perial archives and the letters of Augustus, from which he quotes freely and frequently. His scholastic and secretarial training is evident as he compares and criticizes different accounts to discover the truth. However, detailed dis-cussion of his sources and quotations from emperors' letters decline through the sequence of the *Caesars;* this may reflect limited access, possibly as a result of his dismissal.[60] Philostratus details his sources: traditions from the various cities which Apollonius visited, accounts and letters, as well as the works of his predecessors Maximus of Aegeae, Moiragenes (the 'standard work when Philostratus wrote') and the disputed Damis himself, all of which he claims to have brought together (ξυνήγαγον) carefully (1.3).[61] Conversely, personal knowledge of his subject is used by Lucian, having been Demonax' student for a long period (chapter 1).

7. Methods of Characterization

Direct analysis of Agricola's character comes only in the concluding chapters praising him (*Agr.* 44-46). Elsewhere, character is depicted through the de-scription of events (e.g. his skill in both governing and war, chapter 20) and by the imputation of motives and thoughts ('ceterum animorum provinciae prudens . . .', 19.1). Tacitus uses the latter method regularly in the *Annals* to de-pict the character of emperors like Tiberius. The description of words and deeds is typically ancient: Tacitus says his predecessors 'clarorum virorum facta moresque posteris tradere' (1.1) and concludes by commending Agricola's 'omnia facta dictaque' to his wife and daughter. Martin sees this as typical: 'The way in which a man's "deeds and ways" *(facta moresque)* are re-lated to the ideal of *virtus* is a cardinal element in all Tacitus' writings.'[62] Characterization is thus through the unfolding of the narrative itself.[63]

The classic statement about how character can be discerned from even minor actions comes from Plutarch's introduction to *Alexander and Caesar,*

---

59. See Pelling, 'Truth and Fiction', and *Antony,* pp. 33-6.
60. See Wallace-Hadrill, *Suetonius,* pp. 88-96, and Baldwin, *Suetonius,* pp. 101-213.
61. Bowie, 'Apollonius of Tyana', *ANRW* II.16.2, p. 1673; see n. 18 above, on Damis.
62. Martin, *Tacitus,* p. 41.
63. See Stuart, *Epochs of Greek and Roman Biography,* p. 248.

already discussed. Hamilton has analysed how this works out in the *Alexander* itself:

> Plutarch's artistry consists largely in the way in which he skilfully employs these different methods of illustrating character in combination. Direct statement is confirmed by anecdote, and the major events are related in such a fashion that attention is concentrated on the person of Alexander and the biographer's conception of him gradually emerges through the narrative.[64]

Similarly, in the *Cato Minor*, Plutarch says that small signs of character (τὰ μικρὰ τῶν ἠθῶν σημεῖα) are a good image of the soul (εἰκόνα ψυχῆς, 24.1); indeed, 'such small incidents shed as much light on the manifestation and understanding of character' (πρὸς ἔνδειξιν ἤθους καὶ κατανόησιν) as great and public ones and therefore deserve extended treatment (37.5). Equally in the parallel *Life*, we are told that small events, 'such as a word or a nod' (καὶ ῥῆμα καὶ νεῦμα), are more important than lengthy writing (*Phocion* 5.4). Thus the character of Cato is portrayed through anecdotes, sayings and stories: concern for others through the story of the boy Cato helping a playmate (2.5-6); his self-discipline and obedience to the law in his campaigning for office (8.1-2); his attention to his duties (18) and so on. Direct description (e.g. his character as a child, 1.2-3) is rare, except in comparison with others: 'the character of a hero may be clarified by a succession of comparisons'.[65] Although no formal σύγκρισις exists in the *Cato Minor/Phocion* pair, direct comment on Cato's character and achievement is found in *Phocion* chapter 3.

Suetonius says his non-chronological, topical approach ('neque per tempora sed per species') is to make things clearer ('distinctius', *Div. Aug.* 9), so we might expect direct characterization. The basic categories in all the *Caesars* are military affairs, consulships and offices, general conduct, and virtues and vices, but 'Suetonius' virtue and vice chapters are not to be understood primarily as a means of distinguishing character'.[66] Although we have brief description of the emperor's personal appearance (e.g. *Div. Aug.* 79-80), there is little direct analysis of character: it emerges from the overall account of deeds and words as in our other βίοι, despite the topical arrangement. Lucian considers Demonax' manner of life and temperament in chapters 6-8, but then shows these qualities in all the anecdotes and sayings which follow. Philostratus has a brief comparison of Apollonius' character with other phi-

---

64. Hamilton, *Alexander*, pp. xlii-xliii; see also Gossage, 'Plutarch', pp. 58-60.
65. Russell, 'On Reading', p. 150; see also, Pelling, 'Synkrisis'.
66. Wallace-Hadrill, *Suetonius*, pp. 143-4.

losophers, as he moves from the travels to his imprisonment and trial at Rome (VII.1-4). Elsewhere, however, character emerges from the vast fund of stories about his subject. Thus, we conclude from all our βίοι that the methods of characterization were primarily indirect, through narration of the subject's words and deeds.

8. Summary

The external, structural pattern here confirms that of our early βίοι. Philostratus' *Apollonius of Tyana* diverges most with its excessive length and broader scale. We conclude, therefore, that βίοι are works in prose narrative, often continuous, though not always (e.g. *Demonax*), and of medium length, 5,000 to 25,000 words; into a bare chronological framework of birth/arrival and death are inserted more chronological narrative (especially for statesmen — e.g. Plutarch) and topical material (especially for philosophers or literary men, or as in Suetonius' approach); the scale is narrowly focussed on the subject; a similar range of literary units is used, notably anecdotes, stories, speeches and sayings, taken from a wide range of oral and written sources to display the subject's character indirectly through words and deeds.

E. Internal Features

1. Setting

The geographical settings of the *Agricola* can be as diverse as Anglesey (chapter 18), a hill-side in Scotland (Mons Graupius, 29-38) or the streets of Rome (43), but they all provide a background for Agricola. Even the section concerning Britain (10-17) provides further background for the hero. The *Cato Minor* begins in Rome, moves to Asia for his military tribunate (chapters 9-15), returns to Rome with Cato, then to Cyprus to sort out Ptolemy (34-39), back to Rome again and finally follows the Civil War to Greece and Africa. If the subject was mobile, then so is the setting; indeed, we traverse not just all the known world of the Mediterranean but even beyond, to the unknown climes of India in the footsteps of Apollonius.

As for the dramatic setting, Agricola is usually on stage in person, and he dominates things when absent. Similarly, Plutarch's focus is always on Cato, even when the action is elsewhere; then we wait with Cato for news to arrive (e.g. his not knowing the fate of Pompey after Pharsalus, 55.2, or hearing of the defeat at Thapsus three days later, 58.7). In Suetonius, the topical arrangement of material ensures that 'the subject is always at the centre of the stage. Subsidiary characters enter and exit; they are never developed.'[67] Demonax too is at the centre of the anecdotes as different people come to debate with him; indeed, in such a loosely structured work, this constant focus of the dramatic setting provides a much needed unity. Thus it is clear from all our examples that the subject is the focus of the settings.

2. Topics

Anderson notes similar topical material in Lucian and Philostratus: 'This assembly of parallels can be seen in two ways: either they indicate a common tradition, which would then certainly be a Pythagorean biography, or we are dealing once more with similar mosaics of rhetorical topoi.'[68] We use our previous analysis:

(a) Ancestry

Tacitus mentions Agricola's city, grandfathers, father and mother (*Agr.* 4). Similarly, Plutarch refers to Cato's great-grandfather, the Elder Cato; as Pelling says regarding *Antony:* 'Plutarch deals with his subject's γένος even when there is little to say.'[69] Lucian and Philostratus name the origin of their subjects' family: Cyprus (τὸ μὲν γένος Κύπριος, *Dem.* 3) and Tyana (Ἀπολλωνίῳ τοίνυν πατρὶς μὲν ἦν Τύανα πόλις Ἑλλὰς, *Ap.* I.4). Suetonius always begins with the emperor's family background, except for *Titus* and *Domitian,* where it is covered in the previous *Life* of their father, Vespasian.

(b) Birth

There are no accounts of the births of Agricola, Cato or Demonax. For a really good birth story, we turn to *Apollonius,* with its account of his mother's vision of Proteus and the dance of the swans (I.4-6), which Petzke relates to the birth of Jesus and his ancestry.[70] Suetonius describes the place of Augustus' birth and the shrine built there subsequently in *Div. Aug.* 5-6.

---

67. Baldwin, *Suetonius*, p. 513.
68. G. Anderson, *Studies in Lucian's Comic Fiction*, p. 93.
69. Pelling, *Antony*, p. 117.
70. Petzke, *Die Traditionen*, pp. 162-5.

(c) Boyhood and education

Agricola's ancestry and education are covered briefly with a single story, Agricola's mother's opposition to his early love of philosophy (all in chapter 4). Plutarch has an anecdote about Pompaedius Silo holding the four-year-old Cato out of the window in an attempt to frighten him, and also includes the common motif of childhood play portending the man, with Cato's concern for his unjustly imprisoned playmate (2). Then we have stories of his education under Sarpedon and Antipater the Stoic. The philosophical education of Demonax (I.4-5) and Apollonius (I.7-13) is important for their development.

(d) Great deeds

Agricola's skills in both military strategy and provincial administration are illustrated immediately on his arrival in Britain (18-21). Most of the *Cato Minor* consists of stories relating his great deeds. Suetonius arranges his account of the emperors' deeds under his various headings. As with most philosophers, Demonax' greatness is expressed more in mighty words, seeing a situation and coming up with precisely the right comment (12-62). So too with Apollonius, except that as a miracle-worker, his great deeds are also recorded, like the miraculous removal of his fetters in prison (VII.38); the sheer amount of travelling may also be seen as a mighty deed.

(e) Virtues

In most of our examples, virtues emerge from the account of deeds. Suetonius, however, devotes large parts of his works to direct analysis of the virtues and vices of the emperor, both in his public life and his personal affairs.[71]

(f) Death and consequences

All these works conclude with the subject's death. Agricola's death is carefully described, together with the emperor's interest in it (43); there may be some influence here from the genre of *exitus illustrium virorum*. Cato's death is very detailed, even down to the final minutes (66-70). Suetonius usually has graphic details or memorable last words; as Baldwin points out, 'four assassinations, one lynching, two suicides, two suspected poisonings, and three

---

71. See further Wallace-Hadrill, *Suetonius*, pp. 142-74.

probably natural deaths ought to summon forth the best in any writer'.[72] Subsequent events often include the funeral, and any particular honours accorded are also mentioned, e.g. Demonax' public funeral, honours and garlands, *Dem.* 67.[73] Cato's funeral is described, and honours are bestowed on his body by the inhabitants of Utica, including a statue (71). Suetonius records a praetor seeing Augustus ascending into heaven after his cremation (*Div. Aug.* 100). Finally, Philostratus reports appearances of Apollonius after his death to assure his doubting followers; the different versions of his departure include his assumption into heaven and an appearance to a doubting young man. Philostratus says he has never found any tomb for Apollonius (VIII.30-31). Petzke compares this death and subsequent appearances to those of Jesus.[74]

Thus, βίοι contain a common range of topics and motifs which are not necessarily prescriptive, with some missing in some works, but which make up a commonly recognized group when taken all together.

3. Style

Tacitus was well trained in rhetoric and would also become a leading historiographer, so it is not surprising that this blend of oratory and history should be discerned in his first work: the influence of rhetoric, especially Cicero, upon the opening and concluding sections, and of history, notably Sallust and Livy, upon the rest has already been noted.[75] Such influences can be traced in both stylistic devices and in echoes in vocabulary and technique from Livy, Sallust and Vergil: 'As regards the general literary style of the treatise, we see the beginning of the development which gradually led Tacitus farther and farther away from the popular language of his time till he reached the lofty and strongly individual style of the *Annals*.'[76] One feature showing that public reading was intended is the use of pithy epigrams at the end of a section to give a 'pause for applause', many of which remain as well-known sayings, e.g. the damning indictment of the 'pacification' of Roman imperial-

---

72. Baldwin, *Suetonius,* p. 508.

73. Cancik discusses Demonax' death, 'Bios und Logos', p. 128.

74. Petzke, *Die Traditionen,* pp. 183-7. For his tomb, see the Adana inscription suggesting that it is in Tyana: Bowie, 'Apollonius of Tyana', *ANRW* II.16.2, pp. 1687-8, and C. P. Jones, 'An Epigram on Apollonius of Tyana', *JHS* 100 (1980), pp. 190-4; for an alternative reconstruction, see N. J. Richardson and Peter Burian, *GRBS* 22 (1981), pp. 283-5.

75. Ogilvie, *Agricola,* pp. 21-2.

76. Furneaux-Anderson, p. lxxxiii; for style, see pp. lxxx-lxxxvii, and commentaries by Gudeman, pp. 15-29; Ogilvie, pp. 21-31; and Goodyear, *Tacitus,* pp. 4-5.

ism from Calgacus, 'a wilderness they create, and peace they call it!', 'solitudinem faciunt pacem appellant'.[77]

Plutarch did not follow the contemporary trend of attempting to recreate classical Attic style; his writing draws upon the vocabulary of historiography, rhetoric and moral philosophy, but it remains a form of Koiné, albeit rather literary. He uses the optative (typical of Attic) rather sparingly, but, like Satyrus, he avoids hiatus; his style is more popular and easier to read than that of Tacitus, yet higher than Satyrus'.[78] *Demonax* is also rhetorical writing on a popular level, with a simple and clear style.[79] Suetonius' style is different again, very simple yet precise, often using technical language and accurate quotation from his sources: 'It is the businesslike style of the ancient scholar'.[80] Finally, Philostratus, despite his claim of imperial patronage, is still aiming for an audience which likes a story, and the style befits popular narrative. Thus we conclude that while βίοι could be written in a high literary style, they can have a large element of the popular also.

4. Atmosphere

From the four features of tone, mood, attitude and values, a fairly serious atmosphere emerged for early βίοι, with the exception of Satyrus. A similar atmosphere is seen in Tacitus and Plutarch. The tone of the *Agricola* is fairly serious and respectful. The mood varies according to the story: rejoicing at the dawn of the new age after Domitian's terror in chapter 3, or horror at those recent events in 45, or desolation after the battle in 38. The attitude to the subject is one of respect and, in some places, eulogy (e.g. 46). The values put forward are the traditional Roman values — virtue, courage and piety — together with Tacitus' concern not for vainglorious opposition to bad emperors, but for moderation and the public good (chapter 42), to which themes he returns in the *Annals. Cato Minor* is also serious, its tone reflecting the serious events of the end of the Republic; perhaps Plutarch sympathized with Cato's unsuccessful battle with Fate to prevent the overthrow of the Re-

77. *Agricola* 30.5; see Ogilvie's commentary, p. 30; on the question of truth and fiction in βίοι, while Tacitus has obviously created the saying in Calgacus' mouth, the truth of its challenge has been made clear in our own recent times, perhaps even more than in Roman days.

78. Wardman calls the *Lives* 'popular history' in *Plutarch's Lives*, p. 37; see also Hamilton, *Alexander*, pp. lxvi-lxix on style.

79. 'Die Sprache ist schlicht, klar, einfach', Cancik, 'Bios und Logos', p. 121; see also, Baldwin, *Studies in Lucian*, pp. 72-3.

80. Wallace-Hadrill, *Suetonius*, p. 19; see further pp. 19-25 for Suetonius' style.

public (*Phocion* 3). The mood is somewhat stern and moralistic, almost austere, reflecting perhaps the character of Cato himself. The attitude to the subject is mainly respectful and reverent, as befits one of the last great Romans of the Republic. Yet Cato does not escape without criticism, e.g. for rejecting Pompey's overtures of marriage and thus driving him to an alliance with Caesar (30.6) or his refusal to wear a tunic and shoes when acting as praetor (44.1).[81] The values reflect those of Cato, a mixture of traditional republican values with those of Stoic moral philosophy. Plutarch's own moral and philosophical values may be seen occasionally countering Cato's values such as never compromising (as in his preventing Caesar's triumph in 31.6) or doing so only reluctantly (taking the oath in 32.3-6).

While the usual atmosphere for a βίος is thus somewhat heavy, Lucian is quite different: the tone is never really serious, but he enjoys good witty banter in a generally light-hearted mood. The attitude to the subject is apparent approval of him and of his values of philosophical detachment, but the reader is not exhorted to follow suit as in our previous examples — indeed, one is never quite sure how seriously to take any of it. The atmosphere of *Apollonius* lies somewhere in between these extremes. On the one hand, there is much that is serious and respectful, even eulogistic about Philostratus' approach. The mood is confident in Apollonius' superiority and in the values of later pagan philosophy, but the attraction of the good yarn or interesting story has a constant lightening effect. A similar effect is obtained in Suetonius, where the material is often quite serious, about matters of state; equally, his portrayal of the emperor's virtues and vices indicates a serious moralistic concern. However, the easy style, the racy anecdotes and snatches of court gossip mean that the atmosphere is quite different from Tacitus' or Plutarch's. Thus we may conclude that although the atmosphere of βίοι, derived from the tone, mood, attitude and values tends to be mostly serious and respectful, even encomiastic in some, it can be much lighter in others.

5. Quality of Characterization

The question of stereotype arises here too; Agricola's character is sometimes thought to be overdone, almost too good to be true:

---

81. Plutarch's own criticisms must be distinguished from criticism by others, especially Caesar (e.g. about Cato's drinking and dice playing, meanness or greed in 6, or over his marriage, 52.4), where Plutarch is rebutting the charges (see 11.4, 52.4); see Wardman, *Plutarch's Lives*, pp. 195-6.

So in the *Agricola* a coherent picture of a devoted public servant emerges which is contrasted with the jealous despotism of Domitian. Qualities are attributed to Agricola which are as much conventional hall-marks of the good soldier and the good administrator as particular characteristics of the man himself.[82]

Dorey suggests that Agricola is the 'prototype of a stock character that Tacitus portrays in his later works, the great soldier who falls a victim to the emperor whose jealousy he has incurred', such as Corbulo and Germanicus; so he is endowed with qualities of practical wisdom, statesmanship and fairness, as well as military skill.[83] Nonetheless, the picture of Agricola is convincing and attractive, with enough of the individual and the personal to make it credible, such as his needing to be rescued by his mother from the temptation to drink more deeply of the 'studium philosophiae' than was permissible for a senator (4.3).[84] Something similar happens with Lucian, where the temptation to stereotype is strongest in character analysis: thus the description of Demonax' character is fairly stereotypical (6-11), whereas the picture that emerges from the actual anecdotes has a more 'real' and individual feel about it, as also noted in *Atticus*.

One of Plutarch's main purposes in the *Lives* is to display character, and Cato is depicted clearly as a brilliant, yet rather austere and isolated, conservative figure who never quite manages to control political life, but who has a great effect from the sidelines. This picture begins with Cato as a child (1.2-3) and is developed through the various anecdotes and events, until suicide in the face of defeat is seen as the final evidence of his nobility. Suggestions about the ancients' belief in fixed and unchanging character are still expressed in the secondary literature about Plutarch.[85] However, in the *Lives* there is evidence of character change, for instance in Philip V (*Aratus* 51.4, 54.2) or Sertorius (*Sert.* 10.2-5). Some Plutarchean scholars talk therefore of character 'unfolding' or say that 'Plutarch did not entirely accept the thesis that character was basically unchangeable'.[86] Gill's contrast of character and personality has been mentioned already; modern concern is for psychological personality, whereas Plutarch is interested in moral character as

---

82. Ogilvie, introduction to *Agricola*, p. 20.

83. Dorey, "'Agricola' and 'Germania'", pp. 9-11.

84. See also Martin, *Tacitus*, p. 48, on 'personal information'.

85. 'It is often said that the Greeks and Romans did not conceive of changes of character as the moderns do', Wardman, *Plutarch's Lives*, p. 132; see similarly, Brenk, *In Mist Apparelled*, p. 176; Russell, 'On Reading Plutarch's *Lives*', p. 145; Gossage, 'Plutarch', p. 66.

86. Gossage, 'Plutarch', p. 66; Brenk, *In Mist Apparelled*, p. 177.

he gives examples of virtue and vice — 'for him, as for Aristotle, *ēthos* means 'character' in an evaluative sense, excellence or defectiveness'.[87] This view does allow for development, of the child forming the character (hence the anecdotes about boyhood and education) or the adult reforming his character. Even so, Plutarch does find it difficult to grapple with good character becoming evil (as with Philip or Sertorius). Pelling sees the issue in more literary terms. The moralistic approach is quite clearly there in some *Lives,* such as the *Cato Minor;* others, however, have less moral concern, preferring real psychological interest in the characters, notably *Antony.*[88] Plutarch's characters are very 'integrated', so that their 'different qualities cluster very naturally. . . . The infant Cato is determined, humourless, and intense, and it is not difficult to see how these early traits group naturally with those which develop later, the political inflexibility, the philosophy, the bizarre treatment of his women.'[89]

Thus we should beware of looking for modern concepts of character and psychological analysis in either the gospels or Graeco-Roman βίοι. Instead, we may find some quite carefully drawn characters — some stereotypical and others more realistic — emerging through the narratives.

6. Social Setting and Occasion

Here we are looking for internal clues indicating the social setting. The *Agricola* reveals its setting among the educated upper classes of Roman public life, possibly intended to be read at a dinner party or similar gathering: this is demonstrated by the style and atmosphere, as well as by the *sententiae,* the pithy little maxims concluding each section with a rhetorical flourish. The anecdotal style of the *Demonax* also lends itself to oral delivery, probably in a popular setting or even a public performance, with audience reaction (laughter?) after each story. However, the text itself concludes that from these stories, readers (τοῖς ἀναγινώσκουσι) can deduce what kind of man Demonax was (*Dem.* 67).

Plutarch also reveals his intended audience among the Graeco-Roman educated classes. Wardman concludes from the individuals named and the

---

87. C. Gill, 'The Question of Character-Development', *CQ* 33 (1983), p. 472; see also, his 'Character-Personality Distinction' discussed on p. 120 above.

88. Pelling, 'Plutarch's Adaptation', *JHS* (1980), pp. 136-9, and *Antony,* pp. 12-6.

89. 'Aspects of Plutarch's Characterisation', *ICS* 13.2 (1988), pp. 257-74, quotation from p. 263; see also his 'Childhood and Personality in Greek Biography', in *Characterization and Individuality,* pp. 213-44.

general attitude displayed towards the masses that 'Plutarchean biography was not, in the first place, designed as a *popular* work, without qualification'.[90] Instead, the audience was probably intended to be a circle of 'friends' among the wealthy and educated. The easier style without the rhetorical flourishes suggests that the *Parallel Lives* were intended to be read rather than declaimed. Since Plutarch regularly explains Roman institutions and words, his work was probably intended more for Greeks, despite its dedication to a Roman, Q. Sosius Senecio;[91] perhaps he hoped to stimulate his compatriots to take part in public life. If Philostratus' claim to have been commissioned by the Empress Julia Domna, as a member of her circle, is true, this too sets us firmly in an upper social setting.[92] However, Philostratus adds that he wants to correct widespread ignorance about Apollonius, so a wider audience is intended (I.2-3). A wider social circle may be discerned in Suetonius also: Wallace-Hadrill remarks that his social standpoint is disputed, with some seeing him in a senatorial setting like Tacitus, through to others who see him as representing 'the "man in the street", the reader of the gutter press with a taste for the sensational and sordid'.[93] He suggests that the text reveals the interests of the scholar and the equites, rather than the senate.

We conclude that although these βίοι reflect a social setting within the upper classes, there is evidence within the texts that βίοι can have a variety of social settings and occasions, including those of a more popular level.

7. Authorial Intention and Purpose

We follow the same analysis of intentions as in the last chapter.

(a) Encomiastic

Tacitus' desire to praise is clear at the start, 'hic liber honori Agricolae soceri mei destinatus' (3.3), and again at the end, particularly in the apostrophe of Agricola 'Tu vero felix, Agricola' (45.3). Thus Gudeman, Cousin and Shuler have seen both the intention and genre in encomiastic terms. If we look for other features of a *laudatio*, Ogilvie tells us, 'it lacks some of the fundamental

---

90. Wardman, *Plutarch's Lives*, p. 37, his italics.
91. Pelling, *Antony*, p. 8; for Plutarch's circle, see Jones, *Plutarch and Rome*, pp. 39-64.
92. See G. Anderson, *Philostratus*, pp. 4-7.
93. Wallace-Hadrill, *Suetonius*, p. 99; see also pp. 100-118.

elements'; we should not 'be misled into seeing the *Agricola* as a special kind of "biographical encomium" or as a literary variant of the funeral laudation'.[94] This is just one of its purposes.

(b) Exemplary

Plutarch's stated aim is to portray moral character (*Cato Minor* 24.1; 37.5). As Pelling says, Plutarch's 'theory is clear and consistent. Biography will often concentrate on personal details, and may abbreviate its historical narrative; its concern will be the portrayal of character, and its ultimate purpose will be protreptic and moral.'[95] By imitating (μίμησις) the virtues and avoiding the vices described, the reader will improve his own character (see *Pericles* 1, *Aem. Paul.* 1). This moralistic and didactic exemplary concern for ἦθος and ἀρετή is seen explicitly in the comparison of Cato with Phocion (*Phoc.* 3.3-5).[96] Lucian also aims to provide an example (παράδειγμα) and pattern (κανών) for the young to follow (*Dem.* 2).[97]

(c) Informative

Philostratus states that he wishes to correct people's ignorance (τὴν τῶν πολλῶν ἄγνοιαν) with a true account from which they may learn (I.2-3). Wallace-Hadrill sees this as important for Suetonius, distinguishing the *Caesars* from history: 'It is not history at all. It is biography, written by a scholar in the hellenistic tradition, composed neither to instruct nor to titillate but to inform.'[98]

(d) Entertainment value

Lucian was a professional entertainer and the *Demonax* has satirical undercurrents; likewise, the Apollonius has elements of a good novelistic read in places. Suetonius is often read for his entertainment value: 'The final proof of

---

94. *Agricola*, pp. 12-13; see also, Stuart, *Epochs*, p. 236: 'One must go to extravagant lengths if the *Agricola* is to be reconciled with the normal pattern of encomium.'

95. Pelling, 'Plutarch's Adaptation', *JHS* (1980), p. 135; see also, Russell, *Plutarch*, p. 115.

96. See Wardman, *Plutarch's Lives*, pp. 37 and 47-8; also Hamilton, *Alexander*, pp. xxxvii-xxxix; Brenk, *In Mist Apparelled*, p. 184; Gossage, 'Plutarch', p. 65; Jones, *Plutarch and Rome*, p. 105.

97. See Cancik, 'Bios und Logos', pp. 124-5.

98. Wallace-Hadrill, *Suetonius*, p. 25.

Suetonius' success must be that he is intensely readable.'[99] Connected with this are Tacitus' literary intentions, such as portraying the 'noble savage' against imperial might (see especially Calgacus' speech, 30-32). As Dorey reminds us: 'The *Agricola* represents Tacitus' first attempt at the production of a work of literature.'[100] Similarly, many of Plutarch's *Lives* have various literary intents: for example, *Antony* is full of dramatic and tragic motifs.[101] Plutarch's rhetorical training and skill are demonstrated by his early orations on Alexander, Athens and Rome,[102] and these skills appear in the *Lives*, helping to keep their lasting interest and appeal.

(e) To preserve memory

Like Isocrates, Tacitus tells his wife and mother-in-law that pondering Agricola's deeds and words is better than a statue (46.3). Lucian also claims to be preserving his subject's memory as a student of Demonax (2).

(f) Didactic

Lucian concludes that he wants his readers to realize what sort of man Demonax was (ὁποῖος ἐκεῖνος ἀνὴρ ἐγένετο, 67). Discussion of the subject's teachings occurs in Lucian and Philostratus. Plutarch too has his didactic, semi-religious purposes, to portray his view of the universe. This is seen in the *Cato Minor* when he reflects on justice and the attitude of others to those who are just, such as Cato (44.7-8, see also 9.5), or in Cato's censure of τὰ θεῖα for deserting Pompey now he is fighting for the right (53.2). Brenk shows how Plutarch's moral and religious views come through all the *Lives:* 'The total effect is something quite different from that of an individual biography. . . . Plutarch was at heart a philosopher rather than historian or biographer in the strict sense.'[103] Plutarch is concerned to show the workings of divine justice and retribution in human lives. He uses dreams, oracles and portents to point this out and has more sympathy for those characters who failed (in political terms) than those who were arrogantly successful.

99. G. B. Townend, 'Suetonius and His Influence', in *Latin Biography*, ed. Dorey, p. 93.
100. Dorey, '"Agricola" and "Domitian"', p. 8.
101. Pelling, 'Plutarch's Adaptation', *JHS* (1980), p. 138.
102. See Jones, *Plutarch and Rome*, pp. 67-71, and Hamilton, *Alexander*, pp. xxiii-xxxiii.
103. Brenk, *In Mist Apparelled*, p. 274.

(g) Apologetic and polemic

Furneaux saw the *Agricola* as a political apology for those who, like Agricola and Tacitus, had held office under Domitian.[104] There are polemic against vainglorious opposition and apologia for quiet obedience 'sub malis principibus' (42.4). However, this is not his total purpose: 'The *Agricola* is, then, neither a political pamphlet nor a personal apologia.'[105] Plutarch is aware of the polemic about Cato, and sometimes he corrects false views or accusations made in other *Lives*.[106] Philostratus wishes to defend Apollonius against mistaken views, such as Moiragenes' (I.3). The *Apollonius* has also been seen as pagan polemic against the Christians; certainly βίοι are used in this way soon afterwards by Iamblichus and Porphyry, and similarly with Eusebius' reply, the *Origen*.[107] As for Apollonius himself, Hierocles attempted to draw a parallel between him and Christ, refuted again by Eusebius.

Thus βίοι are written to fulfil many different intentions, from the polemical to laudatory, from didactic to entertainment — and several, or even all, of these can coexist in any one work. As Pelling says, the genre was 'an extremely flexible one',[108] and we should beware of rigid prescriptions about the necessary purpose of the genre or of simplistic deductions from genre to purpose.

8. Summary

From this study of the internal generic features, a clear pattern has emerged: the settings of βίοι focus on the subject, and they include a selection from standard topics. Style and atmosphere can vary: some are high-brow and serious (*Agricola, Cato Minor*), others may be popular and lighter (*Demonax, Apollonius of Tyana*). This is seen in what the text reveals of its social setting and occasion. The quality of the characterization is usually quite good, although always with the possibility of stereotype. Finally, βίοι have many intentions and purposes, often several at the same time.

---

104. Furneaux, 1898 edn, pp. 10-15; see also Dorey, '"Agricola" and "Domitian"', and Syme, *Tacitus*, vol. 1, pp. 26-9 and 125-31.

105. Ogilvie, *Agricola*, p. 19; see also, Goodyear, *Tacitus*, pp. 6-7, and Mattingly's introduction to his translation, pp. 16-17.

106. See n. 81 above and also Wardman, *Plutarch's Lives*, pp. 195-6, and Geiger, 'Munatius Rufus', *Athenaeum* (1979), esp. pp. 54-6.

107. See Cox, *Biography in Late Antiquity*.

108. Pelling, 'Plutarch's Adaptation', *JHS* (1980), p. 139; see also, 'Plutarch and Roman Politics', p. 159.

Conclusion

Three of these βίοι date from soon after the gospels, while the other two have taken us further into the development of the genre. Our survey of ten works in total has provided a clear picture of the βίος genre: there is a family resemblance, yet the overall impression is of a diverse and flexible genre, able to cope with variations in any one work. The major determining feature is the subject; all these works concentrate on one individual. However, there is a high degree of flexibility in the treatment: in some cases there is an even-handed coverage of every area of his life, while others stress just one period; some concentrate on the subject's deeds and the chronology of his life, while others focus on certain topics, teachings or virtues in a non-chronological manner. The βίος genre is often signalled at the outset by using the subject's name in either the title or opening features.

Internal features of content are similar, such as topics and motifs. However, although there are some similarities of style, level, atmosphere, social setting and occasion between these works, there are also indications that the range may vary considerably; Lucian's *Demonax,* and hints elsewhere, suggest that the genre spread further down the social spectrum than extant works might suggest. Features shared are not merely those of content, but include more structural, external features: βίοι tend to be of similar appearance, length and structure, mode of representation and units of composition, which all play an important rôle in communicating the genre, or confirming the initial generic impression mediated by the individual subject, title or opening forms.

However, it should not be assumed that there are no boundaries, or that the genre includes everything. This list of features enables us to see clearly works at the fringes of the genre, especially at the start of its existence *(Evagoras)*, and on its way out into novel and hagiography towards the end of the imperial period: as we have noted, the *Apollonius of Tyana* sometimes shows quite different results from our other examples, e.g. as regards its size and scope, and this indicates generic movement. These features also help us to clarify the blurred frontiers between biographical history and historical bi-ography. Thus the *Agricola,* despite the debate about its genre, is shown to belong to the family nonetheless.

We may conclude, therefore, that there is an overall pattern or family resemblance of generic features which identify this group as the genre of βίος. To belong to this family, a work must show at least as sufficient of the common generic features as these works do, within the limits of diversity, and so now we may turn at last to undertake a similar analysis of the gospels.

━━━━━━━━━━━

CHAPTER 8

The Synoptic Gospels

A third hypothesis about the purpose of the gospels that once was quite popular has now been abandoned altogether: The gospels were not written as biographies of Jesus, nor can a biography be extracted from them.[1]

The form of the gospels most closely resembles that of Hellenistic biographies.[2]

T he fact that general introductions to the New Testament can assert with confidence and certainty such statements which appear blatantly contradictory indicates the continuing disarray concerning the genre of the gospels. Clearly, the idea of the gospels as biographies certainly has *not* 'been abandoned altogether'. On the contrary, after the dominance of the kerygmatic hypothesis for so long, 'more recent discussion of the genre of the gospel has reopened the question of the gospels as biography, however cautiously'.[3] We have suggested consistently that there are two main causes of this disarray: inadequate literary theory of genre and a lack of understanding of Graeco-Roman biography. Therefore, we have identified a range of generic features and used them to analyse Graeco-Roman βίοι, both on

1. John B. Gabel and Charles B. Wheeler, *The Bible as Literature: An Introduction* (OUP, 1986), p. 185.

2. Luke T. Johnson, *The Writings of the New Testament: An Interpretation* (London: SCM, 1986), p. 145.

3. Helmut Koester, 'From the Kerygma-Gospel to Written Gospels', *NTS* 35 (1989), pp. 361-81, quotation from p. 364.

the fringes of the genre and indubitably classic examples. A clear family resemblance has now been established, and so we can proceed with the same exercise on the gospels. Stanton has considered Mark similarly with respect to a number of features, but concludes that several would have 'puzzled readers familiar with the techniques of ancient biographical writing': the concentration on Jesus' death, the enigmatic opening and curiously abrupt ending, and the lack of entertaining anecdotes.[4] His consideration of the question using a number of features is a major step forward; whether the slightly pessimistic conclusion is warranted may emerge from our study. We shall take the three synoptic gospels together and subject them to the same analysis we used for Graeco-Roman βίοι. Since we are dealing with the genre of the final text, issues such as source criticism, oral tradition and the production of the gospels, which are often the usual preoccupation of gospel scholars, may feature occasionally — but our main focus is the text itself, and the generic features it contains, as the primary means of determining genre.

A. Opening Features

1. Title

The Greek titles found in the manuscripts dating from the earliest centuries are variations upon the preposition κατά: e.g., for Luke, MSS B and F have κατὰ Δουκᾶν, A C and D have εὐαγγέλιον κατὰ Δουκᾶν, and others τὸ κατὰ Δουκᾶν εὐαγγέλιον. κατά plus the accusative is not to be seen as equivalent to the normal genitive of the author; thus Plummer says: 'The κατά neither affirms nor denies *authorship:* it implies *conformity to a type.*'[5] A similar range of phrases can be found on manuscripts of Matthew, and Davies and Allison reckon that the title could go back to as early as AD 125.[6] Hengel argues that the unanimity of these descriptions in the manuscripts implies an early date for this formula back into the first century and possibly even to the original

---

4. Graham N. Stanton, *The Gospels and Jesus* (OUP, 1989), p. 19; in his *A Gospel for a New People: Studies in Matthew* (Edinburgh: T&T Clark, 1992), p. 64, n. 3, Stanton suggests that he was 'too cautious' in his assessment of the gospels as biographies in this first edition of *The Gospels and Jesus* in 1989. He has now updated and revised it as *The Gospels and Jesus*, Second Edition (OUP, 2002), where he modifies, but still includes, these four features as 'puzzling' on p. 17.

5. *Luke,* ICC, 4th edn (Edinburgh: T&T Clark, 1901), p. 1; his italics.

6. W. D. Davies and D. C. Allison, *Matthew,* ICC (Edinburgh: T&T Clark, 1988), p. 129, n. 90.

distribution of Mark.[7] Koester, however, is not persuaded by this, while Bovon sees the unanimity as a result of canonization.[8] Whether the titles are original or not, they may suggest that the early church grouped the gospels together into a 'type', but they do not indicate the genre.

The word 'gospel' itself also needs brief consideration; the noun εὐαγγέλιον has religious and salvific connotations in secular Greek from Homer onwards, and within the Old Testament the verb εὐαγγελίζεσθαι has a theological sense, e.g. Isa. 52:7; 61:1 (LXX). Both noun and verb are common in Paul, occurring some fifty and twenty times respectively, for the preaching of the 'good news' of Jesus Christ. In the synoptic gospels too, this link with preaching is clear, e.g. Mark 1:14, Matt. 4:23 and Luke 20:1.[9] Mark may have had a similar meaning in mind when he began his account of Jesus with the words Ἀρχὴ τοῦ εὐαγγέλιου Ἰησοῦ Χριστοῦ (1:1); Christopher Marshall credits him with expanding the original meaning to include 'the whole historical ministry of Jesus', and says that 'Mark's intention is to suggest an equivalence between the preaching of Jesus and that of the church.'[10] For Hengel, this connection of 'preaching and historical narrative' means that Mark's εὐαγγέλιον is meant to be understood as ancient biography.[11] Such linking of the content of early Christian preaching with narrative about Jesus' ministry, death and resurrection changes the word's use. Baird traces this shift from 'the gospel' in the singular (for the content of early Christian belief) to 'the gospels' in the plural (referring to the written documents) through the early Fathers down to Eusebius. Here too, Koester is not persuaded, preferring to see the use of εὐαγγέλιον for a written document as a 'revolutionary innova-

---

7. Martin Hengel, *Die Evangelienüberschriften* (Heidelberg: Winter, 1984); ET, 'The Titles of the Gospels', in *Studies in the Gospel of Mark* (London: SCM, 1985), pp. 64-84, see esp. pp. 66-7 and 83; Hengel has continued his discussion of this in his *The Four Gospels and the One Gospel of Jesus Christ: An Investigation of the Collection and Origin of the Canonical Gospels* (London: SCM, 2000). See also Stuhlmacher's comments in *The Interrelations of the Gospels*, ed. D. L. Dungan, pp. 493-4.

8. Koester, 'From the Kerygma-Gospel to Written Gospels', *NTS* 35 (1989), p. 373; François Bovon, 'The Synoptic Gospels and the Noncanonical Acts of the Apostles', *HTR* 81 (1988), pp. 19-36, see p. 23.

9. See Burridge, 'Gospel', in *SCM Dictionary of Biblical Interpretation*; Lohse, *Formation of NT*, pp. 117-20; Stuhlmacher, *Das Evangelium*, pp. 20-6; J. A. Fitzmyer, 'The Gospel in the Theology of Paul', *Interpretation* 33 (1979), pp. 339-50; Guelich, 'εὐαγγέλιον', *Mark 1–8.26*, pp. 13-14; H. Frankemölle, *Evangelium — Begriff und Gattung*; G. Rau, 'Das Markusevangelium. Komposition und Intention der ersten Darstellung christlicher Mission', *ANRW*, II.25.3 (1985), pp. 2036-257, esp. pp. 2042-72.

10. Christopher D. Marshall, *Faith as a Theme in Mark's Narrative*, SNTSMS 64 (CUP, 1989), p. 45.

11. Hengel, 'The Titles of the Gospels', pp. 72 and 83.

tion' by Marcion; however, Dormeyer's study of Mark 1:1 argues that this is nothing to do with Marcion, but rather the canonization of Mark's combining the literary and theological content of the gospel into a 'Jesus-Biographie'.[12] The situation regarding the titles of the gospels is thus rather complex, but they suggest that *the books were seen as a literary group together, possibly with a connection with βίος.*

2. Opening Formulae/Prologue/Preface

Matthew begins with the genealogy of Jesus, and we have noted how common consideration of the γένος of the subject is in βίοι. The extent of Mark's opening is debated: 1:1, 1:1-8, 1:1-13 and 1:1-15 have all been suggested. Koester sees the opening phrase as a possible scribal insertion; there is nothing to indicate that εὐαγγέλιον is a 'designation of Mark's entire work'. Guelich, however, accepts that εὐαγγέλιον refers to the 'content of the literary work that follows', but prefers to see ἀρχή as just the 'beginning' of the opening section (vv. 1-15), rather than applying to the whole work. Christopher Marshall takes vv. 14-15 as the beginning of Jesus' public ministry, rather than the end of the opening section; like the first verse, they are crucial: 'vv 1, 14, 15 together provide an introduction to the entire ministry of Jesus'.[13] Whatever its extent, Mark's opening section is not a formal prologue or preface. However, Luke's Preface, 1:1-4, is usually seen as a significant attempt to relate his work to contemporary Graeco-Roman literature. Loveday Alexander's detailed study suggested affinities with prefaces in Greek scientific monographs, although such affinities do not negate the 'biographical content of the Gospel and Acts'.[14] The classicist, George A. Kennedy, also points to the Preface, with its 'fine periodic sentence' as evidence that 'Luke in the Gospel comes close to being a classical biographer'.[15]

12. Baird, 'Genre Analysis', pp. 395-400; Koester, 'From the Kerygma-Gospel', *NTS* (1989), p. 381; D. Dormeyer, 'Die Kompositionsmetapher "Evangelium Jesu Christi"', *NTS* (1987), p. 464 (see n. 45, p. 95 above).

13. Koester, 'From the Kerygma-Gospel', *NTS* (1989), p. 370; Guelich, *Mark 1–8.26*, pp. 3-12, quotation from p. 9; Marshall, *Faith as a Theme*, pp. 36-56, quotation from p. 37; see also F. J. Matera, 'The Prologue as the Interpretative Key to Mark's Gospel', *JSNT* 34 (1988), pp. 3-20.

14. L. Alexander, 'Luke's Preface in the Context of Greek Preface-Writing', *NovT* 28 (1986). pp. 48-74; quotation from p. 70; see also her 1977 Oxford D.Phil. thesis, 'Luke-Acts in Its Contemporary Setting, with Special Reference to the Prefaces (Luke 1.1-4 and Acts 1.1)', later published as *The Preface to Luke's Gospel: Literary Convention and Social Context in Luke 1.1-4 and Acts 1.1*, SNTSMS 78 (Cambridge University Press, 1993).

15. G. A. Kennedy, *New Testament Interpretation through Rhetorical Criticism* (University

If we compare the synoptic gospels with our βίοι, we note that Matthew goes straight into the subject's ancestry, like Nepos and Plutarch; Mark, however, like Xenophon, begins with just one sentence, while some of Plutarch's *Lives* start straight in (e.g. *Timoleon* 1). Luke's use of a preface can be parallelled in Lucian and Philo, who have a paragraph each, and in Isocrates, Tacitus and Philostratus, who all have a more extended prologue. Thus the various beginnings of the synoptic gospels reflect the range of possibilities for βίοι with respect to an opening sentence or preface.

Also, like most Graeco-Roman βίοι, Mark and Matthew include the name of their subject at the very start:

Ἀρχὴ τοῦ εὐαγγέλιου Ἰησοῦ Χριστοῦ [υἱοῦ θεοῦ]. (Mark 1:1)

Βίβλος γενέσεως Ἰησοῦ Χριστοῦ υἱοῦ Δαυὶδ υἱοῦ Ἀβραάμ. (Matt. 1:1)

These sentences also allude to the beginning of the Old Testament: Mark's ἀρχή is reminiscent of its opening words and Hebrew title, *b^ere'shith* (ἐν ἀρχῇ LXX), while Matthew's βίβλος γενέσεως picks up ἡ βίβλος γενέσεως in Gen. 2:4 and 5:1 (LXX) and the Greek title, *Genesis.* Further Old Testament allusion appears with Matthew's υἱοῦ Δαυὶδ υἱοῦ Ἀβραάμ and Mark's quotation in 1:2-3. Luke mentions the name at the annunciation (1:31) and the birth (2:21), but it becomes prominent at the start of the main narrative in 3:23 and 4:1. This compares with the use of the subject's name after prologues in *Evagoras* (12 or 21), *Apollonius of Tyana* (I.4) and *Agricola* (4.1). So we can relate the opening features of the synoptic gospels to βίοι in that *Matthew and Mark begin with the subject's name, while Luke has a formal preface, with the name occurring later at the start of the main narrative.*

B. Subject

1. Analysis of Verb Subjects

There is often debate about the 'real' subject of the gospels: for example, Guelich argues 'in short, does the evangelist view his task to write a "biogra-

---

of North Carolina Press, 1984), pp. 107-8; see also, Fitzmyer, *Luke* (New York: Doubleday, 1981), vol. 1, pp, 287-302 for the Preface and contemporary literature, and pp. 172-4 on διήγησις in v. 1 as a 'quasi-title'; V. K. Robbins, 'Prefaces in Greco-Roman Biography and Luke-Acts', *SBL 1978 Seminar Papers,* vol. 2, ed. P. J. Achtemeier (Missoula: Scholars Press, 1978), pp. 193-207; Terrance Callan, 'The Preface of Luke-Acts and Historiography', *NTS* 31 (1985), pp. 576-81.

phy" or to set forth the Christian message about what God was doing in and through Jesus Messiah? Is the ultimate focus not on God rather than on Jesus?[16] Similarly, Sanders and Davies note that 'in the Gospel of Luke, there is a lack of focus on the hero. . . . It is not a biography of Jesus but a story of God bringing salvation to his people. . . . It is God who is the dominant force.'[17] Perhaps, as with our βίοι, analysis of the verb subjects will help us to discern where the 'focus' is and who is the 'dominant force'.

Manual analysis of Mark's gospel reveals immediately our 'skew' effect: Jesus himself is the subject of about a quarter of the verbs (24.4%) and a further fifth occur on his lips, in his teaching or parables (20.2%). These results are very close to Satyrus' where Euripides was the subject of 25.8%, with 17.5% occurring in quotations from his plays. We have the same concentration on the subject: no other individual scores above 1%. Several groups feature: all the references to any individual disciple, and to them as a group, total an eighth (12.2%), while all those to whom Jesus ministered, talked or healed together make up a tenth (9.3%). The Jewish leaders, scribes, Pharisees and Chief Priests are the other significant group, accounting for 5%, while the rest may be termed indefinite or miscellaneous subjects (see Figure 12, Appendix I, p. 318).[18]

Matthew and Luke have similar results, with Jesus dominating the narrative as the subject of over a sixth of the verbs (17.2% and 17.9% respectively); once again, no other individual features, but we have the same groups: disciples (8.8% and 8.3%), those who received ministry from Jesus (4.4% and 7%), and the priests, scribes and Pharisees (4.4% and 3.4%). The amount of verbs contained in Jesus' teaching and parables is more or less doubled from Mark's 20.2% to 42.5% in Matthew and 36.8% in Luke (see Figures 13 and 14, Appendix I, pp. 319-20). The extra material comes mainly from their shared tradition, referred to as 'Q', consisting mostly of 'sayings' and teaching.[19] Matthew tends to collect it all together in five main blocks of teaching, while Luke uses it more widely, but especially in his travel section (9-19). Luke's score for

16. Guelich, 'The Gospel Genre', in *Das Evangelium und die Evangelien*, p. 191; ET *The Gospel and the Gospels*, p. 181.

17. Sanders and Davies, *Studying the Synoptic Gospels*, p. 288; compare 'what the author is primarily interested in presenting is *not* "what sort of person" Jesus is, but rather what sort of action God is effecting through this person', D. P. Moessner, 'And Once Again, What Sort of "Essence"? A Response to Charles Talbert', *Semeia* 43 (1988), p. 80.

18. These figures are based on the full text of the gospel down to 16:20; if one analyses only 1:1-16:8, the effect is to diminish the percentages for Jesus and the disciples by a decimal point or two, which has no significant effect upon the results.

19. On the genre of Q, see Chapter 10, pp. 240-1 and Chapter 11, pp. 258-9 below.

the spoken material is less because, unlike Matthew, he does attempt to provide a *narrative* setting for the blocks of teaching, such as Jesus delivering the speech as a result of being asked a question, or responding to a situation. This is typical of philosophical dialogues and βίοι of philosophers, and may be evidence, therefore, of Luke's attempt to conform his gospel more closely to βίοι, especially philosophical ones. Certainly, these large figures for Jesus' teaching need not prevent the gospels being βίοι. On the contrary, they reveal that approximately half the verbs in the synoptic gospels are taken up with Jesus' words and deeds.

These figures are a clear indicator of a strong biographical tendency in the gospels. They cannot 'prove' that they are βίοι any more than did the results for other works with a biographical interest, such as the *Cyropaedia* or *Memorabilia*; however, these latter works lacked the other features of βίοι and so do not belong to the genre. We must await our consideration of these other features before reaching a final decision about the gospels, but it is evident already that *the gospels belong with other works of a clear biographical interest.*

2. Allocation of Space

X: Content analysis of Matthew's gospel

Chapters	Verses	Topic		Percentage of work
1–2	48	Prologue and infancy		4.5
3–4	42	Preparation and beginnings		3.9
5–7	111	Sermon on the Mount	(Discourse)	10.4
8–9	72	Ministry		6.7
10–11:1	41	Mission of disciples	(Discourse)	3.8
11:2–12	79	Ministry and conflict		7.4
13:1-52	52	Parables of the Kingdom	(Discourse)	4.9
13:53–17:27	136	Ministry and Peter's Confession		12.7
18	35	Christian community	(Discourse)	3.3
19–23	195	Journey to Jerusalem		18.2
24–25	97	Eschatology	(Discourse)	9.1
26–28	161	Last Supper, Passion and Resurrection		15.1
Totals:	1,069			100.0

XI: Content analysis of Mark's gospel

Chapters	Verses	Topic	Percentage of work
1:1-13	13	Preparation and beginnings	2.0
1:14–3:6	66	Ministry in Galilee	9.9
3:7–6:6	119	Call of disciples and ministry	17.9
6:7–8:26	113	Mission and blindness of disciples	17.0
8:27–10:52	113	Journey to Jerusalem	17.0
11–13	114	Ministry in Jerusalem	17.1
14–16:8	127	Last Supper, Passion and Resurrection	19.1
Totals:	665		100.0

XII: Content analysis of Luke's gospel

Chapters	Verses	Topic	Percentage of work
1:1-4	4	Preface	0.4
1:5–2:52	128	Infancy narratives	11.1
3–4:13	51	Preparation and beginnings	4.4
4:14–9:50	275	Ministry in Galilee	23.9
9:51–19:27	406	Journey to Jerusalem	35.3
19:28–21:38	106	Ministry in Jerusalem	9.3
22–24	179	Last Supper, Passion and Resurrection	15.6
Totals:	1,149		100.0

The allocation of space within the gospels is one reason often cited against their being biographies. It is pointed out that we are told little or nothing of the first thirty or so years of Jesus' life, and then there is the large concentration of space devoted to his death.[20] In fact, our analysis of βίοι revealed that the first thirty or forty years of a subject's life can be dealt with very briefly, or even omitted, while the death-scene is usually exaggerated. Matthew and Luke devote just over 15% of their text to the events of the Last Supper, Trial, Passion and Resurrection, while Mark has rather more, 19.1%.[21] If these figures are compared with those given to their subject's last days and death by Plutarch (17.3%), Nepos (15%), Tacitus (10%) and Philostratus (26%), then

20. See, e.g., Stanton, *The Gospels and Jesus,* 1989, p. 19; second edition, 2002, p. 17.

21. The figures in the tables are calculated on the basis of verses, which do vary in length; however, the alternative method, using the number of lines of Greek text, was also tried and produced results which differed only very slightly.

the gospels' allocation of space does not look out of place or puzzling. Of course, the concentration on Jesus' death involves more than just the amount of space describing it; the Cross dominates the whole of Mark, for example, with the various predictions of the Passion. Nonetheless, this is not very different from some Graeco-Roman βίοι; the death of Jesus is as important in understanding his significance for the evangelists as the battle of Mons Graupius was for Agricola (which was given 26%) or the Persian campaign for Agesilaus (given 37%).[22] This means that *the evangelists' concentration on the Passion and death of Jesus can no longer be used as an argument against the gospels being βίοι.*

C. External Features

1. Mode of Representation

The synoptic gospels are in prose narrative. They may have an oral tradition behind them and have been read in public; Mark's primitive Greek may have the occasional oral cadence, but even so, the final written texts are clearly prose works. Metre does not apply therefore. Furthermore, narrative is the best description of the prose: it is not drama, though there are some dramatic elements, nor dialogue, like Satyrus' *Euripides,* although dialogue is contained within the gospels. They are not speeches, like the *Evagoras,* or sermons, although they may exhibit some rhetorical, oral or proclamatory features. Finally, the narrative is mainly continuous; some of the links between sections may be vague or tenuous, but overall the narrative seems intended as a continuous whole. While the gospels may not be as continuous as Lives of statesmen or generals, like Agricola, they are more continuous than those of philosophers, like the *Demonax* with its string of unconnected episodes. Thus *the mode of representation of the synoptic gospels is prose narrative of a fairly continuous nature, like historiography or βίοι.*

22. Note also that a quarter of Acts (24.7%) is taken up with Paul's arrest in Jerusalem, his various hearings and final detention in Rome (Acts 21:17–28:31): 'The space devoted to Paul's arrest and examinations shows the importance attached to these by Luke, and may be compared with the space allotted in the Gospels to the events of Passion Week'. F. F. Bruce, *The Acts of the Apostles,* 2nd edn (London: Tyndale, 1952), pp. 390-1.

2. Size

According to Morgenthaler, Matthew has 18,305 words, Mark 11,242 and Luke 19,428[23] — and this puts them clearly within the medium-length category. This rules out some suggestions for the gospels of genres which lie outside this category. For instance, Kelber suggests that the gospels are to be viewed as 'written parable', while Donahue says that the parables 'give shape, direction, and meaning to the Gospels'.[24] Since parables are often less than 100 words long, and even one as long as the Prodigal Son in Luke 15:11-31 is below 400, they are clearly a short genre: indeed, brevity is part of the essence of their function. Talk of parables 'extended' to 10,000-20,000 words misunderstands how generic features function. This is not to deny, of course, that there may be much of the 'parabolic' about the story of Jesus. However, this is the wider level of mode, as defined in Chapter 2 above, rather than the specific level of genre. The same applies to suggestions that the gospels are tragedy or tragi-comedy.[25] Again, there may be elements of the tragic or tragicomic in the gospels, but these genres are smaller than our texts — as well as possessing other generic features, such as a mode of dialogue and structure of scenes and choruses not in the gospels. We would do better to search for a genre for the gospels among works of medium length. In fact, Matthew and Luke are comparable to the longest of Plutarch's *Lives,* such as *Alexander* or *Antony,* while Mark is similar to Plutarch's average length for his βίοι of 10,000-11,000 words. *Size is thus another shared feature between the gospels and βίοι.*

3. Structure

Most gospel commentaries begin with an elaborate chart of the structure. Here, we are concerned with overall sequence: all three synoptic gospels begin the main narrative with the Baptism of Jesus by John, although it is prefaced

23. Robert Morgenthaler, *Statistik des neutestamentlichen Wortschatzes* (Zurich: Gotthelf, 1958), Table 3, p. 164.

24. See Kelber's section 'The Gospel as Written Parable' in *Oral and Written Gospel,* pp. 117-29, preferring parable to aretalogy or biography as the genre of the gospels; John R. Donahue, *The Gospel in Parable: Metaphor, Narrative, and Theology in the Synoptic Gospels* (Philadelphia: Fortress, 1988), p. ix; see also, James G. Williams, *Gospel Against Parable* (Sheffield: JSOT, 1985) and his 'Parable and Chreia: From Q to Narrative Gospel', *Semeia* 43 (1988), pp. 85-114; Mack, *A Myth of Innocence,* pp. 332-9 is not convinced.

25. E.g. G. G. Bilezikian, *The Liberated Gospel: A Comparison of the Gospel of Mark and Greek Tragedy,* or Dan O. Via's *Kerygma and Comedy in the New Testament;* see pp. 21-2 above.

by birth stories in Matthew and Luke, and all three conclude with the Passion story, Jesus' death and the subsequent events. Martin Kähler's dictum that Mark is a Passion story with an extended introduction is commonly quoted:[26] however, to see over 80% of a work as mere introduction is rather unbalanced, giving insufficient importance to these earlier sections, and is unsatisfactory as an explanation of genre. In between the Baptism and the Passion, all three gospels include a large amount of material concerned with Jesus' ministry. Many commentators deny any connection with biography: so Kümmel says, 'Mk has no biographical-chronological interest'.[27] Such a disjointed approach to Mark is open to lectionary or liturgical theories of genre, seeing the text in terms of units for public reading.[28] Others disagree: thus Nineham accepts that 'he has produced what is, so far as *form* is concerned, a connected historical narrative' with 'a corresponding chronological sequence'. Also, Bilezikian comments 'a consensus has emerged according to which the author of the Gospel intended to write a sequential and progressive narration,' since examination of the links and seams indicates 'that the author was not just copying stories but that he was writing a story'.[29]

Our analysis of the content of the synoptic gospels in the tables above shows that the narrative appears as a chronological account, unfolding from the Baptism to the Passion via Jesus' ministry with its popular success and official opposition. Also, all three have a geographical progression from ministry in Galilee to Jerusalem, most clearly marked in Luke's account.[30] Such a basic chronological structure is not dissimilar from those in βίοι: it is less marked than the datable sequence of Lives of generals like Agricola or Agesilaus, but more structured than the loose string of anecdotes in the *Demonax;* similarly, Porphyry's *Life of Pythagoras* is a collection of stories arranged by theme, such

26. M. Kähler, *The So-Called Historical Jesus and the Historic, Biblical Christ* (Philadelphia: Fortress, 1964), p. 80, n. 11.

27. W. G. Kümmel, *Introduction to NT,* p. 85; see also, 'Mark's order is not . . . determined by a biographical-chronological interest', Hugh Anderson, *The Gospel of Mark,* NCBC (London: Marshall, Morgan & Scott, 1976), p. 33; 'Mark has no interest whatever in precise chronology . . . not [motivated] by the desire to write a biography', E. Schweizer, *The Good News According to Mark* (London: SPCK, 1971), p. 13.

28. E.g. the ideas of Carrington or Goulder, discussed on pp. 19-20 above.

29. D. E. Nineham, *St. Mark* (Harmondsworth: Penguin, 1963), p. 36; Bilezikian, *Liberated Gospel,* p. 14; for Mark's structure, see E. Best, *Mark: The Gospel as Story* (Edinburgh: T&T Clark, 1983), pp. 100-8 and 128-33, and H. Anderson, *Mark,* pp. 32-40; for Matthew, see Johnson, *Writings of NT,* pp. 173-6, and Davies and Allison, *Matthew,* ICC, pp. 58-72: a 'chronological sequence' with teaching 'inserted'.

30. See Fitzmyer, *Luke,* pp. 162-71, on Luke and his use of geography; for history, see also pp. 171-92 and H. Conzelmann, *The Theology of St. Luke* (London: Faber, 1960).

as his communication with animals (23-26) or miracles (27-30). Into their basic chronological structure, all three evangelists insert other material arranged topically: thus Matthew has the five discourses of chapters 5-7, 10, 13, 18 and 24-25, and Mark groups parables together in chapter 4 and has the mini-apocalypse of 13. Luke collects together some teaching in the Sermon on the Plain in 6:12-49 or on the 'Journey to Jerusalem', or the Parables of the Lost in 15. Such insertion of topical material into a chronological structure is very common in βίοι, especially those of philosophers or teachers, like Moses or Apollonius of Tyana. *The gospels' exterior framework of a chronological sequence with topical material inserted is thus a structure typical of Graeco-Roman βίοι.*

4. Scale

The scale of the synoptic gospels is narrowly defined, focussing upon one individual. Jesus is nearly always centre-stage: other characters appear in order to relate with him, in discussion or controversy, or to receive healing from him, or for their needs to be met. On the rare occasions when Jesus is absent from the narrative in person, the characters are still discussing him and what they are going to do about him; see, for example, Herod in Mark 6:14-16 or the discussion about the arrest in Mark 14:1-2. This focus extends even to individual pericopae, as Bornkamm says: 'The circle of light is always sharply defined. The description of those who appear in it is limited to the essential.'[31] This is true of the whole narrative; a wider scale comes in Luke's second volume, Acts — although even here, the focus is still upon certain key individuals, especially Peter and Paul, rather than attempting a comprehensive history of the early church. However, the gospels themselves *all restrict their scale to the person of Jesus in a manner typical of βίος literature.*

5. Literary Units

The use of anecdotal stories, variously termed ἀποφθέγματα or παραδείγματα, from Aristotle onwards has already been noted.[32] Bultmann identified various forms in the gospels: *apophthegms* — subdivided into controversy or scholastic dialogues and biographical apophthegms; *sayings* — teaching,

---

31. Günther Bornkamm, *Jesus of Nazareth* (London: Hodder & Stoughton, 1960), p. 25.
32. See Momigliano, *Development*, pp. 72-3, and p. 168 above; also, R. F. Hock and A. N. O'Neil, *The Chreia in Ancient Rhetoric* (SBL, 1986); on chreiai and education, see Beavis, *Mark's Audience*, pp. 25-31.

prophetic, apocalyptic, legal, or ecclesiastical; *miracle stories, historical stories* and *legends.* Dibelius preferred the terms *paradigms, tales, legends, myths* and *exhortations.* Vincent Taylor pioneered the English terms *pronouncement-stories, miracle-stories* and *sayings,* stressing the link with 'story'.[33] During the 1970s, the SBL Pronouncement Story Work Group under Robert Tannehill studied the use of these literary units in both the gospels and in other Greek, Jewish and Christian literature, culminating in the publication of various essays in *Semeia* 1981. The terms employed for such units include apophthegms, chreiai and pronouncement-stories: their interchangeability is demonstrated by Tannehill's *Semeia* article 'Varieties of Synoptic Pronouncement Stories' appearing in only a slightly revised form as 'Types and Functions of Apophthegms in the Synoptic Gospels' in *ANRW.*[34] Tannehill defines the unit thus: 'A pronouncement story is a brief narrative in which the climactic (and often final) element is a pronouncement which is presented as a particular person's response to something said or observed.'[35] Such units, together with parables and teaching material, are the basic building blocks of the synoptic gospels' central sections, followed by the Passion narrative, a complete unit with its own narrative structure and chronology.

We have seen how βίοι are also composed of stories, anecdotes, sayings and speeches. Lucian, in particular, makes great use of pronouncement-type stories in the *Demonax:* the central section is composed of short stories (50-100 words), which begin with Demonax meeting someone and lead up to a wise or witty pronouncement from the sage.[36] The SBL group examined *Demonax* and Philostratus' *Apollonius,* as well as Plutarch and Philo for comparable units: Robbins analysed 200 pronouncement stories in Plutarch's *Alexander, Caesar, Demosthenes* and *Cicero* alone; more recently, Robbins has teamed up with Mack to compare chreiai with various synoptic units.[37] We

33. Bultmann, *History;* Dibelius, *From Tradition to Gospel;* Vincent Taylor, *The Formation of the Gospel Tradition* (London: Macmillan, 1933), see esp. pp. 29-30 and 63-87.

34. R. Tannehill, 'Varieties of Synoptic Pronouncement Stories', *Semeia* 20 (1981), pp. 101-19, and 'Types and Functions of Apophthegms in the Synoptic Gospels', *ANRW* II.25.2 (1984), pp. 1792-829 — see especially the very similar conclusions with the terms changed, pp. 117 and 1826.

35. R. Tannehill, 'Varieties', *Semeia* (1981), p. 1; for an analysis of Pronouncement Stories in Mark, comparing the lists of Bultmann, Taylor and Tannehill, see Mack, *A Myth of Innocence,* pp. 379-84; also, pp. 172-207.

36. For a comparison of *Dem.* 27 with Mark 2:15-17, see Mack, *Myth,* pp. 181-3; see also, Cancik, 'Bios und Logos', pp. 121-4.

37. V. K. Robbins, 'Classifying Pronouncement Stories in Plutarch's *Parallel Lives', Semeia* (1981), pp. 29-52; B. L. Mack and V. K. Robbins, *Patterns of Persuasion in the Gospels* (Sonoma: Polebridge, 1989).

do not need to enter here the complex analyses of the different types of such stories by Tannehill, Mack and Robbins, except to note that similar types are found in both the gospels and in βίοι. Overall therefore, we may conclude that *the combination of stories, sayings and speeches found in the synoptic gospels is very similar to the basic literary units used by βίοι.*

6. Use of Sources

It was common in prefaces to βίοι to mention any sources used, e.g. Philostratus' and Philo's references to oral and written sources. Luke's Preface also mentions both written accounts (διήγησιν) which many (πολλοὶ) have attempted to compose, and also oral sources, including eyewitnesses (αὐτόπται) and the preachers of the oral kerygmatic tradition (ὑπηρέται τοῦ λόγου) (1:1-4). Much has been written about the sources of the gospels and their relationships, the so-called Synoptic Problem.[38] I assume Markan priority and that both Matthew and Luke used Mark, plus their own material and some shared tradition, which may be conveniently labelled 'Q' but without that necessarily implying that it was all one single document or source. However, whatever solution is used, the consequences for our study are the same: namely, that the evangelists had access to oral and written sources, including notes, collections and in some cases another gospel, from which they selected and edited their material.

This ability to select and edit a wide range of sources is similar to the use of sources by writers of βίοι. Redaction criticism has freed us from seeing the evangelists as mere slaves of the oral tradition; instead, they are creative theologians and literary artists who took their source material and turned it into the gospel *according to* their understanding: 'in its present form, Matt. owes much to the editorial activity of the author who shaped his source material into a unified Gospel'; 'the picture Luke wanted to paint'.[39] *Thus the freedom to select and edit sources to produce the desired pic-*

---

38. See W. G. Kümmel, *Introduction to NT*, pp. 38-80, for a statement of the consensus Two-/Four-Source view; W. R. Farmer, *The Synoptic Problem: A Critical Analysis* (London: Macmillan, 1st edn 1964 or 2nd edn 1976), for an attempt to overturn this; C. M. Tuckett, *The Revival of the Griesbach Hypothesis: An Analysis and Appraisal*, SNTSMS 44 (CUP, 1983) for a defence; and M. D. Goulder, *Luke: A New Paradigm* (SAP, 1989), and M. S. Enslin, 'Luke and Matthew: Compilers or Authors?' in *ANRW* II.25.3, pp. 2358-88, for other attempts.

39. F. V. Filson, *St. Matthew*, 2nd edn (London: A. & C. Black, 1971), p. 10; Fitzmyer, *Luke*, p. 258; see also, Hilton and Marshall, *The Gospels and Rabbinic Judaism* (London: SCM, 1988), p. 13.

ture of the subject is another feature shared by both the gospels and Graeco-Roman βίοι.

7. Methods of Characterization

> A biographer must tell us about his subject's constitution — both physical and mental — and show how it made him the man he became — he must explain what made his subject 'tick'. But on all such matters St Mark and the other Evangelists are completely silent. It is a striking fact that they tell us nothing whatsoever about Our Lord's appearance, physique, and health, or, for that matter, about his personality. . . . From the point of view of the biographer the sheer *amount* of information the Evangelists give us is quite inadequate.[40]

The absence of direct character analysis in the gospels is one of the traditional arguments against the gospels being biographies. However, we have seen that this requirement is a modern predilection; the ancient method was to display character through deeds and words. This is precisely what we find in the evangelists' characterization of Jesus. Luke describes this twofold method clearly when he says that his gospel deals with 'all that Jesus began to do and teach' — ποιεῖν τε καὶ διδάσκειν (Acts 1:1). So the evangelist's picture of Jesus is built up through stories and anecdotes, particularly about how he reacted to those who came to him, as well as by recounting his words. Thus we see his love through his care and ministry to those in pain or need (e.g. Matt. 9:36); his wisdom in outwitting those who try to trap him with clever questions (Mark 12:13-34). His power is revealed in his control of nature and the supernatural, disclosing his identity: 'What sort of man is this, that even winds and sea obey him?' (Matt. 8:27), and it is revealed also by the demonic: 'I know who you are, the Holy One of God' (Mark 1:24). Similarly, the evangelists portray the other characters through their reaction to Jesus: the disciples, constantly misunderstanding him; the crowd, enthusiastic in welcome, decisive in rejection; the provincial governor, interested in the prisoner, but giving in, 'wishing to satisfy the crowd' (Mark 15:15). Such indirect characterization by word and deed is not unique to the gospels, but common in ancient literature, including βίοι. *Therefore the gospels' so-called 'lack of character development' can no longer be used as an argument against their being βίοι.*

---

40. Nineham, *St. Mark,* p. 35; see also, Bultmann, *History,* p. 372; and Kümmel, *Introduction to NT,* p. 37; see pp. 9-10 above.

8. Summary

The external, structural pattern of the gospels is clear: they are works of prose narrative of medium length, with an apparently chronological structure into which topical material is inserted, written on a fairly narrow scale focussed on Jesus, composed from different literary units of stories and sayings selected from both oral and written sources in order to portray the central character of Jesus through his deeds and words and the reactions of others to him. Not all of these generic features are unique to βίοι literature; but *the overall combination of them reflects the same family resemblance as was seen in our study of Graeco-Roman βίοι.*

D. Internal Features

1. Setting

The geographical settings of the synoptic gospels include the countryside in and around Galilee, local towns, the wilderness, and locations in and around the city of Jerusalem, such as the High Priest's house, the Garden of Gethsemane and, of course, the Temple. We move to these settings, however, by following Jesus. The dramatic settings are similarly determined, with Jesus centre stage and the focus of the action; thus, most scenes involve Jesus plus other people who are there because of him. We have didactic settings, where he is teaching his disciples or the crowds; settings of conversation, dialogue or even controversy between Jesus and those who come to him; and active settings, where he is performing a miracle or mighty deed — but he is always the focus of the setting. *This personal focus of the work's settings on an individual, rather than a place or topic, is also a feature of βίοι literature,* and so here we have another generic link between the gospels and βίοι.

2. Topics

Shuler stresses *topoi* as one of his three indicators of genre, applying the lists of Quintilian, Hermogenes and Theon to Matthew.[41] Such lists are designed for school use in rhetorical and encomiastic exercises, rather than for writing, and they are later than most of our works. Therefore, caution is advisable in

---

41. Shuler, *A Genre for the Gospels,* pp. 53-6 and pp. 92-8.

making use of them; instead, we shall apply the same analysis to the gospels as was used for βίοι.

(a) Ancestry

Despite some knowledge of Jesus' family (6:3), Mark begins with John the Baptist and Jesus' baptism. Matthew and Luke include genealogies tracing Jesus' descent back to Abraham (Matt. 1:2-17) or to Adam (Luke 3:23-38).[42] Equally, mention of Bethlehem in Matt. 2:5-16 and Luke 2:4-15 is similar to the frequent mention of the subject's home town at the start of βίοι, particularly if the town linked the subject with a famous hero of the past, such as David.

(b) Birth

Mark has no mention of Jesus' birth. We noted that the birth was also omitted in the *Agesilaus, Atticus, Cato Minor* and *Demonax,* so it is not an essential feature for βίοι. Matthew and Luke do record it, with the various well-known stories of angels, magi and shepherds, Matt. 1:18-2:23 and Luke 1:5-2:40.[43]

(c) Boyhood and education

Luke's story of the twelve-year-old Jesus debating with the teachers in the Temple leads up to his first pronouncement by Jesus, and typically it concerns devotion to his Father's business (2:41-52). Such use of a single childhood anecdote to prefigure the adult's life is common in βίοι, as we saw in the accounts of Evagoras, Agricola and Cato. Bultmann likens the story to Philo's account of Moses outstripping his teachers (*Moses* I.21) and to Apollonius' soaring above his teachers like a young eagle (*Vit. Ap.* I.7).[44] Kennedy sees this anecdote as evidence of 'some awareness . . . of biography' in Luke's treatment.[45]

(d) Great deeds

These usually form the bulk of the narrative of a βίος, and the synoptic gospels are no exception. All three include stories of Jesus' miracles and mighty acts which caused people to wonder at him. Like βίοι of philosophers and

---

42. See Fitzmyer, *Luke,* pp. 488-505 for discussion and bibliography.

43. See Raymond E. Brown, SS, *The Birth of the Messiah: A Commentary on the Infancy Narratives in Matthew and Luke* (London: Geoffrey Chapman, 1977).

44. Bultmann, *History,* pp. 300-301.

45. Kennedy, *NT Interpretation through Rhetorical Criticism,* p. 32; for a full discussion, see Stanton, *Jesus of Nazareth,* pp. 47-51.

teachers, so here sections of the synoptic gospels are devoted to Jesus' teaching, sometimes brought together to form a larger sermon or discourse. The significance of deeds and words for the character of a religious leader is made explicit by Cleopas' comment that Jesus was 'a prophet mighty in deed and word', ἐν ἔργῳ καὶ λόγῳ (Luke 24:19).

(e) Virtues

The synoptic gospels do not have systematic analysis of Jesus' virtues in the manner of *Agesilaus* III-XI, *Atticus* 13-18 or Suetonius' *Caesars;* rather, as with our other βίοι, Jesus' virtues emerge through stories which display his compassion for the crowd who were 'like sheep without a shepherd' (Mark 6:34), or his concern for the outcast by his touching a leper, 'moved with pity' (Mark 1:41), or his quick mind to avoid the questioner's trap (Mark 12:17). Such indirect display of the subject's virtues is common in βίοι.

(f) Death and consequences

Kähler's description of the gospels as a Passion narrative with extended introduction, if wrong about genre, is correct about the crucial significance of the Passion. It is clear from the continuity of the narrative with details of time and place that 'the Passion narratives are the earliest sustained accounts of Jesus' memory, indicating that the part of Jesus' life most requiring interpretation was its last hours'.[46] The concentration on the subject's death has been shown to be common in βίοι; it was particularly important for Plutarch to explain Cato's death in detail, because of his apparent failure.[47] So too here, the declaration of Jesus' innocence by the centurion overseeing his death (Luke 23:47, compare Caesar's comment in *Cato Minor* 72) or the burial in a rich man's tomb with costly spices might be an attempt to offset the ignominy of the death. As well as describing the tomb and final honours, the gospels have the additional stories of the Resurrection. Sanders compares this with the appearance of Apollonius of Tyana after his death (*Vit. Ap.* VIII.31).[48]

The synoptic gospels display, therefore, a similar range of biographical topics to that already noted in βίοι.

46. Johnson, *Writings of NT,* p. 135.

47. See p. 74 and 160-1 above; Pelling compares the posthumous 'rehabilitation' of a hero in tragedy, *Antony,* p. 323; see also, Aune, *Greco-Roman Literature,* pp. 122-3.

48. E. P. Sanders, *Jesus and Judaism* (London: SCM, 1985), p. 320; see also, Petzke, *Die Traditionen,* pp. 183-7.

3. Style

The synoptic gospels, like all the New Testament, are written in a Greek rather different from both classical Attic and that of much contemporary literature. However, since Deissmann's pioneering work in the early 1900s the study of increasing numbers of letters, papyri and manuscripts of the first century AD has shown the prevalence of a simple Greek 'common' to the eastern Mediterranean — and hence known as 'Koiné'. The New Testament books are written in various forms of Koiné, with some clear Semitic influence, while other alleged Semitisms now appear common in contemporary Greek.[49] Mark is often castigated for the poor quality of his Greek style. It is clumsy and with little connection between sections: eighty-eight sections begin paratactically merely with καί, which also links sentences or clauses together endlessly; each new story begins 'immediately', εὐθύς; and there are nineteen examples of no linking at all, asyndeton. He is very fond of the historic present, using it 151 times. Despite these and other technicalities, Mark's style retains an urgency and directness which has its appeal: 'These linguistic usages are not out of place in *koine* Greek, and lend to the account a kind of simple, direct vividness which has been lost in the polishing and editing of the material carried out by Matthew and Luke.'[50] Maloney's examination of Markan syntax has confirmed Semitic influence, while showing that some features are common in Hellenistic writing; Reiser has compared Mark's language and style with that of the *Alexander Romance,* while Beavis has shown from a comparison with contemporary literature that a 'Graeco-Roman reader would have regarded Mark as a well-constructed book with some nice literary touches to lighten its rough prose style'.[51]

Matthew tends to improve Mark's Greek, shortening the stories and replacing the omnipresent καί with the more acceptable δέ. Moule describes him as someone with a sound grasp of Greek and a considerable vocabulary, but capable of Semitisms; Davies and Allison remind us he could have been bi- or trilingual — and a competent but unexciting style would fit in with this.[52] St

---

49. See J. W. Voelz, 'The Language of the New Testament', pp. 893-977; M. Wilcox, 'Semitisms in the New Testament', pp. 978-1029; and S. Segert, 'Semitic Poetic Structures in the New Testament', pp. 1433-62, all in *ANRW* II.25.2 (1984).

50. H. C. Kee, *Community of the New Age* (London: SCM, 1977), pp. 50-1.

51. E. C. Maloney, *Semitic Interference on Markan Syntax*, SBLDS 51 (Scholars, 1980); Marius Reiser, 'Der Alexanderroman und das Markusevangelium', WUNT 33 (1984), pp. 131-63; Beavis, *Mark's Audience*, JSNTSS 33, pp. 42-4.

52. C. F. D. Moule, *The Birth of the New Testament*, 3rd revised edn (London: A. & C. Black, 1981), pp. 276-80; Davies and Allison, *Matthew*, ICC, p. 73; see pp. 72-96 for full discussion.

Jerome described Luke as 'inter omnes evangelistas graeci sermonis eruditis-simus' (*Ep. ad. Dam.* 20.4.4), and he is capable of a wide range of styles: there is the literary Greek of the Preface, followed by the Semitic or Septuagintal flavour of the infancy stories, or the style of Acts becoming less Semitic as the narrative moves away from Jerusalem into the Graeco-Roman world. Like Matthew, he improves Mark's style, but with a greater command of Greek constructions and a wide vocabulary, from both Septuagintal and contemporary settings. Even if Hobart's attempt to demonstrate links with medical vocabulary is less accepted today, much of Luke's style and vocabulary does feature in contemporary treatises and monographs.[53]

We have already seen how Plutarch avoided Attic literary archaicizing, and noted the popular nature of Satyrus and Lucian. Despite some Semitic influence, the style of the synoptic gospels is within the range of contemporary Koiné, and probably similar to popular βίοι no longer extant. *Thus the style of the gospels should not be seen as a feature peculiar to themselves.*

4. Atmosphere

The synoptic gospels have a rather serious atmosphere, befitting important religious works. The tone is serious: although there is humour in Jesus' teaching, it is clear that what is being communicated is important to the writer, and he believes it should be to the reader also. The mood varies according to the action — joy at the birth or a healing, sadness at rejection, impending doom at the arrest or trial, excitement mixed with fear at the Resurrection, but it is usually connected directly with Jesus as the central character: what affects him affects the mood and therefore the reader. The attitude towards the subject is one of reverence and respect, without the desire to praise overtly in the manner of encomium. Likewise, the attitude towards the reader is inviting and expectant of a response, but without the direct apostrophe, hectoring or pleading with the audience in an encomiastic way — so we doubt the link which Shuler makes with encomium. Finally, the values depicted are those of a religious community, with a concern for ethical content and, in Matthew at least, for instructions about relationships within that community. *This somewhat serious and respectful atmosphere, tinged with praise and worship, is reminiscent of the atmosphere of some of our βίοι,* notably the *Agricola* and Philo's *Moses,* as opposed to the lightness of Lucian or Satyrus.

---

53. See Fitzmyer, *Luke,* pp. 107-27, for discussion and bibliography; also A. Plummer, *Luke,* ICC (Edinburgh: T&T Clark, 4th edn 1901), pp. xii-lxvii, is still worth reading.

5. *Quality of Characterization*

The evangelists' selective redaction of their sources has allowed them to paint the portrait of Jesus as they understood him, indirectly through his deeds and words. As regards the quality of characterization in βίοι, we saw a tendency towards the typical and even the stereotypical, but noted that through the actual stories and anecdotes a much more 'real' feel for the character could be obtained. The same pertains to the characterization of Jesus in the synoptic gospels. First, of course, we are talking of *portraits* of Jesus, rather than pictures or photographs; there is an inevitable element of interpretation brought in by the evangelist through his redaction. In doing this, there is a tendency for the typical to emerge, as we found with Tacitus' portrait of Agricola as the good soldier-general, or with Lucian's depiction of Demonax as a typical street philosopher. The portraits drawn by the evangelists are well known: Mark's Jesus is rather enigmatic and secretive, rushing around doing things 'immediately', a miracle-worker, yet one who talks about suffering and who eventually dies terribly alone and forsaken. Matthew shows a Jewish Jesus in continuity with Israel, the 'new Moses' who delivers his teaching from the Mount and reinterprets the Law. Luke, on the other hand, stresses the 'man for others', with his concern for the outcasts and the lost, for Gentiles, women and the poor, who dies with words of forgiveness for his executioners and acceptance of the criminal crucified with him. In developing these portraits, the element of the typical is clear, and contributes to the production and reinterpretation of both words and deeds.

However, having said all this, we cannot leave the discussion merely with the stereotype. That there is a 'real' character which comes through the portraits and the stories is clear from the millions of different people in different situations who, nonetheless, believe that they 'know' this man and try to run their lives as 'he' would wish. Again, this character is communicated by word and deed: by the pithy, paradoxical saying and the short, teasing story as much as by the forgiving acceptance of the sinner and the compassionate healing of the sick. *The tension between the real and the stereotype in the synoptic gospels is thus not dissimilar from characterization in other βίοι.*

6. *Social Setting and Occasion*

The anonymous and traditional nature of the gospels gives us no clear idea of their social setting, geographical provenance or the occasion(s) which prompted their production. Everything has to be gleaned from hints within the texts themselves, which is why this section remains an internal feature. Unfortunately, the hints are so tenuous that there is great debate among gospel scholars over these matters. Traditionally, the social setting of the early Christians was seen as rather lowly; increasingly, however, this is being reconsidered. Kennedy has proposed 'a primarily urban, lower middle class', and Meeks suggests that the early Christian communities included a broad range of social strata, though probably not the extreme top or bottom levels.[54] From the text itself, Mary Beavis has tried to reconstruct a picture of the educational and cultural background of both Mark and his audience, making many links with Hellenistic society.[55]

Mark is traditionally supposed to have written his gospel in Rome, acting as the 'interpreter' of Peter, according to the statement of Papias preserved by Eusebius in *HE* III.39.15; some still hold to this provenance, such as Best, while others have suggested places all over the Mediterranean: Kee prefers 'rural and small-town southern Syria'. Guelich concludes that the internal evidence for authorship, date and place is simply insufficient for any decisions to be made.[56] Matthew's gospel is notable for its Jewish flavour, but here too the date and place of composition and its setting in relationship to both contemporary Judaism and early Christianity are debated: the most common solution involves a setting in Antioch around the time of the 'Birkath ha-Minim' insertion into the Jewish liturgy and the separation of church and synagogue about AD 85, though some prefer somewhere east of the Jordan, such as Pella where the Jerusalem church fled in about AD 66 (Eusebius *HE* III.5.3).[57] Luke's account seems to imply a setting outside Palestine in a more Gentile environment; again, a link with Antioch has been suggested, but nowhere is really agreed, although a date of around 85 does seem likely.[58]

54. *The Relationships among the Gospels: An Inter-disciplinary Dialogue*, ed. W. O. Walker, Jr. (San Antonio: Trinity University Press, 1978), p. 185; see also, Wayne A. Meeks, *The First Urban Christians: The Social World of the Apostle Paul* (New Haven: Yale University Press, 1983), and John Stambaugh and David Balch, *The Social World of the First Christians* (London: SPCK, 1986); further discussion of this issue can be found in Chapter 10, pp. 243-6 below.

55. Beavis, *Mark's Audience*, pp. 13-44.

56. Petr Pokorný, 'Das Markusevangelium: Literarische und theologische Einleitung mit Forschungsbericht', in *ANRW* II.25.3, pp. 1969-2035, see especially pp. 2019-22; Best, *Mark*, pp. 21-36; Kee, *Community of the New Age*, pp. 77-105; Guelich, *Mark 1–8.26*, pp. xxv-xxxii and xi-xliii.

57. A full list of suggested locations is discussed by Davies and Allison, *Matthew*, ICC, pp. 138-47; see also, G. N. Stanton, 'The Origin and Purpose of Matthew's Gospel', in *ANRW* II.25.3, pp. 1889-1951, see esp. pp. 1941-3.

58. See Fitzmyer, *Luke*, pp. 35-62; Robert Maddox, *The Purpose of Luke-Acts* (Edinburgh: T&T Clark, 1982), pp. 6-15.

There is a similar diversity of suggestions about the occasion which led to the composition of the synoptic gospels. Mark may have been prompted by the death of Peter, or other eye-witnesses during Nero's persecutions, or by the Jewish revolt and/or the fall of Jerusalem, by the delay of the Parousia or by his group's conviction of its imminence, or by some internal need of his community.[59] Similar suggestions have been made for Matthew, plus others about the relation of his community to Judaism. Luke-Acts has been seen as part of the brief for the defending counsel at Paul's trial (hence why Acts finishes before Paul's death).[60] Other suggestions include the delay of the Parousia, internal debate about Paul in early Christianity, external debate with the Romans about the legality and acceptability of this new religion and many others.[61] Orchard's suggestion is that Matthew was the gospel of the Jerusalem church AD 30-44, Luke was the product of the 50s crisis over Paul's Gentile churches and that Mark, the latest of the three, is based on lectures in Rome by Peter comparing Matthew and Luke![62] The only sensible conclusion to draw from this diversity is that the texts themselves do not contain sufficient information for us to know the specific settings and occasions which prompted their production, except for a general desire to tell others about Jesus, who he was, what he did and what happened to him in the end.[63] It seems likely that their setting is further down the social scale than our other examples, but perhaps not as far down as used to be thought and certainly not beyond the reach of βίοι, which had a variety of possible settings. At the very least, therefore, *there appears to be nothing about this generic feature preventing them being βίοι.*

59. Best discusses these suggestions in *Mark*, pp. 21-36; Morton Enslin goes for the fall of Jerusalem in his 'Luke and Matthew', *ANRW* II.25.3, p. 2363.

60. A. J. Matill, Jr., 'The Purpose of Acts: Schneckenburger Reconsidered', in *Apostolic History and the Gospel*, ed. W. Ward Gasque and R. P. Martin (Exeter: Paternoster, 1970), pp. 108-22; see also his 'The Jesus-Paul Parallels and the Purpose of Luke-Acts', *NovT* 17 (1975), pp. 15-46.

61. See further, R. Maddox, *The Purpose of Luke-Acts*; or, W. W. Gasque, *A History of the Criticism of the Acts of the Apostles* (Tübingen: J. C. B. Mohr, 1975); Fitzmyer, *Luke*, pp. 8-11 and 57-9.

62. Bernard Orchard and Harold Riley, *The Order of the Synoptics: Why Three Synoptic Gospels?* (Macon: Mercer University Press, 1987), pp. 229-79.

63. For a good treatment of all the various possible settings and communities proposed for the gospels, see Stephen C. Barton, 'Can We Identify the Gospel Audiences?' in *The Gospels for All Christians: Rethinking the Gospel Audiences*, ed. Richard Bauckham (Grand Rapids: Eerdmans, 1998), pp. 173-94.

7. Authorial Intention and Purpose

Here too, we find a range of proposals put forward by gospel scholars; we shall follow the same analysis as for βίοι:

(a) Encomiastic

Shuler tries to claim the gospels as 'encomium biography' and therefore argues that the gospels seek to 'elicit praise' of Jesus from the reader.[64] While this is true to a certain extent, the kind of 'praise' sought within a religious community is rather different from that of an encomiast at a public funeral; furthermore, the attitude of the gospels to both subject and reader has little of the atmosphere of encomium.

(b) Exemplary

The secondary purpose of encomium — to provide a model for the audience to follow — does have more possibilities for the gospel, and Shuler refers to the intention of the evangelists to elicit a response of faith, as well as praise. 1 Peter 2:21 specifically points to Christ as an example to follow, and the most obvious gospel for this is Matthew, whose intention to provide a 'paradigm' for discipleship is noted by many redaction critics.[65]

(c) Informative

Best is unsure about this intention, declaring that Mark 'was not written to provide historical information about Jesus', even though it does do so. Lindars, however, is clear: as the church moved out, away from the eyewitnesses, who were dying anyway, 'public demand to satisfy curiosity about Jesus . . . was bound to arise'; in fact, 'the motive of pious curiosity' also helps to account for items such as the infancy narratives. Moule believes that Luke was 'intended primarily to "tell the story" — and that for the outsider'.[66]

---

64. Shuler, *A Genre for the Gospels*, pp. 103-6, on Matthew's purpose; see also his 1975 Ph.D. dissertation, pp. 221-4 (Matthew), 255-9 (Mark) and 292-8 (Luke).

65. See, for example, Bornkamm's study, 'The Stilling of the Storm in Matthew', see p. 14 above; also Aune, 'The Gospels as Hellenistic Biography', *Mosaic* 20 (1987), p. 7.

66. Best, *Mark*, pp. 51-2; Lindars, *The Study and Use of the Bible*, p. 235; C. F. D. Moule, 'The Intention of the Evangelists', in his *The Phenomenon of the New Testament* (London: SCM, 1967), p. 103.

(d) Entertainment value

Luke, at least, had some literary aims: the quality of his prose in the Preface, his carefully balanced parallels of Jesus, Peter and Paul stretching over the two volumes, the geographical progression to Jerusalem in the first volume and then away to Rome in the second, all show something of his ability. While this may be a secondary aim most of the time, occasionally he is prepared to give it fuller rein, as in the storm and shipwreck of Acts 27. If the gospels were designed to be read aloud, possibly in their entirety, their content and structure needed to be sufficiently interesting to hold the audience's attention.[67]

(e) To preserve memory

If the deaths of many of the first generation and eyewitnesses played a part in stimulating the production of the gospels, then this motive could also be there. However, the belief that Jesus was not dead, but risen and alive among his people, would have made any attempt to 'preserve his memory' rather different from that of, say, Lucian or Xenophon.

(f) Didactic

A common aim of βίοι of philosophers or religious teachers, this is a major purpose here also. Thus Moule sees the gospels as 'ancillary to the preaching', and Best sums up all Mark's purposes as 'pastoral', to teach and to build up his readers in the faith.[68] Similarly, Stanton declares that Matthew is 'primarily concerned to set out the story and significance of Jesus in order to encourage and exhort Christians in his own day', while Hill sees the purpose of the work as something 'from which to teach and to preach'. Luke overtly declares his purpose to help Theophilus to know the reliability (ἀσφάλεια) of what he has been taught (1:4), and Martin argues that 'this expression of intention . . . must be taken seriously'.[69]

---

67. See Beavis, *Mark's Audience*, pp. 124-30.

68. Moule, *Birth of NT,* p. 10; Best, *Mark,* pp. 51-4, 93-9; see also, Guelich, *Mark 1–8.26,* pp. xl-xliii.

69. Stanton, *The Gospels and Jesus,* p. 78 (Second Edition, 2002, p. 76), and see also his article 'Origin and Purpose of Matthew's Gospel' in *ANRW* II.25.3, esp. p. 1938; Hill, NCBC Commentary, p. 43; Martin, *Narrative Parallels to the New Testament,* p. 23.

(g) Apologetic and Polemic

Probably the most common purpose of βίοι in our examples was their use in debate and argument. The titles of Weeden's works on Mark demonstrate this polemical purpose — 'The Heresy That Necessitated Mark's Gospel' and *Mark: Traditions in Conflict* — as Mark struggled against a false view of Jesus as a miracle/wonder-worker.[70] Bilezikian also sees polemic in Mark, directed against the Twelve and traditional Jewish Christianity in the struggle of the 'Gentile-oriented church'; Moule sees this as the backdrop provoking the production of gospel material, while Hill applies this to Matthew's gospel which 'seeks to convince, to instruct and to refute'.[71] As we have just seen, Luke-Acts may have been used as apologetic for Paul at his trial or, more likely, in the later Jewish/Gentile Christian debate, or as apologetic for Christianity itself to a wider Roman audience.

As with other βίοι, it is clearly difficult, if not impossible, to restrict the synoptic gospels to just one purpose. Bilezikian talks of Mark's 'multi-pronged approach' which 'could well have served concurrently a number of purposes, some didactic, others apologetic, polemic, doctrinal, evangelistic, ecclesiological, apocalyptic, etc.', and the same goes for Matthew and Luke.[72] However, the range of possible intentions is similar in both extent and content to that proposed for βίοι. Furthermore, the clearest intentions seem to involve didactic and apologetic purposes, probably the most common aims of βίοι also. These aims do not determine the gospels' genre by themselves; other genres are used for polemic or apologetic, such as Paul's use of Epistles. However, within the overall context of this study, *this congruence of aims between the synoptic gospels and βίοι is another indication of a shared genre.*

8. Summary

The synoptic gospels share the βίος pattern of internal features: the geographical and dramatic settings are focussed on Jesus, and selection is made from

---

70. T. J. Weeden, 'Heresy' in *ZNW* 59 (1968), pp. 145-58, reprinted in *The Interpretation of Mark*, ed. W. Telford (London: SPCK, 1985), pp. 64-77; Weeden, *Mark: Traditions in Conflict* (Philadelphia: Fortress, 1971).

71. Bilezikian, *Liberated Gospel*, p. 145; Moule, *Birth of NT*, pp. 68-106; Hill, NCBC Commentary, p. 44.

72. *Liberated Gospel*, p. 141; see Stanton on Matthew's 'varied' purposes, 'Origin and Purpose', *ANRW* II.25.3, p. 1941, and Ward Gasque similarly on Luke-Acts, *A History of the Criticism of Acts*, p. 303.

the usual biographical topics. The style and social setting are probably more down-market than our other examples, but they have a similarly serious and respectful atmosphere. The quality of characterization is a mix of the real and stereotype, while the range of purposes is also similar, especially the didactic and apologetic. *Overall, therefore, the mixture of internal features is familiar from our study of βίοι.*

Conclusion

It used to be common among New Testament scholars to talk of 'Mark's Unique Literary Contribution' in creating 'a new genre of literature for which, as a whole, there was no precedent'.[73] More recently, however, it has been increasingly suggested that the gospels do not look 'especially strange among all the different kinds of biographical compositions during the Hellenistic era'.[74] Our study has shown that they do share many common biographical features with Graeco-Roman βίοι. The next question, therefore, concerns how many shared features are necessary to make a genre. Davies and Allison accept that 'the gospels do share motifs and themes which also play important rôles in hellenistic biography', but go on to assert that 'common elements do not require a common genre'.[75] We have proposed that the genre of a text is best determined by a wide range of generic features contained within it and that for a work to belong to a genre it needs to display at least as many of these features as other examples do — the 'family resemblance'. We have built up a clear picture of the genre of Graeco-Roman βίοι and the pattern which emerges from a study of their generic features. Using the same sequence of generic features to analyse the synoptic gospels has yielded the following results:

(i) The gospels lack any title which might indicate βίοι, but Luke begins with a formal Preface, while Mark and Matthew commence with the subject's name — both of which are common opening features in βίοι.

(ii) Manual analysis has shown the same pattern of dominance of verb sub-

---

73. H. C. Kee, *Jesus in History: An Approach to the Study of the Gospels,* 2nd edn (New York: Harcourt Brace Jovanovich, 1977), p. 139; see similar comments by E. Schweizer, *Mark* (London: SPCK, 1970), p. 23; W. R. F. Browning, *St. Luke,* 3rd edn (London: SCM, 1972), pp. 17-18; R. Guelich, 'The Gospel Genre', in *Das Evangelium,* p. 213; ET as *The Gospel and the Gospels,* p. 202.

74. V. K. Robbins, *Jesus the Teacher* (Philadelphia: Fortress, 1984), p. 4.

75. Davies and Allison, *Matthew,* ICC, p. 4, n. 9.

jects as was found in Graeco-Roman βίοι: Jesus is the subject of a large number of the verbs with a further portion occurring in his parables and teaching. All three synoptic gospels devote a large amount of their text to his Passion and death; however, such an uneven allocation of space to the subject's important period is common among βίοι.

(iii) As regards external features, the synoptic gospels have a similar mode of representation, size, structure and scale to those found in βίοι; further, they use a similar range of literary units, selected from oral and written sources to provide characterization indirectly by word and deed, as is the case in ancient βίοι.

(iv) Among internal features, the settings, topics, atmosphere, quality of characterization and range of purposes are roughly comparable; the style and social setting are probably further down the social scale than our βίοι, but it is likely that other βίοι were available at these levels which have not survived.

Thus, there is a high degree of correlation between the generic features of Graeco-Roman βίοι and those of the synoptic gospels; in fact, they exhibit more of the features than are shown by works at the edges of the genre, such as those of Isocrates, Xenophon and Philostratus. This is surely a sufficient number of shared features for the genre of the synoptic gospels to be clear: while they may well form their own subgenre because of their shared content, **the synoptic gospels belong within the overall genre of βίοι.** Finally, therefore, we need to ascertain whether this result also pertains to the Fourth Gospel, to which we now turn.

CHAPTER 9

The Fourth Gospel

*The Gospel according to John has so different a character in compar-
ison with the other three, and is . . . the product of a developed theological reflection.*[1]

Jn belongs to the same literary genre, 'gospel', as the Synoptics.[2]

Within New Testament scholarship, separations can sometimes appear
between those who deal with the Epistles and Revelation and those
who specialize in gospel studies; furthermore, the latter may be divided into
synoptic specialists and Johannine scholars. This is understandable for two
reasons: first, those who read and study few ancient texts other than the four
canonical gospels see an immediate difference between the first three and the
Fourth Gospel which grows larger on more study: 'The gospel of John seems
to have come from another tradition entirely — even from another universe
of thought.'[3] Secondly, the vast and ever growing body of secondary literature
makes it increasingly difficult to keep up with both aspects. Nonetheless, such
a gulf is regrettable and leads even more to notions of the isolation and
uniqueness of the Fourth Gospel. We have argued throughout this study that
a wide-ranging and interdisciplinary approach is necessary for a proper appreciation of the place of the gospels within contemporary literature and also
for a correct interpretation of their genre and message, arising from such an

---

1. Bornkamm, *Jesus of Nazareth*, p. 14.
2. Kümmel, *Introduction to NT,* p. 200.
3. J. B. Gabel and C. B. Wheeler, *The Bible as Literature* (OUP, 1986), p. 198.

appreciation. So far, we have discovered that analysis of the main generic features of the synoptic gospels has revealed the same pattern and family resemblance as found in Graeco-Roman βίοι; because it has been viewed often in isolation, it is important that the Fourth Gospel is subjected to our analysis to see if it also belongs to the same genre. The inevitable consequence of such a wide-ranging study is that it is impossible to cover the whole field of Johannine studies and interests. As with the synoptic gospels, so here too our prime concern is with the genre of the final, written text, rather than the major interests of Johannine scholarship, such as the background and composition of the gospel, and its theological understanding of issues such as Christology or eschatology.[4]

However, our basic assumptions about the background and composition of the Fourth Gospel are as follows:[5] the gospel belongs within the syncretistic milieu of the eastern Mediterranean towards the close of the first century AD; within such a culture, those involved with its production would have been influenced by both Jewish and Hellenistic philosophical and religious ideas — everything from Platonic thought and proto-Gnosticism to Rabbinic or 'non-conformist' Judaism — without needing actually to belong to any of these groups. The Jewish-Christian debate and the separation of church and synagogue was probably a significant factor in the background. Secondly, the production and composition of the gospel is best understood within a corporate context, often called the Johannine Community, which developed its distinctive flavour, probably in the course of several editions or versions.[6] Furthermore, the writer(s)/editor(s) had access to some primitive

---

4. For general surveys, see Kümmel, *Introduction to NT,* pp. 188-247; Robert Kysar, *The Fourth Evangelist and His Gospel: An Examination of Contemporary Scholarship* (Minneapolis: Augsburg, 1975), abbreviated and updated as 'The Fourth Gospel: A Report on Recent Research', *ANRW* II.25.3 (1985), pp. 2389-480; Stephen Smalley, *John: Evangelist and Interpreter* (Exeter: Paternoster, 1978); J. A. T. Robinson, *The Priority of John* (London: SCM, 1985); John Ashton (ed.), *The Interpretation of John* (London: SPCK, 1986); Barnabas Lindars, *John* (SAP, 1990); and the introductions to the commentaries by Raymond E. Brown, Anchor Bible, 2 vols. (New York: Doubleday, 1966 and 1970; 2nd edn, 1984); Barnabas Lindars, NCBC (London: Marshall, Morgan & Scott, 1972); C. K. Barrett, 2nd edn (London: SPCK, 1st edn 1955, 2nd edn 1978); Ernst Haenchen, 2 vols., Hermeneia Series (Philadelphia: Fortress, 1984); George R. Beasley-Murray, WBC (Dallas: Word, 1987).

5. See further my introduction to Richard A. Burridge, *John,* The People's Bible Commentary (Oxford: Bible Reading Fellowship, 1998), pp. 12-29.

6. See Brown, *John,* pp. xxiv-li, and his *The Community of the Beloved Disciple* (London: Geoffrey Chapman, 1979); and Kysar, *Fourth Evangelist,* pp. 9-172. Brown has now further revised his understanding of the Johannine Community: see R. E. Brown, *An Introduction to the Gospel of John,* ed. Francis J. Moloney (New York: Doubleday, 2003), esp. pp. 62-89 and 189-219.

and early oral traditions overlapping those used by the synoptic writers, but without knowing their actual texts.[7] With this in mind, we turn to study the generic features of the text itself.

A. Opening Features

1. Title

As with the synoptic gospels, we have no original title preserved to provide an initial indication of genre, just the traditional superscription, κατὰ Ἰωάννην. While the mention of 'John' has caused great debate about the possible authorship or underlying authority of John the Apostle (or Elder) and any connection he may have had with the Beloved Disciple of 13:23, 19:26 etc., the κατὰ construction shows that *the Fourth Gospel was perceived as belonging with the synoptics, and of the same literary type.*

2. Opening Formulae/Prologue/Preface

The gospel begins with a formal prologue of a poetic or hymnic character, concerning ὁ λόγος, identified as personal and coexistent with God from the beginning, but who came to dwell on earth, 'full of grace and truth' (1:1-18). From its peculiar style and because key words like λόγος and χάρις are not mentioned again in the gospel, it is often assumed that the prologue had an independent origin but was taken over and adapted by the evangelist/redactor, perhaps at the final stage or edition of the work; possible backgrounds for the prologue range from the Gnostic to Jewish Wisdom traditions.[8] However, there is little by way of generic guidance for us here.

---

7. Kümmel (*Introduction to NT,* pp. 200-17) and Barrett (Commentary, pp. 34-45 1st edn, or 42-54 2nd edn) remain convinced that John knew at least one of the synoptic gospels; we prefer the general consensus, which has developed since P. Gardner-Smith's *St. John and the Synoptic Gospels* (CUP, 1938) — see surveys in n. 4 above, and P. Borgen, 'John and the Synoptics', in *Tradition and Interpretation in the New Testament,* ed. G. F. Hawthorne and O. Betz (Grand Rapids: Eerdmans, 1987), pp. 80-94. However, now see Richard Bauckham, 'John for Readers of Mark' in *The Gospels for All Christians: Rethinking the Gospel Audiences,* ed. Richard Bauckham (Grand Rapids: Eerdmans, 1998), pp. 147-72.

8. See Brown's commentary, pp. cxxii-cxxviii and 3-37; Haenchen's commentary, pp. 101-40; also, James D. G. Dunn, *Christology in the Making,* 2nd edn (London: SCM, 1989), pp. xxvi-xxxii and 213-50; and Kennedy, *NT Interpretation,* pp. 108-13.

The opening words provide a reminiscence of the opening of Genesis, with their resonant ἐν ἀρχῇ . . . using the two opening words of the Septuagint to place the Logos even before the creation of the world. We noted that both Mark and Matthew have similar allusions at the start of their gospels; this even more exact reference must be designed to link this text in some way with the sacred scriptures and the activity of God.

The other common opening feature for βίος is an early use of the subject's name: here, ὁ λόγος comprises the fourth and fifth words, which is then identified with Ἰησοῦ Χριστοῦ in v. 17, the first mention of Jesus' name at the end of the prologue (and in the genitive case). Our attention is next drawn to John the Baptist's denial of being the Christ (1:20), witnessing instead to Jesus (1:29-34, 35-7). Thus, although Jesus' actual name is not part of the immediate opening words, he is clearly identified as the subject of the prologue, and his name and Messianic identity commence the text itself after the prologue. *The use of the name after the prologue was noted as a common feature in βίοι, such as the Agricola.*

B. Subject

1. Analysis of Verb Subjects

The Fourth Gospel is usually considered to be less interested in Jesus' activity than are the synoptics, seeing him more as a mouthpiece for theological propositions. Manual analysis reveals the surprising result that over a fifth of the verbs have Jesus as their subject (20.2%), occurring in narrative or conversation, with another 1.1% referring to him by means of a title (Word, Son, Lamb, Lord, etc.). Furthermore, over a third of the verbs occur in teaching or discourse material placed on the lips of Jesus (34.0%), including nearly a tenth where Jesus speaks of himself (9.4%). If these self-referring verbs are added to those in the narrative (9.4% + 20.2% + 1.1%), Jesus is the subject of over 30% of the verbs. All together then, over half the verbs are taken up with Jesus' deeds or words, performed by him or spoken by him (55.3%) (see Figure 15, Appendix I, p. 321). These totals make interesting comparisons with those in Mark, where Jesus is the subject of 24.4% and speaks a further 20.2%, and Matthew (17.2% + 42.5%) and Luke (17.9% + 36.8%). Thus the Fourth Gospel occupies a middle position between Mark and Matthew/Luke: despite all John's different 'feel' and discourse material, he places less teaching on Jesus' lips than Matthew and Luke do, and gives Jesus more prominence in his narrative than they have.

The remaining 44.7% is shared by everyone else. Once again, no individuals feature significantly; the two notable groups are the disciples, individually and corporately (9.3%), and those receiving ministry from Jesus (Nicodemus, the Samaritan woman, the official and his son, the paralytic, the adulteress,[9] the blind man, Mary, Martha and Lazarus — 6.4%). The opponents of Jesus form two groups, 'the Jews', οἱ Ἰουδαῖοι, with 3%, occurring mostly in the first section of the gospel, and the Jewish leaders, scribes, Pharisees and priests, who continue their opposition through to the Passion (2.4%). Interestingly, God does not feature significantly as a subject in the narrative, although on the lips of Jesus he is the subject of 3.7% of the gospel's total verbs, often referred to as ὁ πέμψας με; a similar number of 'you plural' verbs spoken by Jesus refer to the Jews (3.6%) or, during the Last Supper Discourses, to the disciples (3.7%). Thus, we may conclude that the Fourth Gospel, far from not being interested in Jesus' activity, *displays the same exaggerated skew effect which is typical of βίοι in both Jesus' activity in the narrative and in the large amount of his teaching.*

2. Allocation of Space

Analysis of the content of the Fourth Gospel reveals a pattern similar to that in the synoptic gospels, with the last week of Jesus' life dominating the work. A fifth of the work (20%) is made up by the Last Supper (4.3%) and the Passion and Resurrection (15.7%); this compares closely with Mark (19.1%), while Matthew and Luke had 15%. Into this final section the Farewell Discourses have been inserted, which occupy over an eighth (13.3%).[10] Thus a third of the total work is devoted to the last week of the subject's life. (See the content analysis on p. 218.) Although this might seem excessive for modern biography, we need to compare it with the *Agricola* (26% devoted to Mons Graupius), *Agesilaus* (37% to the Persian campaign), *Cato Minor* (17.3% to the last days) and *Apollonius of Tyana* (26.3% to the imprisonment dialogues, trial, death and subsequent events).

We conclude from the study of the subject, verbal analysis and allocation of space, that *the Fourth Gospel displays very similar results from these generic features to those already discovered in the synoptic gospels and Graeco-Roman*

9. Since we are dealing with the genre of the whole text, 7:53-8:11 is included; if it is removed, the effect is to reduce the totals for Jesus, recipients and Jewish leaders by less than 0.5%.

10. Since 14:31 ends with 'Rise, let us go hence', but this is not actually done until 18:1, chapters 15-17 are usually seen as an insertion into the narrative at a later revision; see commentaries *ad loc.*

XIII: Content analysis of the Fourth Gospel

Chapters	Verses	Topic	Percentage of work
1:1-18	18	Prologue	2.0
1:19-51	33	Beginnings and call of disciples	3.8
2–10	427	Ministry and Signs	48.6
11–12:11	68	Bethany	7.8
12:12-50	39	Entry into Jerusalem	4.5
13	38	Last Supper	4.3
14–17	117	Discourses	13.3
18–21	138	Passion and Resurrection	15.7
Totals:	878		100.0

βίοι. This provides an initial expectation — to be confirmed or corrected by the other generic features — that the Fourth Gospel may be a βίος 'Ιησοῦ.

C. External Features

1. Mode of Representation

The Fourth Gospel is written in continuous prose narrative, so considerations of metre do not apply. Although there are breaks (or 'aporias') in the narrative (such as the famous jump from 14:31 to 18:1, or the apparent conclusion in 20:30-31, followed by yet another chapter),[11] nonetheless, the story flows in a continuous sequence. Into this narrative, extended discourses and dialogues have been inserted. This is common in βίοι, especially those of philosophers; much of the *Apollonius of Tyana* is similarly occupied with dialogues and long speeches containing the sage's teachings. The feature of dialogue was also noted in Satyrus' *Euripides*. Smalley notes the strongly dramatic feeling in the gospel, describing it as a drama with a prologue, two acts and an epilogue.[12] While this is a helpful insight into its structure, the Fourth Gospel is dramatic only at the level of *mode*, since it lacks the other formal features of the genre of drama, such as poetic metres, choruses and so on. It is significant that John, for all his concern with Jesus' teaching, has still composed in a mode of representation of continuous narrative, *thus making*

11. See Smalley, *John*, pp. 97-100, and Brown's commentary, pp. xxiv-xxv.
12. Smalley, *John*, pp. 192-203.

another link with the synoptic gospels and βίοι, rather than compiling a collection of sayings or discourses, in the manner of some non-canonical gospels or as Q is sometimes supposed to be.

2. *Size*

Morgenthaler reckons the Fourth Gospel to be 15,416 words in length. This is about halfway between Mark's length and the size of Matthew and Luke. It is similar to the length of *Cato Minor* and in the centre of our medium-range category. Thus, *the generic feature of size is also shared with the synoptic gospels and βίοι.* By way of comparison, we note that in the rest of the New Testament, only Acts is comparable (18,382); Revelation is the next longest (9,834). Epistles are much shorter, the longest being Romans (7,105) and 1 and 2 Corinthians (6,811 and 4,469); apart from Hebrews (4,951), the rest range from about 1,000 to 2,000 words.

3. *Structure*

Most analyses of the gospel's structure are variations upon a twofold scheme, like Smalley's two-act drama. Stanton uses another image: 'Like a great mediaeval cathedral, the main body of the gospel is in two sections.'[13] This basic structure is clear from Table XIII above: the work begins with the Prologue and the call of the first disciples (1:1-18 and 1:19-51), followed by the first large section of ministry and signs, alternating between Galilee and Jerusalem (2-10). After the Bethany interlude (11:1-12:11), the second half is devoted to the events of Passion week (12:12-20:31), with the appendix of the lakeside appearance (21). This is a clear chronological framework, from Jesus' pre-existence as the Word with God, through his arrival on the public scene and his ministry, to the death and the events afterwards. This is similar to the synoptic gospels, as Hengel says: 'All the gospels follow a geographical and chronological order, which contains fundamental historical features common in essentials to all the gospels, even if there are differences between the synoptic gospels and John.'[14]

13. Stanton, *The Gospels and Jesus*, p. 112 (Second Edition, 2002, p. 98); for further discussion of John's structure, see Brown's commentary, pp. cxxxviii-cxliv; Haenchen's commentary, pp. 78-86.

14. M. Hengel, *Acts and the History of Earliest Christianity* (London: SCM, 1979), p. 19.

Into this basic chronological outline, John has inserted discourse and dialogue material, arranged topically and often linked to one of Jesus' signs: thus we find eschatology in chapter 5, sacraments, especially the eucharist in 6, light in 8-9 and the farewell discourses at the Last Supper, 14-17. *This structure of a chronological framework with topical material inserted was also noted in the synoptic gospels and is typical of the structure found in many βίοι.*

4. Scale

The Fourth Gospel is written on a narrow scale, with the focus constantly upon Jesus; as we shall see in our discussion of the setting below, he is rarely absent from the centre of the stage and there is no attempt to relate him to wider events and times. The only suggestion of a slightly broader scale comes in the discourses, which build a link between the traditions about Jesus and the needs and concerns of the Johannine community. Generally speaking, however, *the narrow scale is another link with both the synoptic gospels and Graeco-Roman βίοι.*

5. Literary Units

The Fourth Gospel is more of a continuous whole than the synoptic gospels, despite the occasional break or seam in the narrative. It is composed of three main types of unit: stories, dialogue, and speeches or discourses. The stories tend to be a little longer than those of the synoptic gospels, and we do not find anecdotes, or pronouncement stories being used in quite the same way. Nonetheless, some stories are shared with the synoptic tradition, such as the sequence of the miraculous feeding followed by the walking on water in John 6:1-21 (compare Mark 6:32-51). The dialogues are extended conversations, with Jesus responding, sometimes at length, to questions from the crowd or Jewish leaders; such dialogues are typical of philosophical βίοι, such as *Apollonius* or Socratic literature. The discourse material is usually worked carefully into the text, often expounding the meaning of a Sign: thus the eucharistic discourse follows the feeding of the 5,000 in chapter 6, or the debate about light is linked with the healing of the blind man in 8-9. Lindars considers such units of discourse to have originated from homilies by the evangelist.[15] There are a few stray units which seem uncon-

---

15. Lindars, *John*, pp. 36-7; see also his commentary, pp. 51-4.

nected to the main narrative, e.g. 3:16-21 or 3:31-36, but these are exceptions. Finally, we have the large unit of the Passion narrative, like those of the synoptic gospels, into which the Farewell Discourses have been inserted, followed by the stories of the Resurrection. We conclude, therefore, that *the Fourth Gospel is composed mainly of stories, dialogues and speeches or discourses, which are the typical material of βίοι, especially those of philosophers and teachers.*

6. Use of Sources

Source criticism of the Fourth Gospel is more difficult than for the synoptic gospels, since the literary relationship of the latter allows us to compare them and to see what use they may have made of each other, or of shared source material (i.e. Mark and Q on the traditional hypothesis). If John knew any of the synoptics, his revision of them is very radical; if he did not know them, as seems more likely, then we have no external evidence for his sources, nor anything with which to compare him. Most Johannine source theories fall into one of three types: *displacement theories* suggest that the text has somehow become mixed up — hence the breaks in the narrative; rearrangement is required to restore the 'original' order. While pages of a codex may get out of order, it is hard to see this happening to individual verses — and even harder if the first versions were on scrolls; since all our early manuscripts have the same order and reconstructed versions usually reflect the predilections of the scholar, such approaches are not convincing. Theories involving *multiple sources* used to be popular: Bultmann's classic version suggested that the Fourth Evangelist had combined three main sources, Signs, Discourses and Passion, into his gospel which was then revised by the Ecclesiastical Redactor to tone down external influences, like Gnosticism, and to make it more acceptable to the church. Whether it is possible to separate out the different strands from the reasonably unified whole in this way is debatable, although such an approach does still have its exponents, notably Fortna.[16] Most contemporary interpreters prefer some form of *multiple edition* theory, in which the gospel was revised at different stages in the life of the Johannine commu-

16. See Bultmann's commentary on John, originally published in 1941 (Oxford: Blackwell, 1971). Robert T. Fortna, *The Gospel of Signs: A Reconstruction of the Narrative Source Underlying the Fourth Gospel*, SNTSMS 11 (CUP, 1970), and *The Fourth Gospel and Its Predecessor* (Edinburgh: T&T Clark, 1989); for further evaluation of such approaches, see Kysar, *Fourth Evangelist*, pp. 10-37, and 'The Fourth Gospel', *ANRW* II.25.3, pp. 2395-402; Smalley, John, pp. 102-13; Kümmel, *Introduction to NT*, pp. 200-17.

nity in order to address current concerns.[17] While this seems the most likely solution, methodological questions can still be raised about attempts to provide precise reconstructions of the various versions; the sheer multiplicity of proposals suggests that the overall unity of the gospel makes this difficult.[18]

Perhaps some of the proposed source hypotheses have not taken into account the mechanics of production in the ancient world, nor the freedom of writers, especially of βίοι, to revise and alter their sources. It is likely that the writer(s) of the Fourth Gospel had access to oral and written sources from which a selection was made to produce the portrait of Jesus and his teaching which was desired. As Kysar concludes:

> The role of the fourth evangelist appears to be more alike than unlike the role of the synoptic evangelists. Where scholars once set the fourth evangelist apart from his synoptic counterparts, where they once saw him as the unique mystic or the theologian among the four gospel writers, they are now portraying his function as exactly the same as that of the synoptic evangelists: To articulate a Christian tradition in such a manner as to address it with new relevance to a given community.[19]

This is the approach of writers of βίοι, particularly those writing about philosophers and teachers within the context of their particular schools and followers.

7. Methods of Characterization

Characterization in the Fourth Gospel is achieved, as in the synoptic gospels and in Graeco-Roman βίοι, mainly by the indirect means of relating the deeds and words of the subject. Obviously, Jesus' words are of supreme importance here, and through the words he uses and the things he says, John's picture of Jesus' character emerges. Direct characterization of a metaphorical kind is provided by the 'I am' sayings, with their images of light, bread, the vine (6:35,

---

17. The classic version is in Brown's commentary, pp. xxiv-xi, and *Community, passim;* Appendix 1 of *Community* discusses other attempts, pp. 171-82; now updated in R. E. Brown, *An Introduction to the Gospel of John,* ed. Francis J. Moloney (New York: Doubleday, 2003), esp. pp. 62-89 and 189-219. See also, Smalley, *John,* pp. 113-21, and Kysar, *Fourth Evangelist,* pp. 38-81, and 'The Fourth Gospel', *ANRW* II.25.3, pp. 2402-11.

18. See Stephen C. Barton, 'Can We Identify the Gospel Audiences?' in *The Gospels for All Christians: Rethinking the Gospel Audiences,* ed. Richard Bauckham (Grand Rapids: Eerdmans, 1998), pp. 173-94, esp. pp. 189-93; also Bauckham's essay, 'John for Readers of Mark' in *The Gospels for All Christians,* pp. 147-72.

19. Kysar, *Fourth Evangelist,* p. 81,

8:12, 15:1, etc.). Nonetheless, John has not abandoned deeds, in the manner of a 'sayings gospel': the significance given to the Signs is important as a way of earthing both Jesus' message and his character.[20] Finally, we have the occasional suggestion of Jesus' motive or thought to explain his actions, building up his character; e.g., 'perceiving then that they were about to come and take him by force to make him king, Jesus withdrew again to the mountain by himself' (John 6:15). *Deeds and words, sayings and imputed motives are typical devices of characterization in Graeco-Roman βίοι.*

8. Summary

The external structural features of the Fourth Gospel are similar to those of both the synoptic gospels and Graeco-Roman βίοι: it is prose narrative of medium length, with an apparent chronological framework into which topical material, arranged in discourses in the manner of philosophical βίοι, has been inserted. On a narrow scale, the narrative is composed of stories, dialogues and discourses selected from oral and written sources to depict the character of Jesus. So far, these features confirm the initial impression of βίος Ἰησοῦ.

D. Internal Features

1. Setting

As in the synoptic gospels, the geographical setting is largely determined by the whereabouts of Jesus himself, and includes places in Galilee, Judea, Samaria and Jerusalem. The dramatic setting nearly always has Jesus on centre stage with other characters reacting to him. He is only absent from some 9% of the verses of the gospel, and in most of these, those left on stage are discussing Jesus, his identity, or what they are going to do about him: John the Baptist and Jewish leaders (1:19-28); John the Baptist and disciples (3:25-36); officers and Jewish leaders (7:45-52; 11:45-53; 12:9-11); the Jews (10:19-21; 11:55-57); and Thomas with the disciples (20:24-25). The two remaining passages, the debate between the Jewish leaders and the blind man and his parents (9:13-34) and Simon Peter's denial (18:15-18, 25-27), are also strongly influenced by Jesus' presence off-stage. *Such a sharp focus on the person of Jesus was*

---

20. See Brown's commentary, Appendix III, pp. 525-32, on the use of Signs and their relationship to synoptic miracles, and Appendix IV, pp. 533-8, on the 'I am' sayings.

also noted in the synoptic gospels, and the concentration on the subject is a typical feature of βίοι.

2. Topics

Here we follow the same analysis as in previous chapters:

(a) Ancestry

βίοι often begin by tracing the ancestry of the subject back to an impressive forbear in the realm of the legendary or semi-divine; thus Matthew and Luke follow Jesus' origins back to Abraham and Adam or God respectively. John, however, 'leaves the other three far behind in a single super leap by starting its account in the time before creation, in eternity'.[21] Thus Haenchen sees the Prologue as fulfilling this feature by asserting Jesus' origins on the cosmic scale.

(b) Birth, boyhood and education

These are all missing in the Fourth Gospel; presumably all that needed to be said was covered in the majestic sweep of the Prologue. However, the gospel is aware of Jesus' humble earthly origins, and the fact that they were not what was expected of the Christ: see Nathaniel's sneer about Nazareth in 1:46, and the debate among the Jews and the Pharisees about how Jesus' origins prevent him from being the Christ in 7:40-42, 52.[22]

(c) Great deeds

According to most analyses of the Fourth Gospel, Jesus performs seven great deeds, or 'Signs', although which the seven are is not agreed. Seven Signs can be found in the first half of the gospel, often called 'the Book of Signs': changing water into wine (2:1-11); the healing of the official's son (4:46-54), and of the paralytic (5:2-15); the miraculous feeding (6:1-14); walking on water (6:16-21); sight to the blind man (9); and the raising of Lazarus (11:1-44).[23] Unfortu-

21. Haenchen's commentary, p. 101; see also pp. 124-5.
22. See Stanton, *Jesus of Nazareth*, p. 154.
23. See C. H. Dodd, *The Interpretation of the Fourth Gospel* (CUP, 1953), pp. 289-389; and Brown's commentary, Appendix III, pp. 525-32.

nately, the walking on water is not treated like a Sign and no significance or dialogue is attached to it. Smalley rejects it, therefore, and substitutes the miraculous catch of fish in 21:1-14, even though it occurs in the epilogue. Fortna solves this problem by placing it after the official's son in his reconstruction of the pre-Johannine Signs Gospel, thus making it the 'third sign' — the earlier redaction of 'the third time Jesus was revealed' in 21:14.[24] Whichever way the signs are analysed, John, like the synoptic gospels and βίοι, includes narration of his subject's 'mighty deeds'. Equally, as often in βίοι of philosophers and teachers like Demonax and Apollonius of Tyana, the great deeds also include his 'great words', and so we have all the dialogues and discourses.

(d) Virtues

In company with the synoptic gospels and some of our βίοι, John does not analyse his subject's virtues separately, but allows them to emerge through the general narrative.

(e) Death and consequences

Nearly a sixth of the gospel is taken up with Jesus' arrest, trial, death and resurrection appearances, chapters 18–21. All our βίοι returned to chronological narrative for the subject's death and its immediate consequences at the end of their work (with the exception of Isocrates' *Evagoras*). Robinson sees a link between the final section of the Fourth Gospel and the narratives of Socrates' trial, final discourses and execution, and suggests that 'the "trial narrative" as a genre of literature is regularly produced when the need for it is first felt — to set straight the record of what really happened'.[25] We might also compare the huge amount devoted to the imprisonment and trial of Apollonius, as a setting for his final discourses and teaching. Thus, in finishing his gospel with the Farewell Discourses and the events of Jesus' death and their aftermath, John is once more displaying a topic typically used in Graeco-Roman βίοι.

Despite some differences between the narrative of the Fourth Gospel and the synoptic gospels, this feature has shown that *they share a similar range of topics to that found in Graeco-Roman βίοι.*

---

24. Smalley, *John*, pp. 86-8; Fortna, *The Fourth Gospel*, pp. 65-79; for lists of other versions of the Signs, see Kysar, *The Fourth Evangelist*, pp. 25-9.

25. J. A. T. Robinson, *The Priority of John* (London: SCM, 1985), pp. 92-3.

3. Style

Some have seen John's style as containing many Hellenisms while others noted a Semitic quality to the language: in 1922, C. F. Burney even suggested that the Fourth Gospel was originally composed in Aramaic. It does contain various Semitic terms, such as Rabbi, Messiah and Cephas (see 1:37-42), and prefers to connect short sentences paratactically with a simple 'and', or to have no connection at all (asyndeton), rather than using long classical periods. Perhaps this reflects a bi- or trilingual culture, typical of the eastern Mediterranean. The language is fairly uniform, with a limited and repetitive vocabulary; it can be a little flat and ponderous, and displays a unified 'feel' and style to the work, which argues against composite or multiple production theories. John has certain key words, used little in the synoptic gospels but recurring constantly here, e.g. ζωή, ἀλήθεια, or ἀγάπη; the use of dualistic contrasts, such as φῶς and σκοτία, may resonate with Greek philosophical and/or Jewish religious thought, displaying some education. All of this fits the social milieu of the eastern Mediterranean and is typical of other examples of general Koiné more than high-flown or literary levels. *Such a style is comparable to that in which popular βίοι or treatises were written.*[26]

4. Atmosphere

Like the synoptic gospels, the Fourth Gospel has a fairly steady and serious atmosphere. The tone is even, and the mood does not have the variations noted in the synoptics, partly because of Jesus' dominating control: the contrast between the desolation of the Crucifixion in Mark or Matthew followed by the excitement and fear at the Resurrection is flattened out here by Jesus' control and quiet confidence throughout the Passion. The attitude to the subject reflects this high estimation: Jesus is revealed as divine from the opening words of the Prologue through to Thomas' words, 'my Lord and my God', in 20:28. There is a sense of awe which follows from this view of the subject. The attitude to the reader is open and didactic, inviting us to become one of those 'who received him' (1:12) and helping us to be privy to the reality which opponents cannot or will not see. The values expressed are those of the Johannine community, probably a somewhat separate and introspective group, stressing the need to love the 'brethren', more than the

---

26. See further the commentaries by Lindars, pp. 44-6; Haenchen, pp. 52-66; and Brown, pp. cxxix-cxxxvii and Appendix I on key words of Johannine vocabulary, pp. 497-518.

synoptics' 'neighbour'.[27] *This serious and even worshipful approach may be slightly less varied than that found in the synoptic gospels, but it still remains similar to their atmosphere and to that of other βίοι.*

5. Quality of Characterization

Since the writer believes that Jesus is the Christ, the Son of God, in whom is all life and who knows of his own pre-existence and his future return to glory with the Father, any characterization is bound to fall short of a realistic human portrait. The stress on Jesus' divinity and his unity with the Father affects his characterization, making it rather 'unreal' in places. Thus Käsemann attacks John's picture of Jesus as 'naively Docetic', a visitor from another realm who never really touches earth but merely wears 'the absolute minimum of costume' among us for a little while.[28] While this is not really 'stereotypic', it is not realistic characterization either. The sense of unreality is further developed by the long expositions of Johannine theology placed on Jesus' lips.

However, we noticed in both the synoptic gospels and other βίοι that, while characterization can often be stereotypic, a more 'real' picture emerges indirectly through the narrative itself. So too here we see that, despite the divine figure of Christ, the human Jesus has not completely disappeared: he is weary and thirsty in 4:6-7, and weeps at the death of a friend in 11:35, 'snorting with rage' (ἐμβριμώμενος) at what has happened (11:33, 38). Even the calm confidence exhibited in the Passion has to be reached through the nearest John gets to the agony of the synoptics' accounts of Gethsemane, the 'troubling' of Jesus' soul (τετάρακται) in 12:27. Finally, we note the very human and poignant question of one who has been let down: 'Do you also want to leave me?' (6:67). There is, therefore, a creative tension in John's picture and characterization of Jesus between the real and the unreal, the human and the divine. *Such an ambivalent quality is not dissimilar from the mix of stereotype and reality found in both the synoptic gospels and Graeco-Roman βίοι.*

27. For one view of the implications of Johannine Christology and ecclesiology, see Ernst Käsemann, *The Testament of Jesus* (London: SCM, 1968).

28. Käsemann, *The Testament of Jesus*, p. 10; for a critique, see Günther Bornkamm, 'Towards the Interpretation of John's Gospel: A Discussion of *The Testament of Jesus* by Ernst Käsemann', in *The Interpretation of John*, ed. John Ashton, pp. 79-98.

6. Social Setting and Occasion

Since we have no external knowledge of the setting and occasion of this gospel, we are again dependent on hints internal to the text. From these, various social settings and backgrounds have been proposed over the years: for a long time, particularly through Bultmann's work, a 'history of religions' approach dominated, seeing John as influenced by Hellenistic, especially Gnostic, ideas; then the pendulum swung back, placing it within the fuller understanding of Judaism brought by the Qumran material. Increasingly, a better appreciation of the pluralistic and syncretistic nature of the eastern Roman empire during the period is helping us to understand the wide variety of allusions and influences which the text seems to reveal. A social setting is needed in which ideas of traditional Greek philosophy, Platonism and Stoicism, could be coupled at a popular level with those of new cults and sects, including the proto-Gnostics; links are also to be made with the Jewish world of the Old Testament, Rabbinic arguments and the ideas of heterodox or 'non-conformist' Judaism. The work of Philo of Alexandria demonstrates that this heady mixture was available at a sophisticated and educated level; however, such a syncretistic culture spread all the way down the social scale and was thus capable of influencing the early Christian communities.[29]

As regards the occasion of the writing of the gospel, here again we simply do not know. Traditionally, the Fourth Gospel was associated with the apostle John in his old age at Ephesus, and some Johannine Community theories allow for John to have been the *authority* behind the gospel's production, if not the author. On this basis, his death at an old age could have prompted the production of the gospel, or one edition of it. Another possible occasion arises from the gospel's attitude towards 'the Jews'. This phrase, rare in the synoptics, occurs some seventy times in the Fourth Gospel, becoming increasingly prominent as opposition to Jesus grows; Jesus and his disciples, who are all Jews themselves, appear to be set apart from their own people (e.g. 15:25, 'their law'); 9:22 and 12:42 say that any who accept Jesus as Christ will be made ἀποσυνάγωγος. It is argued that this makes no sense in Jesus' own day, but fits perfectly into the increasing separation of church and synagogue around AD 85, with the Council of Yavneh and the insertion of the Benediction against the Heretics ('Birkath ha-Minim') into Jewish liturgy. Perhaps, therefore, the occasion which caused the gospel to be written was the crisis of

---

29. For further discussion, see the commentaries by Lindars, pp. 35-42, and Brown, pp. lii-lxvi; see also, Smalley, *John*, pp. 41-68; Kysar, *Fourth Evangelist*, pp. 102-46, and 'The Fourth Gospel', *ANRW* II.25.3, pp. 2411-25; Kümmel, *Introduction to NT*, pp. 217-28.

confidence which this separation from the synagogue caused the Johannine Community: they needed to be reassured that they were the real people of God, persecuted by 'the Jews' as Jesus himself was. Robinson, however, disagrees, arguing that ἀποσυνάγωγος is not a technical term and that the separation from Judaism was more gradual; the conflict with the Jews in John is no different from that seen in the synoptic gospels — so we need to look elsewhere for the occasion of the gospel's composition.[30]

Thus, the text does not reveal anything definite about its setting and occasion, other than to suggest that it belongs within the rich pluralism of the eastern Mediterranean towards the end of the first century AD, and its occasion was the need to relate Jesus and his teaching to both the Johannine community and those around it. *Such a setting and occasion are well within the scope of βίοι.*

7. Authorial Intention and Purpose

> Now Jesus did many other signs in the presence of his disciples, which are not written in this book; but these are written that you may believe that Jesus is the Christ, the Son of God, and that believing you may have life in his name. (John 20:30-31)

The evangelist's expressed purpose in writing the gospel provides a clear biographical intent with the whole focus upon the person of Jesus: it is an account of 'signs' which *he* did, that people may believe who *he* is, and have life in *him.* Secondly, 20:31 contains two purpose clauses, expressed by ἵνα plus the subjunctive; the first declares an evangelistic aim ('that you may believe') and the second a practical one ('that you may have life'). These aims may be related to our analysis of βίοι: we shall leave aside encomiastic and exemplary intentions, and also the intentions of preserving the subject's memory and providing entertainment, since none of these seem relevant to the expressed purpose or the text itself.

---

30. Robinson, *Priority,* pp. 72-93; see further, Brown's commentary, pp. lxx-lxxv, and *Community,* pp. 40-3, and 66-9; Smalley, *John,* pp. 140-9; Kysar, *Fourth Evangelist,* pp. 149-56, and 'The Fourth Gospel', *ANRW* II.25.3, pp. 2425-8; Kümmel, *Introduction to NT,* pp. 230-4; and Dunn, 'Let John Be John', in *Das Evangelium und die Evangelien,* esp. pp. 318-21, ET as *The Gospel and the Gospels,* pp. 302-4. Johannine scholars are increasingly less sure about the Birkath and any link with the Fourth Gospel: see P. W. van der Horst, 'The Birkat ha minim in Recent Research', *ExpT* 105 (1994-5), pp. 363-68, and Brown, *An Introduction to the Gospel of John* (2003), pp. 157-72 and 213-4.

However, the informative and the didactic aims are relevant to the purpose expressed in 20:31. The writer must provide information about Jesus in order for the reader to come to believe, and he chooses to do this by narrating the Signs. In fact, through the *chronological narrative,* all the necessary information about Jesus' cosmic origins, earthly ministry, Passion and Resurrection is provided for the reader to realize the true identity of Jesus, while through the *discourse material* the reader comes to appreciate the teaching of Jesus and the Christian faith.

Another common purpose of βίοι was as apologetic and polemic, particularly in political or philosophical debate. These purposes can be detected in the Fourth Gospel: thus the gospel's attitude towards 'the Jews' may have its origins in defending the Johannine Community against Jewish attacks, and in its response. Polemic may also be seen in the depiction of John the Baptist telling his followers to leave him and join Jesus (1:29; 1:35-37) since 'he must increase, but I must decrease' (3:30). This may reflect a debate between the Johannine Community and disciples of the Baptist, mentioned as being in Ephesus in Acts 19:1-7. Christian heretics are another possible target: Irenaeus suggested that John was written to counter the arguments of the Christian Gnostic Cerinthus, whereas Bultmann detected pro-Gnostic influence in the gospel. Similarly, 'the Word became flesh' in 1:14 is sometimes considered to be anti-Docetic, like the anti-Docetic polemic in the Epistles, e.g. 1 John 4:2, 2 John 7, possibly directed towards former members of the community who had left (1 John 2:19). However, Käsemann interprets the evidence the other way, stressing 1:14b 'and we beheld his glory', and therefore he sees the gospel as naively Docetic itself. Thus in both Gnosticism and Docetism, the argument for polemic has been interpreted both ways, both pro- and anti-. Likewise, opposing polemical approaches for and against the sacraments and to eschatology have also been noticed. Whichever positions one adopts, the rôle of polemic is clear.[31]

The Fourth Gospel has several intentions and purposes, both those expressed by 20:31 in terms of evangelism and didactic, and those discerned

---

31. Thus Rodney A. Whiteacre entitles his study, *Johannine Polemic: The Role of Tradition and Theology,* SBLDS 67 (Chico: Scholars, 1982), while Lindars has a section headed 'The Use of the Gospel in Debate', *John,* pp. 46-62; see also, David Rensberger, *Overcoming the World: Politics and Community in the Gospel of John* (London: SPCK, 1989). For further discussion of John's purposes, see the commentaries by Lindars, pp. 56-63, and Brown, pp. lxvii-lxxix, and *Community, passim;* and also, Smalley, *John,* pp. 125-36; Kysar, *Fourth Evangelist,* pp. 147-65, and 'The Fourth Gospel', *ANRW* II.25.3, pp. 2425-32; Kümmel, *Introduction to NT,* pp. 228-34; Stanton, *The Gospels and Jesus,* pp. 119-23 (Second Edition, 2002, pp. 116-20); Martin, *Narrative Parallels to the New Testament,* p. 23.

from study of the text itself of apologetic and polemic. *These purposes are also central to the synoptic gospels, and they are some of the most common purposes of Graeco-Roman βίοι, particularly those originating within philosophical schools.*

8. Summary

The Fourth Gospel displays a pattern of internal features similar to that noted in the synoptic gospels; furthermore, many of these features are shared with Graeco-Roman βίοι. The focus of the geographical and dramatic settings upon the person of the subject, the selection of biographical topics, the rather serious atmosphere and the range of purposes are all typical of βίοι. The quality of the characterization reveals a mixture of the human and the divine which is not unlike the usual mix of the real and the stereotype in βίοι. Finally, the style and social setting are consonant with the background of popular Hellenistic βίοι. *The hypothesis that the Fourth Gospel is a βίος Ἰησοῦ is thus confirmed.*

Conclusion

The Gospel writer presents his theology in the form of a *life* of Jesus.[32]

Our analysis of the generic features of Graeco-Roman βίοι and the synoptic gospels showed that these works exhibit a shared pattern or family resemblance. The same analysis has now been applied to the Fourth Gospel with the following results:

(i) Like the synoptic gospels, John lacks any kind of biographical title; it begins with a formal prologue, after which the subject's name is mentioned. These are common opening features in βίοι.

(ii) Verbal analysis of the Fourth Gospel reveals that Jesus is the subject of a fifth of the verbs and a further third are placed on his lips. Such dominance by the subject occurs also in the synoptic gospels and βίοι. Furthermore, the 20% with Jesus as subject demonstrate that, despite all the discourse material, John has not abandoned narrative about Jesus. A

---

32. Oscar Cullmann, *Salvation in History* (London: SCM, 1967), p. 270, his italics; see also, Lindars, *John*, p. 26.

similar proportion of space is allocated to the events of the Passion and Resurrection as in the synoptic gospels, and to crucial periods of the subject's life as in βίοι.

(iii) With respect to external features, the Fourth Gospel shares a similar mode of representation, size, structure and scale to those of the synoptic gospels and βίοι, and makes use of similar literary units, drawn from oral and written sources to display the character of Jesus by means of his deeds, words and sayings in a manner typical of βίοι.

(iv) All four gospels share similar internal features of settings, topics and atmospheres with Graeco-Roman βίοι. The style and social setting of the Fourth Gospel are probably to be located amid groups of the eastern Mediterranean, where popular βίοι were also to be found. John's characterization of Jesus has a mixed quality about it, reminiscent of that found in the synoptics and βίοι. Finally, its purposes of information, didactic, apologetic and polemic are typical of Graeco-Roman βίοι, especially among philosophical schools.

These results place the Fourth Gospel clearly in the same genre as the synoptic gospels, namely βίοι. As Dunn says:

> Another striking fact is that the Fourth Evangelist obviously felt it necessary to retain the format of a *Gospel*. For all its differences from the Synoptics, John is far closer to them than to any other ancient writing . . . he chose, and chose deliberately, to retain the developed discourse material within the framework of a Gospel as laid down by Mark — traditions of Jesus' miracles and teaching building up all the while to the climax of the cross.[33]

Now that we have established the common biographical genre between the synoptic gospels and the Fourth Gospel, this takes us into one further issue: if John is not dependent upon the synoptic gospels nor knew their texts, then 'is it feasible that both Mark and . . . the fourth evangelist independently originated the gospel genre?'[34] Kysar's question leads us into the origins and development of the gospel genre, or more accurately, of the subgenre of βίος literature known as 'gospel' and concerned with βίοι Ἰησοῦ, and also into the hermeneutical implications of this generic identification. These must be the concerns of our concluding chapter.

---

33. Dunn, 'Let John Be John', pp. 338-9; ET *The Gospel and the Gospels*, p. 322.
34. Kysar, *Fourth Evangelist*, p. 69.

CHAPTER 10

Conclusions and Implications

The problem of gospel genre is still a problem and will remain so until it is solved on the basis of sound literary theory and a thorough study of ancient literary history.[1]

This study has been in two parts: the overall review of the problem of the genre of the gospels and the suggestion of a solution. It has been an argument of cumulative weight, with the methodology coming from literary theory and leading to the solution. Concluding summaries have been provided at each stage, leading to the final conclusion that the gospels belong to the genre of Graeco-Roman βίοι. Finally, therefore, we will outline the contribution of this study to gospel studies and some further implications which may flow from its suggestion that the gospels are βίοι. While the latter cannot be dealt with in detail, since they are ancillary to our main argument, they may provoke further studies to build upon our conclusions.

A. Contribution and Results

1. Evaluation of Previous Discussion

The first Chapter provided a general survey and evaluation of attempts to solve the problem of gospel genre over the last century or so. We saw that, al-

---

1. Susan Marie Praeder's conclusion of her review of Shuler's *A Genre for the Gospels* in *CBQ* 45 (1983), p. 709.

though early studies suggested parallels between the gospels and Graeco-Roman biography, this was dismissed by the form critics because of their stress on the oral and *Kleinliteratur* nature of the gospels. However, redaction criticism has renewed interest in the gospel writers as authors in their own right, and with this the debate about the genre of the gospels reappeared. The most common suggestion is that the gospels are in some form of biographical genre. The various proposals for this over the last three decades or so were considered in Chapter 4. None of them has received widespread support as a definitive answer, although the cumulative effect has been an increasing assumption by scholars that some link with Graeco-Roman biography helps in understanding the gospels. Our evaluation is that most of these attempts failed because of either an insufficient grasp of critical literary theory or an inadequate understanding of the nature of Graeco-Roman biography, or both. It was suggested that only a proper interdisciplinary study involving literary theory and Graeco-Roman literature as well as gospel studies would succeed.

2. Establishment of a Proper Methodology

We have set out a methodology taking both literary theory and Graeco-Roman biography into account. Chapter 2 provided a survey of critical literary theory of genre, revealing the way genres form a set of expectations between authors and readers and how they are mediated through a variety of features. In Chapter 3 we considered the use of genre in classical studies and the development of Graeco-Roman biography. We suggested that 'βίος' is a better term for this flexible and widespread ancient genre, rather than 'biography' with all its modern expectations and connotations. One contribution is thus to have provided a study of the disciplines of critical literary theory and Graeco-Roman literature for the benefit of New Testament scholars who do not have this background.

Chapters 5, 6 and 7 then applied the methodology of generic features to various examples of Graeco-Roman βίοι. From this study of ten different authors and periods, some on the fringes of the genre and others at its centre, a clear family resemblance of the genre of βίος emerged. This demonstrated the flexibility of the genre and the room for variation of features within it. However, the genre does have its limits: analysis of some works revealed that they sit on the overlap with other *genera proxima*, or indeed fit better into philosophical treatises or *memorabilia*. To belong to the genre of βίος, it is necessary for a work to demonstrate the same family resemblance with at least as many features in common with βίοι as βίοι tend to have in common with each other.

3. Demonstration of the Genre of the Gospels

Finally, in the last two Chapters, we applied the same, systematic analysis of generic features to the synoptic gospels and to the Fourth Gospel in turn. We discovered a high degree of correlation between the features of the gospels and those noted in βίοι, indicating a shared family resemblance. All four gospels lack any kind of biographical title, but the range of opening features (genealogy, starting directly into narrative, preface or prologue) is also found in βίοι, especially the early use of the subject's name. Analysis of the subjects of the verbs demonstrates that the gospels exhibit the same 'skew' effect noticed in βίοι, caused by the concentration on *one* person as the subject, rather than a range of subjects in the manner of other narrative genres; also the allocation of a reasonably large amount of space to the events of Jesus' death and Passion can be compared with the allocation of space in βίοι to the subject's significant period, including the death in some cases.

Turning to the structural, external features, the mode of representation of prose narrative, the medium-length size, the chronological structure with topical inserts and the narrow scale are all typical of βίοι. Furthermore, the basic literary units of stories, sayings and speeches are not dissimilar from those of βίοι, nor is the deliberate selection from a range of oral and written sources to reveal the particular characterization desired by the author for his portrait. There is, therefore, a high degree of similarity of external features. The study of the internal features, based more on content, revealed both similarity and variation. The wide range of geographical settings caused by the concentration of the dramatic setting on the subject is very similar, and there is a similar selection of topics and motifs. The rather serious and respectful atmosphere of the gospels is quite reminiscent of some βίοι, although other βίοι do have a lighter feel. The style and the apparent social setting of the gospels are both more popular than most of the βίοι studied; this may reflect the general preservation of more upper-class material from the ancient literary world, rather than indicate a significant difference, since there are suggestions that βίοι at a more popular level were actually quite common. The somewhat mixed quality of the characterization in the gospels, and the range of their purposes, can all find parallels within βίοι.

Thus, a wide range of similarities have been discovered between the gospels and Graeco-Roman βίοι; the differences are not sufficiently marked or significant to prevent the gospels belonging to the genre of βίος literature. The increasing tendency among New Testament scholars to refer to the gospels as 'biographical' is vindicated; indeed, the time has come to go on from the use of the adjective 'biographical', for *the gospels are βίοι!*

B. Generic Implications

1. *The Identity of the Gospel Genre*

The first implication from even a brief consideration of their shared generic features is that all four canonical gospels are the same genre, despite the various apparent differences between them, notably the different 'feel' of the Fourth Gospel. Using the idea of 'family resemblance', we may compare the gospels to children of the same family: each child is indeed different, unique and special in its own right, but intimate knowledge of them from the inside and comparison with others outside the family show their shared family features arising from a common ancestry. Such similarities between the gospels have long been recognized, especially between the synoptic gospels with their literary interdependence, but also between John and the rest. This 'group identity' was recognized by the Tübingen Symposium in 1982: Stanton affirmed Matthew's dependency on Mark, saying 'if Mark is an εὐαγγέλιον, so is Matthew . . . he is almost certainly not attempting to create a new *genre*'. Marshall points out that, although there was the alternative pattern of Q, 'the important point is that neither Luke nor Matthew followed its pattern in the composition of their works. Both writers incorporated the Q material in a pattern that is based on Mk.' Finally, Dunn affirmed the identity of John with the others:

> For all its differences from the Synoptics, John is far closer to them than to any other ancient writing (as the Symposium has shown). Although it is the discourses of Jesus which are the most elaborated feature of John's Gospel, the Evangelist did not elect to present a document consisting solely of the discourses or sayings of the redeemer (we may contrast gnostic equivalents like Gospel of Thomas, Thomas the Contender and Pistis Sophia). Rather he chose, and chose deliberately, to retain the developed discourse material within the framework of a Gospel as laid down by Mark.[2]

2. All in *Das Evangelium und die Evangelien*, ed. P. Stuhlmacher, ET as *The Gospel and the Gospels:* Stanton, 'Matthew as a Creative Interpreter', p. 287 (ET, p. 272); Marshall, 'Luke and His "Gospel"', pp. 292-3 (ET, p. 277); Dunn, 'Let John Be John', pp. 338-9 (ET, p. 322).

As already noted, the differences between John and the synoptic gospels emerge when these four works arc studied in isolation; however, as Stanton says, 'when the four gospels are set alongside all the other "gospels" and related writings which flourished for a time in some circles in the early church, it is their similarities rather than their differences which are striking'.[3]

It is necessary to affirm this generic identity of the gospels, since sometimes each gospel is described as its own genre, so that, for example, Matthew turns out to be a manual of church discipline, or Luke is described as a monograph. Even some who recognize the biographical genre of the gospels do not apply this to all four equally. Thus, on Talbert's system, Mark and John are both Type B (Lives written to defend the subject), while Luke and Matthew are different — Type D (written to link the life of the founder with those of his followers) and E (to provide hermeneutical legitimation of his teaching) respectively. Similarly, Aune puts John with Mark and Matthew, but Luke 'does not belong to a type of ancient biography for it belongs with Acts, and Acts cannot be forced into a biographical mold'. Conversely, Barr and Wentling compared Graeco-Roman biography with Luke-Acts alone, ignoring the other three.[4] Given the high degree of family resemblance between all four canonical gospels' generic features, these studies must have made a mistake somewhere in methodology: in Talbert's case, the difference arises from a classification based solely on purpose, whereas Aune insists that both Luke and Acts must be the same genre. Maddox suggests that Luke-Acts is 'theological history'; Hengel calls it 'historical monograph', while Aune prefers 'general history'.[5]

However, we have shown that the borders between the genres of historiography, monograph and biography are blurred and flexible. Medium-length works of prose narrative sharing external features, such as a vague chronological structure made up from units of stories and speeches, belong to one of three related genres: historical monograph or one volume of a larger work of historiography, romance or novel, or βίος. They are differentiated only by internal features such as subject or focus. Richard Pervo has ar-

---

3. Stanton, *The Gospels and Jesus*, p. 135 (Second Edition, 2002, p. 138); see also his *Jesus of Nazareth*, p. 184: 'If the evangelist did not intend, at least in part, to indicate what sort of person Jesus was, why did he write a gospel which, when placed alongside, say, either the *Gospel of Thomas* or *Pirqe Aboth*, looks so much like the synoptics?'

4. Talbert, *What Is a Gospel?*, pp. 134-5, see p. 81 above; Aune, *The New Testament in Its Literary Environment*, p. 77, see p. 99 above; Barr and Wentling, 'Conventions of Classical Biography', see pp. 96-7 above.

5. Maddox, *The Purpose of Luke-Acts*, pp. 15-18; Hengel, *Acts and the History of Earliest Christianity*, pp. 14 and 36; Aune, *The New Testament in Its Literary Environment*, pp. 77ff.

gued that Acts belongs not to historiography but to the genre of the ancient novel, because it is written to entertain as well as for edification. However, these were common purposes also found in much ancient historiography; in the end, Pervo's definition that 'the novel = material + manner + style + structure'[6] is rather vague for identifying genre. Aune criticizes Pervo in that only his use of the term 'fiction' distinguishes his novel from other forms of ancient historiography;[7] furthermore, we have noted already the use of fiction within βίοι. Thus Pervo's identification of the genre of Acts is not persuasive. However, Aune's assertion that 'Luke-Acts must be treated as affiliated with *one* genre' is also problematic.[8] As Parsons replies, 'it is entirely possible that Luke produced works belonging to two distinct genres of literature'.[9] Clearly, the works are closely connected, as is shown by the literary parallels between the characters of Jesus, Peter and Paul, the use of the journey motifs, and, of course, the reference to τὸν πρῶτον λόγον in Acts 1:1. However, the two works are never found together in the manuscripts, but are separated by John (or sometimes by Mark), and even Aune accepts that they could have been published separately.[10] It is possible that Acts, like the gospel, is linked to βίος literature, either as a list of the Lives of the main subject's followers,[11] or as a βίος of the church, in the manner of Dicaearchus' biographical work on Greece, Περὶ τοῦ τῆς Ἑλλάδος βίου, mentioned above. Although Acts and the gospels share many generic features, they differ over their focus and concentration of subject: computer analysis of proper names in Acts shows that God appears in 17% of the sentences or major phrases, Paul in 14.5%, Jesus in 7%, and Peter in 6%. However, Acts and the gospels may be related genres. Both βίος and monograph may be distinguished from history itself by the feature of size: they are medium-length works, whereas

6. Richard J. Pervo, *Profit with Delight: The Literary Genre of the Acts of the Apostles* (Philadelphia: Fortress, 1987), p. 114.

7. Aune, *The New Testament in Its Literary Environment*, p. 153.

8. *Ibid.*, p. 80, his italics.

9. In his review of Pervo, in *Interpretation* 1989, p. 409.

10. Aune, *The New Testament in Its Literary Environment*, p. 77; note also: 'The Acts of the Apostles, though it is Luke's second volume and a sequel to his Gospel, does not belong to that genre. That it is separated from the Gospel of Luke by the Fourth Gospel is significant; the four belonged together, and had to be kept together, even at the cost of splitting Luke's work in two', quotation from F. Kermode, 'Introduction to the New Testament', in *The Literary Guide to the Bible*, ed. Robert Alter and Frank Kermode (London: Collins, 1987), p. 383; J. M. Dawsey, 'The Literary Unity of Luke-Acts', *NTS* 35 (1989), pp. 48-66, notes that Luke and Acts are different genres and are never found together in the manuscripts; for the Western order of the gospels, see Bovon, 'The Synoptic Gospels', *HTR* 1988, p. 20.

11. As Talbert suggests, *Literary Patterns*, pp. 125-43; *What Is a Gospel?*, p. 134.

historiography tends towards large works of several volumes. Although they are of the same size, βίος differs from monograph in that it focusses on one person, while monograph concentrates on a particular situation, war, or period. Thus Cicero suggests to Lucceius that, out of his large overall history ('Italici belli et civilis historia'), he should extract his account of the Catilinarian conspiracy from its start to Cicero's return from exile, which would make a reasonable sized monograph ('modicum quoddam corpus'), so that he can praise Cicero's part in it all (*Ad. Fam.* V.12.2-4). However, the generic boundaries of historiography, monograph and βίοι could get blurred even within one work: thus Diodorus Siculus' massive history of the world in forty books devotes an entire book (XVII) to Alexander the Great, displaying many features of βίος, which is then followed by the 'Acts of his Successors' (τὰς τῶν διαδεξαμένων πράξεις, XVII.118.4); however, his treatment of Agathocles' activity in Sicily is fitted around events elsewhere in Greece or Asia in annalistic fashion, with a wider focus, typical of monograph (XIX.70–XX.101). The differing approach probably results from the sources available to Diodorus for the respective sections.

Thus it is not surprising as Luke moves from the βίος focus on one individual in his gospel to the wider scene of his second work, that generic features shared with history, monograph or romance start to appear in Acts. However, this does not alter the fact that Luke's gospel itself shares the same family resemblance as the other three gospels. Matthew and Luke are the same genre as their source, namely Mark; John, for all its individual 'feel', is also not significantly different from the point of view of genre. Because all four canonical gospels exhibit a high degree of generic similarity, they all belong to the same genre, i.e. βίος, and to the same subgenre, i.e. βίοι Ἰησοῦ.

2. The Nature of the Gospel Genre

Critical literary theory of genre revealed the different levels at which genre and related considerations operate. Fowler had three distinct levels: mode (higher level, vague, based on styles or motifs), genre itself (including features of both form and content) and subgenre (usually differentiated by subject material).[12] If this analysis is applied to the gospels, it clarifies some of the links proposed with other literature. Many possible genres proposed for the gospels are actually modal relationships: thus the dramatic, tragic or tragicomic elements (mode) do not make the gospels into drama or tragedy

---

12. Fowler, *Kinds of Literature*, pp. 106-18, see pp. 39-40 above.

(genre), any more than parabolic concepts make them parables.[13] Below this modal level, we have genre itself, and the genre of the gospels is βίος: no further definition of the genre of the gospels is needed. Below this level again, however, it is possible to be more precise. The subgenres of βίος include political βίοι, literary βίοι, βίοι of philosophers and so forth. The gospels exhibit several features which are also found in philosophical βίοι, such as the use of discourse and teaching material, whereas typical features of political βίοι, such as precise chronology, are missing. Thus there is a similarity with the subgenre of religious or philosophical βίοι. Below this level they are βίοι Ἰησοῦ, and below that is the level of the individual meaning of each gospel.

3. The Development of the Gospel Genre

Our genre theory also showed us that genres emerge from mixed origins, drawing on neighbouring genres and beginning to assemble the pattern of their generic features. The primary stage is reached when someone first puts all these features together, sometimes unconsciously, and often not completely successfully. The secondary stage occurs when others develop the primary model. The tertiary stage involves radical reinterpretation in a new direction. After this the genre 'dies', or ceases to be written in the original form; new genres then develop.[14] Thus βίος moves from its origins in historiography and rhetoric through the primary works of the philosophical schools into secondary Hellenistic βίοι. Roman biography mixes the Roman origins of family honours and traditions with the Greek model to produce new forms of βίοι, which are then modified, developing eventually into the late-imperial genre of hagiography and the new genre of mediaeval biography.

We may apply the model to the development of the gospels within the overall genre of βίος. The origins lie in the oral traditions of the early Christian communities and their preaching, including various contemporary genres; Baird sees twelve different genres, such as polemic, romance, aretalogy, dialogue, etc., reflected in the synoptic gospels.[15] The origins also include proposed sources of the gospels, and *Ur-* or proto-gospels: Robinson saw Q as belonging to the genre of Wisdom sayings, and Kloppenborg sees Q moving from this in the direction of biography. Downing's writings have attempted to show a link between Q and Cynic sayings, although Tuckett is not convinced.

---

13. The suggestions of Kelber, Bilezikian or Via — see p. 194 above.
14. See Fowler, *Kinds*, pp. 149-69 and 'Life and Death', pp. 90-1; see pp. 44-5 above.
15. Baird, 'Genre Analysis', p. 400.

Sato has argued for a prophetic background and genre for Q, while Williams calls it a 'parable-chreia collection'.[16] Similarly, Fortna believes that his Johannine 'Signs Source' is already a 'gospel' in terms of genre through its narrative; however, once it is combined with the Passion Source into the 'Gospel of Signs', then we have the earliest real gospel, 'roughly contemporary with Q' around the 40s/50s AD.[17] Fascinating though these speculations are, they concern texts which, if they existed at all, have not survived; therefore, we cannot be certain about their genre. It is when Mark combines all these various origins and traditions together into a narrative based around Jesus that the βίος form becomes important and we have the primary stage of the subgenre. He may have been consciously writing about Jesus in a way which was similar to βίοι of philosophers, or he may have done it unconsciously, falling into a βίος pattern simply because it is the natural genre for any text concentrating on the deeds and words of a single person.

Matthew and Luke represent the secondary stage: it seems that they did recognize Mark's genre and bring it closer to other Graeco-Roman βίοι: thus the Greek style is tidied up, and ancestry, birth and infancy narratives are added, together with a clearer chronological and topical structure. Berger sees a development towards a 'Königsvita', while the 'philosopher-vita' is suggested by Dieter Georgi.[18] The Fourth Gospel may also be secondary stage; either the evangelist 'reinvented the wheel', as Aune puts it[19] — developing the form separately through his oral sources shared with the synoptics and seeking to blend Jesus' teaching with narrative — or he edits and reinterprets a source which already has this form, such as one of the synoptic gospels (Barrett, Kümmel), the Gospel of Signs (Fortna) or earlier editions from the

---

16. J. M. Robinson, *'Logoi Sophon:* On the Gattung of Q', in *Trajectories*, pp. 71-113; refined by R. Hodgson, 'On the Gattung of Q: A Dialogue with James M. Robinson', *Biblica* 66 (1985), pp. 73-95; Kloppenborg, *Formation of Q*, pp. 262 and 327-8, and 'The Formation of Q and Antique Instructional Genres', *JBL* 105 (1986), pp. 443-62; F. G. Downing, 'Quite like Q: A Genre for "Q": The "Lives" of Cynic Philosophers', *Biblica* 69 (1988), pp. 196-225; C. M. Tuckett, 'A Cynic Q?', *Biblica* 70 (1989), pp. 349-76; Migaku Sato, *Q und Prophetie: Studien zur Gattungs- und Traditionengeschichte der Quelle Q*, WUNT 2.29 (Tübingen: Mohr-Siebeck, 1988); James G. Williams, 'Parable and Chreia: From Q to Narrative Gospel', *Semeia* 43 (1988), pp. 85-114. Downing has subsequently used our method of generic analysis to argue against Tuckett and to conclude that Q is a form of βίος with similarities to Cynic material: F. Gerald Downing, 'A Genre for Q and a Socio-Cultural Context for Q: Comparing Sets of Similarities with Sets of Differences', *JSNT* 55 (1994), pp. 3-26.

17. Fortna, 'Excursus A: The Source's Genre' in *The Fourth Gospel*, pp. 205-16.

18. Berger, 'Hellenistische Gattungen im NT', *ANRW* II.25.2, p. 1245, repeated and affirmed in his *Formgeschichte des NT*, p. 356; Georgi, 'The Records of Jesus', p. 541.

19. Aune, 'The Gospels as Hellenistic Biography', *Mosaic*, 1987, p. 4.

community (Brown *et al.*) — see pages 214 and 221-2 above. The amount of discourse material included begins to push the work towards other genres, such as philosophical dialogues, but sufficient narrative and other biographical features are retained for it still to be a βίος.

The tertiary stage may be discerned in the apocryphal and non-canonical gospels. Again, many of these works are not preserved but are known to us from citations in the Fathers or from papyrus fragments, so genre identification is difficult.[20] However, taken as a whole, they are a mixed group with varying relationships to the canonical gospels. Some examples, especially the 'Jewish-Christian' gospels, such as the *Nazarenes, Ebionites* and *Hebrews,* share stories with both the synoptic gospels and the Fourth Gospel, and may have had a similar overall structure: this can be explained through common oral traditions. These works may have been forms of βίοι; Gero says, 'these works were "complete" gospels, and included much narrative material' and he calls both them and the canonical gospels '*Vitae Jesu*'.[21]

In other cases, however, especially those from the Gnostic tradition, we have different genres: the *Gospel of Thomas* consists of 114 sayings of Jesus. Thus it lacks many generic features of the canonical gospels, such as narrative or chronological and geographical settings.[22] Similarly, the *Gospel of Truth* is related to monograph and 'hortatory, laudatory address' while the *Gospel of Philip* is a collection of sayings, a different pattern of generic features from the canonical gospels.[23] Other documents termed 'gospels' concentrate on one part of the story of Jesus. The *Protevangelium of James,* which begins with the conception of Mary and ends at the birth of Jesus, is described by Gero as

20. See further, E. Hennecke, *New Testament Apocrypha* (London: SCM, 1963), and James H. Charlesworth, *The New Testament Apocrypha and Pseudepigrapha* (London: Metuchen, 1987); also his article with a full bibliography, 'Research on the New Testament Apocrypha and Pseudepigrapha', in *ANRW* II.25.5 (1988), pp. 3919-68.

21. Stephen Gero, 'Apocryphal Gospels: A Survey of Textual and Literary Problems', *ANRW* II.25.5 (1988), pp. 3969-96, quotations from pp. 3975 and 3989; see also, A. F. J. Klijn, 'Das Hebräer- und das Nazoräerevangelium', *ANRW* II.25.5, pp. 3997-4033, and George Howard, 'The Gospel of the Ebionites', pp. 4034-53; P. Vielhauer, 'Jewish-Christian Gospels', in Hennecke, *NT Apocrypha*, pp. 117-65.

22. Hennecke, *NT Apocrypha*, pp. 278-307 and 511-22; 'Evangelium Thomae Copticum', Appendix 1, in *Synopsis Quattuor Evangeliorum*, ed. Kurt Aland, 5th edn (Stuttgart: Württembergische Bibelanstalt, 1968), pp. 517-30; for discussion and bibliography, see F. T. Fallon and R. Cameron, 'The Gospel of Thomas: A Forschungsbericht and Analysis', in *ANRW* II.25.6 (1988), pp. 4195-251.

23. J. Helderman, 'Das Evangelium Veritatis in der neueren Forschung', *ANRW* II.25.5, pp. 4054-106, esp. 'Die Gattung des EV', pp. 4069-72; G. S. Gasparro, 'Il "Vangelo secondo Filippo": rassegna degli studi e proposte di interpretazione', pp. 4107-66, esp. pp. 4113-18, and J. J. Buckley, 'Conceptual Models and Polemical Issues in the Gospel of Philip', pp. 4167-94.

'not really a *Vita Jesu*, but rather a *Vita Mariae*', while the so-called 'infancy gospels' consist of legendary stories about the boyhood of Jesus, designed to fill out the gap we noted in the canonical gospels. Finally, 'Passion gospels' concentrate on the other end of Jesus' life. Thus, none of these documents share the family resemblance of the four canonical gospels.[24]

As Gero concludes, therefore, 'one must guard against an assumption that "apocryphal gospels" or "post-canonical" traditions represent a distinct literary genre'.[25] It is better to see them as part of the tertiary stage of reinterpretation and sophistication away from the basic generic pattern of βίοι Ἰησοῦ. The missing features, such as lack of narrative, settings and chronological development, the scale and focus on the ministry of the earthly Jesus and so on, are the features which place the canonical gospels in the genre of βίος. The use of the word εὐαγγέλιον to describe many of these works is evidence of the early church's recognition of the genre of the gospels, but even then it is sometimes 'so-called' when applied to the non-canonical gospels, as in Bishop Serapion's counterblast περὶ τοῦ λεγομένου κατὰ Πέτρον εὐαγγέλιον (*c.* AD 200).[26] The final evidence that the genre of gospel as βίος Ἰησοῦ has ceased to be composed is that those who wished to write about Jesus without following the Gnostic route out into treatise or sayings/discourse genres chose instead to write in the genre of gospel commentaries, indicating that the canonical gospels have become revered works — and so we have a change of genre.

Thus the canonical gospels form a subgenre of βίοι Ἰησοῦ, possibly related to philosophical βίοι, which displays a clear generic development from its origins in the oral traditions through the primary stage of Mark to the classical secondary versions of Matthew and Luke. John displays some minor variations on the theme, but it is with the development of the non-canonical gospels and commentaries on the canonical gospels that we have moved through the tertiary stage into other related, but different, genres.

4. The Setting of the Gospel Genre

The question of whether Mark wrote in the genre of βίοι deliberately or whether he just fell unconsciously into a natural biographical pattern, and the

---

24. See Hennecke, *NT Apocrypha*, pp. 363-417 and 433-510, and Gero, 'Apocryphal Gospels', *ANRW* II.25.5, pp. 3978-89, for all these gospels; for the *Protevangelium of James*, see p. 3978 and E. Cothenet, 'Le Protévangile de Jacques', *ANRW* II.25.6 (1988), pp. 4252-69.

25. Gero, 'Apocryphal Gospels', *ANRW* II.25.5, pp. 3995-6.

26. See Moule, *Birth of NT*, pp. 251-2.

suggestion made above that Matthew and Luke attempted to conform their work more closely to βίος, both raise the issue of the setting of the gospel genre in contemporary first-century society and of the level of the evangelists' education and literary awareness: would they have known some of these other βίοι and, if so, how did they meet them? A large gulf has been envisaged between classical literature and the New Testament since Schmidt and Bultmann's distinction between *Hochliteratur* and *Kleinliteratur*. This depends upon two ideas: first, that literary knowledge and competence was confined to the upper classes in the ancient world, and second that the early Christians were drawn from the lower classes. The combination of these two ideas implies that the early Christians would not have known 'higher literature' and that their works, such as the gospels, were forms of popular storytelling. If this is true, it causes severe problems for our suggestion that the gospels belong to the genre of Graeco-Roman βίοι.

First, however, the penetration of literary ideas through ancient society was widespread. Francis Cairns points out that awareness of genres and how they operate was taught as part of childhood exercises and would be 'the minimum formal rhetorical equipment of any literate person from the Hellenistic period on'.[27] The content of Hellenistic primary education centred around reading and writing skills based on extracts from classical literature, with moral education being imparted through the choice of elevating stories. These would often be biographical — the great deeds of this or that hero put forward as a model for the children to emulate, and this moral, paradigmatic purpose was typical of βίοι even at a high literary level. Thus the concepts and nature of βίος were taught indirectly at primary level, followed by direct teaching of genres and other aspects of rhetoric and composition at secondary level.[28] Such schools were all over Asia Minor and Syria, and were set up in Palestine, especially in Greek areas like the Decapolis, as part of the process of Hellenization. Their success can be deduced from the response of conservative Jews, in the Maccabean period and later, to safeguard their own school system as 'exclusively a moral and a religious education'.[29] However, even if our early Christian had avoided any contact with Greek literary forms in his schooling, the whole culture of the eastern Mediterranean would have communicated them to him. As Downing argues, literary and cultural awareness was mediated down the social scale from the higher educated classes through

27. Cairns, *Generic Composition*, pp. 37, 70 and 75, see p. 57 above.

28. See further, H. I. Marrou, *A History of Education in Antiquity* (London: Sheed and Ward, 1956), esp. pp. 142-75.

29. E. B. Castle, *Ancient Education and Today* (Harmondsworth: Penguin, 1961), p. 184; see also pp. 160-4 on the clash with Hellenism.

public debates, the Cynic philosopher on the corner and the crowded market-place, the theatre, courts and assembly, as well as the after-dinner entertainment, which the lower classes attended as servants and slaves, if not as guests; he concludes, 'there is no sign of a culture-gap between the highly literate aristocracy and the masses'.[30] Furthermore, Stanton has recently challenged the view that the early manuscripts of the gospels were written by workaday 'documentary hands' in downmarket lower class; the gulf up to literary 'bookhands' has been exaggerated.[31] The first argument for a gap between the gospels and Graeco-Roman literature is thus demolished.

The second argument, that the early Christians were found only in the lower classes, can be traced back to early Marxist analysis of Christianity as a 'working class movement' and to Deissmann's work, linking the insults of Celsus that Christians were 'wool-workers, cobblers, laundry-workers, and the most illiterate and bucolic yokels' (Origen, *Contra Celsum* 3.55) with Paul's admission that 'not many of you were wise according to worldly standards, not many were powerful, not many were of noble birth' (1 Cor. 1:26). However, this suggestion has been criticized in recent years: from the names contained in the New Testament and indirect evidence about travel, slave ownership, money and the tensions within Pauline communities, Meeks has argued that 'a fair cross-section of urban society' is represented, bringing together several social levels, and only 'the extreme top and bottom of the Greco-Roman social scale are missing'. Malherbe has concluded that the quotations and allusions in the New Testament 'help us to establish the lowest educational level that can reasonably be assumed for the New Testament writers who use them, *i.e.*, the upper levels of secondary-school instruction'.[32] Thus neither of the foundations for the suggestion that the early Christians would not have known Graeco-Roman literature is correct, and therefore the form-critical view that the gospels are popular, non-literary and oral in character collapses. There is nothing about either the literary ability or education of the evangelists, nor the social and cultural setting in which they wrote and were interpreted, to prevent the generic link of the gospels with βίοι.

The question of how much of this was conscious is harder to answer

30. F. Gerald Downing, 'A bas les aristos. The Relevance of Higher Literature for the Understanding of the Earliest Christian Writings', *NovT* 30 (1988), pp. 212-30.

31. Graham N. Stanton, *Jesus and Gospel* (Cambridge University Press, 2004); see especially chapter 9, pp. 192ff.

32. Wayne Meeks, *The First Urban Christians*, pp. 51-73, quotations from p. 73; Abraham J. Malherbe, *Social Aspects of Early Christianity*, 2nd edn (Philadelphia: Fortress, 1983), p. 45; see also, Derek Tidball, *An Introduction to the Sociology of the New Testament* (Exeter: Paternoster, 1983), pp. 90-103.

with respect to Mark than to the others. Our study of literary theory stressed that generic conventions and expectations are often mediated unconsciously through society, and that the originators of generic shifts and new types are often not the great writers.[33] Mark's biographical genre may be a natural, if unconscious, consequence of his decision to present his Christian message with such a concentration on the life, deeds and words of Jesus of Nazareth. On the other hand, both Beavis and Tolbert have argued that Mark's educational background and the reader response expected from the audience suggest a basic level of popular education at least.[34] Both Matthew and Luke, however, must have been aware of the similarity between Mark and βίοι: not only do they correct his Greek style, they also expand and develop his work to bring it into greater conformity with the genre. As Kee notes, 'Matthew was also strongly affected by the biographical tradition, especially in his interests in the circumstances of Jesus' birth and infancy. In Luke, however, the impact of Hellenistic and Roman biography is clearly and pervasively apparent.'[35] Finally, it would be strange if the author/editor(s) of the Fourth Gospel did not realize the parallels with βίοι, given the many other links to Graeco-Roman and Jewish philosophical and religious ideas and literature which are found in John.

So we may conclude that the authors of the gospels were aware of the βίος nature of their work. Similarly, their audiences must have realized this; as Hengel says, 'The ancient reader will probably have been well aware of the differences in style and education, say, between Mark and Xenophon; but he will also have noticed what the gospels had in common with the literature of biographical "reminiscences" — and unlike the majority of German New Testament scholars today, he did not mind at all regarding the evangelists as authors of biographical reminiscences of Jesus which went back to the disciples of Jesus themselves.'[36]

5. Summary

Our main study demonstrated that the genre of the four canonical gospels is to be found in βίος literature. These final observations about the generic im-

---

33. See Chapter 2, pp. 42-4 above.

34. Beavis, *Mark's Audience*, pp. 20-44; Tolbert, *Sowing the Gospel*, pp. 301-9.

35. H. C. Kee, *Christian Origins in Sociological Perspective* (London: SCM, 1980), p. 145.

36. M. Hengel, *Acts and the History of Earliest Christianity*, p. 29; see also, Helen Elsom, 'The New Testament and Greco-Roman Writing', in *The Literary Guide to the Bible*, ed. Alter and Kermode, pp. 561-78: 'Such conventions were part of the literature in Greek which was likely to be familiar to the urban citizens of the Roman Empire who read the Gospels', p. 563.

plications of such a result have not revealed anything to oppose this conclusion; the gospels all share an identical genre, that of βίος, and also make up a subgenre within that genre, namely βίοι Ἰησοῦ. This group of literary texts is separate both from its origins and its successors in the non-canonical gospels and gospel commentaries. Finally, New Testament scholarship must not be done in a vacuum: no matter how clear the results of our analysis might be, the idea that the gospels are βίοι would be untenable if no connection with Hellenistic literary culture was possible for their authors and readers. In fact, not only is such a link possible, it is demanded both by the generic features of the texts themselves and also by the social setting of early Christianity within the eastern Roman empire of the first century AD.

C. Hermeneutical Implications

1. Genre — The Key to Interpretation

Our study of the critical literary theory showed that genre plays a crucial rôle in the interpretation of written texts, especially texts from a different period or environment than our own. Genre is a major literary convention, forming a 'contract' between author and reader; it provides a set of expectations for the reader about the author's intentions, which helps in the construction of the meaning on the page and the reconstruction of the author's original meaning, as well as in the interpretation and evaluation of the communication contained within the work itself. To avoid the errors likely in simple application of a text to ourselves without regard for the setting and background of either, appreciation of genre is crucial as a major 'filter' through which the author 'encoded' his message, and through which we may 'decode' the same.

The first implication of all this is that any idea of the gospels as unique, *sui generis* works is a nonsense: authors cannot create, and readers cannot interpret, a total novelty. The second implication is that we must have the same generic expectations as the author and his original readers: trying to 'decode' the gospels through the genre of modern biography, when the author 'encoded' his message in the genre of ancient βίος, will lead to another nonsense — blaming the text for not containing modern predilections which it was never meant to contain. The third implication is that the assignation of different genres to texts results in different interpretations: one listens to the TV News with different expectations than to a fairy story. It has become clear in this study that the narrower the genre proposed for the gospels, the harder it is to prove the case, but the more useful the hermeneutical implications;

whereas the wider the genre, the easier it is to demonstrate that the gospels belong to it, but the less helpful the result. Thus, if Philip Shuler had proved that his genre of 'encomium biography' actually existed and that the gospels belonged within it, we should then have interpreted them encomiastically. However, since he managed to establish neither that the genre existed nor that the gospels belong to it, we are not helped in the hermeneutical quest. On the other hand, our solution may be easier to demonstrate, but produce less direct results, since βίος is a widely diverse and relatively flexible genre within which to place the gospels, without this conclusion dictating all we need to know about their interpretation. Graeco-Roman βίοι could have a variety of purposes from encomium to entertainment, from information to polemic, not all of which are necessarily applicable to the gospels. However, since many βίοι were used by philosophical groups or schools for teaching about their beliefs and founder, as well as for attack and defence in debate with other groups, and some of their generic features are also found in the gospels, we can begin interpreting them with the expectation that we will find didactic, apologetic and polemical purposes and material here also. To this extent, therefore, real progress has been made, even if βίος is a wide and flexible genre.

2. *Jesus — The Key to the Gospels*

If genre is the key to a work's interpretation, and the genre of the gospels is βίος, then the key to their interpretation must be the person of their subject, Jesus of Nazareth. Perrin says that 'the nature of a Gospel is not the ministry of the historical Jesus, but the reality of Christian experience'.[37] Such comments obscure the genre of the gospels; while they include the 'reality of Christian experience', or the Kingdom of Heaven, or the salvation of God in history, and other proposed 'subjects', to place such subjects as their primary concern above the person of Jesus is to miss the fact that they are βίοι. This is clear if we compare the gospels with the Epistles and Rabbinic material.

Paul is also concerned for the reality of Christian experience and the salvation of God in Christ, but he does not write βίοι. Instead, he handles these concerns in the genre of epistle, which has different links with Graeco-Roman literature. The overall message of the writer must not be confused with the genre he uses. The 'reality of Christian experience' can be conveyed in many genres, from gospel and epistle to sermon or drama.

37. Perrin, *What Is Redaction Criticism?*, p. 75.

Paul's choice of the genre of epistle may have been to communicate to a community some distance away, but it is also a genre which is amenable for dealing with a specific event, issue or doctrine; βίος, on the other hand, deals with a specific person. Something similar emerges from a comparison of the gospels with Rabbinic material. Although the individual gospel units often find parallels with Rabbinic stories, Alexander pointed out that there is no parallel to the overall gospel form in the Jewish material, probably because 'the centre of Rabbinic Judaism was Torah; the centre of Christianity was the person of Jesus'.[38]

This emphasis on the centrality of the person of Jesus is a hermeneutical consequence of the gospels being βίοι. That Paul says little about the person of Jesus in his epistles does not necessarily mean that he was not interested in his earthly ministry; it might be that he is writing epistles and not βίοι. If the early church had not been interested in the person and earthly life of Jesus, it would not have produced βίοι, with their narrative structure and chronological framework, but discourses of the risen Christ, like the Gnostic 'gospels', instead. As Bilezikian comments, 'the very existence of the Gospel, and that of Matthew and Luke after Mark, bears witness to the importance attached to the historical Jesus by the early church'.[39] Stanton demonstrated that the early church was interested in the person of Jesus of Nazareth in its preaching and teaching, and our conclusions about the βίος genre of the gospels reinforce this.[40] The centrality of the person of Jesus arising from the βίος genre of the gospels needs to become the central key to their interpretation: Christology, the portrait by each evangelist, affects every area. As Kysar says concerning John's Christology, 'the simple fact that the evangelist has chosen to express himself through the means of a gospel indicates that there is a real historical human life at the root of the central character of his witness. If flesh is irrelevant to the evangelist or if the revealer in no sense really took upon himself fleshly existence, why did the evangelist write a *gospel*?'[41]

Similarly, the βίος genre of the gospels affects the 'Quest for the Historical Jesus', with particular respect to the use of sources by writers of βίοι. The selectivity allowed for an author to produce his portrait of the subject will form part of the redaction critical approach; however, because this is a Life of

38. Alexander, 'Rabbinic Biography', p. 41, see p. 20 above; see also Hilton and Marshall, *The Gospels and Rabbinic Judaism*, p. 13.

39. Bilezikian, *Liberated Gospel*, p. 140.

40. Stanton, *Jesus of Nazareth;* see esp. pp. 186-91.

41. Kysar, *Fourth Evangelist*, p. 191, his italics; similarly, Boring sees Christology as crucial for Mark's genre, *Truly Human/Truly Divine*, pp. 88-9.

a historical person written within the lifetime of his contemporaries, there are limits on free composition. Jack Kingsbury notes this mixture of variety with limits in his suggestion of one gospel about God's saving activity in Jesus in four editions, 'that the early church opted for a plurality of gospels within limits and that it also set considerable store on preserving intact the distinctiveness of each one'.[42] Robert Morgan sees this plurality of gospels as a positive theological opportunity for their interpretation: none of them is the sole Gospel, inviting us to 'faith images of Jesus' over which the canonical gospels act 'both as a stimulus and a control'.[43] Similarly, Stanton concluded that the biographical interest of the early church in the person of Jesus should act as a spur to contemporary evangelism and preaching, which also need to be based on the life and character of Jesus.[44] *It is our contention that this βίος nature of the gospel genre should also restore the centrality of the person of Jesus.*

Conclusion

We began this study with some surprise that such a basic question for the interpretation of the gospels as their genre had not been satisfactorily resolved. Furthermore, we suggested that the biographical hypothesis should either be exposed as a false trail or given a proper, scholarly footing through an interdisciplinary study involving literary theory and Graeco-Roman biography. In fact, such an approach has now demonstrated from an analysis of many generic features that both the four canonical gospels and Graeco-Roman βίος exhibit a clear family resemblance. The genre of βίος is flexible and diverse, with variation in the pattern of features from one βίος to another. The gospels also diverge from the pattern in some aspects, but not to any greater degree than other βίοι; in other words, they have at least as much in common with Graeco-Roman βίοι, as the βίοι have with each other. Therefore, the gospels must belong to the genre of βίος.

Finally, we have outlined some generic and hermeneutical implications of this result. The four canonical gospels belong together as βίοι 'Ιησοῦ, unlike the non-canonical gospels, many of which have lost the generic features of βίος. Furthermore, nothing in the social setting of the gospel texts, writers and audiences prevents them being interpreted as βίοι. Finally, this genre of

42. J. D. Kingsbury, 'The Gospel in Four Editions', *Interpretation* 33 (1979), pp. 363-75.

43. Robert Morgan, 'The Hermeneutical Significance of Four Gospels', *Interpretation* 33 (1979), pp. 376-88, quotations from p. 386.

44. Stanton, *Jesus of Nazareth*, pp. 190-1.

βίος has distinct hermeneutical implications for the gospel studies, reaffirming the centrality of the person of Jesus of Nazareth.

> *Now Jesus did many other signs in the presence of his disciples, which are not written in this book; but these are written that you may believe that Jesus is the Christ, the Son of God, and that believing you may have life in his name.*
> John 20:30-31

CHAPTER 11

Reactions and Developments

*B.'s study . . . brings into conversation the best voices found in classi-
cal studies as well as in gospel criticism. This is a book which should
have been written.*[1]

*This book may produce a sea-change in the problem of the genre of
the Gospels. Whether it produces a sea-change in contemporary interpretations of the Gospels remains to be seen.*[2]

The origins of this research lie in an attempt to bring my background and
training as a classicist to bear upon New Testament studies, originally in
my work as a classics school-teacher, and then in my post-graduate studies
as an ordinand and young priest. It began in the late 1970's in the context of
the domination of the post-Bultmannian, form-critical view of the uniqueness of the gospels. Charles Talbert's *What Is a Gospel?* set out to challenge
this view,[3] and my initial postgraduate studies were intended to critique the
arguments of Talbert and others for the gospels as biography. However, as
noted at the end of Part One, p. 101 above, I became increasingly convinced
that the gospels did belong to the genre of ancient biography, and so my doctoral research through the 1980's attempted to build a more secure foundation for this view, which is laid out in Part Two. While other scholars were

1. Jerome H. Neyrey, review of *What Are the Gospels?* in *CBQ* 55, April 1993, p. 363.
2. Christopher Tuckett, review of *What Are the Gospels?* in *Theology* XCVI No 769 (1993),
pp. 74-5.
3. Charles H. Talbert, *What Is a Gospel? The Genre of the Canonical Gospels* (Fortress 1977/
SPCK 1978) — see pages 80-3 above for fuller assessment.

also beginning to argue for a biographical understanding of the gospels during that decade, the mainstream view still largely remained that they were *sui generis*.

My revised thesis was published at the start of the 1990's and it quickly attracted a lot of reviews and responses. Given that it called for a paradigm shift in gospel studies away from uniqueness to the biographical hypothesis, this was not unexpected. However, it was surprising, if gratifying, how quickly it became accepted, so that by the end of the decade most New Testament scholars seemed to view the gospels within the literary context of Graeco-Roman biography. Indeed, rather than attacking my thesis, most reviewers' main criticism was that the implications of this paradigm shift for the rest of gospel studies had not been sufficiently worked through!

Therefore this new chapter a decade later will first consider the various reactions, reviews and debates sparked off by this book's original publication and then trace how my own further work, and that of others, has developed in the light of the gospels as βίοι. Thus it is inevitable that there will be a biographical element to this final chapter, which begins with the positive initial reviews but which also includes reflections on various papers and debates,[4] as well as the more recently published major treatments of the subject. Finally it will also demonstrate how subsequent work has grown out of these reactions and developed further the implications of their biographical genre for the study and interpretation of the gospels.

A. Reactions and Responses

1. Reviews

The general response to the book has been very encouraging, with reviews in many major New Testament journals, often by scholars already involved in the debate about gospel genre.

Various reviewers noted the combination of detailed study of Graeco-Roman biography and literary theory: thus Jerome Neyrey described it in *CBQ* as 'an immensely learned volume . . . a superb survey of the topic, but also breaks new ground in its nuanced reading of ancient texts and its literary model.'[5] Similarly in *Theology*, Tuckett called it 'a most impressive study, dis-

---

4. As 'live' events, many of these are not easily accessible for others, so I have drawn upon my notes and tapes made of the discussions to put their debates into the public domain.

5. Jerome H. Neyrey, *CBQ* 55, April 1993, pp 361-3.

playing masterly control of the discussion of modern literary theory as well as being at home in a wide range of classical literature'.[6] In *Biblical Interpretation*, Stibbe also agreed: 'a truly astonishing tour de force — interdisciplinary biblical scholarship at its very best'.[7]

Others welcomed its conclusions as the answer to the question of gospel genre. Thus, following his initial work which inspired my research, Talbert argued in *JBL* that 'this volume ought to end any legitimate denials of the canonical Gospels' biographical character. It has made its case.'[8] Bryan goes further: 'a very important book. It will be difficult to take seriously any future study of the gospels' genre which does not come to terms with his arguments'.[9] A similar point was made by Cope: 'an excellent study . . . will serve as a standard for future work'.[10] Several reviewers said that it was 'well-argued';[11] as Clark concluded for *Expository Times*, 'the force lies in the volume of evidence produced and the precision and clarity of its tabling'.[12] In addition, longer reviews in *JTS*, *Journal of Religion* and *Evangelical Quarterly* arose out of debates about the book at various conferences, as will be described shortly.

Because of the comparison with Graeco-Roman biography, there were also some reviews in Classical Studies journals: thus Tim Duff described it in *The Classical Review* as an 'excellent and clearly written study', noting the 'clarity of argument . . . convincingly and with cumulative force'.[13] F. E. Brenk, whose important work on Plutarch was noted above, gave it an extended treatment in *Gnomon*, particularly looking at the sections on Graeco-Roman genres and the development of biography, and concluded that it 'makes out a good case for calling the gospels biography, and adds considerably to our understanding of the specific features of Graeco-Roman biography'.[14]

As well as these academic reviews, there were a number of shorter no-

---

6. Christopher Tuckett, *Theology* (1993), pp. 74-5.

7. Mark W. G. Stibbe, *Biblical Interpretation* 1,3 (1993), pp. 380-81; Rosalind Papaphilippopoulos also discusses the mixture of the classical material and genre theory in *Scottish Journal of Theology* 47.3 (1994), pp. 420-1.

8. Charles H. Talbert, *JBL* 112 (1993), pp. 714-5.

9. Christopher Bryan, *Sewanee Theological Review*, 36.1 (1992), pp. 173-4.

10. Lamar Cope, *Religious Studies Review* 19.3 (July 1993), p. 264.

11. S. E. Porter, *JSNT* 59 (Sept 1993), p. 113; E. Earle Ellis, *Southwestern Journal of Theology* 36.1 (1993), p. 56.

12. Neville Clark, *Expository Times*, Aug. 1992, p. 334.

13. Tim Duff, *The Classical Review*, New Series XLVI.2 (1996), pp. 265-6.

14. F. E. Brenk, *Gnomon* 66 (1994), pp. 492-6.

tices.[15] It was also reviewed and appreciated in the church press, such as Anthony Harvey's verdict in *Church Times,* 'an excellent guide'.[16]

In the midst of the positive appreciation of the book, even at this initial stage various reviewers pointed out some areas for further work. First, Meg Davies accepted the 'general similarities between the gospels and Graeco-Roman biographies' but wondered about comparisons with narratives about Jewish prophets,[17] an area only briefly touched upon in Chapter 1, pp. 19-21 above. While she was the first to raise this area, others later echoed it, so it will become a significant theme as this chapter unfolds.

Secondly, it was noted earlier that the combination of Luke with Acts led Aune to consider it as a form of historiography (pp. 98-9 above) and we discussed the implications of our conclusions for the genre of Acts briefly on pp. 237-9. While David Balch considered my book 'an exciting methodological advance in the study of gospel genre' and was convinced regarding the other gospels, he still argued that 'Luke owes more to ancient historiography than to biography', comparing it with long biographical sections within the histories of Dionysius of Halicarnassus.[18] Downing made a similar point in his review comparing my book with Gregory Sterling's *Historiography and Self-Definition: Josephos, Luke-Acts and Apologetic Historiography,*[19] and others were to follow suit.

Finally, while agreeing that the gospels are ancient biographies, some reviewers wanted further developed or stronger conclusions. Thus, Müller argued for an individual treatment of one or more gospels separately.[20] Brian Mountford was more direct: 'clearly written, easily used, beautifully printed . . . but how much does it matter?'[21] Although he called it 'a powerful and

---

15. See, for example, *Theology Digest* 39.4 (Winter 1993), p. 354; *Theological Studies,* 53 (1992), pp. 780-1; *Theological Book Review* 5.3 (June 1993), p. 24; *The Chronicle of Higher Education,* March 18th 1992, p. A15; *New Testament Abstracts* 36.3 (1992), pp. 419-20. A more extended treatment in Polish appeared in *Collectanea Theologica* 64 (Warsaw: 1994), pp. 168-70, by Michal Wojciechowski.

16. Anthony Harvey, *Church Times,* 10th April 1992, p. 13; see also, the assessment of 'the importance of his work . . . writes with clarity and zest' in *Priests and People* 10.1 (Jan 1996); 'a book which fulfils its promises'. *Discourse,* March 1993, p. 7.

17. Meg Davies, *New Blackfriars* No. 868, Vol. 74 (Feb. 1993), pp. 109-110.

18. David Balch, unpublished review article; see also his 'ΜΕΤΑΒΟΛΗ ΠΟΛΙΤΕΙΩΝ. Jesus as Founder of the Church in Luke-Acts: Form and Function' in *Contextualising Acts: Lukan Narrative and Greco-Roman Discourse,* ed. Todd Penner & Caroline Van der Stichele (Symposium Series; Scholars Press & Brill, in press), pp. 137-86.

19. F. Gerald Downing, *JTS* 44.1 (April 1993), pp. 238-40.

20. Ulrich B. Müller, *Theologische Literaturzeitung* 118.6 (1993), pp. 514-15.

21. Brian Mountford, *Theological Book Review,* 5.3 (June 1993), p. 24.

convincing study', Tuckett implied a similar question when he described my stress on the focus on the subject of the Lives as 'of course, true, but almost trite', and wanted more hermeneutical consequences.[22] Christopher Southgate raised the same issue, 'the reader may ask — so what?' and looked for 'more of a hint as to the theological implications' in 'a second book to evaluate Burridge's own reading of four Gospels'.[23] This was something of a prophetic call and became a major incentive for my next book.

Thus, while these reviews gave an encouragingly positive initial response, they also included some helpful observations and set the tracks for further work. While some possible hermeneutical and theological implications were briefly considered on pp. 247-50 above, these questions have dominated my own writing and thinking over the last decade, including the issue of the gospels and Jewish writings, as we shall see below. Meanwhile, the relationship of Luke-Acts to both biography and historiography has continued to be debated, together with the implications of the biographical hypothesis for the interpretation of the gospels.

2. Debates and Conferences

In addition to these reviews, the book was also the subject of papers and debates at various seminars and conferences over the next few years.

(a) The British New Testament Conference, September 1992

The first was a paper given by Loveday Alexander at the British New Testament Conference.[24] After a survey of recent work on the question of the genre of Luke-Acts, covering F. Bovon, C. H. Talbert, D. Moessner, R. Pervo, C. Hemer, O'Feaghail, and V. K. Robbins, she turned to an extended treatment of my book, much of which was later published as a review article.[25]

She begins with a domestic answer to my title, 'What are the Gospels? To my teenage son the answer is obvious: the Gospels are books about Jesus'

---

22. Christopher Tuckett, *Theology* (1993), pp. 74-5.

23. Christopher C. B. Southgate, *Exeter Diocesan News* (August 1992), p. 6.

24. Loveday Alexander, 'Ancient Biography and the Social Function of Luke-Acts', British New Testament Conference, University of Exeter, 19th Sept 1992; the BNTC is modelled on the international meetings of the SNTS for those teaching in British universities and colleges and their postgraduate students.

25. Loveday Alexander, *Evangelical Quarterly* 66 (1994), pp. 73-6; also reprinted in *European Journal of Theology* 3.1 (1994), pp. 84-6.

— but notes that New Testament scholarship from Bultmann onwards disagreed. She then describes the methodology of combining classical scholarship and literary theory, welcoming the latter as 'most useful'. She appreciates that the list of Graeco-Roman Lives for comparison 'is clearly chosen to encompass a wide variety of *Bioi* from different periods and language-groups: it is designed to be inclusive rather than discriminatory'. When the gospels and the Lives are compared against the 'checklist' of my generic features, the conclusion is clear: 'the Gospels turn out to be *as much* Bioi *as any of the others*'. Almost anticipating Tuckett's criticism of the book's conclusion as 'trite', Alexander prefers to call it 'deliberately understated . . . his aim is (if I read him rightly) simply to clear the ground methodologically for future study of the Gospels within the broad classification *Bios* . . . overall the cumulative effect of his analysis is impressive'. She accepts that 'if there is a sense of dissatisfaction on reaching the end of the book, it is probably simply because the classification of the Gospels as *Bioi* is too broad to answer many of the precise questions which many readers want answered'.

Recognizing that 'this is very much a book which opens up possibilities rather than one which solves problems', she went on to discuss helpfully some of those possibilities, both in her review article and more fully in the seminar. These included the relationship of biographical writing to history and that 'which is described simply as "fiction" by classical scholars like Mary Lefkowitz', and the question of authorial intentionality within the generic 'contract' and whether Mark knew he was writing a *bios*. Perhaps her most stimulating remarks concerned the implications for the 'social location' of *bios,* especially within the standards of ancient literacy (drawing on the work of Harris[26]), and for its 'social function', especially within the context of the philosophical schools, providing them with a 'succession narrative' (referring to the work of Talbert[27]). In conclusion, she returned to the question of the gospels' subject, and suggested that 'it may be that he himself has underestimated the hermeneutical gain to be made from his demonstration of the centrality of Jesus to the Gospel form. . . . There is a lot to be said for reminding ourselves again of the obvious (but too easily forgotten) fact that first and foremost the Gospels are "books about Jesus"'.

The following debate ranged widely around the hermeneutical implications of the gospels being 'about Jesus' and questions of intentionality, truth

---

26. William V. Harris, *Ancient Literacy* (Cambridge, Mass.: Harvard University Press, 1989).

27. Alexander particularly noted the article by C. H. Talbert, 'Ancient Biography' in *The Anchor Bible Dictionary,* ed. D. N. Freedman (New York: Doubleday, 1992), Vol. I, pp. 745-9.

and fiction. I note Alexander's comments that I had 'understated' or even 'underestimated' my conclusions; I suspect that this hesitation was a consequence of challenging the established scholarly consensus about the gospels' uniqueness! However, this discussion was the first encouragement to develop the conclusions further. Perhaps the most important issue to arise from this seminar concerned social settings, location and function of the gospels — which, as will be shown later below, was later to lead to articles by both Loveday Alexander and myself in *The Gospels for All Christians*.[28]

(b) American Lecturing Tour, April-May 1993

During some study leave in April and May 1993, I gave various papers and seminars on the issues raised by my book at a number of American universities and seminaries.[29] Once again, it was encouraging how quickly the proposal that the gospels are a form of Graeco-Roman biography was accepted. Rather than arguing about it, most of the discussions centred on its implications for their interpretation.

Firstly, there are *the literary implications*. As noted in some reviews above, my work compared the gospels only to Graeco-Roman literature, especially ancient biography. However, since Jesus, his first followers and most (if not all) of the New Testament writers were Jews, one might expect Jewish literature rather than the Graeco-Roman background to be the obvious place for generic parallels for the gospels. This was an area for further work, which I was later to undertake as discussed later below.

Also, our concentration on the four canonical gospels left open the question of genre for both any preceding texts (such as Q, and possible *Ur-* or proto-gospels) and the non-canonical gospels. Genre, however, is a feature of a text as a whole; given the difficulty we have had with the four texts we possess, it is even harder to speculate on the genre of non-extant or hypothetical documents reconstructed from our canonical texts or papyrus fragments. Nonetheless, the debate about the form and dates of Q, Thomas and other

28. Richard Bauckham, ed., *The Gospels for All Christians: Rethinking the Gospel Audiences* (Grand Rapids: Eerdmans/T&T Clark, 1998).

29. This included visits to Southwestern Baptist Theological Seminary, Fort Worth; the University of the South, Sewanee, Tennessee; Vanderbilt University; Duke Divinity School; University of North Carolina, Chapel Hill; Princeton University and Seminary; Yale Divinity School; General Theological Seminary, New York; Loyola University, Chicago. I am grateful to all who invited me, and showed me warm hospitality — but also to all those who participated in the discussions which stimulated much further thought about the genre of the gospels. The paragraphs which follow are based upon tapes of those debates and seminars.

non-canonical gospels has intensified over recent years, and genre may well have a part to play in those debates.[30] The same goes for the literary relationships between the four gospels, and questions of Markan priority, the relationship of the fourth gospel to the other three and so forth. There was also some discussion about the implications of the biographical hypothesis for the genre of Acts, especially if Luke and Acts are seen as a two-volume work — and this area too has seen subsequent debate.

Secondly, *the sociological implications* provoked much comment, reflecting the issues raised by Loveday Alexander above. These concern to what extent ancient βίοι may have existed within a community setting, such as the early philosophical schools, and how they functioned with regard to apologetic or legitimation for their own group and polemic against others. The social levels at which βίοι were produced and read might also provide some interesting insights into possible settings for the gospels. These discussions provided further stimulus for future work on this area, as will again be seen later below.

Thirdly, the biographical hypothesis has some significant *historical implications* for the issues of authenticity and truth. We saw early in this study that ancient βίοι nestled between historiography and rhetorical encomium, taking from history the combining of stories and events into a written narrative, with the concentration on **one** person coming from encomium (beginning with the shift from an oral speech, *Evagoras,* to an account written for circulation, *Agesilaus*). Even ancient historiography had more opportunities for interpretation than modern canons of accurate reporting, but the writer of βίος appears to have had more selectivity for his treatment of a subject than would be true for history. Thus, Xenophon shows that he knows, and disapproves, of certain aspects of Agesilaus' conduct (such as his dealings with Pharnabazus or Sphodrias) when writing his *Hellenica,* yet he suppresses these when he writes his separate account of *Agesilaus.*[31] Even more freedom was allowed for encomium: Isocrates conveniently omits to mention the fact, embarrassing for his encomium, that Evagoras was actually murdered! The novel has the most scope for invention, as is seen in the way Philostratus' *Apollonius* has moved significantly in the direction of a travelogue or a novel.[32] Therefore, simply discovering that the gospels are βίοι does not an-

30. See F. Gerald Downing, 'A Genre for Q and a Socio-Cultural Context for Q: Comparing Sets of Similarities with Sets of Differences', *JSNT* 55 (1994), pp. 3-26, which takes my categories of generic features and tries to apply them to Q.

31. See J. K. Anderson, *Xenophon* (London: Duckworth, 1974), pp 167-71.

32. See E. L. Bowie, 'Apollonius of Tyana: Tradition and Reality' in *ANRW* II.16.2, 1978, p. 1665.

swer all our questions about their historicity or truth, but it may give an indication of the freedom each of the evangelists has in constructing a portrait of Jesus.

Lastly, there are *theological implications*. K. L. Schmidt's article on 'Jesus Christus' in *Die Religion in Geschichte und Gegenwart* reveals that the form-critical view of the uniqueness of the gospels was linked to theological implications about Christ: the *sui generis* gospels were the product of the oral tradition within the unique cultic communities witnessing to God's unique revelation of himself in Jesus Christ.[33] John Meagher argues that not only does this have implications for the evangelists themselves (as compilers of the tradition with no personality, theology or authorial intentions), but also for theology in general: 'the Schmidt hypothesis is radically gnostic'. In other words, the unique hypothesis implies that the heart of the Christian message is untranslatable into human culture.[34] However, interpreting the gospels as biography not only saves them from the literary nonsense of unique texts but also rescues Christian theology from such thoroughgoing gnosticism. The biographical hypothesis leads to Christological hermeneutics, for the gospels are narratives about a person — which is why the rise of Narrative Criticism was so vital for gospel studies.[35] If the gospels are βίοι of Jesus and theology is to be done through narrative and story, then interpreters need to pay much more attention to the four portraits of Jesus of Nazareth which are offered. Thus the different Christologies of the gospels will become the hermeneutical key, both to the works as a whole and to individual pericopae: a central question concerns what this passage is trying to say about the character of Jesus in the light of this evangelist's overall portrait. It certainly argues against a typical response to plurality which goes back to Tatian's *Diatessaron,* namely the habit of harmonization which bedevilled nineteenth-century 'Lives of Jesus' and still affects much use of the gospels today.

Thus this American study leave and lecture tour not only provided

33. ET of RGG is *Twentieth Century Theology in the Making,* ed. J. Pelikan (London: Collins, 1969); Schmidt's article 'Jesus Christ' is pp. 93-168.

34. John C Meagher, 'The Implications for Theology of a Shift from the K. L. Schmidt Hypothesis of the Literary Uniqueness of the Gospels', in Bruce Corley (ed.), *Colloquy on New Testament Studies: A Time for Reappraisal and Fresh Aproaches* (Macon: Mercer University Press, 1983), pp. 203-33, see especially pp. 206-19.

35. See David Rhoads and Donald Michie, *Mark as Story: An Introduction to the Narrative of a Gospel* (Philadelphia: Fortress, 1982); Jack Dean Kingsbury, *Matthew as Story* (Philadelphia: Fortress, 1986, 2nd edn 1988); Robert C. Tannehill, *The Narrative Unity of Luke-Acts: A Literary Interpretation,* 2 vols. (Philadelphia and Minneapolis: Fortress, 1986 and 1990); R. Alan Culpepper, *Anatomy of the Fourth Gospel: A Study in Literary Design* (Philadelphia: Fortress, 1983).

more encouraging reactions but also gave rise to some stimulating debates. Although these happened in different places, similar issues kept coming up which helped set the direction for my further work on the biographical and Christological interpretation of the gospels in following years.

(c) Society of Biblical Literature
International Meeting, August 1994

The Twelfth International Meeting of the SBL had the usual range of interesting topics under discussion.[36] However, a lot of attention was given to the gospels and genre issues through a main paper on Luke-Acts as Historiography from Hubert Cancik and a morning of papers about the New Testament and Ancient Romances; an afternoon on the genre of Luke-Acts featured detailed review papers of my book from Richard Pervo and Adela Yarbro Collins, while Gregory Sterling's *Historiography and Self-Definition: Josephos, Luke-Acts and Apologetic Historiography*[37] was critiqued by Loveday Alexander and Albrecht Dihle, followed by responses from both authors and general discussion.

As with other reviews, Pervo's paper welcomed my book's combination of genre theory (especially the statistical material) and classical scholarship as 'the best argument to date for aligning these works with Greco-Roman biography'; he also echoed Alexander's comments, concluding 'one may compliment this author for not attempting to say or to claim too much.'[38] He then discussed some of the generic features, including the subject analyses and length of works, as well as the relationship with monograph and the connection of Luke's gospel to Acts. Collins agreed that my genre theory with classical material was 'more systematic and profound' than previous attempts; while she accepted most of my arguments about genre, she disputed the statistical analysis and maintained that the gospels are more like historical monographs than βίοι; she argued for a much closer relationship to Jewish literature and debated how literate and educated the evangelists and their audiences were. Collins subsequently revised her paper in the light of the debate,

36. This took place in Leuven, alongside the 43rd Colloquium Biblicum Lovaniense, 7th-10th August, 1994; it included a major debate on the Historical Jesus between N. T. Wright and John Dominic Crossan.

37. Gregory E. Sterling, *Historiography and Self-Definition: Josephos, Luke-Acts and Apologetic Historiography*, SupNT 64 (Leiden: Brill, 1992); Gerald Downing had already compared my work with Sterling's in his joint review of both books in *JTS* 44.1 (April 1993), pp 238-40.

38. Richard I. Pervo, 'Review of Burridge, *What Are the Gospels?*', SBL International Meeting, 9/8/1994, quotations from p. 5.

omitting the criticism of the statistical material, and published it as a review article in the *Journal of Religion*.[39]

Collins' and Pervo's points, and my responses, were then debated in general discussion. This helped to clarify my *methodology:* in my discussion of genre theory, I argued that we must not apply modern expectations of biography to ancient βίοι (which was, in part, Bultmann's error, see pages 9-12 and 51 above). However, we must use modern literary theory to understand what genres actually are, and how they function, grow and develop (which is the point of Chapter 2 above), while respecting the ancient theorists and writers for their generic expectations of a classical genre such as βίοι (see Chapter 3). In both, we need to remember the flexible nature of genre.

Discussion of methodology also helped to clarify my use of *statistical material,* especially the verbal analysis. Pervo did some computer analysis of Luke (and got worryingly low results for Jesus), while Collins, who was less impressed with it, did some manual analysis of sections from Sallust to show some interest in a person there. Others have also attempted further analyses, and, as with Pervo and Collins, it has become clear that it is important not to confuse the figures and results from the two different methods which I used. Computer analysis is a quick and easy way of looking for distribution of verbal subjects through the nominative cases of proper names and nouns; indeed, such are the advances of technology with laptops and CDs of the whole corpus of ancient literature, that it is even quicker and easier now, than when I was pioneering such techniques on mainframes and magnetic computer tape in the mid 1980's! However, such analyses will include only those with nominative nouns — and thus miss many instances where the subject is contained within the verb, or is understood from the previous verb or sentence (note carefully the discussion and warnings about this on pages 110-12 above). Given that Luke uses the proper name of Jesus much less than other evangelists, but often uses the title 'the Lord' and just links with 'he', Pervo's low computer result is not surprising. There is, therefore, no substitute for doing the analysis by hand, as we did for the four gospels and some of the βίοι. Such manual analysis shows that Luke's concentration on Jesus through his name, titles and the third person pronoun and verbs, is very similar to Matthew's, and together they fit well within the results for other βίοι (see the charts of statistical analysis in the Appendix below).

Furthermore, while some other books may show a similar concentration on the subject, especially sections from ancient historiography about a particular person, as Collins found with parts of Sallust, this does not neces-

---

39. Adela Yarbro Collins, 'Genre and the Gospels', *JR* 75.2 (1995), pp. 239-46.

sarily make them βίοι; again note the comments on pages 33-4, 130-1 and 239 above. It must be stressed that genre is mediated through the whole range of generic features, and analysis of verbal subjects is just *one* of those — although it is particularly useful for disentangling *genera proxima* which share many features in common, like biography and historical monograph, where the subject of the former is a person's life and character, while the latter is more focussed on a single topic, often involving many people.

Regarding the book's *content,* various topics familiar from previous debates emerged during this discussion. Collins thought that the use of 'purpose' as a generic feature was 'most promising' but ended up as 'not especially helpful'.[40] This is inevitable given the wide range of purposes of ancient βίοι, but it does at least give us some possibilities for the gospels, such as didactic, apologetic and polemic within the concentration on the person of the subject. Alexander's comments about 'understated' conclusions and Pervo's about 'not claiming too much' are important here — but these observations reinforced the need to consider further the Christological purposes of the gospels.

Both Pervo and Collins raised points about the *social setting of the gospels,* especially the levels of literacy and education of the evangelists and their first audiences. Collins argued that the writers were 'more likely to have been familiar with Greek historiography than with βίοι.'[41] It is not clear why this should be so, as the moral stories of βίοι were told at a much earlier stage of childhood, and encomia were read in school before historiography, which tended to feature later in tertiary rhetorical studies. Even if the evangelists knew them, it is less likely that their audiences would have been familiar with such higher studies — hence my comments about audience levels on pages 243-6 above. Once again, these comments echoed Alexander's questions about social location and function and provided further stimulus to reflect upon those topics.

One of the most interesting sections of Collins' review was her claim that my comparison with Graeco-Roman biography 'did not seriously consider any alternative', such as within *Jewish literature.*[42] She then discusses biographical sections within Jewish historiography in the scriptures, as part of her argument for the genre of 'historical monograph'. While the Jewish background was briefly considered (pp. 19-21 above), we concentrated on Graeco-Roman biography since that was the current genre proposal which I

---

40. Collins, *JR* 1995, p. 241.
41. Collins, *JR* 1995, p. 245.
42. Collins, *JR* 1995, p. 241.

initially tried to criticise! However, Collins' comments were a further incentive to compare the Jewish milieu with the gospels.

The most important topic concerned *the genre of Luke-Acts*. In her important chapter on the genre of Mark in *The Beginning of the Gospel,* Collins had already argued against the biographical approach of Aune and Talbert, preferring historiography instead, although she did admit that 'the most obvious difficulty for the hypothesis that Mark is a historical monograph is its focus on the person of Jesus'.[43] She pressed her case again here: 'I believe that the genre "historical monograph" has as good a claim as the ancient bios to be recognized as the genre chosen by Mark.'[44] Pervo also suggested that 'on the perplexing subject of monography Burridge is rather cloudy'.[45] Both of them go on to refer to Cicero's request to Lucceius that he should write a monograph on Cicero's role in the Catilinarian conspiracy (*Ad Fam* V.12). However, we have already seen above (p. 239) that this is where the generic boundaries of history, monograph and bios can get very blurred: after all Cicero himself mixes up Xenophon's *Agesilaus* with Polybius here! There is bound to be a continuum between these genres, which is why it is important to remember the flexible nature of genre and to use a wide range of generic features. Even where there is a similar concentration on a particular person, Talbert distinguishes between the concern of history about how people are involved in an event and biography's interest 'in what sort of person the individual is'.[46]

Gregory Sterling's book, *Historiography and Self-Definition: Josephos, Luke-Acts and Apologetic Historiography,*[47] devotes most of its extensive research to arguing for a specific genre of 'apologetic historiography' into which Luke-Acts is then assigned. Both Loveday Alexander and Albrecht Dihle complimented Sterling's detailed work in their reviews, but were unsure about the actual genre. As Dihle pointed out, apologetic tendencies can certainly play a part in ancient historiography, as in other genres, and they may well be there in Luke-Acts without 'the discovery of a new, distinct literary genre'.[48] Alexander agreed that Sterling's new category might not be recognized by first-century readers, but could be useful for critics today. In re-

43. Adela Yarbro Collins, *The Beginning of the Gospel: Probings of Mark in Context* (Minneapolis: Fortress, 1992); see pp. 10-38, quotation from p. 27.

44. Collins, *JR* 1995, p. 244.

45. Richard I. Pervo, 'Review of Burridge', SBL 9/8/1994, p. 8.

46. C. H. Talbert, 'Ancient Biography' in *The Anchor Bible Dictionary,* ed. D. N. Freedman (New York: Doubleday, 1992), Vol. I, p. 746.

47. Gregory E. Sterling, *Historiography and Self-Definition: Josephos, Luke-Acts and Apologetic Historiography, SupNT* 64 (Leiden: Brill, 1992).

48. Albrecht Dihle, 'Review of Sterling', SBL 9/8/1994, p. 6.

sponse, Sterling compared Luke-Acts' purpose with 'Dee Brown's effort to tell the story of the American West from the perspective of a native American in *Bury My Heart at Wounded Knee*'; he concluded that this is what Josephos was doing for the Jews and 'the Hellenistic historians and the author of Luke-Acts attempted to do the same by telling their stories to their own people who had to make sense of their world.'[49]

This all confirms the importance of the approach to genre theory which we have stressed throughout. Genre is to be distinguished from 'mode', which functions at the adjectival level more like 'tragic' than 'tragedy'; further, genre is identified through a wide range of generic features (see pages 40-2 above). Apologetic tendencies and purposes, whether addressed to people within the author's community or beyond to wider society, are *modal* — and can be found in many different genres, including both ancient biography and historiography. It is important to recognize such intentions but they do not determine the assignation of genre, nor are they required by it. Monograph was closely related to wider ancient historiography, and distinguished from it only by its more limited scale (usually one scroll long) and focus on a single topic, group or city; thus it was also closely linked to βίος, which differed in its concentration on a particular individual. On this basis, Luke belongs with the other gospels as βίοι, while Acts is closer to monograph. As we shall show later below, the continuing debate about the genre of Luke-Acts as a two-volume work arises from their closely related, but different genres as separate works.

The careful attention and debate given to our work at this international meeting of the SBL thus confirmed the clear directions emerging from the book reviews and other conferences and seminars, both with regard to the general welcome for my approach and also to the various issues for further study.

(d) 'Biographical Limits in the Ancient World', Dublin, Sept. 2001

Some classical specialists joined New Testament scholars in the above discussions — and classicists initiated our final debate, which began with *Portraits*, a collection of essays looking at biographical representation across a wide range of Graeco-Roman literature, and not just ancient biography (which is mostly ignored in the book). One of the editors, Mark Edwards, explained in his epilogue 'Biography and the Biographic' that they intended 'to illustrate a significant phenomenon of the Roman world, and one for which the scope of

---

49. Gregory E. Sterling, 'Response to Dihle and Alexander', SBL 9/8/1994, p. 10.

the word "biography", under any definition, would be too narrow.'[50] He prefers the word 'biographic' to describe the way 'biographic tendencies' spread across different literary forms.

A critique of my book follows, in which Edwards says 'I cite Burridge as an example of common falsehoods', although he does admit that 'he is often less inaccurate than others'![51] Regrettably, however, Edwards' criticisms are themselves inaccurate: for instance, he claims that I regard Theocritus as 'the father of pastoral', while I merely instance him as 'an early practioner' (p. 44 above); he says that my account of 'biography in the Classical period rests upon four documents', omitting to include Satyrus in citing the *five* examples taken from before the gospels (Chapter 6), and ignoring the five later examples altogether (Chapter 7); he accuses me of calling the *Evagoras* and *Agesilaus* 'not only biographies, but βίοι', when in fact I explicitly avoid this when describing their rhetorical origins on pages 125-6 and 129 above.

Such incorrect attacks are odd given that my approach agrees with Edwards' main distinction between biography and the biographic: 'whereas biography is a form of literature, the biographic is a trend in literature'.[52] This is exactly the distinction noted above, using Alastair Fowler's terms 'mode' and 'genre' to convey the difference between an adjective like biographic and a noun like biography (see pp. 39-40), and I agree about the importance of the distinction. However, this is best done by utilising a full range of generic features, rather than restricting the genre merely to 'writings . . . employing the title βίος' as Edwards seems to do.[53] Thus while Greg Camp cites Edwards as the 'one significant challenge' which he could find, he concludes that it is 'not one that is sufficient to discredit the approach taken by Burridge'.[54]

The rest of *Portraits* contains some very useful discussions of the effect of the 'biographic' across classical literature. Pelling's chapter on 'Biographical History' looks at how Cassius Dio writes about the early Principate, where his interest in the first emperors brings in some biographical features.[55] His use of 'biostructuring', however, does not obscure the fact there are still

50. M. J. Edwards, 'Biography and the Biographic' in *Portraits: Biographical Representation in the Greek and Latin Literature of the Roman Empire*, ed. M. J. Edwards and Simon Swain (Oxford: Clarendon, 1997), pp. 227-36; quotation from p. 227.

51. Edwards, 'Biography and the Biographic', p. 229.

52. Edwards, 'Biography and the Biographic', p. 228.

53. Edwards, 'Biography and the Biographic', p. 229.

54. Greg Alan Camp, 'Woe to You, Hypocrites! Law and Leaders in the Gospel of Matthew', Ph.D. Thesis, University of Sheffield, Sept. 2002, pp. 64-5.

55. C. B. R. Pelling, 'Biographical History? Cassius Dio on the Early Principate', in *Portraits*, pp. 117-44.

'trans-regnal themes' and a tendency to generalize across the emperors. Thus Pelling helpfully demonstrates that while biography and historiography are very close genres and the 'biographic' does invade histories centred on individuals like emperors, it is still possible to differentiate between the two. This has obvious implications for the historiographical tendencies in Luke and the biographic in Acts.

Edwards and Pelling were then both involved in the conference on 'Biographical Limits in the Ancient World: Form and Content'.[56] Its overall theme of the limits and expressions of biography brought together both classicists and biblical scholars to work together on defining the genre and determining its boundaries. The first afternoon was spent on some general papers, including one from Loveday Alexander on 'Anecdote and *Chreia* in the ancient biographical tradition'. The second day was devoted to biography and the Bible, including papers on the story of the Rise of David in the Hebrew Scriptures, Philo's *Moses*, Cynicism in the Gospels, the Acts of the Apostles as Biography, and on Mark and Ancient Biography, culminating in papers from Edwards and myself. The third day considered more Graeco-Roman biographies and biographical writings from Philostratus, Lucian and Plutarch, concluding with papers on the last day about letters, writing, travel and culture. The interdisciplinary conversation of classicists and biblical scholars was extremely stimulating and most illuminating.[57]

Despite his critique of my book in *Portraits*, Edwards' paper on 'Sense and Sensitivity: Reflections on the Genre of the Gospels' curiously chose not to engage with my work at all. Instead, he concentrated on the development of genres in the ancient world and how the gospels came to be written, before discussing the work of Christopher Bryan on Mark, and Morton Smith and H. C. Kee on aretalogy. Regrettably, his assessment of Bryan is as inaccurate as his treatment of my own work. He criticized Bryan for a mechanical view of genre, examining Bryan's four 'common motifs' of the hero's origins, education, great deeds and death.[58] Edwards then called these four 'criteria' and argued that they are not met in Mark. Yet Bryan himself recognizes the differences here, and only views these four as 'common motifs', which is how he translates τόποι. This is only *one* of eleven different generic features which Bryan considers, drawn mainly from our list of features used above, all of

56. This was organized by Judith Mossman at Trinity College, Dublin 5-8 September 2001.

57. The collected papers are being published as *The Limits of Biography*, ed. Brian McGing and Judith Mossman (Swansea: The Classical Press of Wales, forthcoming).

58. Christopher Bryan, *A Preface to Mark: Notes on the Gospel in Its Literary and Cultural Settings* (Oxford University Press, 1993), pp. 50-53.

which Bryan considers at greater length.[59] Unfortunately, Edwards did not discuss the other ten features, nor Bryan's detailed treatment of Mark as oral presentation. Thus it is Edwards who is being mechanical here, rather than Bryan.

My own paper attempted to respond to the various reviews and reactions to my book, and to sketch out how the biographical hypothesis has enabled my work and that of others to develop.[60] Discussion afterwards ranged widely over my use of statistical analysis of verbal subjects, comparison with Jewish literature and the absence of Rabbinic biography, the Christological implications for interpreting the gospels, and issues regarding the public reading of the gospels and whether their 'performance' in worship or early church meetings was analogous to that of Lucian or the sophists. It is significant that in this interdisciplinary context similar issues arose as from the reviews and other seminars mentioned earlier.

Other very interesting papers included Brian McGing on Philo's *Moses* and Sean Freyne on Mark. Justin Taylor's analysis of the Acts of the Apostles as biography revisited Talbert's ideas of succession narrative, and found this 'fruitful for interpretation'. On its own, Acts conforms well enough to historiography, while Luke is a biography; but in bringing them together, we notice a number of biographical elements in Acts, especially about Peter and Paul. Among the more classical papers, Christopher Pelling's analysis of writings about Caesar showed how Dio, Appian and Plutarch pressed on the boundaries of the genres of history and biography. The fact that a boundary is 'porous' does not mean that there is not a difference: thus night turns to day gradually, but we can still distinguish them — as we can between historiography and βίος.[61] Mike Tapp looked at the boundary between biography and letters, which he considered 'an inherently (auto)biographical medium', going on from classical examples to consider the epistles of St Paul.

The concluding plenary discussion considered some issues which had arisen from many papers throughout the conference. The first was *the whole*

59. Bryan, *A Preface to Mark*, pp. 27-64; Edwards seems to have missed Bryan's careful conclusions about some of the 'unusual features' in Mark, which do not prevent it being received as a 'life', pp. 61-2.

60. It appears in *The Limits of Biography*, ed. McGing and Mossman, and forms an early basis for what has become this extended last chapter of my book.

61. See also C. B. R. Pelling, 'Epilogue' in *The Limits of Historiography: Genre and Narrative in Ancient Historical Texts*, ed. Christina Shuttleworth Kraus (Leiden: Brill, 1999), pp. 325-60; in note 14, p. 329, Pelling contrasts my book with Edwards' position and reiterates the importance of genre as a 'useful shorthand' even when the 'distinctions between biography and its *genera proxima* (as he [Burridge] but not Edwards would put it) are blurred'.

concept of 'limits' and how one defines the boundaries of a genre like ancient biography, particularly when its modal influence as 'biographical' affected so many other forms of writing. Yet it had become clear that some sense of genre is necessary to investigate how works are written and how they function in relation to other writings, as was seen in Pelling's paper. This fits well into the flexible approach to genre we have used throughout. This led on to discussion of the issues of *social function and ancient performance of texts,* especially the way in which apologetic and polemic affected many genres.

Finally, we reflected on the experience of bringing together the two disciplines: as one classicist asked, 'are the NT folk on, or from, Planet Zog?'! It was recognized that the interaction had been fruitful and we noted how the two groups seemed to operate with different 'canons', with the classicists looking at Plutarch, Suetonius and other highly literary works, while the New Testamenters study Philo, Diogenes Laertius, the Alexander Romance and so forth, further down the social ladder. However, this was not as simple as the old Bultmannian *Hoch-* v. *Kleinliteratur* debate: it was noted that there were differing societies within the ancient world with different approaches to biographical literature from Athenian democracy or Persian letters to the Great King, to the later Republic and early Principate, with differing reactions ranging from Philo's emulation of Xenophon in his *Moses* to the absence of Rabbinic biography. Furthermore, even within the same time period different sections of the same society were writing different works in the same language — which reinforces the need for proper literary theory and a flexible understanding of genre which still recognizes the reality of 'limits' or boundaries within a good awareness of Graeco-Roman literature.

In many ways, this conference brings us back full circle to our initial proposals about tackling the nature of the gospels through genre theory and a comparison with other contemporary works within the Graeco-Roman and Jewish world. It is now clear that this approach has won widespread acceptance and that most scholars on both sides of the Atlantic and across the disciplines accept that the gospels are a form of ancient biography. These reviews and debates have also identified a number of issues where the implications of the biographical hypothesis have stimulated new and continuing research, to which we now turn.

3. Continuing Work and Scholarship

Reviews and conference papers are the quickest way in which reactions and responses appear to any work, particularly if it is calling for a new paradigm or model. However, what is really crucial is how it is incorporated into the continuing task of New Testament research in general and gospel studies in particular. Therefore in this third section, we need to consider how the debate about gospel genre and the biographical hypothesis has developed over the last decade or so.

(a) Articles on the Genre Debate

At the end of Part One, we saw that some scholars were beginning to argue that the gospels were a form of ancient biography, but that this still needed to be properly established (see pages 100-101 above). So it is not surprising that some dictionary articles about the gospels and biography appeared around the same time as my book. Frans Neirynck could still say that 'according to the modern critical consensus, the Gospels constitute their own literary genre: they are sui generis, sharing a distinctive form and content'. However, he went on to describe 'a growing dissatisfaction with this form-critical approach' and a 'renewed interest' in the search for 'parallels to Mark's genre, especially for possible associations with Hellenistic biographical literature, in its variegated forms, including the popular biography'.[62] Larry Hurtado provided a succinct discussion of the genre theory and a summary of the debate about the gospels, and then considered each gospel briefly in turn to argue that they 'constitute a distinctive group of writings within early Christianity' likened to Graeco-Roman popular biography 'in very general terms'.[63] Willem Vorster took a similar line in his *ABD* article, outlining the traditional form-critical arguments for the uniqueness of the gospels, but arguing that the canonical gospels are members of 'the same genre . . . narratives about the life, deeds and words of Jesus' with analogies to biography as the 'only generic text type with which the gospel genre can be compared'; the gospels 'reveal features of ancient biographies'.[64]

However, in the special edition of *Neotestamentica* commemorating

---

62. Frans Neirynck, 'Gospel, Genre of' in *The Oxford Companion to the Bible*, ed. Bruce M. Metzger and Michael D. Coogan (Oxford University Press, 1993), pp. 258-9; reprinted in *The Oxford Guide to Ideas and Issues of the Bible*, ed. Bruce M. Metzger and Michael D. Coogan (Oxford University Press, 2001), pp. 184-6 — but even more out of date now than it was originally!

63. L. W. Hurtado, 'Gospel (Genre)', in *Dictionary of Jesus and the Gospels*, ed. J. B. Green et al. (Downers Grove, Ill.: InterVarsity, 1992), pp. 276-82.

64. Willem Vorster, 'Gospel Genre', in *The Anchor Bible Dictionary*, ed. D. N. Freedman (New York: Doubleday, 1992), Vol. 2, pp. 1077-9; the *ABD* also contains a good article from Charles Talbert on 'Biography, Ancient', Vol. 1, pp. 745-9.

Vorster, Norman Petersen disagreed with him — and also criticised my book.[65] Petersen's important work on literary criticism for the New Testament in general and his early contribution to the 1970 SBL Task Force on Gospel Genre were noted at the start above (pp. 16 and 21). Against Vorster, Petersen now argued that the gospels did not belong to the same genre at all, and that none of them are biography: Mark and John are more like parodies of aretalogy, and it is their plot-type which is crucial, while Matthew is more like a 'community rule' and Luke-Acts belongs with historiography as a two-volume work. He notes my comments about the difficulty of proving a narrow genre identification which could be hermeneutically helpful, and the converse about broader definitions (pp. 247-8 above), but then attacks 'the very triviality' of my conclusion regarding the gospels' central focus on Jesus.[66] This echoes comments made in some reviews discussed above, which led to my further work on the Christological implications of the gospels as biography. Ironically, Petersen concludes by moving away from genre to explain the gospels through their 'sociology of common knowledge'.

On the other hand, John Fitzgerald picked up my arguments and those of David Aune to argue for 'a "new" or "emerging" consensus in regard to the Gospels' biographical character.'[67] As with other reactions above, the biographical view is accepted as the basis for new work building upon it, as Fitzgerald concentrates on ancient lives of Aristotle. He concludes 'this suggests that the recent trend towards viewing the Gospels as a subtype of Hellenistic biography is warranted and that additional study of Greco-Roman biographies would enhance our understanding of the canonical Gospels.' Equally, two general articles in *The New Interpreter's Bible* also show this move. Tannehill compares the gospels with narrative literature, noting that they share 'with ancient biography some general similarities of content, form and function', drawing on Aune's work, but also noting Adela Yarbro Collins' arguments for historiography.[68] This is followed immediately by Tuckett's article on 'Jesus and the Gospels' which refers to Aune but also to my work to accept that 'it is now becoming clear . . . that the NT Gospels could be placed within the wide parameters that accommodate ancient biography', although he does go on once again to ask how and whether this helps in their interpre-

---

65. Norman Petersen, 'Can one speak of a gospel genre?' *Neotestamentica* 28.3 (1994) (Special Edition), pp. 137-58.

66. Petersen, 'Can one speak of a gospel genre?' *Neotestamentica* 1994, pp. 146-7.

67. John T. Fitzgerald, 'The Ancient Lives of Aristotle and the Modern Debate about the Genre of the Gospels', *Restoration Quarterly* 36 (1994), pp. 209-21; quotation from p. 211.

68. R. C. Tannehill, 'The Gospels and Narrative Literature' in *The New Interpreter's Bible*, Volume VIII (Nashville: Abingdon, 1995), pp. 68-70.

tation.[69] This shift towards the gospels as biography is demonstrated in the new edition of the *Oxford Classical Dictionary,* where Pelling's article on Greek biography included the gospels, referring to my work.[70] Meanwhile, in the *Oxford Bible Commentary,* Henry Wansbrough notes the change in that as late as 1987 the 'majority opinion' was 'that there was no close parallel to the genre of the gospels', but that 'Burridge (1992) has shown that the gospels fall within the varied and well-attested Graeco-Roman concept of biography'.[71] Finally, Tuckett answers his own questions about the usefulness of the bio-graphical genre by drawing upon my work in his general introduction to the gospels in the new *Eerdmans Bible Commentary.*[72] Thus these discussions and dictionary articles resemble the reviews and conferences both in accepting generally the biographical hypothesis and moving the debate on to its impli-cations.

(b) Matthew

Garland was one of the first commentators to make use of my material. In his Introduction to *Reading Matthew,* he begins with traditional questions about authorship, date and provenance — but finds it hard to come to definite con-clusions. Instead, he suggests that a comparison with other ancient literature may help to illumine its genre and purpose, and quotes my conclusion which Petersen (and others) found trivial that the gospels are motivated by a 'gen-eral desire to tell others about Jesus'; he then goes on to apply my list of possi-ble purposes for ancient lives and the gospels (pp. 207-10 above) specifically to Matthew.[73] As the external examiner of my thesis, Graham Stanton quickly incorporated its insights into his work on Matthew, giving a whole section to 'Genre' in his chapter on Literary Criticism, including a discussion of Mat-thew as a biography.[74] Having been the first modern scholar to compare the

69. Christopher M. Tuckett, 'Jesus and the Gospels', *NIB* VIII, pp. 71-86; quotation from p. 72; compare his review in *Theology* (1993), pp. 74-5; see notes 2, 6 and 22 above and his conclu-sions, note 72 below.

70. C. B. R. Pelling, 'Biography, Greek' in *The Oxford Classical Dictionary* (Oxford Uni-versity Press, 1996), pp. 241-2.

71. Henry Wansbrough, 'The Four Gospels in Synopsis' in *The Oxford Bible Commentary,* ed. John Barton and John Muddiman (Oxford University Press, 2001), pp. 1001-2.

72. Christopher Tuckett, 'Introduction to the Gospels', in *Eerdmans Commentary on the Bible,* ed. James D. G. Dunn and John Rogerson (Grand Rapids: Eerdmans, 2003), pp. 989-93.

73. David E. Garland, *Reading Matthew: A Literary and Theological Commentary on the First Gospel* (London: SPCK, 1993); see pp. 5-9.

74. G. N. Stanton, *A Gospel for a New People: Studies in Matthew* (Edinburgh: T&T Clark, 1992); see pp. 59-71.

gospels to biographical writings (see the assessment of his work on pp. 79-80 above), he now accepts that 'the gospels are a type of Graeco-Roman biography', kindly describing my book as 'a careful and thorough study which will remain the standard discussion for a long time to come'.[75] He continues with a critique of Shuler's idea that Matthew is an encomium biography and discusses how Matthew adapts the genre of Q, before going on to the gospel's social setting and function, adapting suggestions from Aune and myself to argue that Matthew provides a social legitimation in his 'biography of Jesus'. In his extensively revised second edition of *The Gospels and Jesus,* Stanton again begins with the question of genre and the gospels as biographies, noting that his biographical approach in 1974 'was then unfashionable'. He then discusses my book, and concludes 'there is little doubt that early Christian readers of the gospels did read them as biographies'.[76]

(c) Mark

Christopher Bryan is a good example of a scholar who welcomed and agreed with my work, but then developed it in new directions which I had not expected. In his innovative *A Preface to Mark,* he draws heavily on my material for Part I, 'What Kind of Text Is Mark?' before going on to consider 'Was Mark Written to Be Read Aloud?' in Part II. This is an excellent instance of what we noted at the start of this work, that genre is a crucial guide to the production and reception of writings, and therefore we need to determine the genre of the gospels before progressing to their interpretation. Bryan uses my book to demonstrate that 'Mark is a Hellenistic "Life"'.[77] He then adapts our list of generic features in his detailed analysis of Mark's eleven features, particularly appreciating my statistical material on verbal subjects, the allocation of space and the length of ancient works about which other reviewers were less enthusiastic.[78] Having thus demonstrated that Mark is a type of 'Hellenistic "Life"', Bryan turns in his larger second part to consider oral composition, transmission and performance of texts in the ancient world, discussing the oral characteristics of Mark's style and presentation, concluding with some interesting comments about its performance both then and today.

Ezra Shim from Stellenbosch also draws extensively upon my work in

75. Stanton, *A Gospel for a New People,* p. 64.

76. Graham Stanton, *The Gospels and Jesus,* Second Edition (Oxford University Press, 2002), pp. 16-17; see n. 8 on p. 80 above.

77. Christopher Bryan, *A Preface to Mark: Notes on the Gospel in Its Literary and Cultural Settings* (Oxford University Press, 1993), pp. vii, 27-30.

78. Bryan, *A Preface to Mark,* pp. 36, 41, 56.

his analysis of the history of the issue of gospel genre and genre theory.[79] He then goes on to consider the specific genre of Mark, concluding with three possible proposals: the *sui generis* approach of the form critics, a genre similar to other contemporary genres (including our suggestions about biography) or a third, 'middle position' of a 'new, but synthesized genre'. In suggesting this third option, he argues that Mark is a form of narrative, utilizing earlier genres and showing the influences of both Judaism and Hellenism with various modal applications. While I am sure that he is correct about the way Mark can have 'modal' tendencies such as 'realistic narrative', 'kerygmatic' or 'dramatic', locating its genre in something as broad as 'narrative' does not really help; such modal tendencies are better understood arising out of its biographical genre.

Telford similarly begins his chapter on 'Mark as Literature' with a consideration of genre, and then goes on to the genre of Mark with the same three options as Shim — *sui generis,* a parallel genre (like biography) or a middle choice of 'a new type of "evolved" literature'.[80] In his discussion of Mark as biography, he discusses only Talbert, and concludes that 'there are still many who would hold that the Graeco-Roman biography hypothesis fails to account for certain major and special features of Gospels such as Mark'; perhaps if he had considered the approach taken throughout this book, he might have been able to account for these features. Telford then considers apocalyptic drama, Greek tragedy, Hellenistic romance, and tragic-comedy before concluding that 'the Gospel of Mark constitutes for many scholars a distinctive type of ancient biography combining Hellenistic form and function with Jewish content'.[81] In the light of this generic conclusion, he goes on to analyse Mark's structure and arrangement, literary techniques and rhetorical devices, and his narrative, plot and characters.

Finally, Ben Witherington III also begins with genre and then moves to interpretation in his socio-rhetorical commentary on Mark. His discussion of genre briefly considers suggestions that Mark might be dramatic and Collins' proposal for historiography, but goes on to argue strongly for Mark as 'an example of an ancient *bios*', drawing on my material to examine its external and internal features.[82] The implications of this for the interpretation of the gos-

---

79. Ezra S. B. Shim, 'A Suggestion about the Genre of Text-Type of Mark', *Scriptura* 50 (1994), pp. 69-89; see especially pp. 70-5.

80. W. R. Telford, *Mark* (Sheffield Academic Press, 1995), Chapter 3, pp. 86-119; see p. 95 for three options.

81. Telford, *Mark,* pp. 97, 100.

82. Ben Witherington III, *The Gospel of Mark: A Socio-Rhetorical Commentary* (Grand Rapids: Eerdmans, 2001), pp. 1-9; see especially n. 18, p. 6.

pel arise from 'the author's biographical focus' which seeks 'to ask and answer the questions: Who was Jesus, what was he like, and why is he worth writing a biography about?' Thus, as noted above with Garland's commentary on Matthew, our conclusions about the biographical focus on Jesus are far from Petersen's 'trivial', but rather reveal the importance of Christology: 'the *who* question was very important for Mark'.[83] This insight is then crucial for Witherington throughout the rest of his commentary.

Therefore, over the last decade, various scholars have demonstrated both the importance of beginning Markan study with the question of genre and also how the biographical hypothesis helps with its interpretation.

(d) Luke-Acts

Our original conclusions upon the generic implications of the biographical hypothesis included some brief reflections about the generic relationship of Luke and his second volume, Acts (see pages 237-9 above). This raised the question of whether the two volumes had to be the same genre, or whether Luke's gospel is a biography while Acts is more of a historical monograph, while maintaining many biographical generic features such as the focus on Peter and Paul (appearing in 6% and 14.5% of the sentences according to our statistical analysis), or even perhaps a βίος of the church in the manner of Dicaearchus' biographical work on Greece. We also noted the tendency for some biographical material to appear within sections of a larger historiographical work. All of these issues have continued to be debated over the last decade as the focus has shifted more to the genre of Luke's second volume.

After I completed my doctoral thesis, but prior to its publication, the SBL Acts group gave particular attention to this question at their 1989 meeting. Richard Pervo protested 'Must Luke and Acts Belong to the Same Genre?' arguing that the modern stress on the unity of Luke-Acts leads to absurdity if it requires generic unity.[84] We have already noted that Aune's demand that 'Luke and Acts *must* be treated as affiliated with *one* genre' leads to the odd conclusion that Luke cannot be the same biographical genre as the other three gospels,[85] hence Pervo's critique. Greg Sterling gave a taster of his later work with 'Luke-Acts and Apologetic Historiography' as did David Balch with his 'preliminary comparison' of Luke-Acts with Dionysius of

83. Witherington, *The Gospel of Mark*, pp. 10, 5, and 42.

84. Richard Pervo, 'Must Luke and Acts Belong to the Same Genre?', in *SBL 1989 Seminar Papers* (Atlanta: Scholars Press, 1989), pp. 309-16.

85. David Aune, *The New Testament in Its Literary Environment* (Cambridge: James Clarke & Co., 1988), pp. 77-80; see pages 98-9 above.

Halicarnassus.[86] In addition, Edwards looked at 'narrative communication' and Jones at 'historical chronology'.[87] A couple of years later, Pervo and Parsons returned to this issue as one of the questions which led them to question the assumption of the unity of Luke and Acts.[88]

This mixture of historiography and literary questions can be seen in Bruce's revised Introduction to the 1990 edition of his important commentary. Although he never addresses the question of genre directly, he does discuss Luke as an apologist and as a historian; significantly, he notes that while 'it is in Acts rather than in his "former treatise" that Luke is recognizable as a Hellenistic historian', yet 'Luke develops his theme biographically: he records what might be called the Acts of Stephen and Philip, the Acts of Peter, and the Acts of Paul'.[89] Marshall picks this up in his contribution to *The Book of Acts in Its Ancient Literary Setting* in his section on 'the genre of Luke-Acts' where he looks at Aune's argument for historical monograph and Talbert's biographical succession narrative and concludes that 'the whole work demonstrates affinities both to historical monographs and to biographies, but it appears to represent a new type of work, of which it is the only example'.[90] Elsewhere in the same volume, Palmer considers the genre of Acts alone and argues against Pervo's romance, Sterling's apologetic history and Alexander's technical treatise in favour of 'historical monograph' following Polybius' definition.[91] On the other hand, Alexander considers 'Acts and Ancient Intellectual Biography', revisiting Talbert's succession narrative thesis and Diogenes Laertius to sug-

86. Gregory E. Sterling, 'Luke-Acts and Apologetic Historiography', *SBL 1989 Seminar Papers*, pp. 326-42; David L. Balch, 'Comments on the Genre and a Political Theme of Luke-Acts: A Preliminary Comparison of Two Hellenistic Historians', *SBL 1989 Seminar Papers*, pp. 343-61. Balch followed this the next year with 'The Genre of Luke-Acts: Individual Biography, Adventure Novel or Political History?', *Southwestern Journal of Theology* 33 (1990), pp. 5-19; see also note 18 earlier in this chapter for Balch's current work on the genre of Luke-Acts, ΜΕΤΑΒΟΛΗ ΠΟΛΙΤΕΙΩΝ.

87. Douglas R. Edwards, 'Acts of the Apostles and the Graeco-Roman World: Narrative Communication in Social Context', *SBL 1989 Seminar Papers*, pp. 362-77; David L. Jones, 'Luke's Unique Interest in Historical Chronology', *SBL 1989 Seminar Papers*, pp. 378-87.

88. M. C. Parsons and R. I. Pervo, *Rethinking the Unity of Luke and Acts* (Minneapolis: Fortress, 1993).

89. F. F. Bruce, *The Acts of the Apostles: The Greek Text with Introduction and Commentary*, revised edition (Leicester: IVP/Grand Rapids: Eerdmans, 1990), pp. 22-34; quotations from pp. 28 and 30.

90. I. Howard Marshall, 'Acts and the "Former Treatise"', in *The Book of Acts in Its Ancient Literary Setting*, ed. Bruce W. Winter and Andrew D. Clarke (Carlisle: Paternoster/Grand Rapids: Eerdmans, 1993), pp. 163-82; see esp. pp. 178-80.

91. Darryl W. Palmer, 'Acts and the Ancient Historical Monograph' in *The Book of Acts in Its Ancient Literary Setting*, pp. 1-29.

gest that the Socratic paradigm may have influenced the genre of Acts; however, she does make use of my work, especially the statistics about Peter and Paul already mentioned, to point out the biographical focus whereby 'Paul is in fact the sole hero of the narrative . . . for more than half the book'.[92]

We have already discussed the International Meeting of the Society of Biblical Literature in August 1994 with the contributions from Pervo, Alexander, Sterling and Collins in section 2.c above — and these debates have continued subsequently. Cancik's main paper (in German) on Luke-Acts as the 'history of an institution' at that conference was subsequently translated and published in *JBL*; he applies this theme to both books *('logoi')* and states about the gospel that 'the first *logos* is not a biography'.[93] Mark Reasoner criticised him for not addressing the issue of genre directly, using our material to argue that the 'theme' or content of Acts cannot determine its genre alone.[94] Alexander's paper at the 1997 meeting of the SNTS at Birmingham about the genre of history in Acts pointed out that modern readers often confuse 'history' with 'truth' or 'fact', while actually there was a large amount of 'historical fiction' within ancient historiography as well as in the early novel; this would have been recognized by the first readers of Acts.[95]

Similarly, it was left to Talbert to fly the biographical flag in a volume about Acts and historiography, in which he cites similar biographical passages in ancient historians to those we have already noted, but still distinguishes history from biography. He then summarises my book, concluding that 'it is difficult to see how, after this careful study, the biographical nature of the canonical gospels can be denied'.[96] However, the problem for Luke comes from the supposed historiographical nature of Acts: Talbert first exposes some of the problems with this, and then rehearses his argument for Acts as a biographical succession narrative. He also considers my suggestion that Acts might be a βίος of the early church like Dicaearchus' 'life' of Greece (see pp. 70 and 238 above); he describes this option as 'a novel one' and brings together

---

92. L. C. A. Alexander, 'Acts and Ancient Intellectual Biography', in *The Book of Acts in Its Ancient Literary Setting*, pp. 31-63; see esp. pp. 33-4 and note 6.

93. Hubert Cancik, 'The History of Culture, Religion and Institutions in Ancient Historiography: Philological Observations concerning Luke's History', *JBL* 116 (1997), pp. 673-95; quotation from p. 673.

94. Mark Reasoner, 'The Theme of Acts: Institutional History or Divine Necessity in History?', *JBL* 118.4 (1999), pp. 635-59; see p. 649, n. 52, and p. 659, n. 95.

95. Loveday Alexander, 'Fact, Fiction and the Genre of Acts', *NTS* 44 (1998), pp. 380-99.

96. Charles H. Talbert, 'The Acts of the Apostles: Monograph or Bios?' in *History, Literature, and Society in the Book of Acts*, ed. Ben Witherington III (Cambridge University Press, 1996), pp. 58-72; quotation from p. 62.

his approach and my suggestion to argue that 'some combination of the two biographical hypotheses would work better than either taken alone'. He concludes by observing that 'the biographical genre, no less than historiography, offers no guarantees about historicity.'[97] Finally, Daniel Marguerat, who also participated in the discussions at SBL 1994, has tried to move the argument about Luke as a historian away from the 'true/false quagmire' to a literary discussion of ancient historiography within its own framework and rules.[98]

Meanwhile commentaries on Acts have also begun to take the issue of genre seriously. Thus Spencer's introduction to his volume in Sheffield's 'Readings' series moves rapidly from the question of authorship to that of genre. He considers the proposals from historical monograph, biblical history, biographical narrative and succession and popular romance and concludes, 'the push to fit Acts into one of these slots — and in some cases to fit in the Lukan Gospel along with it — has fostered considerable debate, but little consensus.'[99] Fitzmyer's introduction begins with 'Title' even before 'Author' and argues that 'the ancient title *Praxeis* was a term designating a specific Greek literary form', linked also to the Roman *Res Gestae;* this relates 'this NT writing to a well-known Hellenistic genre, a "historical monograph"', but 'a biographical concern is not excluded' for the *'diegēsis'* of the Third Gospel. Against Talbert's biographical genre for the whole work and Pervo's novel, Fitzmyer is content to take *Praxeis* to indicate the genre of 'historical monograph'.[100] As with Mark, so Witherington also begins his socio-rhetorical commentary on Acts with the question of genre, again making use of my work as he discusses both the biographical and historiographical character of Luke and Acts.[101]

These issues are also at the heart of a collection of essays on Luke as a Hellenistic writer claiming to interpret the history and heritage of Israel through his two volumes. It begins with the questions of the Prologues with an essay from Alexander on 'Formal Elements and Genre' comparing Luke 1.1-4 and Acts 1.1ff with historiography, apologetic and technical prose to argue that they give the first-century reader 'a socio-literary framework for reading Luke's work'.[102] However, Schmidt considers Luke's Preface against

---

97. Talbert, 'The Acts of the Apostles: Monograph or Bios?' pp. 64, 70, 72.

98. Daniel Marguerat, *The First Christian Historian: Writing the 'Acts of the Apostles',* SNTSMS 121 (Cambridge University Press, 2002).

99. F. Scott Spencer, *Acts* (Sheffield Academic Press, 1997), pp. 13-14.

100. Joseph A. Fitzmyer, SJ, *The Acts of the Apostles: A New Translation with Introduction and Commentary,* The Anchor Bible (New York: Doubleday, 1998), pp. 47-9.

101. Ben Witherington III, *The Acts of the Apostles: A Socio-Rhetorical Commentary* (Grand Rapids: Eerdmans, 1998), pp. 2-39; see esp. pp. 15-21.

102. L. C. A. Alexander, 'Formal Elements and Genre: Which Greco-Roman Prologues

the rhetoric of Hellenistic historiography and argues that 'it seems unlikely that attempts to settle once and for all whether Luke and/or Acts are really "history" or "biography", or something else, can be successful', although in the end he settles for 'the rather wide spectrum of "Hellenistic historiography"'.[103] Meanwhile, Pervo sees the problem arising from the modern determination to read the two volumes as one work and one genre; he discusses all the various options and scholars mentioned above, including our work, and argues for Luke and Acts as two monographs, where 'Acts is a sequel rather than a second volume'.[104] Finally, Howard Marshall draws upon my book to agree that for Luke 'it is correct to call it a biography with a religious purpose or motivation', but then he goes on to see what difference knowing Acts is to follow as a sequel makes to reading Luke.[105]

Clearly, the issues of genre relating to Luke and Acts will continue to be debated. Most scholars seem to accept the obvious point that Luke's genre belongs with that of the other gospels, as we argued originally — but this is complicated by how one sees Acts. Our biographical understanding of Luke continues to have relevance to the debates about Acts, not least because of the biographical interest shown in its heroes like Peter and Paul. If the decade since the publication of my book began with Alexander picking up my statistics about the verbal subjects in Acts, it is interesting to note that it ended with a paper from Steve Walton on his current research project to the British New Testament Conference in Sept. 2003, using my method of statistical analysis of the nominatives and nouns throughout the New Testament to demonstrate that the 'key actor' in Acts is actually God![106]

(e) John

The fourth gospel has long been treated by biblical scholars in a separate category from the other three, perhaps even a different world! From the

---

Most Closely Parallel the Lukan Prologues?' in *Jesus and the Heritage of Israel: Luke's Narrative Claim upon Israel's Legacy*, ed. David P. Moessner (Harrisburg: Trinity Press International, 1999), pp. 9-26; quotation from p. 24.

103. Daryl D. Schmidt, 'Rhetorical Influences and Genre: Luke's Preface and the Rhetoric of Hellenistic Historiography' in *Jesus and the Heritage of Israel*, pp. 27-60; quotations from pp. 51 and 59.

104. Richard Pervo, 'Israel's Heritage and Claims upon the Genre(s) of Luke and Acts: The Problems of a History' in *Jesus and the Heritage of Israel*, pp. 127-43.

105. I. Howard Marshall, '"Israel" and the Story of Salvation: One Theme in Two Parts' in *Jesus and the Heritage of Israel*, pp. 340-58; quotation from p. 348 and n. 27.

106. Steve Walton, 'The Acts — of God? What is the "Acts of the Apostles" All About?', British New Testament Conference, Birmingham, Sept. 2003.

point of view of genre, it has been compared with drama, beginning with Hitchcock's analysis of it in five divisions like tragedy, complete with *anagnorisis*, discovery, and *peripateia*, reversal of fortunes.[107] This was most fully worked out by Mark Stibbe, comparing John to Euripides' *Bacchae* to argue that John's genre or *mythos* is tragedy.[108] Yet John lacks all the formal characteristics to belong to the genre of tragedy, such as being written in verse with three actors and a chorus.[109] So in his second book, Stibbe accepted that 'the genre of the Gospel as a whole I understand to be *bios*, ancient biographical writing' which moves through four *mythoi*, or plot-types, including tragedy.[110]

Although we discussed the genre of the fourth gospel separately from the Synoptics in chapter 9, we concluded that it shared so many generic features of both form and content with the other three that they all belong to the same genre, namely βίοι (see pages 232 and 236 above). Comparisons to drama, like those of Stibbe, belong to the level of mode, where one can talk of the 'dramatic' or 'tragic' character of John.[111] Significantly, Culpepper, who pioneered narrative criticism of John, notes that his 'discussion of plot in *Anatomy of the Fourth Gospel* does not adequately relate it to the issue of the genre of the Gospel or its structure'. He proceeds to discuss Stibbe's arguments for tragedy, followed by considering my book, noting that 'the conclusion that John is biography has fuelled several significant analyses of its plot'. After analysing John's plot, Culpepper concludes that 'the Gospel of John, therefore, is an ancient biography in dramatic form' — which again makes clear both John's genre of biography and its dramatic mode.[112]

Andrew Lincoln also draws upon our distinction of mode and genre to argue for a 'testimony' mode within John's genre of ancient biography, as a

---

107. F. R. M. Hitchcock, 'Is the Fourth Gospel a Drama?', *Theology* 7 (1927), pp. 307-17; reprinted in the useful collection edited by Mark W. G. Stibbe, *The Gospel of John as Literature: An Anthology of Twentieth-Century Perspectives*, NTTS (Leiden: Brill, 1993), pp. 15-24.

108. Mark W. G. Stibbe, *John as Storyteller: Narrative Criticism and the Fourth Gospel*, SNTSMS 73 (Cambridge University Press, 1992), see esp. pp. 30-49; Stibbe and I both did our doctorates while training for ordination together at Nottingham, which provoked much helpful debate about literary theory and genre!

109. See further my review of Stibbe, *John as Storyteller* in *Journal of Theological Studies* 44 (2) 1993, pp. 654-8.

110. Mark W. G. Stibbe, *John* (Sheffield Academic Press, 1993), see pp. 13-14.

111. See, for instance, Richard A. Burridge, *John*, The People's Bible Commentary (Oxford: Bible Reading Fellowship, 1998), pp. 38 and 40, for modal use of John's dramatic way of writing.

112. R. Alan Culpepper, 'The Plot of John's Story of Jesus' in *Gospel Interpretation: Narrative-Critical & Social-Scientific Approaches*, ed. Jack Dean Kingsbury (Harrisburg: Trinity Press International, 1997), pp. 188-99; quotations from pp. 189, 192, 198.

key part of his argument for the 'lawsuit motif in the fourth gospel.'[113] As with the debates about the historicity of Luke-Acts, so Lincoln also applies our discussion of the conventions of ancient biography to the issues of truth and facticity in John.[114] Lincoln argues that viewing the fourth gospel as ancient biography provides a 'middle way' between those who view it as historical and those who believe it has no historicity.[115]

Thus as with the other gospels, the recognition that John belongs within the genre of ancient biography is increasingly producing fruitful results for both its interpretation and for the debates about its theology and history.

(f) Books and Major Treatments

In recent years, there have been several book-length treatments of the genre of the gospels which have dialogued with my work, either to take it forward or to critique it. Lawrence Wills' *The Quest of the Historical Gospel* attempts to set Mark and John within the context of both Graeco-Roman and Jewish literature. The first chapter discusses the genre of the gospels, beginning with the two-source hypothesis about Mark and Q and the independence of John, from which he argues that Mark and John 'both utilized an independent narrative tradition'.[116] There follow a brief discussion about 'approaches to genre' and an account of 'investigations of the gospel genre', drawing on most of the major writers in the field, such as Schmidt, Dodd, Dihle, Talbert, Berger and my own book, which is criticised for lacking 'any significant reference to Jewish literature'.[117] Consideration of possible sources of Mark and John leads Wills to his two theses: that Mark and John have both used 'an extensive gospel narrative' which is recoverable, and that this was a 'cult narrative of a dead hero', 'influenced by both Jewish and pagan tradition'.[118] To illustrate such a biographical cult narrative, Wills considers the *Life of Aesop,*

113. Andrew T. Lincoln, *Truth on Trial: The Lawsuit Motif in the Fourth Gospel* (Peabody: Hendrickson, 2000), pp. 169-71.

114. Lincoln, *Truth on Trial,* p. 370, referring to pages 59-67 above, and also our discussion of Calgacus' speech in Tacitus' *Agricola* in Burridge, *Four Gospels, One Jesus?* (Eerdmans/SPCK, 1994), pp. 167-8; see also page 176, note 77 above.

115. Lincoln, *Truth on Trial,* pp. 370-8 and 389-97; he argues for a 'middle of the road' approach in a recent paper, '"We know that his testimony is true": Johannine Truth Claims and Historicity', delivered at the SBL Annual Meeting, Atlanta, 22nd November 2003, again drawing on our approach.

116. Lawrence M. Wills, *The Quest of the Historical Gospel: Mark, John and the Origins of the Gospel Genre* (London: Routledge, 1997), p. 4.

117. Wills, *The Quest of the Historical Gospel,* p. 18.

118. Wills, *The Quest of the Historical Gospel,* p. 21.

and then the rest of the book is devoted to a detailed synoptic comparison between Mark and John to reconstruct their shared original source, a form of
'aretalogical biography associated with cult'.[119] He concludes with a useful
English translation of the *Life of Aesop* in an Appendix.

It is an interesting and thought-provoking study, even if it is eventually
not convincing in either of its main theses. Many of the parallels Wills cites
are instructive, well rooted in both classical literature and Jewish studies. Unfortunately, in the end he fails to establish either of his main theses about the
gospel genre or the shared source of Mark and John. Wills is aware that 'no
single model of aretalogy exists from early antiquity',[120] and merely calling it
'aretalogical biography' neither creates nor defines this genre, or sub-genre of
ancient biography. Furthermore, all his detailed comparisons of Mark and
John with each other and with *Aesop* merely demonstrate how different they
all are. It is rather an odd conclusion that Mark is related more to John and to
Aesop than to Matthew and Luke, which he declares at the outset to be 'a different kind of biography'.[121] Thus although Wills' two main theses both fail to
be convincing, his study does reinforce the need for debate about gospel
genre to be well rooted in both genre theory and contemporary literature.
Finally, while our approach and conclusions have been criticised for being
too broad, Wills, like Shuler (see pages 85-6 and 248 above), is a salutary reminder of the difficulties of trying to force the gospels into a more well-
defined sub-genre.

Michael Vines similarly takes issue with my work and then tries to
move the debate towards the ancient novel. He begins with 'a brief history
of the problem of gospel genre', drawing on my analysis and concentrating
on Votaw, Schmidt and Bultmann, before turning to a more detailed account of my work as a 'revival of Votaw's thesis', which at least he terms 'the
most significant attempt'.[122] He then moves to discuss Aune, Wills, Mary
Ann Tolbert and Collins, from which he concludes that Mark is only
'loosely' related to Graeco-Roman biography, preferring instead to follow
Wills and Tolbert towards the novel and popular literature, together with
Collins' stress on apocalyptic.[123] He concludes with a brief discussion of the
'nature of genre', in which he accuses Aune and myself of beginning with
the 'assumption that the gospels are biographical in nature', which leads to

119. Wills, *The Quest of the Historical Gospel*, p. 156.
120. Wills, *The Quest of the Historical Gospel*, p. 35.
121. Wills, *The Quest of the Historical Gospel*, p. 10.
122. Michael E. Vines, *The Problem of the Markan Genre: The Gospel of Mark and the Jewish Novel* (Atlanta: SBL, 2002), see pp. 1-12.
123. Vines, *The Problem of the Markan Genre*, pp. 12-22.

the 'inherent circularity' of our conclusions; we are also criticised for not looking for possible Jewish comparisons, and these two complaints are repeated later through the book.[124] In fact, it is patently not the case that I began by assuming that the gospels are biography; as mentioned at the end of Part One (page 101 above), I set out initially to criticise the biographical hypothesis, which was chosen because it was beginning to gain scholarly approval. However, it is true that this focus meant that possible Jewish parallels received only brief attention (pp. 19-21 above); the fact that many reviewers have pointed this out led to my further work on Jewish biography which will be discussed later below.

Having made these criticisms, Vines sets off on 'a new investigation' not into the genre of the gospels all together, but merely that of Mark, which he wants to compare with both Graeco-Roman and Hellenistic-Jewish literature. In fact, what he does is to take us into a lengthy discussion of the literary theory of Mikhail Bakhtin, especially his understanding of genre as determined by 'chronotype' which fixes a work in time and space, though not the real time and space of its composition and performance so much as the work's artistic or literary world.[125] We then move towards 'Greco-Roman literature in the Hellenistic period' in Chapter 3, considering epic, novel, biography, romance and Menippean satire — but only with Bakhtin as our guide.[126] We only come to Mark eventually in the shorter last chapter, in which its chronotype is argued to be none of biography, Greek romance or satire. Finally, its last sixteen pages try to cover 'Jewish novelistic literature in the Hellenistic period' to show that 'the chronotype of the Gospel of Mark most closely resembles that of the Jewish novels'; while Vines has to admit that Mark's episodic structure and his use of chreia and anecdote are different from the Jewish novel, these are only 'superficial differences' compared with the 'realistic-apocalyptic chronotype' which establishes their 'generic connection'.[127] It is rather curious that an account of Mark as a Jewish novel should contain so little about either Mark or the Jewish novels, while giving well over half its space to Bakhtin; but only by using his 'chronotype', which the ancients would not have recognised, can such different works be generically related. This both Wills and Vines conclude by relating the gospels to various forms of the ancient novel, despite the fact that, as Graham Stanton said even of Mary Ann Tolbert's more careful attempt, 'the differences in form and con-

124. Vines, *The Problem of the Markan Genre*, pp. 25-8; see also pp. 122-5, 144.

125. Vines, *The Problem of the Markan Genre*, pp. 30-67; see esp. p. 61.

126. Vines, *The Problem of the Markan Genre*, pp. 69-120.

127. Vines, *The Problem of the Markan Genre*, pp. 121-60; concluding quotations from p. 159.

tent between the gospels and ancient novels are much more striking than the similarities'.[128]

Further debate has come from John Riches' stimulating Introduction to a new English translation of K. L. Schmidt's important 1923 article.[129] Byron McCane has translated Schmidt's 'affected, wordy, convoluted and bombastic' German with its frequent neologisms into clear, plain and very readable English, though apparently not without a struggle;[130] such a translation is as overdue as it is welcome. Like Schmidt's original essay, John Riches' Introduction attacks those who compare the gospels to ancient biography, with my book as the chief of sinners. He accuses me of conflating Schmidt and Bultmann, and seeks to exonerate Schmidt from the charge of considering the gospels to be *sui generis,* like Bultmann.[131] It is true that, while we outlined the work of Schmidt and Bultmann separately at the start of our study above, they were evaluated together in their distinction of *Hochliteratur* and *Kleinliteratur* (see pages 8-12 above), although I hope without conflating their other views. Of course, Schmidt was looking for analogies for the gospels in his 'Stellung' — place or setting — of the gospels within literature, while Bultmann particularly stressed their uniqueness. Yet McCane's translation ends with Schmidt talking about the 'uniqueness of "early Christian literature"' with the 'various parallels adduced here . . . sharpening the eye for that which is unique to primitive Christianity' (pp. 85-6). Overall, Riches' provocative article is an attempt to defend form-critical approaches, against an 'English-speaking world's resistance'.[132] In contrast, I think the mood of gospel studies has moved even further in the direction of literary studies of the gospels as finished products of conscious authors over the last decade or so — and thus further away from Schmidt's conclusions. Even Riches who considers that 'whatever else the evangelists were, they were not ancient biographers', admits that 'in compiling and presenting the traditions of Jesus' words and sayings, of his life and death, they were inevitably inviting comparison with ancient biographies'.[133] This comparison is at the heart of our current

---

128. Stanton, *A Gospel for a New People,* p. 69, n. 2.

129. Karl Ludwig Schmidt, *The Place of the Gospels in the General History of Literature,* translated by Byron R. McCane (University of South Carolina Press, 2002), with an introduction by John Riches, pp. vii-xxviii; see pp. 8-12 above for details and discussion of the German original.

130. See McCane's comments as translator, in Schmidt, *The Place of the Gospels,* pp. xxix-xxxiii.

131. Riches, 'Introduction', in Schmidt, *The Place of the Gospels,* p. xviii.

132. Riches, 'Introduction', in Schmidt, *The Place of the Gospels,* p. vii.

133. Riches, 'Introduction', in Schmidt, *The Place of the Gospels,* p. xxi.

work, but something which Schmidt would not have accepted. However, I agree with Riches that Schmidt's work has been 'neglected' and share his hope that this translation and introduction will contribute to the continuing debate about the genre of the gospels.

Riches' concern for the traditionally thorough methods of the German form-critics finds an echo in Frickenschmidt's massive treatment of *Gospel as Biography*.[134] A student and research assistant of Klaus Berger, Frickenschmidt has revised his 1996 Heidelberg Dissertation in this immensely thorough analysis of over 550 closely-printed and tightly argued pages of German! He begins with an analysis of research from the early form-critics through classicists' treatments of ancient biography (Leo, Steidle, Dihle, Stuart, Momigliano, etc.) to an assessment of others' attempts to compare the gospels with biography from Renan and Votaw through Stanton and Talbert to Shuler, Aune, Dihle, Berger, Cancik, Dormeyer and Frankemölle. In this respect, his work resembles our own analysis in Chapters 1 and 4 above, and indeed he culminates his account by describing my work as 'a detailed and extensive contribution'.[135] He then provides a detailed summary of our approach and argument, concluding that my 'results are very similar in several important points' to his own work which was already 'in an advanced stage' when my book came to him. The discovery that my 'quite different methods and procedures' produced results 'in clear agreement' with his is seen as encouraging: he takes this as an indication that 'this consensus of research is well-grounded in actual fact'.[136]

His own study begins with a list of some 142 ancient biographies which is the basis for his comparison, echoing Berger's own analysis (see pages 94-5 above). Frickenschmidt then sets off on his 'method of comparison' with an account of the origins of Greek biography (Aristotle, Isocrates and Xenophon) and discusses biographical material which appears in historiography, both within the Old Testament (including Moses, Joshua, Samuel, David, Elijah and Elisha, and Jeremiah) and within classical historians like Herodotus, Polybius, Velleius Paterculus and Josephus. This is followed by a detailed account of early biographical fragments from the fifth to the second century BC, through

---

134. Dirk Frickenschmidt, *Evangelium als Biographie: Die vier Evangelien im Rahmen antiker Erzählkunst* (Tübingen: Francke Verlag, 1997).

135. Frickenschmidt, *Evangelium als Biographie*, p. 65: 'ein ausführlicher und weiterführender Beitrag zum kompletten Vergleich zwischen Evangelien und antiken Biographien kam schließlich von Burridge.'

136. Frickenschmidt, *Evangelium als Biographie*, pp. 65-68: 'trotz ganz verschiedener Verfahrensweisen deutliche Übereinstimmungen . . . als Indiz für einen in der Sache gut begründeten Forschungskonsens', p. 68.

to the 'blooming of ancient biography' with Nepos, Plutarch, Philo, Suetonius, Tacitus, Lucian, Diogenes Laertius, Philostratus, etc. He concludes that ancient biography has an 'integrative, three-fold overall form' comprising the opening sections (including opening words, genealogies, names, childhood stories and preparations for the main story), the middle part (deeds and activities, stories and anecdotes, reputation and assessment by friends and foes) and the closing section (the way to the end, intrigues or plots, farewell speeches and last words, death, reactions, signs, ascension or deification) with possibilities for prologues and epilogues at the beginning and end. Such analysis is indeed not dissimilar to our own in Part Two above. He then gives a detailed analysis of Mark, John, Matthew and Luke to show this three-fold form at work in each of them, concluding with a discussion of Luke-Acts as a 'biographical-historiographical double-work'.[137] Finally, he summarises the whole work and his results and finishes with a few remarks about the 'biographical function' of the gospels for the churches. In contrast, therefore, to books like Vines, this is a good example of how another thorough and detailed treatment of genre theory rooted in careful analysis of the gospels with contemporary ancient texts can emerge with similar results to our own.

In addition to such major treatments concentrating on gospel genre in general and my work in particular, the biographical hypothesis has begun to be accepted within other aspects of New Testament scholarship, such as the continuing Quest(s) for the Historical Jesus. Tom Wright's blockbuster multi-volume series, *Christian Origins and the Question of God,* has dominated Jesus scholarship over the last decade, often in debate with the Jesus Seminar.[138] In his first volume, Wright provides the setting within the first-century world, stressing the importance of stories within early Christianity, which leads him to consider the nature of the gospels. He draws upon my work in his discussion of the narrative of Luke-Acts 'within the broad genre of Hellenistic biography' and in stating that there is 'no doubt that Matthew has written the story of Jesus as a Hellenistic-style *bios,* a biography'; equally, 'though Mark's book is clearly more than a typical Hellenistic biography, it is certainly not less'; and the same goes for John, told 'with great subtlety' as 'a Hellenistic-style *bios*'.[139] The same assumption is then made a few years later about 'why

---

137. Frickenschmidt, *Evangelium als Biographie,* pp. 498-500: 'Lk und Apg als biographisch-historiographisches Doppelwerk'.

138. N. T. Wright, *Christian Origins and the Question of God:* Vol. 1, *The New Testament and the People of God* (London: SPCK/Fortress, 1992); Vol. 2, *Jesus and the Victory of God* (London: SPCK/Fortress, 1996); Vol. 3, *The Resurrection of the Son of God* (London: SPCK/Fortress, 2003).

139. Wright, *The New Testament and the People of God,* pp. 373, 381, 390, 391, 411-12.

are the Gospels what they are' in his next volume.[140] Similarly, Dunn uses my work to argue for the biographical genre of the gospels as a basis for his latest reconstruction of Jesus.[141] In this way, the biographical hypothesis is taking its place within broader debate about Jesus and the gospels.

We began this section with Larry Hurtado's article about Gospel genre,[142] and we conclude by returning to his work. His interest in the genre of the gospels arises out of his main work over many years on early devotion to Jesus and worship of him.[143] In part, of course, this is a response to Bousset's early magisterial treatment, *Kyrios Christos*,[144] with its history of religions approach to the development of Christology from a Palestinian setting for Jesus as a rabbi through to his worship as Lord arising from a Gentile, Hellenistic context. Hurtado's enormous and detailed study, *Lord Jesus Christ: Devotion to Jesus in Earliest Christianity*, has recently appeared.[145] The whole book is a careful reappraisal of the history of religions approach, with detailed study of Jewish monotheism, the earliest forms of Judean Jewish Christianity, Pauline groups through the writing of the gospels and other Jesus books to Johannine Christianity and on to the second century with its radical diversity and proto-orthodox devotion. After some 650 pages of painstaking research and argument, Hurtado concludes that devotion to Jesus as 'Lord' is not a later or Hellenistic development; rather worship of Jesus as divine 'erupted suddenly and quickly' in the earliest Jewish Christian circles. It was the struggle to work out this devotion and belief within monotheism which led to the diversity of approaches within the New Testament and the first centuries, but devotion to Jesus was central then — and the key question today remains, 'Who do you say that I am?'[146]

Within this major treatment of Christology and early devotion to Jesus, Hurtado has a very interesting chapter on 'Jesus Books', a description which he prefers to 'gospels'.[147] He compares the four canonical gospels as 'the earliest narrative portraits of Jesus' with Q, Thomas and other non-canonical

140. Wright, *Jesus and the Victory of God*, pp. 112-13.

141. J. D. G. Dunn, *Jesus Remembered* (Grand Rapids: Eerdmans, 2003), pp. 184-6.

142. L. W. Hurtado, 'Gospel (Genre)', in *Dictionary of Jesus and the Gospels*, ed. J. B. Green et al. (Downers Grove, Ill.: InterVarsity, 1992), pp. 276-82.

143. Larry Hurtado, *One God, One Lord: Early Christian Devotion and Ancient Jewish Monotheism* (Philadelphia: Fortress, 1988); second edition (Edinburgh: T&T Clark, 1998).

144. Wilhelm Bousset, *Kyrios Christos: A History of the Belief in Christ from the Beginnings of Christianity to Irenaeus* ET (Nashville: Abingdon, 1970); German original, Göttingen, 1913.

145. Larry Hurtado, *Lord Jesus Christ: Devotion to Jesus in Earliest Christianity* (Grand Rapids: Eerdmans, 2003).

146. Hurtado, *Lord Jesus Christ*, pp. 650-3.

147. Hurtado, *Lord Jesus Christ*, chapter 5, pp. 259-347.

writings which seem to lack this narrative focus; these four share many features which make them into a 'particular kind of dedicated literary expression of devotion to Jesus',[148] which causes him to discuss their literary genre, compared both with other early Christian writings and with Jewish literature and 'the Roman-era literary environment'. Here he concludes that 'the Gospels do have a number of formal similarities to various examples of *bios* writings of the Greco-Roman era', as is shown by my work, since 'the choice to write books about Jesus in the *bios* shape likely seemed to the Gospel authors an effective way to focus attention on the person of Jesus'.[149]

Thus, the shift from Hurtado's acceptance of the gospels as biography only 'in very general terms' in his 1992 article not only to the use being made of their biographical genre but also to the consequent Christological focus upon the person of Jesus in his most recent book is a good illustration of what has been happening over the last decade in reaction, at least in part, to my work. Now that the biographical genre of the gospels is increasingly accepted and taken for granted by many scholars, the focus is moving towards the implications of this for Christology and for the gospels' setting both within Graeco-Roman society and in relation to Jewish literature.

B. Implications and Further Developments

So far we have surveyed the reviews of my original book and the various debates, conferences, reactions and responses to it. This has shown that while the gospels are now widely viewed as a form of ancient biography, a number of issues about the implications of this have recurred regularly. These include the Christological consequences of their focus upon Jesus, their sociological setting, and their relationship to Jewish writings as well as to Graeco-Roman literature. In fact, these issues became the driving force behind most of my subsequent research and writing over the years, which will now be summarised briefly in this final section.

1. The Gospels as Christological Narrative

We noted above that reactions were divided about our final conclusion that their biographical genre means that the person of Jesus is the focus of the gos-

---

148. Hurtado, *Lord Jesus Christ*, p. 270.
149. Hurtado, *Lord Jesus Christ*, pp. 279 (see esp. n. 45) and 281-2.

pels and thus the key to their interpretation (as laid out on pp. 247-50 above). Tuckett thought this was 'trite' while Petersen criticised its 'very triviality'.[150] However, Alexander considered it 'deliberately understated', while Garland and Witherington used this focus upon Jesus for their commentaries on Matthew and Mark.[151] I am convinced that the latter is the correct approach. If the gospels are a form of ancient biography, then we must study them with the same biographical concentration upon their subject, to see the particular way each portrays an understanding of Jesus. The gospels are nothing less than Christology in narrative form.

However, most traditional scholarly approaches to the gospels have tended to ignore this basic fact, preferring instead to concentrate upon their sources and internal literary relationships, the forms of individual pericopae and their settings within the early church, or the theological concerns of the author and his presumed community. Thus within the terms of communication theory of author-text-audience, the gospels have been interpreted as written by committees about concepts for communities! On the other hand, biography is a genre written by a person about a person for other people. Therefore the hermeneutical key for understanding the gospels as biography is not to be found in presumed problems in hypothetical communities, settings or textual relationships, but rather in their Christology. Every passage, pericope or verse must be interpreted in the light of the biographical genre of the whole: what this story tells us about the author's understanding of Jesus.

This Christological approach can be illustrated easily by considering the notorious problem of Mark's depiction of the disciples as lacking in faith. Despite the suggestion that the disciples are given the secret (μυστήριον) of the Kingdom of God (4.11), they fail to understand, and Jesus gets increasingly frustrated with them especially in the three boat scenes (4.40-41; 6.50-52; 8.14-21); James and John want the best seats in heaven (10.35-45), while they all fail to understand the Passion predictions (8.32-33; 9.32; 10.32-41). Eventually, they fall asleep in Gethsemane and desert Jesus, leaving Judas to betray him and Peter to deny him (14.37-50, 66-72). Not only scholars find this picture rather harsh; even Matthew and Luke 'improve' it, so that Matthew turns Mark's 'no faith' (Mk. 4.40) into 'men of little faith' (Matt. 8.26), while in Luke the disciples ask Jesus, 'increase our faith' (Lk. 17.5).

Form- and redaction-critical approaches seek to solve this problem by

---

150. Tuckett, *Theology* (1993), pp. 74-5; Petersen, *Neotestamentica* 1994, pp. 146-7.

151. Alexander, *Evangelical Quarterly* 66 (1994), pp. 73-6; Garland, *Reading Matthew,* pp. 5-9; Witherington, *The Gospel of Mark,* pp. 10, 5, and 42.

relating it to certain groups in the early church. Thus, Weeden's account is actually entitled *Mark: Traditions in Conflict;* he sees the slow-witted disciples as standing for other leaders, particularly those with a *theios anēr* Christology to whom Mark is opposed.[152] Quite apart from the fact that there are problems over the concept of *theios anēr*, such an approach does not do justice to the positive material about the disciples in Mark: Jesus continues to explain things to them (e.g. 7.17-23; 8.34-38; 10.23-31; 11.20-25; 13); he has pity on their exhausted sleep (14.38); and Peter has at least followed Jesus into danger after the others fled, as he promised (14.29). If the disciples represent the wrong leaders, why does Jesus promise to meet them in Galilee (14.28; 16.7)?

Once we read the gospels through the genre of ancient biography, then the Christological key can be used to interpret such passages. The point of each passage is to tell us *not* about the disciples, but about the biography's subject — namely, Jesus of Nazareth — in this case, that he is someone who is hard to understand and tough to follow. Given both the positive and the negative aspects of the disciples' portrayal, the readers should not be surprised if they find discipleship difficult; yet it is such struggling disciples whom Jesus calls and teaches, despite the difficulties. Thus, reading the gospels in their biographical genre has immediate benefit for their interpretation.

Traditional form-critical approaches to the gospels saw them as a collection of individual pericopae, separated or 'cut off' (περι-κόπτω) from their contexts, strung together like beads on a string with little overall coherence. Redaction critics looked at the evangelists' theological treatment of each story, thus bringing back the author, while narrative critics have redirected our attention back to the story as a whole. Studies such as those by Rhoads and Michie on Mark, Kingsbury on Matthew, Tannehill on Luke-Acts and Culpepper on John have analysed the plot lines throughout each gospel, looking at how the characters develop, how repetition and reference back or forward in the narrative can lead to irony, and how the main themes are resolved in a climax.[153] Unfortunately, narrative critics did not grapple with the issue of genre in their initial studies until recently. Thus Rhoads says 'genre criti-

---

152. T. J. Weeden, *Mark: Traditions in Conflict* (Philadelphia: Fortress Press, 1971).

153. David Rhoads and Donald Michie, *Mark as Story: An Introduction to the Narrative of a Gospel* (Philadelphia: Fortress, 1982); Jack Dean Kingsbury, *Matthew as Story* (Philadelphia: Fortress, 1986, 2nd edn 1988); Robert C. Tannehill, *The Narrative Unity of Luke-Acts: A Literary Interpretation*, 2 vols. (Philadelphia and Minneapolis: Fortress, 1986 and 1990); R. Alan Culpepper, *Anatomy of the Fourth Gospel: A Study in Literary Design* (Philadelphia: Fortress, 1983). See also, Mark Stibbe, *John as Storyteller: Narrative Criticism and the Fourth Gospel*, SNTSMS 73 (CUP, 1992); Mark Allen Powell, *What Is Narrative Criticism? A New Approach to the Bible* (Minneapolis: Fortress, 1990; and London: SPCK, 1993).

cism is increasingly important for narrative analysis'.[154] Similarly, Culpepper admits that his 'discussion of plot in *Anatomy of the Fourth Gospel* does not adequately relate it to the issue of the genre of the Gospel or its structure'; therefore he proceeds to summarise and discuss my book, applying his recognition that 'the Gospel of John, therefore, is an ancient biography in dramatic form' to his account of John.[155]

Thus, the biographical genre for the gospels takes these narrative approaches another step forward, leading us to expect the depiction of one person, the subject, as understood by another person, the author, leading up to the climax of the subject's death, which according to ancient conventions should be the culmination of the portrait as the subject dies as he has lived. Instead of a form-critical approach to the gospels as Passion narratives preceded by disjointed pericopae strung together or redaction-critical reconstructions of early communities, biographical-narratological readings show how each evangelist traces his various themes through the gospel to be resolved in his account of the Passion.

Therefore, I set out deliberately to demonstrate the usefulness of the biographical genre in the interpretation of the gospels by writing *Four Gospels, One Jesus?* Here I provided such a biographical narrative reading of each gospel, using the traditional images of lion, human, ox and eagle found in books like the Book of Kells, but using them as 'images of the Son of God' (as Irenaeus put it, *Against the Heresies,* III. 11.8-9) rather than of the evangelists.[156] Thus Mark depicts Jesus like a lion who appears almost from nowhere (1.9), who then rushes around, being misunderstood by everybody, including his family and friends and the authorities (3.20-35). The descriptions of Jesus as an enigmatic wonder-worker who binds people to secrecy, the eschatological prophet who will suffer and die in Jerusalem as both Son of God and Son of Man, are held together in complementary tension in a biographical narrative, rather than explaining them as deriving from different historical traditions. Jesus finds Jerusalem and the Temple as barren as the fig-tree and prophesies their same destruction (11-13). He suffers and dies alone in dark desolation: 'my God, my God, why have you forsaken me?' (15.34) as the Pas-

154. David Rhoads, 'Narrative Criticism: Practice and Prospects' in *Characterization in the Gospels: Reconceiving Narrative Criticism,* ed. David Rhoads and Kari Syreeni, JSNTSS 184 (Sheffield Academic Press, 1999), p. 275.

155. R. Alan Culpepper, 'The Plot of John's Story of Jesus' in *Gospel Interpretation: Narrative-Critical & Social-Scientific Approaches,* ed. Jack Dean Kingsbury (Harrisburg: Trinity Press International, 1997), pp. 188-99; quotations from pp. 189 and 198.

156. Richard A. Burridge, *Four Gospels, One Jesus? A Symbolic Reading* (Grand Rapids: Eerdmans/London: SPCK, 1994); second edition due 2005.

sion brings to a climax all Mark's themes. Even the ending is full of enigma, fear and awe with an empty tomb and an absent Jesus (16.1-8).

In Matthew, however, we have the human face of Jesus' Jewish background, genealogy and birth (1-2). He is another Moses, who teaches from mountains (5.1) and fulfils the law and the prophets, giving his teaching in five great blocks like the Pentateuch (5-7, 10, 13, 18, 24-25). Unfortunately, this brings him into conflict with the leaders of Israel which unfolds through the gospel. In the Passion, the cry of abandonment is answered by an earthquake as *everyone* realizes this was truly the Son of God (27.51-54, cp. Mk. 15.39). Finally, the Resurrection continues with further divine earthquakes as the old Israel takes bribes and tells lies while a new community is commissioned on a mountain to go to the Gentiles (28.1-20).[157] Again, the climax resolves all the themes of the gospel.

Luke begins with a Greek periodic Preface (Lk. 1.1-4) and sets Jesus within the history of both Israel and contemporary Roman rule (Lk. 1.5-80; 2.1; 3.1). As the traditional image of the ox, the bearer of burdens, illustrates, Jesus is concerned for the poor, the lost, outcasts, women, Samaritans and Gentiles. He is also the man of prayer (11.1-4). At the Passion he cares for women (23.27-31) and prays for the soldiers and the penitent thief (23.34, 43), committing himself in trust to his Father (23.46). After the resurrection, history looks forward from Israel's past to the world's future (24.44-47). The gospel ends as it began 'in Jerusalem with great joy, in the Temple blessing God' (24.51-52, cp. 1.5-23). Such a clear balanced biographical narrative reflects a single author and purpose.

As the high-flying, all-seeing eagle, John begins with Jesus existing before all time, in the beginning, with God (Jn. 1.1-18). Jesus is constantly centre stage and he is characterized as the author interweaves 'signs' and discourse, revealing the effect of meditation and theological reflection upon the person of Jesus. Opposition from "the Jews" develops through the first half (2-12); at the climax, Jesus gathers his disciples, washes their feet and explains what will happen (13-17). The 'hour of glory' is also the Passion: throughout Jesus is serenely in control, directing events (19.11), organizing his mother and disciple (19.26-27), fulfilling scripture (19.28) until finally 'it is accomplished' (19.30). After the resurrection he appears as he wishes to comfort Mary (20.14), challenge Thomas (20.26) and restore Peter (21.15-19). Once again, we have a clear portrait through the ministry of Jesus culminating in his death and resurrection.

---

157. For a good comparison of Matthew with Mark, see J. L. Houlden, *Backward into Light: The Passion and Resurrection of Jesus according to Matthew and Mark* (London: SCM Press, 1987).

So *Four Gospels, One Jesus?* laid out these four individual accounts, each concerned with the resolution of their particular themes, as composed by four writers, each portraying a particular view of Jesus in the manner of ancient biography. Subsequently, other general introductions to the four gospels have also looked first at the issue of genre, drawing on our work, followed by a chapter on each gospel separately. Thus Reddish began with a section on 'What is a Gospel?' before going on to discuss each gospel, while Marsh and Moyise picked up our use of the traditional images; Houlden discusses both the first edition of this book and our use of the four symbols in *Four Gospels, One Jesus?* in his stress on taking each gospel as a whole.[158]

I concluded *Four Gospels, One Jesus?* with a discussion of the fact that the fathers chose to keep four separate accounts in the canon, despite the problems of possible conflict between them.[159] This demonstrates that they recognized these works as coherent single accounts of Jesus, yet which belong together — and therefore they need to be read in that way today. There has been renewed interest in the idea of the 'fourfold gospel' and its theological implications, even suggesting that the early church's preservation of four gospels together may have stimulated the development of the codex.[160] This also raises interesting theological questions about plurality and diversity within the limits of the canon. Morgan sees this as offering both a 'stimulus' to produce more 'faith images of Jesus' and a 'control' upon them.[161] Wolterstorff draws upon my work on biographical genre to argue that 'the gospel narratives are best understood as portraits of Jesus' in his arguments for 'the illocutionary stance of biblical narrative',[162] while Barton similarly uses my material to reflect upon 'Many gospels, one Je-

---

158. Mitchell G. Reddish, *An Introduction to the Gospels* (Nashville: Abingdon, 1997), see esp. pp. 18-26; Clive Marsh and Steve Moyise, *Jesus and the Gospels: An Introduction* (London: Cassell, 1999), esp. pp. 9, 46, 115; Leslie Houlden, *The Strange Story of the Gospels: Finding Doctrine Through Narrative* (London: SPCK, 2002), esp. pp. 2-4, 17.

159. Burridge, *Four Gospels, One Jesus?*, 25-7, 164-79; see also Oscar Cullmann, 'The Plurality of the Gospels as a Theological Problem in Antiquity' in his collection, *The Early Church: Studies in Early Christian History and Theology*, ed. A. J. B. Higgins (Philadelphia: Westminster Press, 1956), 37-54, translated from the original German article in *TZ* i (1945), 23-42.

160. See T. C. Skeat, 'Irenaeus and the Four-Fold Gospel Canon', *NovT* 34.2 (1992), 194-99; Graham N. Stanton, 'The Fourfold Gospel', *NTS* 43 (1997), pp. 347-66; Martin Hengel, *The Four Gospels and the One Gospel of Jesus Christ: An Investigation of the Collection and Origin of the Canonical Gospels* (London: SCM, 2000).

161. Robert Morgan, 'The Hermeneutical Significance of Four Gospels', *Interpretation* 33.4 (1979), pp. 376-88; see esp. p. 386.

162. Nicholas Wolterstorff, *Divine Discourse: Philosophical Reflections on the Claim That God Speaks* (Cambridge University Press, 1995), see pp. 249-60.

sus?'[163] All of this demonstrates that the biographical focus upon the person of Jesus in interpreting the gospels as Christological narrative is indeed anything but trite or trivial!

2. The Gospels in Their Social Setting

Another area which came up regularly throughout the various debates about my book concerned the implications of the biographical hypothesis for the social setting of the gospels. New Testament scholars often assume that the gospels were written within the context of a community and produced specifically for that community. In fact, these are two separate issues, since it is possible for a work to be written within one group, but aimed at people outside that community, or conversely, to be directed at a community by an individual writing from outside it. The genre of letters is ideally suited for both these situations — but the biographical genre of the gospels may imply a different approach. Loveday Alexander and I debated these questions in her seminar at the British New Testament Conference in Sept. 1993 (see section 2.a above), and we both then contributed to a volume edited by Richard Bauckham, *The Gospels for All Christians*, which provided a critique of such community approaches.[164]

It all began with a paper from Bauckham at the British New Testament Conference at the University of Bangor in September 1995. Bauckham provided a critique of the consensus view about gospel communities by suggesting that such theories treated the gospels almost as allegories of their communities, through the 'two-level' approach to their narratives adopted by scholars like Martyn on John or Kee and Weeden on Mark.[165] Yet the sheer diversity of the reconstructions of these communities rendered them not really credible. Furthermore, Bauckham argued that these approaches rested upon a genre mistake and treated the gospels like letters; drawing upon my book,

---

163. Stephen C. Barton, 'Many Gospels, One Jesus?' in *The Cambridge Companion to Jesus*, ed. Markus Bockmuehl (Cambridge University Press, 2001), pp. 170-83, esp. pp. 178-9.

164. Richard Bauckham (ed.), *The Gospels for All Christians: Rethinking the Gospel Audiences* (Grand Rapids: Eerdmans, 1998); for responses to this volume as a whole, see P. Esler, 'Community and Gospel in Early Christianity: A Response to Richard Bauckham's *Gospels for All Christians*', *Scottish Journal of Theology* 51.2 (1998), pp. 235-48, and Bauckham's reply, pp. 249-53, and David C. Sim, 'The Gospels for All Christians? A Response to Richard Bauckham', *JSNT* 84 (2001), pp. 3-27.

165. Bauckham, *The Gospels for All Christians*, pp. 13-22, referring to J. L. Martyn, *History and Theology in the Fourth Gospel* (Nashville: Abingdon, 1979), H. C. Kee, *Community of the New Age* (Philadelphia: Westminster, 1977) and T. J. Weeden, *Mark: Traditions in Conflict* (Philadelphia: Fortress Press, 1971).

he argued that ancient biographies were written for wider audiences.[166] Against the consensus view of isolated self-sufficient communities, Bauckham showed how early church leaders moved around the Mediterranean with good mobility and communications, writing letters and keeping in contact with each other. Therefore it is a mistake to give the hermeneutical key for the gospels to these hypothetical communities; the gospels were written for more indefinite audiences than specific isolated groups.[167]

Following Bauckham's original lecture, a number of those present offered to write further papers exploring these themes, including Loveday Alexander on the methods of ancient book production, Michael Thompson on the speed and types of communication in the ancient Mediterranean, Stephen Barton on the variety of reconstructions of the gospel communities, concluding with a literal, theological reading from Francis Watson.[168]

Building on Bauckham's use of my argument that the gospels are a form of Graeco-Roman biography, my contribution contrasted the traditional consensus that the gospels were written 'by committees, about concepts, for communities' with the consequences of the biographical hypothesis — that they were written by a person, about a person, for other persons.[169] One question which had surfaced regularly in the responses to my work was whether other Lives functioned in such a community-based way in the ancient world and whether their biographical genre could tell us anything about the social level or function of the gospels — so this provided an opportunity to explore these questions.[170]

(a) Communities or Audiences?

One parallel may be the philosophical schools of the fourth and third centuries BC. Various βίοι of philosophers date from this period, although since the works themselves are not preserved, we cannot be sure how fully they fit the

166. Bauckham, *The Gospels for All Christians*, pp. 27-30; see esp. p. 28, n. 31.

167. Bauckham, *The Gospels for All Christians*, pp. 30-48.

168. Bauckham, *The Gospels for All Christians*, containing Michael B. Thompson, 'The Holy Internet: Communication Between Churches in the First Christian Generation', pp. 49-70; Loveday Alexander, 'Ancient Book Production and the Circulation of the Gospels', pp. 71-112; Stephen C. Barton, 'Can We Identify the Gospel Audiences?', pp. 173-94; Francis Watson, 'Toward a Literal Reading of the Gospels', pp. 195-218.

169. Richard A. Burridge, 'About People, by People, for People: Gospel Genre and Audiences' in Bauckham, *The Gospels for All Christians*, pp. 113-45.

170. The sections which follow summarise part of my chapter, 'About People, by People, for People: Gospel Genre and Audiences', pp. 131-7 and 140-3; see Bauckham, *The Gospels for All Christians* for the full argument.

genre.[171] However, they are still written for a wider audience — to attract people outside the author's own group.

Closer in time to the Gospels, we have already noted the sequence of 'Cato literature': from Cicero's panegyric, the *Cato,* Caesar's reply the *Anti-Cato* and a succession of works by Brutus, Hirtius, Augustus and Thrasea Paetus as 'Catonism' became 'an ideological hallmark of the Early Principate'.[172] However, this was more of a sequence of Lives than a 'school' or 'Cato community'. Something similar happens in Tacitus' *Agricola;* it may have been written after Domitian's fall as a political apology for people like Tacitus and Agricola who worked with evil emperors (42.4).[173] Thus while the book is written within one group (Tacitus and his family) it is aimed at others involved in Roman politics; in biographies, it is the portrait of the subject which matters more than the readership.

This should make us hesitate about hypothetical 'Matthean' or 'Johannine' communities without further specific evidence. Interpreting the Gospels as βίοι provides a critique of too much community-based sociological analysis of the gospel audiences. Instead, scholars have moved away from reconstructing the evangelists' communities to what Mary Ann Beavis describes as a 'more general audience of early Christian missionary teaching/ preaching'.[174] Reading the Gospels as βίοι confirms that this development is more helpful than imagined communities.

(b) Social Function

Genre can sometimes be a clue to both the social context and the function for which a work was composed — as, for example, encomia were delivered on

171. As discussed on pages 69-70 above; see Fritz Wehrli, *Die Schule des Aristoteles,* 10 vols. (Basel: Schwabe & Co., 1967-69) for the fragments; for further discussion of the schools, see A. Momigliano, *The Development of Greek Biography* (Cambridge, Mass.: Harvard University Press, 1971), pp. 66-79; and for a comparison of Hellenistic school biographies with Acts, see Alexander, 'Acts and Ancient Intellectual Biography'.

172. J. Geiger, 'Munatius Rufus and Thrasea Paetus on Cato the Younger', *Athenaeum* 57 (1979), p. 48; see page 153 above.

173. See H. Furneaux, *Cornelii Taciti, Vita Agricolae* (Oxford: Clarendon, 1898), 10-15; also Dorey, '"Agricola" and "Domitian"' in his *Tacitus* (London: Routledge & Kegan Paul, 1969), 1-18; Syme, *Tacitus* (OUP, 1958), vol. 1, 26-9, 125-31; see page 183 above.

174. Mary Ann Beavis, *Mark's Audience: The Literary and Social Setting of Mark. 4.11-12,* JSNTSS 33 (Sheffield Academic Press, 1989), p. 171; see also Mary Ann Tolbert, *Sowing the Gospel: Mark's World in Literary-Historical Perspective* (Minneapolis: Fortress Press, 1989), esp. pp. 59-79 and 303-6, and Dwight N. Peterson, *The Origins of Mark: The Markan Community in Current Debate* (Leiden: Brill, 2000).

certain specific social occasions. The problem with the biographical hypothesis for the gospels is that we have discovered a variety of functions for ancient βίοι, and different lives appear to have been used in different ways — including praise and blame (Xenophon's *Agesilaus*), but also for exemplary, moral purposes (Plutarch), for didactic or information (Satyrus), to preserve the memory of a great man (Tacitus' *Agricola*) or even, in the case of Lucian or Philostratus, simply to entertain.[175] Therefore, it is true that simply putting the gospels into this genre does not automatically answer all our questions about purpose and social function within a community setting.

However, one possible parallel for the use of the gospels arises from the social functions of apologetic and polemic, as was the case with early βίοι in the philosophical schools through to the later debate between Christians and Pagans at the end of the third and beginning of the fourth century AD with lives like Porphyry's *Plotinus* and Eusebius' *Origen*.[176] This function also suggests a wider audience for 'social legitimation' whereby an author seeks to explain or justify the position taken by himself or his social grouping, as in the lives of Cato or the *Agricola*. Referring to my suggestions about apologetic and polemic in βίοι, Graham Stanton has declared that 'this is precisely the social function I envisage for Matthew's βίος of Jesus' and he goes on to argue for a wider audience than just one single 'Matthean community'.[177] Similarly in Luke-Acts, we have the constant declaration of the 'innocence' of Jesus (by Pilate 23.4, 14-15, 22 and also in Luke's redaction of the centurion in 23.47), and this is then repeated frequently of the early church leaders like Peter and Paul in Acts. This implies that the author envisaged a wider public, aiming to legitimate the church in the eyes of contemporary society. Thus the social functions of apologetic and polemic suggest that the gospels, like other βίοι, are written for wider audiences than just single communities.

---

175. See pages 145-7 and 180-3 above; also, C. H. Talbert, 'Biographies of Philosophers and Rulers as Instruments of Religious Propaganda in Mediterranean Antiquity', *ANRW* II.16.2 (1978), 1620-3.

176. See Patricia Cox, *Biography in Late Antiquity: A Quest for the Holy Man* (University of California Press, 1983), especially p. 135.

177. Graham N. Stanton, 'Revisiting Matthew's Communities', *SBL Seminar Papers, 1994*, ed. E. H. Loverington (Atlanta: Scholars Press, 1994), 9-23, quotation from 10; see also Stanton, *A Gospel for a New People: Studies in Matthew* (Edinburgh: T&T Clark, 1992), 70, also 104-7 and 378-9 for more on legitimation, and 232-55 for the use of Matthew in early Christian-Jewish polemic and apologetic.

(c) Social Setting of Delivery and Publication

It is often assumed that the gospels were read in church, either in worship (hence the various lectionary hypotheses) or for instruction (hence suggestions about manuals of teaching).[178] This takes us straight into questions about the production and publication of ancient texts and the extent to which people were able to read them, which Loveday Alexander discussed extensively with photographic illustrations in her contribution to *The Gospels for All Christians*.[179] Reading aloud was one of the main ways of 'publication' in the ancient world, often as entertainment after dinner. To this extent we can see a 'communal setting' (rather than the tighter definition of a sectarian community) as a frequent feature of ancient literature. The *Agricola* contains many *sententiae*, pithy little maxims which conclude each section with a rhetorical flourish — allowing a 'pause for applause'. Similarly, the style of Lucian's *Demonax* lends itself to oral delivery, with space for audience reaction (even laughter?) after each anecdote.

One of the reasons for the division of ancient works into 'books' is that one scroll is about the amount which can be delivered in one 'sitting' — with allowance for comfort breaks! The average length of a book of Herodotus or Thucydides is about 20,000 words, which would take around two hours to read. We noted on pages 114-15 above that after the Alexandrian library reforms, an average 30-35-foot scroll would contain 10,000 to 25,000 words — exactly the range into which both the gospels and many ancient βίοι fall. We are so used to hearing the gospels in lectionary use in small sections of twelve to twenty verses or studying individual pericopae that we forget that the entire text can be read out aloud in a couple of hours. It is significant that Alec McCowen's dramatic solo rendition of Mark's Gospel (in the King James' Version) has been an evening's entertainment on stage on both sides of the Atlantic; the video recording of his performance runs for only 105 minutes in total.[180] Building on our work, and inspired by McCowen, Christopher Bryan's *A Preface to Mark* provides an

178. For worship, see M. Goulder, *The Evangelist's Calendar: A Lectionary Explanation of the Development of Scripture* (London: SPCK, 1978), discussed on page 19 above; see also Mary Ann Beavis' comprehensive discussion of proposals for Mark's audience in terms of worship (*Mark's Audience*, pp. 46-50) and teaching (pp. 50-66)

179. Loveday Alexander, 'Ancient Book Production and the Circulation of the Gospels' in Bauckham (ed.), *The Gospels for all Christians*, pp. 71-105.

180. The video of Alec McCowen's solo performance of St Mark's Gospel is produced by Arthur Cantor Films, 2112 Broadway, Suite 400, New York, NY 10023; he wrote about his experiences of performing Mark in Alec McCowen, *Personal Mark* (London: Hamilton, 1984).

interesting study of that gospel as a Hellenistic life designed to be read aloud.[181]

Consideration of how βίοι, like those of Tacitus and Lucian, were read aloud or performed can benefit gospel studies, illuminating how they may have been read, not just in one community, but in many different groups across a wide geographical area. Thus viewing the gospels as ancient biographies can liberate us from the circularity of deducing the communities from the text and then interpreting the text in light of these (deduced) communities. Instead, this generic comparison can provide external evidence of social groupings and levels in which βίοι functioned.

The book has provoked some interesting reactions, including a fascinating session at the SBL Annual Meeting in November 2003.[182] Most of the debate has naturally concentrated on the gospel audiences rather than some of the other issues raised by Loveday Alexander and myself about social levels, function, delivery and production. Margaret Mitchell's paper 'Patristic Counter-Evidence to the Claim That "The Gospels Were Written for All Christians"' collected together a range of fascinating extracts from the Fathers to show how the gospels were associated with different audiences, rather than being for 'all' Christians. However, I have not argued that all the gospels were written for all Christians everywhere, but that the implications of our work on the gospels as biography do suggest that they were designed for a wider audience than just their own small community. Just as Tacitus or Plutarch would have envisaged their writings being of interest to a wider audience than just their own circles, so the evangelists write for a more general audience. This is what I have termed 'market niche' or 'target audience' and it allows for Matthew to be directed at Christians from a more Jewish background, while Luke is aimed more at a Gentile 'market'.[183] Nonetheless, these groups are 'indefinite' audiences, rather than a specific, separate community.

Here again, therefore, our work on the biographical genre has provided a basis which has provoked interesting debates about the social setting and functions of the gospels which look likely to continue for some time yet.

181. Christopher Bryan, *A Preface to Mark,* as discussed in section 3.c, see notes 77-8 above.

182. Society of Biblical Literature, Session S22-118 on 'Gospels for All Christians?', in which I introduced the book's arguments (in the absence of Richard Bauckham through illness) and Loveday Alexander, Mark Matson, Margaret Mitchell and Theodore J. Weeden participated; Atlanta, 22nd November 2003.

183. Richard A. Burridge, 'About People, by People, for People: Gospel Genre and Audiences' in Bauckham, *The Gospels for All Christians,* p. 143.

3. Gospel Genre and the Absence of Rabbinic Biography

We have noted throughout this chapter that various reviewers or those debating my book drew attention to the absence of any proper comparison of the gospels with Jewish literature. We did consider this briefly, but concluded that because of the absence of Rabbinic biographies, we should follow Philip Alexander's suggestion that the origins of the gospel genre should be sought within the Graeco-Roman world — see pages 19-21 above. The other reason for concentrating on Graeco-Roman biography was that this was the genre increasingly being proposed for the gospels, but often with poor literary theory or little understanding of the classical literature to back it up. Therefore we argued that it needed either to be given a proper scholarly basis, or exposed as a false trail (see pages 24 and 100-101 above). After having demonstrated the generic relationship of the gospels with Graeco-Roman biography, however, the question of why the evangelists used this genre and not a Jewish one still needed to be faced. I therefore took the opportunity of contributing to a Festschrift in honour of David Catchpole on the theme of *Christology, Controversy and Community* to investigate this area, which proved to be very illuminating.[184] After arguing that the biographical genre of the gospels leads us to their Christological subject, I discussed the part played by Christological controversy in the parting of the ways between the synagogue and early church. This led naturally to the question about Rabbinic biography.

(a) The Absence of Rabbinic Biography

First, we must note that it is very common to compare individual pericopae in the gospels with rabbinic material. Thus, Rabbi Michael Hilton and Fr. Gordian Marshall OP in *The Gospels and Rabbinic Judaism: A Study Guide* compare Jesus' sayings with rabbinic sources. The Great Commandment (Mark 12.28-34 and the parallels in Matt. 22.34-40 and Luke 10.25-28) is compared with a *Sifra* passage from Rabbi Akiba on Lev. 19.18, Genesis Rabba 24.7 (on Gen. 5.1) and the famous story from the Babylonian Talmud, *Shabbat* 31A, of the different reactions from Shammai and Hillel when asked to teach the whole law to a Gentile enquirer while standing on one leg: Shammai chased the questioner away, while Hillel repeated the Golden Rule as the sum of the

---

184. Richard A. Burridge, 'Gospel Genre, Christological Controversy and the Absence of Rabbinic Biography: Some Implications of the Biographical Hypothesis' in *Christology, Controversy and Community: New Testament Essays in Honour of David Catchpole*, ed. David G. Horrell and Christopher M. Tuckett (Leiden: Brill, 2000), pp. 137-56; I am grateful to Brill for permission to reproduce this article as Appendix II to this book, pages 322-40 below.

whole Torah, with the rest as commentary, but still to be learned. Hilton concludes that 'Jesus at his most "rabbinic" engaged in lively debate and answering some of the same questions as the rabbis'.[185]

An international symposium on Hillel and Jesus held in Jerusalem in June 1992 devotes some 170 pages to comparisons of their sayings![186] Philip Alexander notes that 'the overriding feeling is one of astonishment at the convergence of the two traditions'.[187] Alexander has written extensively on such rabbinic writings, and how New Testament scholars should use this material.[188] He collected together some rabbinic stories to compare 'Rabbinic Biography and the Biography of Jesus', concluding, 'there are parallels to the individual pericopae, and at this level similarities are very strong. In terms of form, function, setting and motif, the Rabbinic anecdotes are very close to the Gospel pericopae, and there can be little doubt that both belong to the same broad Palestinian Jewish tradition of story-telling.'[189]

Since Bultmann and other Form Critics saw the gospels as strung together like beads on a string, we might expect rabbinic stories to form similar accounts of Hillel, Shammai or others. Yet, this is precisely what we do *not* find, much to everybody's surprise. Thus Philip Alexander concludes his study of 'Rabbinic Biography and the Biography of Jesus' thus: 'there are no Rabbinic parallels to the Gospels as such. This is by far the most important single conclusion to emerge from this paper. . . . There is not a trace of an ancient biography of any of the Sages. . . . This is a profound enigma.'[190]

Jacob Neusner has devoted much study to this question. In 1984's *In Search of Talmudic Biography* he states that 'there is no composition of tales and stories into a sustained biography'.[191] He followed this with an analysis of *Why No Gospels in Talmudic Judaism?* The stories about sages were never compiled into biographical narratives or gospels: they are 'the compositions

185. Rabbi Michael Hilton with Fr. Gordian Marshall OP, *The Gospels and Rabbinic Judaism: A Study Guide* (London: SCM, 1988), p. 34.

186. James H. Charlesworth and Loren L. Johns, eds., *Hillel and Jesus: Comparative Studies of Two Major Religious Leaders* (Minneapolis: Fortress, 1997).

187. P. S. Alexander, 'Jesus and the Golden Rule' in *Hillel and Jesus*, pp. 363-88; quotation from p. 388.

188. See, for example, Philip S. Alexander, 'Rabbinic Judaism and the New Testament', *ZNW* 74 (1983), pp. 237-46.

189. Philip S. Alexander, 'Rabbinic Biography and the Biography of Jesus: A Survey of the Evidence' in *Synoptic Studies: The Ampleforth Conferences of 1982 and 1983*, ed. C. M. Tuckett, JSNTSS 7 (Sheffield: JSOT, 1984), pp. 19-50; quotation from p. 42.

190. Philip S. Alexander, 'Rabbinic Biography and the Biography of Jesus', p. 40.

191. Jacob Neusner, *In Search of Talmudic Biography: The Problem of the Attributed Saying*, Brown Judaic Studies 70 (Chico: Scholars, 1984), p. 2.

no one made'.[192] In *The Incarnation of God* again he stresses: 'While the two Talmuds present stories about sages, neither one contains anything we might call a "gospel" of a sage or even a chapter of a gospel. There is no sustained biography of any sage'.[193] Finally, he answered the claim of similarities between the gospels and Jewish material with *Are There Really Tannaitic Parallels to the Gospels?*[194]

In the symposium on *Jesus and Hillel*, Gottstein notes the 'basic differences between the nature of Talmudic literature and the nature of the Gospels. We have no Talmudic Gospel of any Rabbi.' He then discusses my book and accepts its conclusions: 'following Burridge's discussion, the present discussion assumes Gospel writing to be a form of biography'; however, he too then raises the question, 'one could therefore ask why we do not have any instances of rabbinic biography'.[195]

(b) Possible Literary Reasons for This Absence

Most rabbinic material is comprised of anecdotes, which are more about a rabbi's teaching than his actions. Many of the stories are dialogue which leads up to actual saying, with any narrative at the start to set the scene. Thus in some ways, the rabbinic material is more like Q or Gospel of Thomas, i.e. it has the genre of sayings, *logia*, more than biographical narrative. Yet, in debate with my original version of this material, Hurtado argues that 'unlike the rabbinic texts', even 'Q and Thomas are entirely about Jesus'.[196] Philip Alexander notes that the rabbinic stories have an 'intensely oral character . . . against the more prosy "written" style of the gospels'. They are 'extremely compressed, allusive, witty, dramatic and learned'; more like bits from a play to be performed than a text to be read, intended for oral circulation, not in written form.[197] In *The Incarnation of God*, Neusner applies a 'taxonomy of narrative' to the material and finds 'five species of the genus narrative'.[198] The problem

---

192. Jacob Neusner, *Why No Gospels in Talmudic Judaism?* BJS 135 (Atlanta: Scholars, 1988), pp. 33-8.

193. Jacob Neusner, *The Incarnation of God: The Character of Divinity in Formative Judaism* (Philadelphia: Fortress, 1988), p. 213.

194. Jacob Neusner, *Are There Really Tannaitic Parallels to the Gospels? A Refutation of Morton Smith*, South Florida Studies in the History of Judaism, No. 80 (Chico: Scholars, 1993).

195. A. Goshen Gottstein, 'Jesus and Hillel: Are Comparisons Possible?' in *Hillel and Jesus*, pp. 31-55; quotations from pp. 34-5.

196. Hurtado, *Lord Jesus Christ*, pp. 275-6.

197. Philip S. Alexander, 'Rabbinic Biography and the Biography of Jesus', p. 42.

198. Jacob Neusner, *The Incarnation of God*, p. 214.

with this is that 'narrative' is neither a genus nor a genre in itself according to most literary theories of genre, and his five 'species' are not clearly identified as subgenres.

However, the basic point is clear, that the rabbinic anecdotes are directed more towards sayings than actions. This would not prevent their being compiled into an ancient biography. Lucian's *Demonax* has a brief preface and account of the philosopher's life, followed by a large number of anecdotes all strung together, each composed mainly of dialogue leading up to a pronouncement or decision by the great sage — yet it is still called a 'life', βίος. In fact, as we saw in our discussion on pages 162 and 166 above, the *Demonax* is more loosely structured with less integration of teaching and activity than even Mark's gospel.

Thus although the rabbinic material is more anecdotal than are the gospels and some ancient lives, it still contains enough biographical elements (through sage stories, narratives, precedents and death scenes) to enable an editor to compile a 'life of Hillel' or whoever. Such an account would have been recognisable as ancient biography and have looked like the *Demonax*. Yet nobody actually ever did so. Literary and generic reasons alone are therefore not sufficient to explain this curious absence of rabbinic biography.

(c) Theological Reasons — The Christological Focus

Biography directs the audience's attention to the life and character of the subject. We have already seen throughout this chapter that the decision to write a biographical account of Jesus has important Christological implications. Equally, the failure to write, or even compile from the anecdotes, any biographies of the rabbis also has significant implications.

Neusner argues that this is because the individual sages are not at the centre of attention. '*Sage-stories turn out not to tell about sages at all; they are stories about the Torah personified.* Sage-stories cannot yield a gospel because they are not about sages anyway. They are about the Torah. . . . The gospel does just the opposite, with its focus on the uniqueness of the hero.'[199] Alexander makes the same point: 'The obvious answer is that neither Eliezer nor any other Sage held in Rabbinic Judaism the central position that Jesus held in early Christianity. The centre of Rabbinic Judaism was Torah; the centre of Christianity was the person of Jesus, and the existence of the Gospels is, in itself, a testimony to this fact.'[200] Similarly Rabbi Michael Hilton says: 'The

---

199. Jacob Neusner, *Why No Gospels in Talmudic Judaism?*, pp. 52-3; his italics.
200. Philip S. Alexander, 'Rabbinic Biography and the Biography of Jesus', p. 41.

Gospels can thus be regarded as a kind of commentary on Jesus' life, in much the same way as the Rabbis comment on biblical texts'.[201] Similarly, Gottstein in comparing Jesus and Hillel stresses that 'Gospel writing would be the product of the particular religious understanding of the messianic, and therefore salvific, activity of Jesus. The lack of Gospels in rabbinic literature would then be a less significant issue, since no salvific claim is attached to any particular Rabbi.'[202]

Thus the literary shift from unconnected anecdotes about Jesus, which resemble rabbinic material, to composing them together in the genre of an ancient biography is not just moving from a Jewish environment to Graeco-Roman literature. It is actually making an enormous Christological claim. Rabbinic biography is not possible, because no rabbi is that unique; each rabbi is only important in as much as he represents the Torah, which holds the central place. To write a biography is to replace the Torah by putting a human person in the centre of the stage. The literary genre makes a major theological shift which becomes an explicit Christological claim — that Jesus of Nazareth is Torah embodied.[203] Furthermore, Crispin Fletcher-Louis points out that the stories about the sages showed how the Torah, or the wisdom of God himself, could be temporarily embodied in different rabbis, as is also seen in Neusner's work on incarnation.[204] However, as we have seen, Neusner himself points out that this was never true of any *one* sage in and of himself and for his life in all its aspects. Therefore, writing a biography of Jesus implies the claim that not only is the Torah embodied, but that God himself is uniquely incarnated in this one life, death and resurrection.

4. The Gospels' Biographical Narrative and Ethical Debate

The final area to which we want to apply the biographical genre of the gospels concerns New Testament ethics. As we have shown, the biographical-narrative approach to the gospels reminds us that the gospels are not just collections of Jesus' teachings, like those of the rabbis. Such documents did exist,

---

201. Hilton and Marshall, *The Gospels and Rabbinic Judaism*, p. 13.

202. Goshen Gottstein, 'Jesus and Hillel', p. 35.

203. Jacobus Schoneveld, 'Torah in the Flesh: A New Reading of the Prologue of the Gospel of John as a Contribution to a Christology without Anti-Semitism' in *The New Testament and Christian-Jewish Dialogue: Studies in Honor of David Flusser*, ed. Malcolm Lowe, Emmanuel 24/25 (Jerusalem: Ecumenical Theological Research Fraternity in Israel, 1990), pp. 77-93.

204. I am grateful to Dr. Crispin Fletcher-Louis for this comment in a personal email responding to my chapter, 10th Feb 2003; see above notes for Neusner on incarnation.

such as the Gospel of Thomas, or some later Gnostic gospels, which were just sayings and had no narrative about Jesus' life, actions — or even his death. It is probable that Q, if it existed as a document, was a similar collection of sayings; the narrative context of the Q sayings is usually supplied by Luke or Matthew — and there is no Q material in the Passion narratives. However, many approaches to the ethics of Jesus treat the canonical gospels as though they were like these collections of sayings and just concentrate on his teaching and words. Central to all ancient biography is that the picture of the subject is built up through both his words *and* his deeds. So to find the heart of Jesus' ethic we need to consider both his ethical teaching *and* his actual practice. This leads to the question of the relation of Jesus' ethical teaching (often strict and rigorous) to his pastoral practice (so open and accepting that it offends religious and moral authorities).

In using the gospels in ethics, it is vital to note that the gospels are ancient biographies, not primarily ethical texts (as, say, Aristotle's *Nicomachean Ethics*), nor is Jesus portrayed as just a moral teacher, despite so many people's estimation of him as such. Jesus' ethical teaching is not a separate and discrete set of maxims, but is part of his proclamation of the kingdom of God. It is primarily intended to elicit a response from his hearers to live as disciples within the community of others who also respond and follow. In his appeal for the eschatological restoration of the people of God, Jesus intensified the demands of the Law with his rigorous ethic of renunciation and self-denial in the major human experiences of money, sex, power, violence, and so forth, while at the same time his central stress on love and forgiveness opened the community to the very people who had moral difficulties in these areas. Hence he was regularly accused of being 'a glutton and a drunkard, a friend of tax collectors and sinners' (Matt. 11.19; Luke 7.34).[205]

Ancient biographies held together both words and deeds in portraying their central subject. Many were written explicitly to give an example to others to emulate: Xenophon composed his *Agesilaus* to provide an example (παράδειγμα) for others to follow to become better people (ἀνδραγαθίαν ἀσκεῖν, X.2). Equally, Plutarch aims to provide examples so that by imitating (μίμησις) the virtues and avoiding the vices described, the reader can improve his own moral character (*Pericles* 1; *Aem. Paul.* 1). Equally in the gospels, the readers are exhorted to follow Jesus' example in accepting and welcoming others (Mark 1.17; Luke 6.36). Paul also stresses the theme of imitation: 'be imitators of me, as I am of Christ' (1 Cor. 11.1; Phil. 3.17; 1 Thess. 1.6), following

---

205. See E. P. Sanders, *Jesus and Judaism* (London: SCM, 1985), pp. 206, 283, 323 for the accusation that Jesus allowed the 'wicked' into the kingdom.

the 'example to imitate' (τύπον μιμεῖσθαι) (2 Thess 3.7, 9).[206] Therefore, as befits a biographical narrative, we must confront this paradox between Jesus' teaching and his activity and behaviour.

In studying Jesus' ethics, therefore, it is not enough just to outline the main points of his teaching. The biographical genre of the gospels with its ancient idea of imitation suggests that it must be earthed in his practical example, not only of calling people to repentance and discipleship — but also his open pastoral acceptance of sinners. All too often those who apply New Testament ethics to today end up doing one or the other: that is, teaching a rigorist ethic with strenuous demands which seems condemnatory and alienates people from the church — or having an open acceptance of sinners and being accused of having no ethics at all! Thus even here, the biographical genre of the gospels has significant implications for today.[207]

Conclusion

The original conclusion to this book, pages 247-51 above, argued that the gospels were a form of Graeco-Roman biography, and suggested that there might be some generic and hermeneutical implications to follow from this result. As this survey has shown, those conclusions have been more than amply demonstrated over the decade since the book's first publication. Despite the fact that it was against the scholarly consensus of the uniqueness of the gospels which had prevailed for the previous half a century, our arguments for the biographical genre of the gospels have rapidly become part of a new consensus. I am grateful to all those who reviewed or engaged with the book, or who joined in the various seminars and conferences discussed in this new concluding chapter.

Out of these reactions there quickly developed a number of areas for further study, especially concerning the Christological implications of the biographical genre of the gospels, as well as their setting within Graeco-Roman and Jewish society and their relationship to Jewish literature, especially the rabbinic material. These areas therefore became the focus for my own further research and writing, which has followed these implications and

206. See A. McGrath, 'In What Way Can Jesus Be a Moral Example for Christians?' *Journal of the Evangelical Theological Society* 34 (1991), pp. 289-98; McGrath compares this with Luther's idea of 'being conformed to Christ' and Calvin's being 'incorporated into Christ' (p. 296).

207. These last few paragraphs are a summary of part of a major research project on *New Testament Ethics Today* upon which I have been working over recent years, to be published by Eerdmans as *Imitating Jesus: An Inclusive Approach to New Testament Ethics,* hopefully in 2005.

consequences of the genre of the gospels, as summarised above, as well as that of many others. Therefore these final remarks should not be seen as any kind of 'last word' on the subject: rather, I very much hope and expect that this revised and updated publication of my thesis will provoke further reaction and debate in the years ahead.

Analysis Charts of Verb Subjects

Homer's *Iliad*
Computer analysis

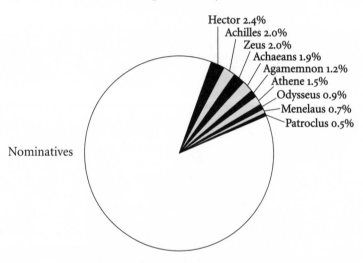

Hector 2.4%
Achilles 2.0%
Zeus 2.0%
Achaeans 1.9%
Agamemnon 1.2%
Athene 1.5%
Odysseus 0.9%
Menelaus 0.7%
Patroclus 0.5%

Nominatives

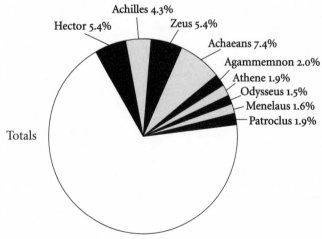

Achilles 4.3%
Hector 5.4%   Zeus 5.4%
Achaeans 7.4%
Agammemnon 2.0%
Athene 1.9%
Odysseus 1.5%
Menelaus 1.6%
Patroclus 1.9%

Totals

Figure 2

Homer's *Odyssey*
Computer analysis

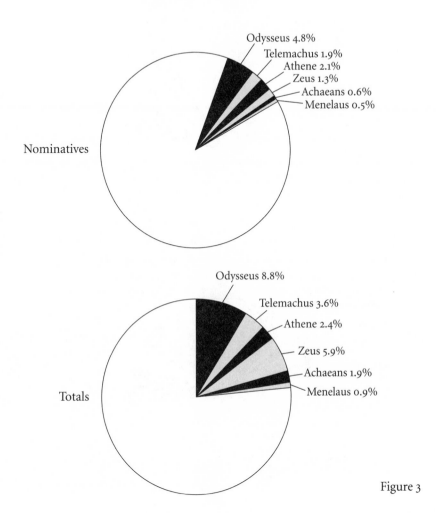

Nominatives

Odysseus 4.8%
Telemachus 1.9%
Athene 2.1%
Zeus 1.3%
Achaeans 0.6%
Menelaus 0.5%

Totals

Odysseus 8.8%
Telemachus 3.6%
Athene 2.4%
Zeus 5.9%
Achaeans 1.9%
Menelaus 0.9%

Figure 3

Herodotus' *Histories* VI and VII
Computer analysis

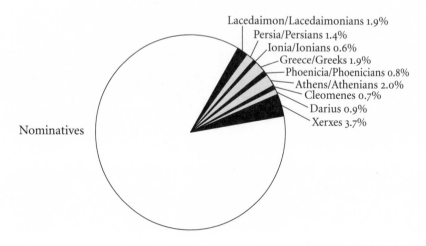

Nominatives

Lacedaimon/Lacedaimonians 1.9%
Persia/Persians 1.4%
Ionia/Ionians 0.6%
Greece/Greeks 1.9%
Phoenicia/Phoenicians 0.8%
Athens/Athenians 2.0%
Cleomenes 0.7%
Darius 0.9%
Xerxes 3.7%

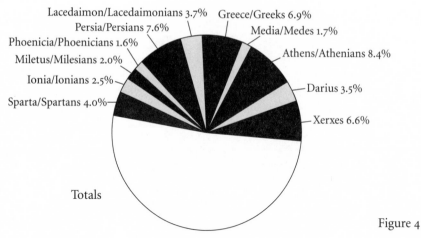

Totals

Lacedaimon/Lacedaimonians 3.7%   Greece/Greeks 6.9%
Persia/Persians 7.6%   Media/Medes 1.7%
Phoenicia/Phoenicians 1.6%   Athens/Athenians 8.4%
Miletus/Milesians 2.0%
Ionia/Ionians 2.5%   Darius 3.5%
Sparta/Spartans 4.0%   Xerxes 6.6%

Figure 4

Xenophon's *Agesilaus*
Computer analysis

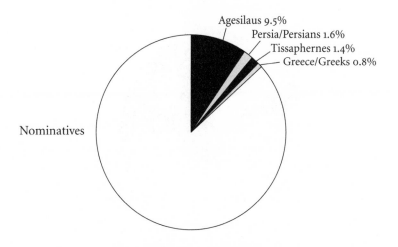

Agesilaus 9.5%
Persia/Persians 1.6%
Tissaphernes 1.4%
Greece/Greeks 0.8%

Nominatives

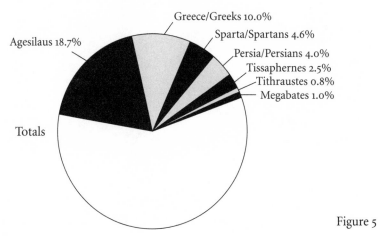

Greece/Greeks 10.0%
Sparta/Spartans 4.6%
Persia/Persians 4.0%
Tissaphernes 2.5%
Tithraustes 0.8%
Megabates 1.0%

Agesilaus 18.7%

Totals

Figure 5

Satyrus' *Euripides*
Manual analysis

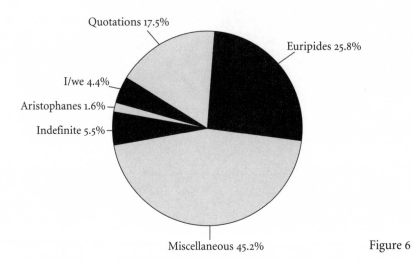

Quotations 17.5%

Euripides 25.8%

I/we 4.4%

Aristophanes 1.6%

Indefinite 5.5%

Miscellaneous 45.2%

Figure 6

Xenophon's *Cyropaedia*
Computer analysis

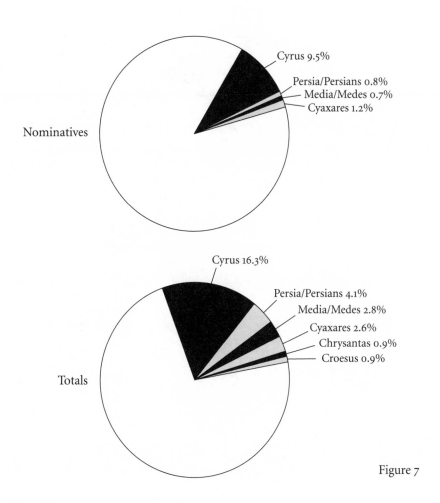

Figure 7

Xenophon's *Memorabilia*
Computer analysis

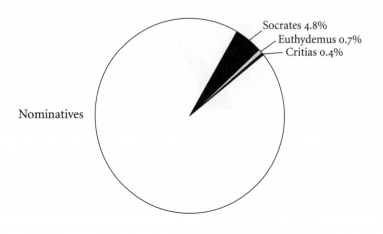

Nominatives

Socrates 4.8%
Euthydemus 0.7%
Critias 0.4%

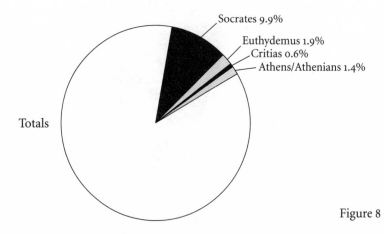

Totals

Socrates 9.9%
Euthydemus 1.9%
Critias 0.6%
Athens/Athenians 1.4%

Figure 8

Tacitus' *Agricola*
Manual analysis

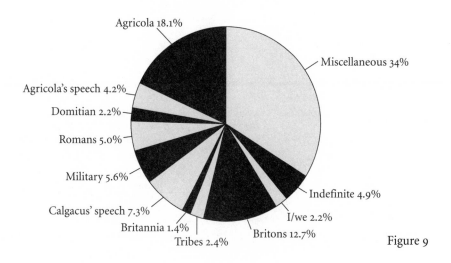

Agricola 18.1%

Miscellaneous 34%

Agricola's speech 4.2%

Domitian 2.2%

Romans 5.0%

Military 5.6%

Calgacus' speech 7.3%

Britannia 1.4%

Tribes 2.4%

Britons 12.7%

I/we 2.2%

Indefinite 4.9%

Figure 9

Plutarch's *Cato Minor*
Computer analysis

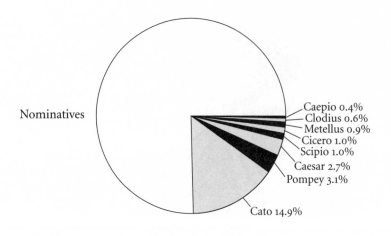

Nominatives

Caepio 0.4%
Clodius 0.6%
Metellus 0.9%
Cicero 1.0%
Scipio 1.0%
Caesar 2.7%
Pompey 3.1%

Cato 14.9%

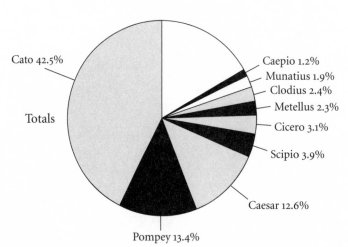

Cato 42.5%

Totals

Caepio 1.2%
Munatius 1.9%
Clodius 2.4%
Metellus 2.3%
Cicero 3.1%
Scipio 3.9%

Caesar 12.6%

Pompey 13.4%

Figure 10

Lucian's *Demonax*
Manual analysis

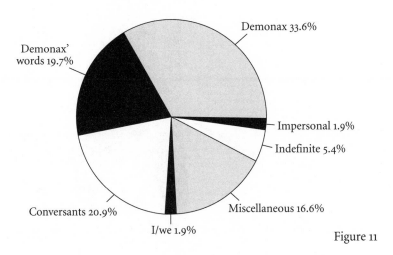

Demonax 33.6%

Demonax' words 19.7%

Impersonal 1.9%

Indefinite 5.4%

Conversants 20.9%

Miscellaneous 16.6%

I/we 1.9%

Figure 11

Mark's gospel
Manual analysis

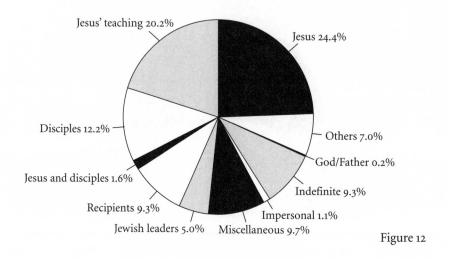

Jesus' teaching 20.2%

Jesus 24.4%

Disciples 12.2%

Others 7.0%

God/Father 0.2%

Jesus and disciples 1.6%

Indefinite 9.3%

Recipients 9.3%

Impersonal 1.1%

Jewish leaders 5.0%

Miscellaneous 9.7%

Figure 12

Matthew's gospel
Manual analysis

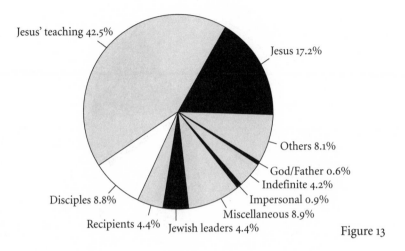

Jesus' teaching 42.5%

Jesus 17.2%

Others 8.1%

God/Father 0.6%

Indefinite 4.2%

Impersonal 0.9%

Miscellaneous 8.9%

Disciples 8.8%

Recipients 4.4%   Jewish leaders 4.4%

Figure 13

Luke's gospel
Manual analysis

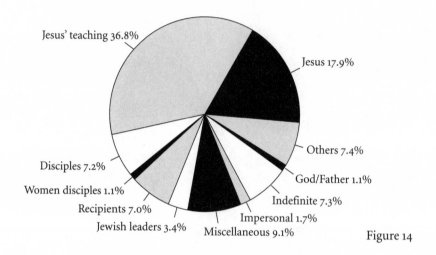

Figure 14

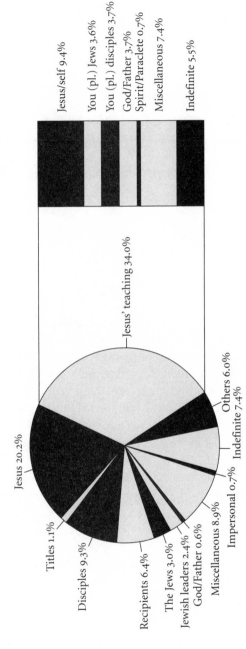

John's gospel
Manual analysis

Jesus/self 9.4%
You (pl.) Jews 3.6%
You (pl.) disciples 3.7%
God/Father 3.7%
Spirit/Paraclete 0.7%
Miscellaneous 7.4%

Indefinite 5.5%

Jesus' teaching 34.0%

Others 6.0%
Indefinite 7.4%
Impersonal 0.7%
Miscellaneous 8.9%
God/Father 0.6%
Jewish leaders 2.4%
The Jews 3.0%
Recipients 6.4%
Disciples 9.3%
Titles 1.1%
Jesus 20.2%

Figure 15

321

Gospel Genre, Christological Controversy and the Absence of Rabbinic Biography: Some Implications of the Biographical Hypothesis

Introduction

It is a privilege and a delight to contribute this essay in honour of David Catchpole. I first met him at the British New Testament Conference in September 1986, when I was delivering a paper which contained the first public airing of the substantive idea of my doctoral work on the genre of the gospels.[1] I little expected to find myself a year later appointed as Lazenby Chaplain to the University of Exeter, whereupon David invited me to do some New Testament teaching with him in the Department of Theology. It was through this experience of teaching together both in the university and in extra-mural activities that I came to appreciate David's passion for the traditio-historical method of studying the gospels. At the same time his support and encouragement for me to finish my doctorate and get it published was as constant as it was helpful.

Therefore I have chosen to draw on this material and develop it further in this essay to look at how my work on gospel genre might affect our chosen area of Christological controversy. It will begin with a brief summary of my argument about gospel genre and biography, which leads to the concentrated Christological focus on the person of Jesus. We then consider some

---

1. I have to admit it was David's Somerset County Cricket Club sweatshirt which attracted my attention as a fellow supporter! Many of our subsequent debates on the New Testament, including some of the ideas in this chapter, were conducted on days out at the cricket — and I wish him many happy days at the Taunton ground in his future retirement.

implications of this for Christological development and controversies. Finally we will discuss the question of why no biographies were written of other Jewish rabbis in the first century; this notable absence suggests that the biographical genre of the gospels itself contains a Christological claim about Jesus of Nazareth.

A. The Genre of the Gospels

The major focus of David Catchpole's work has been to use the historical method to analyse the gospels, to understand the redactional interests of the evangelists and to get behind them to their sources, especially the 'double tradition' of material shared by Matthew and Luke, known as 'Q'.[2] The ultimate aim, however, is to go further into the process to discover the original teachings of the historical Jesus: thus, in a typical Catchpole phrase, he says of the sermon by Jesus in Nazareth, 'while the words are the words of Luke, the voice is surely the voice of Jesus.'[3] Many a time I have watched David take a class through a complex section of gospel material, such as the Beatitudes, on the blackboard, analysing it and reducing it to the pure, golden nugget of authentic material from Jesus. Such an approach is often described as treating the gospels as though they are 'windows' through which we look to that which lies 'beyond' or 'behind the text'. Thus Q is to be found behind the canonical gospels — and the historical Jesus beyond that. The gospels are seen as windows onto both the early Christian communities and their debates and also to Jesus himself.

One problem with such an approach is the sheer diversity of reconstructions offered by those who look 'through' the 'window' — see for example the multitude of interpretations of Q itself.[4] Equally the variety of accounts of the historical Jesus are sometimes thought to 'reflect' as much of the scholar's own views as those of Jesus. Thus the image moves from window to 'mirror' in which what one may think is seen through or 'behind' the text is actually one's own concerns 'before' the text, like a mirror reflecting back what is actually 'in front' of it. The traditional historical method depends

2. David Catchpole's major articles on Q are collected together and expanded in his *The Quest for Q* (Edinburgh: T&T Clark, 1993).

3. David R. Catchpole, 'The Anointed One in Nazareth' in *From Jesus to John: Essays on Jesus and New Testament Christology, in Honour of Marinus de Jonge*, ed. M. C. de Boer (Sheffield: JSOT, 1993), pp. 230-51; quotation from p. 251.

4. Contrast, for example, Catchpole's work with that of J. S. Kloppenborg, *The Formation of Q: Trajectories in Ancient Wisdom Collections* (Philadelphia: Fortress, 1987).

upon a communication model of author — text — reader, where the reader attempts to get back through the text to the original author's intention or situation. Since we do not know who wrote the gospels, when, where or why, more recent literary approaches have stressed the impossibility of getting back behind the text to the author; instead there is just text and reader.[5] But, it may be asked, are all responses made by a reader to the text equally valid? Can we make texts mean what we want them to mean in such Humpty Dumpty fashion?

Both approaches tend to ignore the question of genre: what kind of glass is the text, window or mirror — or something different? The issue of genre is absolutely crucial to any kind of communication theory. TV or radio broadcasts must be decoded by a receiver using the same frequency or system as that in which they were transmitted. Interpreting legends as though they were history, or soap operas as though they were real life, leads to misunderstanding them. Thus genre is a key convention governing both the composition and interpretation not just of texts, but of all communication. It is an 'agreement', often unspoken or even unconscious, between writer and audience, author and reader, about the expectations and conventions in which the work communicated is composed and understood.

Thus before we can read the gospels, we have to discover what kind of books they might be. It is therefore rather a shock to discover scholars like Karl Ludwig Schmidt and Rudolf Bultmann affirming that the gospels are 'unique' forms of literature, *sui generis,* of their own genre — and that this approach dominated gospels studies for most of the last century.[6] In contrast to this approach, I compared the gospels with ten examples of ancient biography from fourth century BC rhetorical encomia (Isocrates and Xenophon) through the major biographical writers (like Plutarch and Suetonius) to the 3rd century AD forerunners of the novel (Lucian and Philostratus). This showed that while ancient biography was a diverse and flexible genre, it still had a recognizable 'family resemblance' in both form and content.

From a formal or structural perspective, they are written in continuous prose narrative, between 10,000 and 20,000 words in length, the amount on a single scroll; unlike much modern biography, they do not cover every part of

5. See, for example, Stephen D. Moore, *Literary Criticism and the Gospels: The Theoretical Challenge* (New Haven: Yale University Press, 1989).

6. See K. L. Schmidt, 'Die Stellung der Evangelien in der allgemeinen Literaturgeschichte', in *EUCHARISTERION: Studien zur Religion und Literatur des Alten und Neuen Testaments,* ed. Hans Schmidt (Göttingen: Vandenhoeck und Ruprecht, 1923), vol. 2, 50-134; R. Bultmann, *The History of the Synoptic Tradition* (Oxford: Blackwell, 1972), see especially p. 374.

the subject's life and times in detail, preferring a barely chronological outline starting with the birth or public debut and ending with the death, with topical material inserted to portray a particular understanding of the subject. Given the ancient interest in how a person's death encapsulates one's life, often this will be dealt with in great detail. The gospels' narrative structure, length and mixture of anecdote and sayings fit quite happily in this genre, and their concentration on Jesus' last days and death is typical of ancient biographies.[7] This means that the gospels have a particular focus on the person of Jesus of Nazareth derived from their literary genre.

B. The Christological Subject of the Gospels

However, the subject of the gospels has produced considerable debate over the years which takes a different view. Various proposals for their 'real' subject include God, the Kingdom of Heaven, the early Christian preaching, discipleship, or specific concerns of each different community, assumed to be behind the gospel. Nonetheless, for most of the last century, the one thing most scholars agreed was that they were not about Jesus: 'there is a lack of focus on the hero. . . . It is not a biography of Jesus but a story of God bringing salvation to his people.'[8]

In fact, detailed analysis of the verbal structure of the gospels reveals exactly the opposite. Every sentence in English and in ancient languages must have a subject — the person or thing doing the action of the verb. Analysis of the subjects of the verbs can be extended from one sentence to a paragraph and then across a whole work. Most narratives, ancient or modern, have a wide variety of subjects, as different people come to the fore at different times. It is particularly characteristic of biography that the attention stays focused on one person. My analysis has demonstrated that in ancient biography around a quarter or a third of the verbs are dominated by one person, the hero; furthermore, another 15% to 30% of the verbs can occur in sayings, speeches or quotations from the person. So too in the gospels: Jesus is the subject of a quarter of the verbs in Mark's Gospel, with a further fifth spoken by him in his teaching and parables. Matthew and Luke both make Jesus the subject of nearly a fifth of their verbs, while about 40% are

7. This is a very brief summary of the argument of my doctoral studies; see Richard A. Burridge, *What Are the Gospels? A Comparison with Graeco-Roman Biography,* SNTSMS 70 (CUP 1992) for fuller detail.

8. E. P. Sanders and M. Davies, *Studying the Synoptic Gospels* (London: SCM, 1989), p. 288.

spoken by him. About half of John's verbs either have Jesus as the subject or are on his lips.[9]

Thus we can see clearly that, as in other ancient biographies, Jesus' deeds and words are of vital importance for the four evangelists as they each paint their different portraits of Jesus of Nazareth. Since the gospels are a form of ancient biography, we must interpret them with the same biographical concentration upon their subject to see how each evangelist portrays his understanding of Jesus. For this reason, I followed up my work at Exeter on the genre of the gospels with a study of the four gospels as Christological narratives, using the traditional images of the four faces or living creatures (the human, lion, ox and eagle of Ezekiel 1 and Revelation 4–5) as symbols not of the evangelists themselves, but rather of their understandings of Jesus.[10]

To return to our earlier images, they are not primarily a window onto the historical Jesus or the early Christian communities, nor a mirror to reflect anything we place before them. They are more like a piece of stained glass. Of course, we can look through stained glass to that which lies the other side — but what we see is shadowy and coloured by the glass. Equally, we can sometimes catch our own reflection in the glass. But principally, stained glass is about the image in the glass — the picture or portrait, assembled by the artist within a relatively limited compass and using all the various possible colours and shapes to communicate their particular understanding of the subject or person depicted. In the case of the gospels as ancient biography, that subject is Jesus — and so the gospels are nothing less than Christology in narrative form, the story of Jesus. This is true at micro-level of every word, passage or pericope as well as the macro-level of the overall narrative flow.

C. Christological Controversy and Genre

Given this biographical concentration upon the person of Jesus in the gospels, one would expect the genre of the gospels to play a major part in studies of Christology — both in terms of its own development and its role in controversy among early Christians and Jews. Surprisingly, these are two notable areas where there is very little discussion of the genre of the gospels.

---

9. For diagrams of all these data, see Appendix I, pages 308-21 above.

10. Richard A. Burridge, *Four Gospels, One Jesus? A Symbolic Reading* (London: SPCK/ Grand Rapids: Eerdmans, 1994).

1. *The Development of Christology*

The development of New Testament Christology has been a very productive area with many key books published over recent decades. The emphasis has moved from the development 'of' Christology, to the 'Christology in the New Testament' and more recently to a stress on the 'Christologies' of the New Testament. What is common to most of them is the use of various tools of historical analysis — using the texts as 'windows' to reconstruct the understandings of Jesus which lie behind the various texts. Any literary analysis is confined mostly to things like the Christological titles used in the various New Testament books to describe Jesus — but even here the emphasis is upon which titles may have been used by which groups among the early Christians, again what we are calling the 'window' approach.

This began with an evolutionary approach to Christology, pioneered by the History of Religions theories of Wilhelm Bousset and, later, Rudolf Bultmann.[11] Taking the texts as windows, they looked 'through' them to the origins of Christology in a Palestinian primitive Christianity believing in Jesus as a messianic figure, descended from David and being the Son of Man, as opposed to the primitive Hellenistic Christianity which saw Jesus in terms similar to pagan deities.

A typical study of the Christological 'titles' is seen in C. F. D. Moule's *The Origin of Christology*, looking first at four 'descriptions of Jesus' as Son of Man, Son of God, Christ and Kurios; he then goes on to the 'corporate Christ', looking particularly at Pauline phrases, including the body and the temple. After a survey of the rest of the New Testament, he goes on to the death of Christ and the theme of fulfilment and a discussion of Christ's 'distinctiveness'. He concludes by arguing against the History of Religions approach of Bultmann and others that 'development is a better analogy than evolution for the genesis of New Testament Christology'.[12] While Moule recognises a variety of understandings of Jesus in the New Testament, the different genres of the various books do not feature at all, nor whether any particular type of book lends itself particularly to the argument. Instead, the various books are like quarries from which to extract the titles.

James Dunn follows a similar strategy for *Christology in the Making*,

---

11. W. Bousset, *Kyrios Christos: A History of the Belief in Christ from the Beginnings of Christianity to Irenaeus,* German original published in 1913 and revised in 1921; ET was not until 1970 by John Steely (Nashville: Abingdon, 1970); R. Bultmann, *The History of the Synoptic Tradition.*

12. C. F. D. Moule *The Origin of Christology* (Cambridge: CUP 1977); quotation from p. 135.

looking at the titles of Son of God, Son of Man, last Adam, Spirit or Angel, the Wisdom of God and the Word of God. He also talks of 'development' over the first century,[13] but once again there is no attempt to look at the different genres of literature. Raymond Brown provides an introduction for lay people into high and low, conservative and liberal Christologies and traces a development from Jesus' own Christology, or self-understanding, to a variety of Christologies in the New Testament in terms of Jesus' second coming, resurrection or pre-existence.[14] Despite Brown's general concentration on the gospels, here too there is no attempt to deal with their overall form or genre as Christological narrative; instead, once again they are merely a source for the various Christological ideas Brown discusses.

Ben Witherington III began by looking at *The Christology of Jesus,*[15] but more recently stresses plurality in his *The Many Faces of the Christ: The Christologies of the New Testament and Beyond.*[16] This begins with some historical background on pre-Christian Jewish Messianism and moves on to Jesus' self-understanding, drawing on his previous work. When he comes to the rest of the New Testament, Witherington argues against any developmental or evolutionary view, preferring to describe a variety of Christologies, or 'many faces of the Christ', where early views of Jesus do not necessarily imply a 'low' Christology, nor later writings a 'high' one. Like the other books of this type, he also makes no use of the genre of the gospels, nor of any other New Testament literature.

Another blow to the History of Religions type of evolutionary accounts of Christology arising slowly from pagan sources was dealt by Larry Hurtado. In his *One God, One Lord,* he looks at the interest in angels and personified divine attributes in Judaism, and the shift given to Christology very early on by the first Christians' religious experience of Jesus.[17] This time the 'window' is particularly directed towards early Christian worship. Unfortunately, such an account also has no room for the literary nature of the gospels.

Most recently, the development of genre and narrative approaches to the gospels have finally begun to impinge on this debate. Thus, in a new set of

---

13. James D. G. Dunn, *Christology in the Making* (London: SCM 1980, 2nd edn 1989); quotation from p. 248.

14. Raymond E. Brown, *Introduction to New Testament Christology* (London: Chapman, 1994).

15. Ben Witherington III, *The Christology of Jesus* (Minneapolis: Fortress, 1990).

16. Ben Witherington III, *The Many Faces of the Christ: The Christologies of the New Testament and Beyond* (New York: Crossroad Herder, 1998).

17. Larry Hurtado, *One God, One Lord: Early Christian Devotion and Ancient Jewish Monotheism* (London: SCM, 1988),

Essays on Christology in Honor of Jack Dean Kingsbury, entitled *Who Do You Say That I Am?,* Ben Witherington recognizes that one area where 'distinct progress has been made' since his previous work 'is in genre studies'. He notes that 'the crucial work of R. A. Burridge has provided a strong case' for the biographical genre of the gospels.[18] In the same volume, Leander Keck rightly notes that there is no such thing as a 'single "Christology of the New Testament"', but many Christologies, and goes on to point out that they are 'expressed in quite diverse literary forms', from titles and parables right up to entire gospels. Furthermore, not only do the gospels contain Christological forms, but 'they also build Christology into their narrative structures, thereby creating a "show and tell" Christology'.[19] In another collection sharing the same title, David Hancock argues that not only do the gospels provide a sufficient and authoritative source for Christology, but that they also give it 'narrative force', stressing that story should 'form the genre in which the Gospels are read and interpreted'.[20]

Thus the history of the study of Christology in the New Testament over the last century has mostly concentrated on the gospels as 'windows' into the historical development, although with the occasional attempt to 'reflect' in them some contemporary descriptions of Jesus. Given the Christological nature of the biographical genre of the gospels, it is surprising that this aspect has made so little impact on the discussion. However, the last examples might lead us to begin to expect more literary use of the gospels' biographical genre in future discussions of Christology.

2. The Parting of the Ways

The second area of surprising omission concerns the debate about the so-called 'Parting of the Ways' as the early Christian movement and what became Rabbinic Judaism grew apart after the Jewish war of 66-70 and the Bar Kochba revolt of 132-35. Many accounts of this separation stress the importance of Christology as a dividing factor. Therefore, one might have expected

---

18. Ben Witherington III, 'The Christology of Jesus' in M. A. Powell and D. R. Bauer, eds., *Who Do You Say That I Am? Essays on Christology in Honor of Jack Dean Kingsbury* (Louisville: Westminster John Knox 1999), pp. 1-13; quotations from p. 2.

19. Leander E. Keck, 'Christology of the New Testament: What, Then, Is New Testament Christology?' in Powell and Bauer, *Who Do You Say?,* pp. 185-200; quotation from p. 186.

20. David Hancock, 'The Christological Problem' in *Who Do You Say That I Am? Christology and the Church,* ed. Donald Armstrong (Grand Rapids: Eerdmans, 1999), pp. 1-24; quotation from pp. 12-13.

the biographical nature of the gospels with their concentrated Christological focus to feature in the various discussions, but actually this is not the case.

Thus Bruce Chilton and Jacob Neusner use the New Testament as a window into first century Jewish practices and beliefs, describing early Christianity as '(a) Judaism'.[21] Dunn's account of *The Partings of the Ways* works his way through the four pillars of Second Temple Judaism, Jesus and the Temple, Paul and the Covenant to reach the climax of his discussion of the Christological issues in the relationship of Jesus to God in chapters 9–11.[22] Throughout, the New Testament documents are treated as a source for the period, but not their literary form. This omission is all the more surprising in the light of Dunn's earlier article 'Let John Be John: A Gospel for Its Time' where he does bring together Christology and relationships among Christians and with "the Jews" in his consideration of John as a gospel.[23]

In the same 1982 symposium, Graham Stanton argued for Matthew as a creative 'interpreter' of the sayings of Jesus.[24] By the 1989 Durham-Tübingen symposium, Stanton is stressing the role 'Matthew's Christology' plays in the separation between Jews and Christians, looking particularly at the charges that Jesus was a magician and a deceiver — but again with no treatment of the writing or genre of the gospel as a whole.[25]

The oddity of this omission of the role played by the Christological nature of the gospels in the parting of the ways is further strengthened by the recognition that both Christians (especially Jewish Christians) and their (non-Christian) Jewish opponents shared a respect for and use of the scriptures. Judith Lieu indicates one possible answer in her account of Justin Martyr's use of the scriptures in Christological debate with Trypho, where she notes that Justin knows he must debate 'on the basis of the scriptures accepted by the Jews (56.16; 68.2)', unlike later writers who use the gospels.[26] Martin Hengel discusses the way Christians claimed the Septuagint for their

21. Bruce Chilton and Jacob Neusner, *Judaism in the New Testament: Practices and Beliefs* (London: Routledge, 1995), passim, e.g. pp. 4-9.

22. James D. G. Dunn, *The Partings of the Ways: Between Christianity and Judaism and Their Significance for the Character of Christianity* (London: SCM 1991)

23. James D. G. Dunn, 'Let John Be John: A Gospel for Its Time' in the 1982 Tübingen symposium, *The Gospel and the Gospels*, ed. Peter Stuhlmacher (Grand Rapids: Eerdmans, 1991), pp. 293-322.

24. Graham Stanton, 'Matthew as a Creative Interpreter of the Sayings of Jesus' in *The Gospel and the Gospels*, ed. Stuhlmacher, pp. 257-72.

25. Graham Stanton, 'Matthew's Christology and the Parting of the Ways' in *Jews and Christians: The Parting of the Ways, AD 70 to 135*, ed. James D. G. Dunn (Grand Rapids: Eerdmans, 1999), pp. 99-116.

26. Judith M. Lieu, *Image and Reality* (Edinburgh: T&T Clark, 1996), p. 125.

scriptures, while Philip Alexander notes that 'the books of the heretics', *sifrei minim,* alludes to Torah scrolls copied out by Christian scribes which *Tosefta Yadayim* 2.13 and *Tosefta Shabbat* 13 (14).5 did not consider to have the same sanctity as 'genuine Torah scrolls'.[27] Dunn sees this shared experience of interpreting scripture as a common heritage even for Jews and Christians today and a 'cause for hope in Jewish/Christian relations'.[28] However, such comments do run the risk of reflecting in the mirror of the text a modern concern placed in front of it, namely relationships between Jews and Christians today.

One person who does examine the implications of this shared use of scriptures for the literary form of the gospels is Wolfgang Roth. He examines the use of what he calls 'the Pharisaic canon', the 'law and the prophets' in the gospels to contrast what he considers are two types of gospel — the Synoptics and John.[29] While the contrast he draws is interesting, it is not sufficient to demonstrate different genres for John and the Synoptics.

Thus despite the significance of the biographical genre for the Christological focus of the gospels, this aspect hardly features in the usual accounts both of the development of New Testament Christology/ies and of the debates between early Christians and Jews over Christology which led to the parting of the ways. Instead, nearly all the scholars discussed have been using the gospels as windows to get behind the text to the first-century debate and parting of the ways, although there are also hints of a 'mirror approach' when modern concerns about anti-Semitism after the holocaust are reflected in the discussion. Once again, however, the 'picture in the stained glass', the portrait of Jesus determined by the genre of the text, is almost totally missing. In both of these areas, the Christological implications of the biographical hypothesis could make a significant contribution.

D. Rabbinic Material and the Absence of Biography

This almost total ignoring of any consideration of the overall form and story of the gospels in the light of their biographical genre is all the more remark-

---

27. Martin Hengel, 'The Septuagint as a Collection of Writings Claimed by Christians: Justin and the Church Fathers before Origen' in *Jews and Christians*, pp. 39-83; Philip S. Alexander, '"The Parting of the Ways" from the Perspective of Rabbinic Judaism' also in *Jews and Christians*, pp. 1-25, see especially pp. 11-15.

28. James D. G. Dunn, *The Partings of the Ways*, pp. 252-3.

29. Wolfgang Roth, 'To Invert or Not to Invert: The Pharisaic Canon in the Gospels' in *Early Christian Interpretation of the Scriptures of Israel: Investigations and Proposals,* ed. Craig A. Evans and James A. Sanders, JSNTSS 148 (Sheffield Academic Press, 1997), pp. 59-78.

able given the frequent comparison of individual gospel stories with rabbinic material. In our work together, David Catchpole would often give students gospel pericopae in parallel with comparable rabbinic anecdotes to assist with traditio-historical analysis. Once again, both the gospel texts and the rabbinic material are being used as windows to get behind the text to the kinds of stories and events typical of teachers in the first century.

Thus, Rabbi Michael Hilton and Fr. Gordian Marshall OP worked together to produce *The Gospels and Rabbinic Judaism: A Study Guide* to demonstrate the similarities between some of Jesus' sayings and passages from rabbinic sources. They begin with the Great Commandment, comparing Mark 12.28-34 and the parallels in Matt. 22.34-40 and Luke 10.25-28 with a *Sifra* passage from Rabbi Akiba on Lev. 19.18, Genesis Rabba 24.7 (on Gen. 5.1) and the famous story from the Babylonian Talmud, *Shabbat* 31A, of the different reactions from Shammai and Hillel when asked to teach the whole law to a Gentile enquirer while standing on one leg: Shammai chased the questioner away, while Hillel repeated the Golden Rule as the sum of the whole Torah, with the rest as commentary, but still to be learned. Further passages are noted, leading up to Hilton's conclusion that here is 'Jesus at his most "rabbinic" engaged in lively debate and answering some of the same questions as the rabbis'.[30] Subsequent chapters compare passages from the gospels with rabbinic material on the synagogue, parables, halakhah in the saying about an ox in the pit (Matt. 12.11-12; Luke 14.5), the sabbath, divorce and forgiveness.

Similar comparisons emerge from the results of an international symposium comparing Hillel and Jesus held in Jerusalem in June 1992.[31] No less than eight chapters or 170 pages of the published papers are devoted to comparisons of just the sayings of Jesus and Hillel! Once again the Golden Rule traditions are carefully compared, here by Philip Alexander who concludes that 'the overriding feeling is one of astonishment at the convergence of the two traditions'.[32] Similarly, B. T. Viviano compares and contrasts Hillel and Jesus' teaching on prayer, concluding that Hillel is more creation-centred and sapiential as against Jesus' apocalyptic urgency.[33] Other chapters examine the difficulties in reconstructing sayings of both Jesus and Hillel, as well as some Qumran material and questions of transmission and interpretation.

---

30. Rabbi Michael Hilton with Fr. Gordian Marshall OP, *The Gospels and Rabbinic Judaism: A Study Guide* (London: SCM, 1988), p. 34.

31. James H. Charlesworth and Loren L. Johns, eds., *Hillel and Jesus: Comparative Studies of Two Major Religious Leaders* (Minneapolis: Fortress, 1997).

32. P. S. Alexander, 'Jesus and the Golden Rule' in *Hillel and Jesus*, pp. 363-88; quotation from p. 388.

33. B. T. Viviano, 'Hillel and Jesus on Prayer' in *Hillel and Jesus*, pp. 427-57.

Philip Alexander has devoted many studies elsewhere to such rabbinic writings, and is keen to enable New Testament scholars to handle this material carefully.[34] He has collected together some rabbinic stories and anecdotes to compare 'Rabbinic Biography and the Biography of Jesus'. He concludes, 'there are parallels to the individual pericopae, and at this level similarities are very strong. In terms of form, function, setting and motif, the Rabbinic anecdotes are very close to the Gospel pericopae, and there can be little doubt that both belong to the same broad Palestinian Jewish tradition of story-telling.'[35]

Thus, at the level of Form Criticism, looking through the 'window' of the text to the first-century context, the parallels between the gospel pericopae and the rabbinic anecdotes are very close. Since Bultmann and other Form Critics saw the gospels as just a collection of such stories, strung together like beads on a string, we might expect the rabbinic stories to be similarly strung together to form accounts of Hillel, Shammai or others, to give us some more stained-glass portraits.

Yet, this is precisely what we do *not* find, much to everybody's surprise. Thus Philip Alexander concludes his study of 'Rabbinic Biography and the Biography of Jesus' thus: 'there are no Rabbinic parallels to the Gospels as such. This is by far the most important single conclusion to emerge from this paper. . . . There is not a trace of an ancient biography of any of the Sages. . . . This is a profound enigma.'[36]

Jacob Neusner has devoted much study to this question. In 1984 he began with *In Search of Talmudic Biography* in which he notes the importance of attributing a saying to a particular rabbi — notably Eliezer. Yet despite this material, he states that 'there is no composition of tales and stories into a sustained biography'.[37] He followed this with an analysis of *Why No Gospels in Talmudic Judaism?*, confronting why the rabbinic traditions contain no biographies and nothing like the gospels about Jesus. He provides many examples of the stories about sages, but which were never compiled into biographical narratives or gospels: they are 'the compositions no one made'.[38] His next

---

34. See for example, Philip S. Alexander, 'Rabbinic Judaism and the New Testament', *ZNW* 74 (1983), pp. 237-46.

35. Philip S. Alexander, 'Rabbinic Biography and the Biography of Jesus: A Survey of the Evidence' in *Synoptic Studies: The Ampleforth Conferences of 1982 and 1983*, ed. C. M. Tuckett, JSNTSS 7 (Sheffield: JSOT, 1984), pp. 19-50; quotation from p. 42.

36. Philip S. Alexander, 'Rabbinic Biography and the Biography of Jesus', p. 40.

37. Jacob Neusner, *In Search of Talmudic Biography: The Problem of the Attributed Saying*, Brown Judaic Studies 70 (Chico: Scholars, 1984), p. 2.

38. Jacob Neusner, *Why No Gospels in Talmudic Judaism?* (Atlanta: Scholars, 1988), pp. 33-8.

study on *The Incarnation of God* was a detailed treatment of the idea of incarnation, both of the Torah and of God — but he stresses as before: 'While the two Talmuds present stories about sages, neither one contains anything we might call a "gospel" of a sage or even a chapter of a gospel. There is no sustained biography of any sage.'[39] Finally, he answered the claim of some similarities between the gospels and other Jewish material with *Are There Really Tannaitic Parallels to the Gospels?*[40]

Lastly, we return again to the symposium on *Jesus and Hillel.* In Chapter 2, A. Goshen Gottstein from the University of Tel Aviv deals with the question, 'Jesus and Hillel: Are Comparisons Possible?' He comes to the same conclusions as Neusner: 'We must be reminded of some basic differences between the nature of Talmudic literature and the nature of the Gospels. We have no Talmudic Gospel of any Rabbi.' He then refers to my book, *What Are the Gospels?* and accepts its conclusions: 'Following Burridge's discussion, the present discussion assumes Gospel writing to be a form of biography.' Thus Goshen connects the two main parts of this essay together, linking my work on the gospels' genre to that of Alexander and Neusner on rabbinic stories: 'One could therefore ask why we do not have any instances of rabbinic biography'.[41] To this question, therefore, we must now turn at long last. Why is it that, while both rabbinic stories and gospel pericopae can be used as windows onto the first-century context, biographical portraits were painted only of Jesus?

E. Literary Reasons: The Genre of Rabbinic Material

The first area to consider for possible reasons why there are no rabbinic biographies is literary. We argued above that genre is crucial for the composition and interpretation of texts. Therefore, as with the gospels, we need to start with the issue of the genre of the rabbinic traditions.

Most of the rabbinic material is comprised of anecdotes, which are more about a rabbi's teaching than his actions. Many of the stories are composed mostly of dialogue which leads up to an actual saying or ruling of the rabbi, with any narrative just at the start to set the scene. In this way, the rab-

39. Jacob Neusner, *The Incarnation of God: The Character of Divinity in Formative Judaism* (Philadelphia: Fortress, 1988), p. 213.

40. Jacob Neusner, *Are There Really Tannaitic Parallels to the Gospels? A Refutation of Morton Smith,* South Florida Studies in the History of Judaism, No. 80 (Chico: Scholars, 1993).

41. A. Goshen Gottstein, 'Jesus and Hillel: Are Comparisons Possible?' in *Hillel and Jesus,* pp. 31-55; quotations from pp. 34-5.

binic material is more like Q or Gospel of Thomas, i.e. it has the genre of say-ings, *logia*, more than biographical narrative. Thus Philip Alexander tries var-ious methods to provide an analysis of rabbinic anecdotes, attempting to use form, point and content in his classification of seven main types:

- Precedents — stories which may begin with *ma'aseh* and lead up to a ruling.
- Exempla — stories commending certain virtues.
- Responsa — answering a question from a disciple or enquirer.
- Scholastic debates — disputes between authorities over halakhah.
- Encomia — aiming to praise a certain master.
- Miracle-stories — stories often told of the earlier masters.
- Death stories — developing later, especially of martyrdoms.[42]

He also argues that the rabbinic stories have an 'intensely oral character . . . against the more prosy "written" style of the gospels'. They are 'extremely compressed, allusive, witty, dramatic and learned'; more like bits from a play to be performed than a text to be read, intended for oral circulation, not in written form.[43]

Neusner makes a similar point. *In Search of Talmudic Biography* is subti-tled 'the problem of the attributed saying' — and it is 'sayings' which com-prise this material. In *The Incarnation of God*, Neusner applies a 'taxonomy of narrative' to the material and finds 'five species of the genus narrative'. He calls them parable, precedent, narrative setting for a saying, scriptural story and sage story.[44] The problem with this is that 'narrative' is neither a genus nor a genre in itself according to most literary theories of genre, and his five 'species' are not clearly identified by generic features as subgenres.

However, the basic point is clear, that the rabbinic anecdotes are di-rected more towards sayings than actions. The question then needs to be asked whether this generic character would prevent their being compiled into an ancient biography. However, ancient biography was not all com-posed of narrative and actions. One possible comparison is with Lucian's *Demonax* which has a brief preface and account of the philosopher's life, fol-lowed by a large number of anecdotes all strung together, each composed mainly of dialogue leading up to a pronouncement or decision by the great sage — yet it is still called a 'life', *bios*. In fact, the *Demonax* is more loosely

---

42. Philip S. Alexander, 'Rabbinic Biography and the Biography of Jesus', pp. 21-4.
43. Philip S. Alexander, 'Rabbinic Biography and the Biography of Jesus', p. 42.
44. Jacob Neusner, *The Incarnation of God*, p. 214.

structured with less integration of teaching and activity than even Mark's gospel.[45]

However, the concern particularly for precedent does tend towards a more narrative biographical form. The Jews believed that a teacher's example could be as important as his words. Thus, in the absence of a ruling by a legal authority, it was permissible to report a rabbi's actions and to deduce from them what his legal position would be on the matter. This gives the precedent, or *ma'aseh:* 'it happened that Rabbi X did such and such'. From the master's action, something of the Torah could be learned. Thus stories are told of Rabbi Akiba following his master, Rabbi Joshua, into the toilet to see how he relieved himself and there he learned three things (to sit north and south, to sit not stand, and to wipe with the left hand, not the right). When Ben 'Azzai expressed some surprise that he should 'take such liberties with your master', R. Akiba explained that 'it was a matter of Torah, and I needed to learn'. Ben 'Azzai then followed R. Akiba into the toilet and learned the same three things, which he duly passed on to R. Judah. Similarly, R. Kahana hid under his master's bed and was so impressed with what is euphemistically termed his master's 'chatting with his wife, and joking and doing what he required' that he cried out 'One would think that Abba's mouth had never before supped the cup!' When his master, somewhat surprised to find his pupil under the marital bed, told him to get out 'because it is rude', Kahana's reply was also 'Master, it is Torah, and I need to know'.[46]

So the imitation of the master is a way of knowing Torah, and so it becomes an imitation of God. Thus the crucial point here, as Neusner says of the sage-story, is that it provides 'a good example of how one should behave'.[47] He repeats the same point elsewhere: 'The sage is always represented as exemplary'.[48] Similarly, Alexander notes how these stories 'hold up the conduct of the rabbis for emulation'.[49]

One obvious example of this sort is the story of the death of a sage. Alexander notes that rabbinic literature is not interested in 'wonderful birth-stories' but 'does show a steady interest in how the Sages died'. Usually it is either a death-bed scene which allows for the last instructions or 'ethical last will and testament' or a martyrdom, which provide another form of exempla.[50] This exemplary purpose was very common for much of ancient

---

45. See my discussion of the *Demonax* on pages 162 and 166 above.
46. Babylonian Talmud, *Berakoth* 62a (London: Soncino Press, 1948), p. 388.
47. Jacob Neusner, *The Incarnation of God*, p. 216.
48. Jacob Neusner, *Why No Gospels in Talmudic Judaism?*, p. 52.
49. Philip S. Alexander, 'Rabbinic Biography and the Biography of Jesus', p. 38.
50. Philip S. Alexander, 'Rabbinic Biography and the Biography of Jesus', p. 24.

biography, and we noted above the tendency to describe the subject's death at some length to reveal the true character. Neusner sees the stories of the deaths of sages with a similar function: 'How a sage died — the death-scene, with its quiet lessons — likewise presented a model for others.'[51]

Thus although the rabbinic material is more anecdotal and based more on sayings than are the gospels and some other ancient lives, it still contains enough biographical elements (through sage stories, narratives, precedents and death scenes) which would have enabled an editor to compile a 'life of Hillel' or whoever. Such an account would have been recognisably in the genre of ancient biography and have looked quite like works like the *Demonax*. Literary and generic reasons alone are therefore not sufficient to explain this curious absence of rabbinic biography.

F. Theological Reasons:
The Christological Focus of the Gospels

In the end, biography directs the audience's attention at the life and character of the person being described. We are back to the image of stained glass, where the skill of the artist is in representing a portrait through limited means and the focus must be centred on the subject. The decision to write a biographical account of Jesus thus has important Christological implications. Equally, the failure to write, or even compile from the various anecdotes available, any biographies of the rabbis also has significant implications.

Neusner argues that this is because the individual sages are not at the centre of attention. '*Sage-stories turn out not to tell about sages at all; they are stories about the Torah personified.* Sage-stories cannot yield a gospel because they are not about sages anyway. They are about the Torah. Gospels by contrast tell the life of a human being. . . . The sage story, dealing with the individual, homogenizes sage with sage. The gospel does just the opposite, with its focus on the uniqueness of the hero.'[52] Neusner's answer thus has two key components — that the sages or rabbis are seen as a collective group, being not significant as individuals, and that centre stage belongs not to them as human beings but to the Torah.

Alexander makes the same point: 'The obvious answer is that neither Eliezer nor any other Sage held in Rabbinic Judaism the central position that Jesus held in early Christianity. The centre of Rabbinic Judaism was Torah;

---

51. Jacob Neusner, *Why No Gospels in Talmudic Judaism?*, p. 62.
52. Jacob Neusner, *Why No Gospels in Talmudic Judaism?*, pp. 52-3; his italics.

the centre of Christianity was the person of Jesus, and the existence of the Gospels is, in itself, a testimony to this fact.'[53] Similarly Rabbi Michael Hilton says: 'The Gospels can thus be regarded as a kind of commentary on Jesus' life, in much the same way as the Rabbis comment on biblical texts. What is central to the Gospel writers is the experience of resurrection. . . . And what is central to the rabbinic texts is the experience of revelation, the feeling that God's will is known and available to be derived from the text of the Torah'.[54]

This is not to say that sages are not important. Indeed, notes Neusner, they can be seen as 'equivalent to a scroll of the Torah: He who sees the disciple of a sage who has died is as if he sees a scroll of the Torah that has been burned (y. Moed Qatan 3:7.X).' The Sage is 'at the same level of authority as the Torah'.[55] However, this is only true in as much as he represents and embodies the Torah and the whole community; there is no uniqueness or individuality about the rabbi to commemorate for his own sake. So he concludes his study thus: 'our rapid comparison of the Gospels of Jesus Christ and the Torah of our sages of blessed memory yields a simple point of difference. Individual authors, Matthew, Mark, Luke, John, tell the story of the unique individual. A consensus of an entire community reaches its full human realization in the sage, and the writing down of that consensus will not permit individual traits of rhetoric.'[56]

Similarly, Goshen Gottstein in comparing Jesus and Hillel stresses that individual rabbis are not to be venerated, nor separated from other rabbis. Furthermore, 'Gospel writing would be the product of the particular religious understanding of the messianic, and therefore — salvific, activity of Jesus. The lack of Gospels in rabbinic literature would then be a less significant issue, since no salvific claim is attached to any particular Rabbi.'[57] Further on in the same symposium, David Flusser from the Hebrew University of Jerusalem compares the 'self awareness' of Jesus and Hillel; while Hillel understood himself as a representative of humanity and an exemplar, Jesus had a high self-awareness of himself as Messiah.[58]

Thus the literary shift from unconnected anecdotes about Jesus as a teacher, which resemble so much of the rabbinic material, to composing them together carefully in the genre of an ancient biography is making an enor-

---

53. Philip S. Alexander, 'Rabbinic Biography and the Biography of Jesus', p. 41.

54. Hilton and Marshall, *The Gospels and Rabbinic Judaism,* p. 13.

55. Jacob Neusner, *Why No Gospels in Talmudic Judaism?,* pp. 20 and 45.

56. Jacob Neusner, *Why No Gospels in Talmudic Judaism?,* p. 72.

57. Goshen Gottstein, 'Jesus and Hillel', p. 35.

58. D. Flusser, 'Hillel and Jesus: Two Ways of Self-Awareness' in *Jesus and Hillel,* pp. 71-107.

mous Christological and theological claim. In the end, rabbinic biography is not possible, because no rabbi is that unique and is important only as he represents the Torah, which continues to hold the central place. To write a biography is to replace the Torah by putting a human person in the centre of the stage. The literary genre makes a major theological shift which becomes an explicit Christological claim — that Jesus of Nazareth is Torah embodied, or as Schoneveld puts it, 'Torah in the Flesh'.[59]

Conclusion: Gospel Genre as Christological Claim

This paper has suggested that many traditio-historical studies treat the gospels as 'windows' through which they look to what lies behind or beyond the text in the first-century context of the historical Jesus or early Christian communities. More recent literary approaches see the text more like a mirror, reflecting our concerns from in front of it. However, the study of literary genre confronts us with the question of what is the nature of the text itself. Genre analysis shows that the gospels are written in the form of an ancient biography, with a concentrated focus on the person of Jesus of Nazareth. Like a piece of stained glass, it is their portrait which is most important. Yet the Christological implications of this literary genre have been ignored in most recent writing on New Testament Christology.

Furthermore, it is common to see Christology as a boundary marker, helping to develop a sense of identity and separation from Judaism in the construction of early Christian identity during the period of 'the parting of the ways'. However, in this debate too, the Christological implications of the gospels' biographical genre have also not been realized.

The significance of these implications is increased by a comparison of the gospels with rabbinic material. Both gospel pericopae and rabbinic anecdotes can be used as windows into the first-century context. However, although the rabbinic tradition contains all the biographical anecdotes and raw material, no 'Lives of Hillel' or Eliezer were ever compiled. Only with respect to Jesus were the various individual pieces assembled to form a portrait in their own right — a fact of theological and Christological importance. In concentrating the readers' attention upon the person of Jesus through writing

---

59. Jacobus Schoneveld, 'Torah in the Flesh: A New Reading of the Prologue of the Gospel of John as a Contribution to a Christology without Anti-Semitism' in *The New Testament and Christian-Jewish Dialogue: Studies in Honor of David Flusser*, ed. Malcolm Lowe, Emmanuel 24/25 (Jerusalem: Ecumenical Theological Research Fraternity in Israel, 1990), pp. 77-93.

a biography, the early Christian gospel writers were asserting something which was never said of a rabbi — that he was centre stage as the embodiment, or even replacement of Torah, a unique individual revealing God in his deeds and words, life, death and resurrection.

The desire to make this deliberate Christological claim forces the early Christian writers to move out from the Jewish tradition of stories and anecdotes to use a Greek genre of continuous biographical narrative. The actual writing of a gospel was a Christological claim in itself and also contributed towards the 'parting of the ways' between the early Christians and the developing rabbinic tradition.

Select Bibliography

Full bibliographical details are given to all works when first mentioned in the notes. The primary Graeco-Roman sources are collected below; the standard editions and commentaries (in addition to those mentioned in the notes) are assumed for biblical texts. The list of secondary sources includes only works frequently cited or of major significance for the subject.

Primary Sources

Aristophanes: The Frogs, ed. W. B. Stanford, 2nd edn, London: Macmillan, 1963 (1971 reprint with alterations).

Aristotle: Ars Rhetorica, ed. W. D. Ross, *OCT*, OUP, 1959.

Aristotle: Poetics, Introduction, Commentary and Appendixes by D. W. Lucas, OUP, 1978 reprint of 1968.

Horace on Poetry, vol. 1: *Prolegomena to the Literary Epistles*, ed. C. O. Brink, CUP, 1963.

Horace on Poetry, vol. 2: *Ars Poetica*, ed. C. O. Brink, CUP, 1971.

Horace on Poetry, vol. 3: *Epistles Book II*, ed. C. O. Brink, CUP, 1982.

Isocrates: Cyprian Orations, ed. Edward S. Forster, OUP, 1912.

Isocrates, with an English translation by George Norlin (vols. 1 and 2), and Larue Van Hook (vol. 3), 3 vols., Loeb Classical Library, London: Heinemann, 1928/1945.

Luciani Opera, ed. M. D. MacLeod, 4 vols., *OCT*, OUP, 1972-87.

Lucian, with an English translation by A. M. Harmon, in 8 vols., Loeb Classical Library, London: Heinemann, 1913.

Cornelius Nepos, ed. E. O. Winstedt, *OCT*, OUP, 1904.

Cornelius Nepos, with an English translation by John C. Rolfe, Loeb Classical Library, London: Heinemann, 1984.

Cornelius Nepos: A Selection, including the Lives of Cato and Atticus, ed. Nicholas Horsfall, OUP, 1989.

Philo, with an English translation by F. H. Colson, 11 vols., Loeb Classical Library, London: Heinemann, 1950.

Select Bibliography

Philostratus: The Life of Apollonius of Tyana, with an English translation by F. C. Coneybeare, 2 vols., Loeb Classical Library, London: Heinemann, 1917.

Plutarch: Alexander, A Commentary, ed. J. R. Hamilton, OUP, 1969.

Plutarch: Life of Antony, ed. C. B. R. Pelling, CUP, 1988.

Plutarch: Cato the Younger, ed. J. Murrell, *LACTOR* 14, London: Association of Classical Teachers, 1984.

Plutarch's Lives, with an English translation by Bernadotte Perrin, 11 vols., Loeb Classical Library, London: Heinemann, 1919.

'Satyrus, *Life of Euripides*', *P.Oxy.* No. 1176, in *The Oxyrhynchus Papyri* IX, ed. Arthur S. Hunt, London: Egypt Exploration Fund Graeco-Roman Branch, 1912, pp. 124-82.

De Satyro Peripatetico, ed. Casimirus Felix Kumaniecki, Polska Akademja Umiejętności Archiwum Filologiczne Nr. 8, Cracow: Gebethner et Wolff, 1929.

Satiro, Vita di Euripide, ed. Graziano Arrighetti, Studi Classici e Orientali, vol. 13, Pisa: Libreria Goliardica Editrice, 1964.

Suetonius, with an English translation by J. C. Rolfe, 2 vols., Loeb Classical Library, London: Heinemann, 1914.

Suetonius: Divus Augustus, ed. John M. Carter, Bristol: Classical Press, 1982.

Suetonius: Claudius, ed. J. Mottershead, Bristol: Classical Press, 1986.

Suetonius: Nero, ed. B. H. Warmington, Bristol: Classical Press, 1977.

Suetonius' Life of Nero, ed. K. R. Bradley, Brussels: Collection Latomus 157, 1978.

Cornelii Taciti, Vita Agricolae, ed. H. Furneaux, Oxford: Clarendon, 1898.

Taciti: De Vita Iulii Agricolae, ed. Ioannes Forni, Rome: Athenaeum, 1962.

Cornelii Taciti: De Vita Agricolae, ed. R. M. Ogilvie and I. A. Richmond, OUP, 1967.

Tacitus: The Agricola and the Germania, trans. H. Mattingly, revised edition by S. A. Handford, Harmondsworth: Penguin, 1970.

Kommentar zum Agricola des Tacitus, ed. Heinz Heubner, Göttingen: Vandenhoeck and Ruprecht, 1984.

Xenophon: Opera Omnia, ed. E. C. Marchant, 5 vols., *OCT,* OUP, 1910.

Xenophon's Cyropaedia, with an English translation by Walter Miller, 2 vols., Loeb Classical Library, London: Heinemann, 1943 and 1947.

Kommentar zu Xenophons Memorabilien, ed. Olof Gigon, 2 vols., Basel: Friedrich Reinhardt, 1953 and 1956.

Xenophon: Scripta Minora, with an English translation by E. C. Marchant, Loeb Classical Library, London: Heinemann, 1925.

Ancient Literary Criticism: The Principal Texts in Translation, ed. D. A. Russell and M. Winterbottom, OUP, 1972.

The Chreia in Ancient Rhetoric, vol. 1: *The Progymnasmata,* ed. Ronald F. Hock and Edward N. O'Neil, SBL, 1986.

Secondary Sources

Alexander, Loveday C. A., *The Preface to Luke's Gospel: Literary Convention and Social Context in Luke 1.1-4 and Acts 1.1,* SNTSMS 78, Cambridge University Press, 1993.

———'Acts and Ancient Intellectual Biography', in *The Book of Acts in Its Ancient Literary*

Setting, ed. Bruce W. Winter and Andrew D. Clarke, Carlisle: Paternoster/Grand Rapids: Eerdmans, 1993.

———— 'Fact, Fiction and the Genre of Acts', *NTS* 44 (1998), pp. 380-99.

———— 'Ancient Book Production and the Circulation of the Gospels' in *The Gospels for All Christians: Rethinking the Gospel Audiences*, ed. Richard Bauckham, Grand Rapids: Eerdmans, 1998, pp. 71-105.

———— 'Formal Elements and Genre: Which Greco-Roman Prologues Most Closely Parallel the Lukan Prologues?' in *Jesus and the Heritage of Israel: Luke's Narrative Claim upon Israel's Legacy*, ed. David P. Moessner, Harrisburg: Trinity Press International, 1999, pp. 9-26.

Alexander, Philip S. 'Midrash and the Gospels', in *Synoptic Studies: The Ampleforth Conferences of 1982 and 1983*, ed. C. M. Tuckett, JSNTSS 7, Sheffield: JSOT Press, 1984, pp. 1-18.

———— 'Rabbinic Biography and the Biography of Jesus: A Survey of the Evidence', in *Synoptic Studies*, 1984, pp. 19-50.

———— 'Rabbinic Judaism and the New Testament', *ZNW* 74 (1983), pp. 237-46.

Alter, Robert, and Frank Kermode (eds.). *The Literary Guide to the Bible*, London: Collins, 1987.

Anderson, Graham. *Studies in Lucian's Comic Fiction*, Mnemosyne Supplementum 43, Leiden: Brill, 1976.

———— *Philostratus: Biography and Belles Lettres in the Third Century* A.D., London: Croom Helm, 1986.

Anderson, Hugh. *The Gospel of Mark*, NCBC, London: Marshall, Morgan & Scott, 1976.

Anderson, J. K. *Xenophon*, London: Duckworth, 1974.

Ashton, John (ed.). *The Interpretation of John*, London: SPCK, 1986.

Auerbach, Erich. *Mimesis: The Representation of Reality in Western Literature*, Princeton: University Press, 1953.

Aune, David E. 'The Problem of the Genre of the Gospels: A Critique of C. H. Talbert's *What Is a Gospel?*', in *Gospel Perspectives II: Studies of History and Tradition in the Four Gospels*, ed. R. T. France and D. Wenham, Sheffield: JSOT Press, 1981, pp. 9-60.

———— 'The Apocalypse of John and the Problem of Genre', *Semeia* 36 (1986), pp. 65-96.

———— 'The Gospels as Hellenistic Biography', *Mosaic* 20 (1987), pp. 1-10.

———— (ed.) *Greco-Roman Literature and the New Testament: Selected Forms and Genres*, SBL Sources for Biblical Study 21, Atlanta: Scholars, 1988.

———— *The New Testament in Its Literary Environment*, Cambridge: James Clarke & Co., 1988.

Baird, J. Arthur. 'Genre Analysis as a Method of Historical Criticism', in *SBL Proceedings 1972: Book of Seminar Papers for 108th Annual Meeting*, ed. Lane C. McGaughy, vol. 2, pp. 385-411.

Balch, David L. 'Comments on the Genre and a Political Theme of Luke-Acts: A Preliminary Comparison of Two Hellenistic Historians', in *SBL 1989 Seminar Papers*, Society of Biblical Literature, Atlanta: Scholars Press, 1989, pp. 343-61.

———— 'The Genre of Luke-Acts: Individual Biography, Adventure Novel or Political History?', *Southwestern Journal of Theology* 33 (1990), pp. 5-19.

Baldwin, Barry. *Studies in Lucian*, Toronto: Hakkert, 1973.

———— *Suetonius*, Amsterdam: Hakkert, 1983.

Barr, David Laurence, and Judith L. Wentling. 'The Conventions of Classical Biography and the Genre of Luke-Acts: A Preliminary Study', in *Luke-Acts: New Perspectives from the SBL Seminar*, ed. Charles H. Talbert, New York: Crossroad, 1984, pp. 63-88.

Barrett, C. K. *The Gospel According to St. John*, London: SPCK, 1st edn 1955, 2nd edn 1978.

Bauckham, Richard (ed.). *The Gospels for All Christians: Rethinking the Gospel Audiences*, Grand Rapids: Eerdmans/T&T Clark, 1998.

Beasley-Murray, George R. *John*, WBC, Vol. 36, Dallas: Word, 1987.

Beavis, Mary Ann. *Mark's Audience: The Literary and Social Setting of Mark 4.11-12*, JSNTSS 33, SAP, 1989.

Benario, Herbert W. 'Recent Work on Tacitus: 1974-1983', *Classical World* 80 (1986), pp. 73-147.

Berger, Klaus. 'Hellenistische Gattungen im Neuen Testament', in *ANRW* II.25.2, 1984, pp. 1031-432.

Best, Ernest. *Mark: The Gospel as Story*, Edinburgh: T&T Clark, 1983.

Bilezikian, Gilbert G. *The Liberated Gospel: A Comparison of the Gospel of Mark and Greek Tragedy*, Grand Rapids: Baker, 1977.

Bockmuehl, Markus (ed.). *The Cambridge Companion to Jesus*, Cambridge University Press, 2001.

Boring, M. Eugene. *Truly Human/Truly Divine: Christological Language and the Gospel Form*, St. Louis: CBP Press, 1984.

Bornkamm, Günther. *Jesus of Nazareth*, London: Hodder & Stoughton, 1960.

Bousset, Wilhelm. *Kyrios Christos: A History of the Belief in Christ from the Beginnings of Christianity to Irenaeus*, ET Nashville: Abingdon, 1970.

Bowie, Ewen Lyall. 'Apollonius of Tyana: Tradition and Reality' in *ANRW* II.16.2, 1978, pp. 1652-99.

Brenk, Frederick E., S.J. *In Mist Apparelled: Religious Themes in Plutarch's Moralia and Lives*, Mnemosyne Supplementum 48, Leiden: Brill, 1977.

Brown, Raymond E., S.S. *The Gospel According to John*, Anchor Bible, 2 vols., New York: Doubleday, 1966 and 1970; 2nd edn, 1984.

———— *The Birth of the Messiah: A Commentary on the Infancy Narratives in Matthew and Luke*, London: Geoffrey Chapman, 1977.

———— *The Community of the Beloved Disciple*, London: Geoffrey Chapman, 1979.

———— *Introduction to New Testament Christology*, London: Chapman, 1994.

———— *An Introduction to the Gospel of John*, ed. Francis J. Moloney, New York: Doubleday, 2003.

Bruce, F. F. *The Acts of the Apostles: The Greek text with Introduction and Commentary*, revised edition, Leicester: IVP/Grand Rapids: Eerdmans, 1990.

Bryan, Christopher. *A Preface to Mark: Notes on the Gospel in Its Literary and Cultural Settings*, Oxford University Press, 1993.

Bultmann, Rudolf. *The History of the Synoptic Tradition* (1921), revised edn with Supplement, trans. John Marsh, Oxford: Blackwell, 1972.

———— 'Evangelien', in *Die Religion in Geschichte und Gegenwart*, ed. H. Gunkel et al., 2nd edn, Tübingen: J. C. B. Mohr, 1928, vol. 2, cols. 418-22; ET as 'The Gospels (Form)', in

Twentieth Century Theology in the Making, ed. Jaroslav Pelikan, London: Collins, Fontana, 1969, vol. 1, pp. 86-92.

———— *Theology of the New Testament,* trans. K. Grobel, London: SCM, 1952, vol. 1.

Burridge, Richard A. 'Gospel', in *A Dictionary of Biblical Interpretation,* ed. R. Coggins and J. L. Houlden, London: SCM, 1990, pp. 266-8.

———— *Four Gospels, One Jesus? A Symbolic Reading,* Grand Rapids: Eerdmans/London: SPCK, 1994; second edition 2005.

———— *John,* The People's Bible Commentary, Oxford: Bible Reading Fellowship, 1998.

———— 'About People, by People, for People: Gospel Genre and Audiences' in *The Gospels for All Christians: Rethinking the Gospel Audiences,* ed. Richard Bauckham, Grand Rapids: Eerdmans, 1998, pp. 113-45.

———— 'Gospel Genre, Christological Controversy and the Absence of Rabbinic Biography: Some Implications of the Biographical Hypothesis' in *Christology, Controversy and Community: New Testament Essays in Honour of David Catchpole,* ed. David G. Horrell and Christopher M. Tuckett, Leiden: Brill, 2000, pp. 137-56.

Cairns, Francis. *Generic Composition in Greek and Roman Poetry,* Edinburgh: University Press, 1972.

Callan, Terrance. 'The Preface of Luke-Acts and Historiography', *NTS* 31 (1985), pp. 576-81.

Cancik, Hubert (ed.). *Markus-Philologie: Historische, literargeschichtliche und stilistische Untersuchungen zum zweiten Evangelium,* WUNT 33, Tübingen: J. C. B. Mohr, 1984.

———— 'The History of Culture, Religion and Institutions in Ancient Historiography: Philological Observations concerning Luke's History', *JBL* 116 (1997), pp. 673-95.

Castle, E. B. *Ancient Education and Today,* Harmondsworth: Penguin, 1961.

Catchpole, David R. *The Quest for Q,* Edinburgh: T&T Clark, 1993.

———— 'The Anointed One in Nazareth' in *From Jesus to John: Essays on Jesus and New Testament Christology, in Honour of Marinus de Jonge,* ed. M. C. de Boer, Sheffield: JSOT, 1993, pp. 230-51.

Charlesworth, James H. *The New Testament Apocrypha and Pseudepigrapha,* London: Metuchen, 1987.

———— 'Research on the New Testament Apocrypha and Pseudepigrapha', in *ANRW* II.25.5, 1988, pp. 3919-68.

———— and Loren L. Johns (eds.). *Hillel and Jesus: Comparative Studies of Two Major Religious Leaders,* Minneapolis: Fortress, 1997.

Chilton, Bruce, and Jacob Neusner. *Judaism in the New Testament: Practices and Beliefs,* London: Routledge, 1995.

Collins, Adela Yarbro. *The Beginning of the Gospel: Probings of Mark in Context,* Minneapolis: Fortress, 1992.

———— 'Genre and the Gospels', *JR* 75.2 (1995), pp. 239-46.

Conzelmann, Hans. *The Theology of St. Luke,* trans. G. Buswell, London: Faber and Faber, 1960.

Cox, Patricia. *Biography in Late Antiquity: A Quest for the Holy Man,* University of California Press, 1983.

Culler, Jonathan. *Structuralist Poetics: Structuralism, Linguistics and the Study of Literature,* London: Routledge & Kegan Paul, 1975.

Cullmann, Oscar. 'The Plurality of the Gospels as a Theological Problem in Antiquity' in

The Early Church: Studies in Early Christian History and Theology, ed. A. J. B. Higgins, Philadelphia: Westminster Press, 1956, pp. 37-54.

———— *Salvation in History,* London: SCM, 1967.

Culpepper, R. Alan. *Anatomy of the Fourth Gospel: A Study in Literary Design,* Philadelphia: Fortress, 1983.

———— 'The Plot of John's Story of Jesus' in *Gospel Interpretation: Narrative-Critical & Social-Scientific Approaches,* ed. Jack Dean Kingsbury, Harrisburg: Trinity Press International, 1997, pp. 188-99.

Davies, W. D., and D. C. Allison, *Matthew,* ICC, Edinburgh: T&T Clark, 1988.

Dibelius, Martin. *Die Formgeschichte des Evangeliums,* 2nd edn, Tübingen: J. C. B. Mohr, 1933. ET *From Tradition to Gospel,* trans. B. L. Woolf, London: James Clarke, 1971.

Dihle, Albrecht. *Studien zur griechischen Biographie,* 2nd edn, Göttingen: Vandenhoeck & Ruprecht, 1970.

———— 'Die Evangelien und die griechische Biographie', in *Das Evangelium und die Evangelien: Vorträge vom Tübinger Symposium 1982,* ed. Peter Stuhlmacher, WUNT 28, Tübingen: J. C. B. Mohr, 1983, pp. 383-411; ET 'The Gospels and Greek Biography', pp. 361-86.

Dodd, C. H. *The Interpretation of the Fourth Gospel,* Cambridge University Press, 1953.

Donahue, John R. *The Gospel in Parable: Metaphor, Narrative, and Theology in the Synoptic Gospels,* Philadelphia: Fortress, 1988.

Dorey, T. A. 'Agricola and Domitian', *Greece and Rome* 7 (1960), pp. 66-71.

———— (ed.) *Latin Biography,* London: Routledge & Kegan Paul, 1967.

———— '"Agricola" and "Germania"' in T. A. Dorey (ed.), *Tacitus,* London: Routledge & Kegan Paul, 1969.

Dormeyer, Detlev. 'Die Kompositionsmetapher "Evangelium Jesu Christi, des Sohnes Gottes" Mk. 1.1. Ihre theologische und literarische Aufgabe in der Jesus-Biographie des Markus', *NTS* 33 (1987), pp. 452-68.

———— *Evangelium als literarische und theologische Gattung,* Darmstadt: Wissenschaftliche Buchgesellschaft, 1989.

Doty, William G. 'The Concept of Genre in Literary Analysis', in *SBL Proceedings 1972: Book of Seminar Papers for 108th Annual Meeting,* ed. Lane C. McGaughy, vol. 2, pp. 413-48.

Downing, F. Gerald. 'Contemporary Analogies to the Gospels and Acts: "Genres" or "Motifs"?', in *Synoptic Studies: The Ampleforth Conferences of 1982 and 1983,* ed. C. M. Tuckett, JSNTSS 7, Sheffield: JSOT Press, 1984, pp. 51-65.

———— 'Cynics and Christians', *NTS* 30 (1984), pp. 584-93.

———— 'Ears to Hear', in *Alternative Approaches to New Testament Study,* ed. A. E. Harvey, London: SPCK, 1985, pp. 97-121.

———— 'A bas les aristos. The Relevance of Higher Literature for the Understanding of the Earliest Christian Writings', *NovT* 30 (1988), pp. 212-30.

———— 'Quite like Q. A Genre for "Q": The "Lives" of Cynic Philosophers', *Biblica* 69 (1988), pp. 196-225.

———— *Christ and the Cynics: Jesus and Other Radical Preachers in First-Century Tradition,* JSOT Manuals 4, SAP, 1988.

———— 'A Genre for Q and a Socio-Cultural Context for Q: Comparing Sets of Similarities with Sets of Differences', *JSNT* 55 (1994), pp. 3-26.

Dubrow, Heather. *Genre,* The Critical Idiom Series 42, London: Methuen, 1982.

Dungan, David L. (ed.). *The Interrelations of the Gospels,* Leuven: University Press, 1990.

Dunn, James D. G. 'Let John Be John: A Gospel for Its Time', in *Das Evangelium und die Evangelien: Vorträge vom Tübinger Symposium 1982,* ed. Peter Stuhlmacher, WUNT 28, Tübingen: J. C. B. Mohr, 1983, pp. 309-39; ET pp. 293-322.

———— *Christology in the Making,* 2nd edn., London: SCM, 1989.

———— *The Partings of the Ways: Between Christianity and Judaism and Their Significance for the Character of Christianity,* London: SCM, 1991.

———— *Jesus Remembered,* Grand Rapids: Eerdmans, 2003.

Edwards, Douglas R. 'Acts of the Apostles and the Graeco-Roman World: Narrative Communication in Social Context', in *SBL 1989 Seminar Papers,* Society of Biblical Literature, Atlanta: Scholars Press, 1989, pp. 362-77.

Edwards, M. J. 'Biography and the Biographic' in *Portraits: Biographical Representation in the Greek and Latin Literature of the Roman Empire,* ed. M. J. Edwards and Simon Swain, Oxford: Clarendon, 1997, pp. 227-36.

Esler, Philip. 'Community and Gospel in Early Christianity: A Response to Richard Bauckham's *Gospels for All Christians*', *Scottish Journal of Theology* 51.2 (1998), pp. 235-53.

Eucken, Christoph. *Isokrates: Seine Positionen in der Auseinandersetzung mit den zeitgenössischen Philosophen,* Untersuchungen zur antiken Literatur und Geschichte 19, Berlin: Walter de Gruyter, 1983.

Evans, Craig A., and James A. Sanders, eds., *Early Christian Interpretation of the Scriptures of Israel: Investigations and Proposals,* JSNTSS 148, Sheffield Academic Press, 1997.

Filson, F. V. *St. Matthew,* 2nd edn., London: A. & C. Black, 1971.

Fitzgerald, John T. 'The Ancient Lives of Aristotle and the Modern Debate about the Genre of the Gospels', *Restoration Quarterly* 36 (1994), pp. 209-21.

Fitzmyer, Joseph A., S.J. *Luke,* The Anchor Bible, New York: Doubleday, 1981.

———— *The Acts of the Apostles: A New Translation with Introduction and Commentary,* The Anchor Bible, New York: Doubleday, 1998.

Fortna, Robert T. *The Gospel of Signs: A Reconstruction of the Narrative Source Underlying the Fourth Gospel,* SNTSMS 11, CUP, 1970.

———— *The Fourth Gospel and Its Predecessor,* Edinburgh: T&T Clark, 1989.

Fowler, Alastair. 'The Life and Death of Literary Forms', in *New Directions in Literary History,* ed. Ralph Cohen, London: Routledge & Kegan Paul, 1974, pp. 77-94.

———— *Kinds of Literature: An Introduction to the Theory of Genres and Modes,* OUP, 1982.

Frankemölle, H. *Evangelium — Begriff und Gattung: ein Forschungsbericht,* Stuttgart: Katholisches Bibelwerk, 1988.

Frickenschmidt, Dirk. *Evangelium als Biographie: Die vier Evangelien im Rahmen antiker Erzählkunst,* Tübingen: Francke Verlag, 1997.

Frye, Northrop. *Anatomy of Criticism: Four Essays,* Princeton: University Press, 1957.

———— *The Great Code: The Bible and Literature,* London: Routledge & Kegan Paul, 1982.

Gabel, John B., and Charles B. Wheeler, *The Bible as Literature: An Introduction,* Oxford University Press, 1986.

Gadamer, Hans-Georg. *Truth and Method,* London: Sheed and Ward, 1975.

Garland, David E. *Reading Matthew: A Literary and Theological Commentary on the First Gospel,* London: SPCK, 1993.

Gasque, W. Ward. *A History of the Criticism of the Acts of the Apostles,* Tübingen: J. C. B. Mohr, 1975.

Geiger, Joseph. 'Cornelius Nepos, *De Regibus Exterarum Gentium*', *Latomus* 38 (1979), pp. 662-9.

———— 'Munatius Rufus and Thrasea Paetus on Cato the Younger', *Athenaeum* 57 (1979), pp. 48-72.

———— 'Plutarch's Parallel Lives: The Choice of Heroes', *Hermes* 109 (1981), pp. 85-104.

———— *Cornelius Nepos and Ancient Political Biography,* Historia Einzelschriften 47, Stuttgart: Franz Steiner, 1985.

Georgi, Dieter. 'The Records of Jesus in the Light of Ancient Accounts of Revered Men', in *SBL Proceedings 1972: Book of Seminar Papers for 108th Annual Meeting,* ed. Lane C. McGaughy, vol. 2. pp. 527-42.

Gerhart, Mary. 'Generic Studies: Their Renewed Importance in Religious and Literary Interpretation', *JAAR* 45 (1977), pp. 309-25.

———— 'Generic Competence in Biblical Hermeneutics', *Semeia* 43 (1988), pp. 29-44.

Gero, Stephen. 'Apocryphal Gospels: A Survey of Textual and Literary Problems', in *ANRW* II.25.5, 1988, pp. 3969-96.

Gill, Christopher. 'The Question of Character-Development: Plutarch and Tacitus', *CQ* 33 (1983), pp. 476-87.

Goodenough, Erwin R. *An Introduction to Philo Judaeus,* 2nd edn, Oxford: Basil Blackwell, 1962.

Goodyear, F. R. D. *Tacitus,* Greece and Rome New Surveys in the Classics 4, OUP, 1970.

Goulder, M. D. *Midrash and Lection in Matthew,* London: SPCK, 1974.

———— *The Evangelist's Calendar: A Lectionary Explanation of the Development of Scripture,* London: SPCK, 1978.

———— *Luke: A New Paradigm,* Sheffield Academic Press, 1989.

Griffin, Jasper. 'Genre and Real Life in Latin Poetry', *JRS* 71 (1981), pp. 39-49.

Guelich, Robert A. 'The Gospel Genre', in *Das Evangelium und die Evangelien: Vorträge vom Tübinger Symposium 1982,* ed. Peter Stuhlmacher, WUNT 28, Tübingen: J. C. B. Mohr, 1983, pp. 183-219; ET pp. 173-208.

———— *Mark 1–8.26,* Word Biblical Commentary, Vol. 34A, Dallas: Word, 1989.

Gundry, Robert H. 'Recent Investigations into the Literary Genre "Gospel"', in *New Dimensions in New Testament Study,* ed. R. N. Longenecker and M. C. Tenney, Grand Rapids: Zondervan, 1974, pp. 97-114.

Hack, R. K. 'The Doctrine of Literary Forms', *Harvard Studies in Classical Philology* 27 (1916), pp. 1-65.

Hadas, Moses, and Morton Smith. *Heroes and Gods: Spiritual Biographies in Antiquity,* London: Routledge & Kegan Paul, 1965.

Haenchen, Ernst. *Gospel According to John,* 2 vols., Hermeneia Series, Philadelphia: Fortress, 1984.

Hägg, Tomas. *The Novel in Antiquity,* Oxford: Blackwell, 1983.

Halliwell, Stephen. 'Traditional Greek Conceptions of Character', in *Characterization and Individuality in Greek Literature*, ed. C. B. R. Pelling, OUP, 1990, pp. 32-59.

Harris, William V. *Ancient Literacy*, Cambridge, Mass.: Harvard University Press, 1989.

Hawthorn, Jeremy. *Unlocking the Text: Fundamental Issues in Literary Theory*, London: Edward Arnold, 1987.

Hengel, Martin. *Acts and the History of Earliest Christianity*, London: SCM, 1979.

———— *Studies in the Gospel of Mark*, London: SCM, 1985.

———— *The Four Gospels and the One Gospel of Jesus Christ: An Investigation of the Collection and Origin of the Canonical Gospels*, London: SCM, 2000.

Heffernan, Thomas J. *Sacred Biography: Saints and Their Biographers in the Middle Ages*, Oxford University Press, 1988.

Hennecke, E. *New Testament Apocrypha*, vol. 1, ed. W. Schneemelcher, London: SCM, 1963.

Hilton, Michael, with Gordian Marshall OP. *The Gospels and Rabbinic Judaism: A Study Guide*, London: SCM, 1988.

Hirsch, E. D., Jr. *Validity in Interpretation*, New Haven: Yale University Press, 1967.

———— *The Aims of Interpretation*, Chicago: University Press, 1976.

Hitchcock, F. R. M. 'Is the Fourth Gospel a Drama?', *Theology* 7 (1927), pp. 307-17.

Houlden, J. Leslie. *Backward into Light: The Passion and Resurrection of Jesus according to Matthew and Mark*, London: SCM Press, 1987.

———— *The Strange Story of the Gospels: Finding Doctrine Through Narrative*, London: SPCK, 2002.

Hurtado, Larry W. 'Gospel (Genre)', in *Dictionary of Jesus and the Gospels*, ed. J. B. Green et al. Downers Grove, Ill.: InterVarsity, 1992.

———— *One God, One Lord: Early Christian Devotion and Ancient Jewish Monotheism*, Philadelphia: Fortress, 1988; second edition, Edinburgh: T&T Clark, 1998.

———— *Lord Jesus Christ: Devotion to Jesus in Earliest Christianity*, Grand Rapids: Eerdmans, 2003.

Johnson, Luke T. *The Writings of the New Testament: An Interpretation*, London: SCM, 1986.

Jones, C. P. 'Towards a Chronology of Plutarch's Works', *JRS* 56 (1966), pp. 61-74.

———— *Plutarch and Rome*, OUP, 1971.

———— *Culture and Society in Lucian*, Cambridge, Mass.: Harvard University Press, 1986.

Jones, David L. 'Luke's Unique Interest in Historical Chronology', in *SBL 1989 Seminar Papers*, Society of Biblical Literature, Atlanta: Scholars Press, 1989, pp. 378-87.

Kähler, M. *The So-Called Historical Jesus and the Historic, Biblical Christ*, Philadelphia: Fortress, 1964.

Käsemann, Ernst. *The Testament of Jesus*, London: SCM, 1968.

Kee, Howard C. 'Aretalogy and Gospel', *JBL* 92 (1973), pp. 402-22.

———— *Jesus in History: An Approach to the Study of the Gospels*, 2nd edn, New York: Harcourt Brace Jovanovich, 1977.

———— *Community of the New Age: Studies in Mark's Gospel*, London: SCM, 1977.

———— *Christian Origins in Sociological Perspective*, London: SCM, 1980.

Kelber, Werner H. *The Oral and Written Gospel: The Hermeneutics of Speaking and Writing in the Synoptic Tradition, Mark, Paul, and Q*, Philadelphia; Fortress, 1983.

Kennedy, George A. *New Testament Interpretation through Rhetorical Criticism,* University of North Carolina Press, 1984.

Kingsbury, Jack Dean. 'The Gospel in Four Editions', *Interpretation* 33 (1979), pp. 363-75.

———— *Matthew as Story,* Philadelphia: Fortress, 1986, 2nd edn., 1988.

Kloppenborg, John S. *The Formation of Q: Trajectories in Ancient Wisdom Collections,* Philadelphia: Fortress, 1987.

Koester, Helmut. 'From the Kerygma-Gospel to Written Gospels', *NTS* 35 (1989), pp. 361-81.

Kroll, Wilhelm. 'Die Kreuzung der Gattungen', Chapter 9 in his *Studien zum Verständnis der römischen Literatur,* 2nd edn, Stuttgart: J. B. Metzler, 1964 reprint of 1924, pp. 202-24.

Kümmel, W. G. *Introduction to the New Testament,* London: SCM, 1975.

Kysar, Robert. *The Fourth Evangelist and His Gospel: An Examination of Contemporary Scholarship,* Minneapolis: Augsburg, 1975.

Lefkowitz, Mary R. *The Lives of the Greek Poets,* London: Duckworth, 1981.

Leo, Friedrich. *Die griechisch-römische Biographie nach ihrer literarischen Form,* Leipzig: Teubner, 1901.

Lieu, Judith M. *Image and Reality,* Edinburgh: T&T Clark, 1996.

Lieu, Judith M., John North and Tessa Rajak. *The Jews Among Pagans and Christians in the Roman Empire* (London: Routledge, 1992).

Lincoln, Andrew T. *Truth on Trial: The Lawsuit Motif in the Fourth Gospel,* Peabody: Hendrickson, 2000.

Lindars, Barnabas, SSF. *The Gospel of John,* NCBC, London: Marshall, Morgan & Scott, 1972.

———— *John,* Sheffield Academic Press, 1990.

Louw, J. P. *Semantics of New Testament Greek,* Philadelphia: Fortress, 1982.

Mack, Burton L. *A Myth of Innocence: Mark and Christian Origins,* Philadelphia: Fortress, 1988.

Mack, Burton L., and Vernon K. Robbins. *Patterns of Persuasion in the Gospels,* Sonoma: Polebridge, 1989.

Maddox, Robert. *The Purpose of Luke-Acts,* Edinburgh: T&T Clark, 1982.

Malherbe, Abraham J. *Social Aspects of Early Christianity,* 2nd enlarged edn, Philadelphia: Fortress, 1983.

Marguerat, Daniel. *The First Christian Historian: Writing the 'Acts of the Apostles',* SNTSMS 121, Cambridge University Press, 2002.

Marrou, H. I. *A History of Education in Antiquity,* ET George Lamb, London: Sheed and Ward, 1956.

Marsh, Clive, and Steve Moyise. *Jesus and the Gospels: An Introduction,* London: Cassell, 1999.

Marshall, Christopher D. *Faith as a Theme in Mark's Narrative,* SNTSMS 64, CUP, 1989.

Marshall, I. Howard. 'Acts and the "Former Treatise"', in *The Book of Acts in Its Ancient Literary Setting,* ed. Bruce W. Winter and Andrew D. Clarke, Carlisle: Paternoster/ Grand Rapids: Eerdmans, 1993, pp. 163-82.

———— '"Israel" and the Story of Salvation: One Theme in Two Parts' in *Jesus and the Heritage of Israel,* ed. David P. Moessner, Harrisburg: Trinity Press International, 1999, pp. 340-58.

Martin, Francis (ed.). *Narrative Parallels to the New Testament,* SBL Resources for Biblical Study 22, Atlanta: Scholars, 1988.

Martin, Ronald. *Tacitus,* London: Batsford, 1981.

Martyn, J. L. *History and Theology in the Fourth Gospel,* Nashville: Abingdon, 1979.

Marxsen, Willi. *Der Evangelist Markus,* Göttingen: Vandenhoeck & Ruprecht, lst edn 1956, 2nd edn 1959; ET *Mark the Evangelist,* New York and Nashville: Abingdon Press, 1969.

———— *Introduction to the New Testament: An Approach to Its Problems,* Oxford: Blackwell, 1968.

Matera, F. J. 'The Prologue as the Interpretative Key to Mark's Gospel', *JSNT* 34 (1988), pp. 3-20.

Matill, A. J., Jr. 'The Purpose of Acts: Schneckenburger Reconsidered', in *Apostolic History and the Gospel,* ed. W. Ward Gasque and R. P. Martin, Exeter: Paternoster, 1970, pp. 108-22.

McCowen, Alec. *Personal Mark,* London: Hamilton, 1984.

McGing, Brian, and Judith Mossman, eds. *The Limits of Biography,* Swansea: The Classical Press of Wales, forthcoming.

Meagher, John C. 'The Implications for Theology of a Shift from the K. L. Schmidt Hypothesis of the Literary Uniqueness of the Gospels' in *Colloquy on New Testament Studies: A Time for Reappraisal and Fresh Approaches,* Bruce Corley (ed.), Macon: Mercer University Press, 1983, pp. 203-33.

Meeks, Wayne A. *The First Urban Christians: The Social World of the Apostle Paul,* New Haven: Yale University Press, 1983.

———— *The Moral World of the First Christians,* London: SPCK, 1987.

Meyer, Eduard. 'Apollonius von Tyana und die Biographie des Philostratos', *Hermes* 52 (1917), pp. 371-424.

Momigliano, Arnaldo. *The Development of Greek Biography,* Cambridge, Mass.: Harvard University Press, 1971.

———— 'Second Thoughts on Greek Biography', in *Mededelingen der Koninkluke Nederlandse Akademie van Wetenschappen, AFD. Letterkunde,* NR 34.7, pp. 245-57; published separately, Amsterdam: North-Holland, 1971.

Moore, Stephen D. *Literary Criticism and the Gospels: The Theoretical Challenge,* Yale University Press, 1989.

Morgan, Robert. 'The Hermeneutical Significance of Four Gospels', *Interpretation* 33.4 (1979), pp. 376-88.

Morgenthaler, Robert. *Statistik des neutestamentlichen Wortschatzes,* Zurich: Gotthelf, 1958.

Moule, C. F. D. *The Phenomenon of the New Testament,* London: SCM, 1967.

———— *The Origin of Christology,* Cambridge: CUP, 1977.

———— *The Birth of the New Testament,* 3rd revised edn, London: A. & C. Black, 1981.

Murray, G. *Euripides and His Age,* 2nd edn., Oxford University Press, 1965.

Neirynck, Frans. 'Gospel, Genre of' in *The Oxford Companion to the Bible,* ed. Bruce M. Metzger and Michael D. Coogan, Oxford University Press, 1993, pp. 258-9; reprinted in *The Oxford Guide to Ideas and Issues of the Bible,* ed. Bruce M. Metzger and Michael D. Coogan, Oxford University Press, 2001, pp. 184-6.

Neusner, Jacob. *In Search of Talmudic Biography: The Problem of the Attributed Saying,* Brown Judaic Studies 70, Chico: Scholars, 1984.

———— *Why No Gospels in Talmudic Judaism?* BJS, 135, Atlanta: Scholars, 1988.

———— *The Incarnation of God: The Character of Divinity in Formative Judaism,* Philadelphia: Fortress, 1988.

———— *Are There Really Tannaitic Parallels to the Gospels? A Refutation of Morton Smith,* South Florida Studies in the History of Judaism, No. 80, Chico: Scholars, 1993.

Nineham, D. E. *St. Mark,* Harmondsworth: Penguin, 1963.

Oliver, Revilo P. 'The First Medicean MS of Tacitus and the Titulature of Ancient Books', *TAPA* 82 (1951), pp. 232-61.

Palmer, Darryl W. 'Acts and the Ancient Historical Monograph' in *The Book of Acts in Its Ancient Literary Setting,* ed. Bruce W. Winter and Andrew D. Clarke, Carlisle: Paternoster/Grand Rapids: Eerdmans, 1993, pp. 1-29.

Parsons, M. C., and R. I. Pervo, *Rethinking the Unity of Luke and Acts,* Minneapolis: Fortess, 1993.

Pelling, C. B. R. 'Plutarch's Method of Work in the Roman Lives', *JHS* 99 (1979), pp. 74-96.

———— 'Plutarch's Adaptation of His Source Material', *JHS* 100 (1980), pp. 127-40.

———— 'Synkrisis in Plutarch's Lives', in *Miscellanea Plutarchea,* ed. Frederick E. Brenk and Italo Gallo, *Quaderni del Giornale Filologico Ferrarese* 8 (1986), pp. 83-96.

———— 'Aspects of Plutarch's Characterisation', *Illinois Classical Studies* 13.2 (1988), pp. 257-74.

———— (ed.). *Characterization and Individuality in Greek Literature,* OUP, 1990.

———— 'Truth and Fiction in Plutarch's Lives', in *Antonine Literature,* ed. D. A. Russell, OUP, 1990, pp. 19-52.

———— 'Biography, Greek' in *The Oxford Classical Dictionary,* Oxford University Press, 1996.

———— 'Biographical History? Cassius Dio on the Early Principate', in *Portraits: Biographical Representation in the Greek and Latin Literature of the Roman Empire,* ed. M. J. Edwards and Simon Swain, Oxford: Clarendon, 1997, pp. 117-44.

———— 'Epilogue' in *The Limits of Historiography: Genre and Narrative in Ancient Historical Texts,* ed. Christina Shuttleworth Kraus, Leiden: Brill, 1999, pp. 325-60.

Perrin, Norman. *What Is Redaction Criticism?* London: SPCK, 1970.

———— 'The Literary Gattung "Gospel" — Some Observations', *ExpT* 82 (1970), pp. 4-7.

Pervo, Richard I. *Profit with Delight: The Literary Genre of the Acts of the Apostles,* Philadelphia: Fortress, 1987.

———— 'Must Luke and Acts Belong to the Same Genre?', in *SBL 1989 Seminar Papers,* Society of Biblical Literature, Atlanta: Scholars Press, 1989, pp. 309-16.

———— 'Israel's Heritage and Claims upon the Genre(s) of Luke and Acts: The Problems of a History' in *Jesus and the Heritage of Israel,* ed. David P. Moessner, Harrisburg: Trinity Press International, 1999, pp. 127-43.

Petersen, Norman R. 'So-called Gnostic Type Gospels and the Question of the Genre "Gospel"', Working Paper for the Task Force on Gospel Genre, SBL, 1970.

———— *Literary Criticism for New Testament Critics,* Philadelphia: Fortress, 1978.

———— 'Can one speak of a gospel genre?' *Neotestamentica* 28.3 (1994) (Special Edition), pp. 137-58.

Peterson, Dwight N. *The Origins of Mark: The Markan Community in Current Debate,* Leiden: Brill, 2000.

Petzke, G. *Die Traditionen über Apollonius von Tyana und das Neue Testament,* Studia ad Corpus Hellenisticum Novi Testamenti, vol. 1, Leiden: Brill, 1970.

Powell, Mark Allen. *What Is Narrative Criticism? A New Approach to the Bible,* Minneapolis: Fortress, 1990 and London: SPCK, 1993.

Rawson, Elizabeth. *Intellectual Life in the Late Republic,* London: Duckworth, 1985.

Reasoner, Mark. 'The Theme of Acts: Institutional History or Divine Necessity in History?', *JBL* 118.4 (1999), pp. 635-59.

Reddish, Mitchell G. *An Introduction to the Gospels,* Nashville: Abingdon, 1997.

Reiser, Marius. 'Der Alexanderroman und das Markusevangelium', WUNT 33 (1984), pp. 131-63.

Renan, Ernest. *Life of Jesus,* ET, London: Kegan Paul, 1893.

Rensberger, David. *Overcoming the World: Politics and Community in the Gospel of John,* London: SPCK, 1989.

Resseguie, James L. 'Reader-Response Criticism and the Synoptic Gospels', *JAAR* 52 (1984), pp. 307-24.

Rhoads, David. 'Narrative Criticism: Practice and Prospects' in *Characterization in the Gospels: Reconceiving Narrative Criticism,* ed. David Rhoads and Kari Syreeni, JSNTSS 184, Sheffield Academic Press, 1999.

Rhoads, David, and Donald Michie. *Mark as Story: An Introduction to the Narrative of a Gospel,* Philadelphia: Fortress, 1982.

Ricoeur, Paul. 'The Hermeneutical Function of Distanciation', *Philosophy Today* 17 (1973), pp. 129-41.

——— *Hermeneutics and the Human Sciences: Essays on Language, Action and Interpretation.* Edited, translated and introduced by John B. Thompson, CUP, 1981.

Robbins, Vernon K. 'Prefaces in Greco-Roman Biography and Luke-Acts', *SBL 1978 Seminar Papers,* vol. 2, ed. P. J. Achtemeier, Missoula: Scholars Press, 1978, pp. 193-207.

——— 'Mark as Genre', *SBL Seminar Papers,* Chicago: Scholars, 1980, pp. 371-99.

——— *Jesus the Teacher: A Socio-Rhetorical Interpretation of Mark,* Philadelphia: Fortress, 1984.

Robinson, James M. 'The Problem of History in Mark, Reconsidered', *Union Seminary Quarterly Review* 20 (1965), pp. 131-47.

——— 'On the *Gattung* of Mark (and John)', in *Jesus and Man's Hope,* vol. 1, Pittsburgh Theological Seminary, 1970, pp. 99-129.

Robinson, James M., and Helmut Koester. *Trajectories through Early Christianity,* Philadelphia: Fortress, 1971.

Robinson, J. A. T. *The Priority of John,* London: SCM, 1985.

Rogerson, John, Christopher Rowland and Barnabas Lindars (eds.). *The Study and Use of the Bible,* Basingstoke: Marshall Pickering, 1988.

Rosenmeyer, Thomas G. *The Green Cabinet: Theocritus and the European Pastoral Lyric,* University of California Press, 1969.

Rossi, L. E. 'I Generi Letterari e Le Loro Leggi Scritte e Non Scritte Nelle Letterature Classiche', *Bulletin of the Institute of Classical Studies* 18, University of London (1971), pp. 69-94.

Russell, D. A. 'On Reading Plutarch's Lives', *Greece and Rome* 13 (1966), pp. 139-54.

———— *Plutarch*, London: Duckworth, 1972.

———— *Criticism in Antiquity*, London: Duckworth, 1981.

Sage, M. M. 'Tacitus' Historical Works: A Survey and Appraisal', *ANRW* II.33.2 (1990), pp. 851-1030, Indexes, pp. 1629-47.

Sanders, E. P. *Jesus and Judaism*, London, SCM, 1985.

Sanders, E. P., and Margaret Davies. *Studying the Synoptic Gospels*, London: SCM, 1989.

Schmidt, Daryl D. 'Rhetorical Influences and Genre: Luke's Preface and the Rhetoric of Hellenistic Historiography' in *Jesus and the Heritage of Israel*, ed. David P. Moessner, Harrisburg: Trinity Press International, 1999, pp. 27-60.

Schmidt, Karl Ludwig. *Der Rahmen der Geschichte Jesu*, Berlin: Trowitzsch und Sohn, 1919; reprinted, Darmstadt: Wissenschaftliche Buchgesellschaft, 1964.

———— 'Die Stellung der Evangelien in der allgemeinen Literaturgeschichte', in *EYXAPIΣTHPION: Studien zur Religion und Literatur des Alten und Neuen Testaments*, ed. Hans Schmidt, Göttingen: Vandenhoeck und Ruprecht, 1923, vol. 2 (= *FRLANT*, NF 19.2), pp. 50-134. ET as *The Place of the Gospels in the General History of Literature*, translated by Byron R. McCane, University of South Carolina Press, 2002, with an introduction by John Riches.

———— 'Jesus Christ' in *Die Religion in Geschichte und Gegenwart*, ed. H. Gunkel et al., 2nd edn, Tübingen: J. C. B. Mohr, 1928, vol. 2, cols. 418-22; ET in *Twentieth Century Theology in the Making*, ed. Jaroslav Pelikan, London: Collins, Fontana, 1969, vol. 1, pp. 93-168.

Schoneveld, Jacobus. 'Torah in the Flesh: A New Reading of the Prologue of the Gospel of John as a Contribution to a Christology without Anti-Semitism' in *The New Testament and Christian-Jewish Dialogue: Studies in Honor of David Flusser*, ed. Malcolm Lowe, Emmanuel 24/25, Jerusalem: Ecumenical Theological Research Fraternity in Israel, 1990, pp. 77-93.

Seck, Friedrich (ed.). *Isokrates*, Darmstadt: Wissenschaftliche Buchgesellschaft, 1976.

Shim, Ezra S. B. 'A Suggestion about the Genre of Text-Type of Mark', *Scriptura* 50 (1994), pp. 69-89.

Shuler, Philip L. *A Genre for the Gospels: The Biographical Character of Matthew*, Philadelphia: Fortress, 1982.

Sim, David C. 'The Gospels for All Christians? A Response to Richard Bauckham', *JSNT* 84 (2001), pp. 3-27.

Skeat, T. C. 'Irenaeus and the Four-Fold Gospel Canon', *NovT* 34.2 (1992), 194-9.

Smalley, Stephen. *John: Evangelist and Interpreter*, Exeter: Paternoster, 1978.

Spencer, F. Scott. *Acts*, Sheffield Academic Press, 1997.

Stambaugh, John, and David Balch. *The Social World of the First Christians*, London: SPCK, 1986.

Standaert, B. H. M. G. M. *L'Evangile selon Marc: composition et genre littéraire*, Zevenkerken, Brugge, 1984.

Stanton, Graham N. *Jesus of Nazareth in New Testament Preaching*, SNTSMS 27, CUP, 1974.

———— 'Matthew as a Creative Interpreter of the Sayings of Jesus', in *Das Evangelium und die Evangelien: Vorträge vom Tübinger Symposium 1982*, ed. Peter Stuhlmacher, WUNT 28, Tübingen: J. C. B. Mohr, 1983, pp. 273-87; ET, pp. 257-72.

—————— *The Gospels and Jesus,* OUP, 1989; Second Edition, Oxford University Press, 2002.

—————— *A Gospel for a New People: Studies in Matthew,* Edinburgh: T&T Clark, 1992.

—————— 'Revisiting Matthew's Communities', *SBL Seminar Papers, 1994,* ed. E. H. Loverington, Atlanta: Scholars Press, 1994, 9-23.

—————— 'The Fourfold Gospel', *NTS* 43 (1997), pp. 347-66.

—————— *Jesus and Gospel,* Cambridge University Press, 2004.

Steidle, Wolf. *Sueton und die antike Biographie,* 2nd edn, Munich: C. H. Beck, 1963.

Sterling, Gregory E. 'Luke-Acts and Apologetic Historiography', in *SBL 1989 Seminar Papers,* Society of Biblical Literature, Atlanta: Scholars Press, 1989, pp. 326-42.

—————— *Historiography and Self-Definition: Josephos, Luke-Acts and Apologetic Historiography,* SupNT 64, Leiden: Brill, 1992.

Stibbe, Mark W. G. *John as Storyteller: Narrative Criticism and the Fourth Gospel,* SNTSMS 73, Cambridge University Press, 1992.

—————— *The Gospel of John as Literature: An Anthology of Twentieth-Century Perspectives,* NTTS, Leiden: Brill, 1993, pp. 15-24.

—————— *John,* Sheffield Academic Press, 1993.

Strelka, Joseph P. (ed.). *Theories of Literary Genre,* Pennsylvania State University Press, 1978.

Stuart, Duane Reed. *Epochs of Greek and Roman Biography,* Berkeley: University of California Press, 1928.

Stuhlmacher, Peter (ed.). *Das Evangelium und die Evangelien: Vorträge vom Tübinger Symposium 1982,* WUNT 28, Tübingen: J. C. B. Mohr, 1983; ET as *The Gospel and the Gospels,* ed. Peter Stuhlmacher, Grand Rapids: Eerdmans, 1991.

Suggs, M. J. 'Gospel, Genre', in *The Interpreter's Dictionary of the Bible,* Supplementary volume, Nashville: Abingdon Press, 1976, pp. 370-2.

Syme, R. *Tacitus,* Oxford University Press, 1958.

Talbert, Charles H. *Literary Patterns, Theological Themes and the Genre of Luke-Acts,* SBLMS 20, Missoula, Montana: Scholars, 1974.

—————— *What Is a Gospel? The Genre of the Canonical Gospels,* Philadelphia: Fortress, 1977; London: SPCK, 1978.

—————— 'Biographies of Philosophers and Rulers as Instruments of Religious Propaganda in Mediterranean Antiquity', in *ANRW* II.16.2, 1978, pp. 1619-51.

—————— 'Once Again: Gospel Genre', *Semeia* 43 (1988), pp. 53-73.

—————— 'Ancient Biography' in *The Anchor Bible Dictionary,* ed. D. N. Freedman, New York, Doubleday, 1992, Vol. I, pp. 745-9.

—————— 'The Acts of the Apostles: Monograph or Bios?' in *History, Literature, and Society in the Book of Acts,* ed. Ben Witherington III, Cambridge University Press, 1996, pp. 58-72.

Tannehill, Robert C. (ed.). *Pronouncement Stories, Semeia* 20 (1981).

—————— *The Narrative Unity of Luke-Acts: A Literary Interpretation,* 2 vols., Philadelphia and Minneapolis: Fortress, 1986 and 1990.

—————— 'The Gospels and Narrative Literature' in *The New Interpreter's Bible,* Volume VIII, Nashville: Abingdon, 1995, pp. 68-70.

Taylor, Vincent. *The Formation of the Gospel Tradition,* London: Macmillan, 1933.

Telford, W. R. *Mark,* Sheffield Academic Press, 1995.

Thistleton, Anthony C. *The Two Horizons,* Exeter: Paternoster, 1980.

Todorov, Tzvetán. *Introduction à la littérature fantastique,* Paris: Seuil, 1970. ET: *The Fantastic: A Structural Approach to Literary Genre,* New York: Cornell University Press, 1975.

Tolbert, Mary Ann. *Sowing the Gospel: Mark's World in Literary-Historical Perspective,* Minneapolis: Fortress, 1989.

Tronson, Adrian. 'Satyrus the Peripatetic and the Marriages of Philip II', *JHS* 104 (1984), pp. 116-26.

Tuckett, C. M. *Reading the New Testament: Methods of Interpretation,* London: SPCK, 1987.

———— 'A Cynic Q?', *Biblica* 70 (1989), pp. 349-76.

———— 'Jesus and the Gospels' in *The New Interpreter's Bible,* Volume VIII, Nashville: Abingdon, 1995, pp. 68-70.

———— 'Introduction to the Gospels' in *Eerdmans Commentary on the Bible,* ed. James D. G. Dunn and John Rogerson (Grand Rapids: Eerdmans, 2003), pp. 989-99.

Via, Dan O., Jr. *Kerygma and Comedy in the New Testament: A Structuralist Approach to Hermeneutic,* Philadelphia: Fortress, 1975.

Vines, Michael E. *The Problem of the Markan Genre: The Gospel of Mark and the Jewish Novel,* Atlanta: SBL, 2002.

Vivas, Eliseo. 'Literary Classes: Some Problems', *Genre* 1 (1968), pp. 97-105.

Vorster, Willem. 'Gospel Genre', in *The Anchor Bible Dictionary,* ed. D. N. Freedman, New York: Doubleday, 1992, Vol. 2, pp. 1077-79.

Votaw, C. W. 'The Gospels and Contemporary Biographies', *American Journal of Theology* 19 (1915), pp. 45-73 and 217-49; reprinted (with an Introduction by John Reumann) as *The Gospels and Contemporary Biographies in the Graeco-Roman World,* Philadelphia: Fortress, Facet Books, 1970.

Walker, William O., Jr. (ed.). *The Relationships Among the Gospels: An Interdisciplinary Dialogue,* San Antonio: Trinity University Press, 1978.

Wallace-Hadrill, Andrew. *Suetonius: The Scholar and His Caesars,* London: Duckworth, 1983.

Wansbrough, Henry. 'The Four Gospels in Synopsis' in *The Oxford Bible Commentary,* ed. John Barton and John Muddiman, Oxford University Press, 2001, pp. 1001-2.

Wardman, Alan. 'Plutarch's Methods in the *Lives*', *CQ* 21 (1971), pp. 254-61.

———— *Plutarch's Lives,* London: Paul Elek, 1974.

Weeden, Theodore J. *Mark: Traditions in Conflict,* Philadelphia: Fortress Press, 1971.

Wehrli, Fritz. *Die Schule des Aristoteles,* 10 vols. Basel: Schwabe & Co., 1967-69.

Wellek, René, and Austin Warren. *Theory of Literature,* 3rd edn, Harmondsworth: Penguin, Pelican, 1982 reprint of 1963 edn.

West, Stephanie. 'Satyrus: Peripatetic or Alexandrian?', *GRBS* 15 (1974), pp. 279-87.

Whiteacre, Rodney A. *Johannine Polemic: The Role of Tradition and Theology,* SBLDS 67, Chico: Scholars, 1982.

Williams, James G. *Gospel Against Parable: Mark's Language of Mystery,* Bible and Literature Series 12, Sheffield: JSOT Press, 1985.

———— 'Parable and Chreia: From Q to Narrative Gospel', *Semeia* 43 (1988), pp. 85-114.

Wills, Lawrence M. *The Quest of the Historical Gospel: Mark, John and the Origins of the Gospel Genre,* London: Routledge, 1997.

Witherington, Ben, III. *The Christology of Jesus,* Minneapolis: Fortress, 1990.

———— *The Acts of the Apostles: A Socio-Rhetorical Commentary,* Grand Rapids: Eerdmans, 1998.

———— *The Many Faces of the Christ: The Christologies of the New Testament and Beyond,* New York: Crossroad Herder, 1998.

———— *The Gospel of Mark: A Socio-Rhetorical Commentary,* Grand Rapids: Eerdmans, 2001.

Wolterstorff, Nicholas. *Divine Discourse: Philosophical Reflections on the Claim That God Speaks,* Cambridge University Press, 1995.

N. T. Wright, *Christian Origins and the Question of God:* Vol. 1, *The New Testament and the People of God,* London: SPCK/Fortress, 1992; Vol. 2, *Jesus and the Victory of God,* London: SPCK/Fortress, 1996; Vol. 3, *The Resurrection of the Son of God,* London: SPCK/Fortress, 2003.

Index of Passages

Index of Names and Subjects

Page numbers in italic type denote major treatment of subject